DÉRICOURT

JEAN OVERTON FULLER

SAPERE
BOOKS

DÉRICOURT

Published by Sapere Books.

24 Trafalgar Road, Ilkley, LS29 8HH

United Kingdom

saperebooks.com

ISBN: 978-1-80055-831-1.

TABLE OF CONTENTS

1: ENTRY TO THE MAZE

I believe I knew Déricourt better than anybody. I must explain how this came to be. I have never been an agent. Before the war I knew Noor Inayat Khan and her brother Vilayat, children of an Indian Sufi mystic and an American mother, brought up in France. When the Germans overran France in June 1940, they fled to England, spoiling to enter a British service, part of a great wave of escapees from the Continent. Vilayat enlisted in the RAF. Noor followed him into the light blue of the WAAF. Mrs Inayat Khan took a flat a few doors from mine, near to my wartime job in the postal censorship, and Noor came to me when on leave. In March 1943 she changed her WAAF uniform for the khaki of the FANY. In May she told me, glowing, 'I'm being sent on foreign service.' Then she vanished. In May 1949, six years after she had left us, she was awarded a posthumous George Cross. She had been landed by Lysander aircraft on 16 June 1943 to work with the French Resistance as a radio operator, 'Madeleine'. The Gestapo had made mass arrests in the group she had been sent to join, but she refused an offer of repatriation and carried on for three and a half months, until betrayed to the Gestapo. She had made a daring attempt to escape from the headquarters at 84 Avenue Foch, had on recapture refused parole, and on 12 September 1944 had been shot at Dachau. It was reported that her commanding officer had been Colonel Maurice Buckmaster, head of the 'French Section'.

French Section of what I did not know, but I wrote to Buckmaster, care of the War Office, saying I had been a friend of Miss Inayat Khan and would like to know a little more, and perhaps write something about her. He replied by telephone, referring me to a Miss Vera Atkins. She received me in her flat on 3 August 1949. She said she did not know if the names of the schools in which my friend had trained had yet been taken off the security list. Nor could she tell me anything about the people Noor had been sent out to work with, who were, in any case, all dead. She had suggestions, however, about people I might contact.

On 14 September I met the first of them, Captain John Starr, at his home in Paris. He had been a fellow prisoner with 'Madeleine' at the Avenue Foch. He said he would have to tell me a bit of his story so that I would understand how the part concerning my friend fitted in. On his second mission, in May 1943, he was parachuted 'blind'. Agents were infiltrated in three ways, by boat, by aircraft that came down on to the ground or — as in the majority of cases — by parachute. One might be parachuted in two ways, blind or to reception committee. Blind meant with no one to meet one; one had to bury one's own parachute and find one's own way. A reception committee meant two or three people standing on the field to help one out of one's harness, bury the parachute, present a bicycle and indicate the way to the nearest railway station. This was supposed to be a great help, but in fact safety lay in jumping blind. It was the reception committee that could prove a trap.

After his arrest on 1 July at Dijon, betrayed by a double agent, 'Martin', Starr was brought to 84 Avenue Foch. On first being taken up to the little guard-room, on the fifth floor, he was surprised to see a British officer apparently very much at his ease. Later this officer told Starr that his code-name was 'Archambaud' and he was a radio operator.

Whenever the Germans captured a radio operator, complete with radio-set and crystals, the great thing was to get from him his code and security check, and play the set back to London, as if it were the captured agent still operating. Appointments were made with London for the parachute delivery of arms, munitions, money, supplies of all sorts and further agents, straight to a German reception committee. The Germans called this the 'radio-game'. The expert of the German radio department at Avenue Foch was Joseph Goetz.

Starr said he had been there a couple of months when 'Madeleine' was brought in. He would like, first of all, to assure me she was not ill-treated — 'so long as she was *there*'. 84 Avenue Foch was not a prison. It was a big private house the Germans had commandeered. Kieffer, the commandant, had his living quarters on the fourth floor. The fifth floor was the attic — all small rooms that had been used as maids' bedrooms. One was occupied by Ernst Vogt, the interrogator, for his office. One was the guard-room. The others — seven if he remembered rightly — were used as cells for prisoners, including 'Madeleine' and himself. The food was amazingly good — grilled lamb chop, grilled pork chop, grilled steak. This was probably because the prisoners were so few in proportion to the staff that it was less trouble to give the same to everybody. There did not appear to be a canteen but obviously there was a kitchen below. There was no lift, so that a trolley could not be used, but at meal-times SS orderlies would bring plates to the rooms on the different floors. Arrived at the fifth, they would take in two plates — one for Vogt and one for whichever prisoner he was at that moment interrogating. They would then go on to the guardroom and the cells. Ironically, 'as prisoners, we ate better than the free people outside, or the people at home'.

The few prisoners kept by the Sicherheitsdienst (SD) at their headquarters were special ones. Ordinary prisoners — the rank and file of the Resistance — were kept in Fresnes and other prisons, from which they were brought up for questioning lasting only a few hours. Those kept permanently on the premises were ones the Germans wanted handy for re-questioning at any moment. 'Madeleine' was a radio operator, and they were playing her set back to London, impersonating her over the air. Most likely she did not know. From her bearing, it was unlikely that she gave them any help knowingly. But Vogt had her in his office for questioning for some part of every day for certainly over a month. If he was just chatting her up, it would be in the hope she might let slip some unguarded word he could pass to Goetz, to help him impersonate her. Vogt would pour out cups of tea for his English prisoners, trying to relax them. This partially succeeded, though one never really relaxed. There was always the anxiety. Where was all this leading? They could at any time be sent somewhere very different. He saw 'Madeleine' when she was escorted to Vogt's, to the lavatory or to the separate bathroom, next to Vogt's office, in which prisoners were permitted to take a bath. There was hot water and soap. She also came into the guard-room to change her 'library' book. There was a shelf with a few French novels and thrillers. Whereas in Fresnes lights were out after the evening meal, here one could have one's light on in one's cell as late as one wanted. She was, of course, always closely escorted by one of the guards. Nevertheless, when she came in to change her book they exchanged smiles and a few words. They began tapping to each other in morse through the partition wall between their cells. She was in similar communication with the prisoner on her other side, a Colonel Faye, head of the independent network, L'Alliance. Between the three of them, they organised a simultaneous break-out from their cells, through the skylights, on to the roof. Unfortunately, they were recaptured. Kieffer asked each of them if they would give him their word of honour never again to try to escape, otherwise he would have to send them somewhere else. 'Madeleine' and Faye refused, and disappeared from the scene. Starr gave his, hoping to be able to pass his information about the radio-game to another prisoner or to put a spoke in it. He was able to do the latter, when, in the spring of 1944, London must at least have become suspicious of one of the radio circuits that had been run by the Germans for about a year, for they asked the supposed organiser to speak through the S-phone to someone in a plane that would circle over. The Germans asked Starr to impersonate him. By temporising until the very last minute before refusing, he forced von Kapri to attempt the communication, in English so heavily German the game must have been given away, for no more drops were made to that circuit. Had he not led them along, they could have used the time to find someone who spoke proper English. After D-Day, when the Germans knew they were going to have to retreat and could not take prisoners with them, he was sent to Germany with the rest and found himself in the Extermination Camp at Mauthausen, where the inmates were being gassed in order of weakness at about 500 a day. He was rescued in the last days of the war by the Belgian Red Cross, which obtained permission to enter the camp and take out Belgians — and found room in their ambulance to take a few non-Belgians as well.

Miss Atkins, when she gave me Starr's name, had contrasted his behaviour most unfavourably with Noor's, and warned me not to believe him if he should begin to spin some kind of a story 'in which he is perfectly justified and the Section seems to have done everything wrong'. Now, I was troubled. Starr's story sounded credible enough to me, and I had a sinking feeling that I had learned something it was not wished in London I should know. The public at home had no inkling of this. I had stumbled upon what must be an inconvenient secret.

On my return to London, I had, on 11 October, my only interview with Colonel Buckmaster. It was on a landing of the premises of Ford Motor Co Ltd, of which he was Publicity Manager. His office, he explained, had a conference going on in it, which he had left for a few minutes in order to see me. There was really nothing he could tell me about my friend. He was not sure he even remembered her. He remembered that, from the field, her transmissions went on and on and on. It was Miss Atkins who knew everything.

Next on my list from Miss Atkins was a French patriot, not a member of the Section, called Robert Gieules. He offered me an interview in Paris on 5 November to which he brought his lawyer. He had seen my letter to Starr, which I had inadvertently transposed with his. It had prompted him to go to the Department de la Surveillance du Territoire (DST) to ask for Starr to be charged with Intelligence with the enemy. He said he was angry with 'Madeleine', because she had presented him to two 'Canadians', who turned out to be Germans who had substituted themselves through the radio-game. He was angry, too, with Bodington (another on my list from Miss Atkins, who had not replied to my letter) for some other reason. He spoke some violent words. I was dazed by all his charges, but took his words down. Right at the end he mentioned that a woman was coming up for trial in ten days' time, charged with having sold 'Madeleine' to the Gestapo. Her name was Renée Garry.

I could not stay. I was at that time a freelance teacher of English, and had been booked to take a series of classes at a college in London. However, I dropped a note for Vilayat Khan, at his home in Suresnes, and on my return to London I called on Miss Atkins and told her. At first she was dismissive, but when I told her the name of the woman, she said this was so serious she would need to think. She did not wish to talk about it with me.

On the evening of the 17th Vilayat arrived at my London flat, at 4 Guilford Place. He said the witnesses for the prosecution had been first, a German, Ernst Vogt (of whom Starr had spoken), who said the accused had telephoned his service to offer the address of 'Madeleine', for a price. Vogt had been sent by his chief, Kieffer, to conduct the negotiation and was taken by Renée Garry to the address at which he later arrested 'Madeleine', and, a few days afterwards, Garry and his wife, Marguerite.

Vogt was followed into the box by Mme Garry, survivor of Ravensbrück, sister-in-law of the accused, widow of E. H. Garry, hanged in Buchenwald. Then a Mme Aigrain testified, likewise a survivor of Ravensbrück; and then Vilayat himself. Renée Garry told the court she had been in love with a man called 'Antoine' who had returned her affection until the arrival of 'Madeleine'. Nevertheless, she said, Vogt must have made a mistake. He may have had dealings with some woman but it was not with her.

The sole but effective witness called by the defence was Robert Gieules. He told the court 'Madeleine' did not need anyone to betray her, as she was already in contact with two 'Canadians' who were Germans. They met her constantly, and could have arrested her at any time. Vilayat did not understand this very well, but gathered there had been two real Canadians,

15

whom she thought she was meeting, but they had been captured and these two Germans had substituted themselves. The master-stroke for the defence was, however, the production by Renée Garry's counsel of a letter from Colonel Buckmaster, written to her shortly after the end of the war thanking her for her services to his organisation. Counsel had waved this in the air, asking rhetorically, 'Which are you going to believe, that German or the English Colonel Buckmaster?' The panel of nine military judges had acquitted Renée Garry by five votes to four.

Vilayat showed me the piece about the trial in *France Soir*, which he had brought back. The reporter inclined to prefer Vogt's evidence. Renée Garry was described as a woman who 'had been beautiful and had not altogether renounced pretensions to beauty'. He interpreted the case as one of love and jealousy. Vilayat was extremely upset, and wanted to talk to Miss Atkins. We rang her and she agreed to let us come over straight away. She was very interested that Vilayat had seen Renée Garry, and asked him, 'Was she a big woman, with high colour, florid?'

'Yes,' said Vilayat.

That was what Kieffer had told her, Miss Atkins said. He had given her a detailed description of the woman who came to their offices after 'Madeleine' had been arrested, to collect the money. It was Miss Atkins who had interrogated Kieffer before the evidence was brought on which he was eventually condemned.[1] 'If that hadn't come up, he would have been a

---

[1] On receipt of teleprint orders from Berlin, Kieffer had five uniformed commandos changed into civilian clothes before being executed It was for carrying out this order that he was hanged. There was no other charge against him

16

free man today. We had nothing else on him.' The brain of the Avenue Foch, she maintained, was Goetz.

She dropped a reference to another acquittal, an acquittal which had particularly sickened her. 'The motives were so base.' She did not name a name, but I remembered the words and the tone and later realised that her reference had been to Déricourt.

Amongst Vilayat's papers concerning his sister I found one which showed that while a prisoner at Pforzheim, Germany, she had talked about the escape from Avenue Foch in a way that confirmed Starr's story. I took this with me on my next visit to Paris, on 30 December 1949. Starr told me that evening that his *juge d'instruction* was a Captain Mercier, who had accepted his word of honour to hold himself available for questioning, so that he might continue to live at his home during the investigation. Mercier had asked him if he could give the real name of a colleague he had mentioned only by his code-name. Starr had not been sure, so he had gone to the British Consulate, explained his circumstances and asked whether he would have permission. When he called back in a few days for the answer, the Consul told him the reply he had from London was 'Leave the country immediately'.

Perhaps because I was a soldier's daughter, I was profoundly shocked a man in his position should have been advised to break his parole and flee. Moreover, I could think of no explanation of it, other than the one Starr preferred, that they did not want him to tell Mercier about the radio-game, as it was obvious he would have to, in his own defence.

On 3 January 1950 I went with Starr to the Tribunal Militaire Permanent de Paris at the Caserne de Reuilly. Forming three sides of a square, it was like a college quad, except for the *Tricolore* and the sentry who challenged us at the big iron gate.

17

We went up one of the staircases, to Mercier's office. Captain Mercier rose to greet us, tall, blond, smartly military. I showed him the paper with 'Madeleine's' information which he borrowed for copying by his *gréffier*.

Mercier said to Starr, 'I wrote to Colonel Buckmaster, telling him we were making this investigation, and asking him if he would like to tell me anything about you. I have not had a reply.'

Starr said, 'I don't think you will.'

'It is not indispensable,' said Mercier.

I said I had heard French magistrates sometimes came out to look at the scene of an alleged crime. Could we not all go to the Avenue Foch? Starr could show him the skylights and the roofs and I could see everything, so as to be able to describe it in my book. Mercier agreed at once, and after lunch we all went in his car, taking his ever-attendant *gréffier*.

84 Avenue Foch had reverted to private occupation, but as we were the military we were let in without question, and Starr led the way up the very grand staircase to the suite of rooms on the fourth floor which had been Kieffer's office. There, beneath the heavy chandelier he had sat at his massive desk, on the puce-purple carpet. Then we made up the little white staircase to the servants' quarters, where Vogt had had his office, near to the prisoners whom he had to interrogate.

During the same visit to Paris I went to see Mme Garry, widow of E. H. Garry and sister-in-law of the woman who had recently stood trial. She described to me how 'Madeleine' had arrived at their flat, having come straight from the landing-field … to the right address but confused, because she had understood the contact with whom she had to exchange passwords was an elderly lady. Anyhow it was Garry to whom the other half of her pass-phrase had been given, and identities were established. Garry's sister Renée shared the flat with them, and recently they had had as their guest a South African major, 'Antoine'. They asked 'Madeleine' to stay with them too. In a low trembling voice she unfolded to me her interpretation of the betrayal.

I knew there was no point in trying to see Renée Garry. Vilayat had called on her advocate, who told him he had not seen or heard from her since she left the court. He had inquired at her domicile, but had been told she had not returned to it, even to fetch her things. (That is how it remains to this day. She has simply vanished.)

Mme Garry did, however, tell me of two people whom I ought to meet, Professor Serge Balachowsky, of the Institut Pasteur, and his wife. They could tell me more than she about 'Madeleine's' actual work. They lived at Viroflay, on the Versailles line, and on 7 January I took the train out to see them. It was Mme Balachowsky, red-haired and fierce, who at last told me what I had sought for so long to discover, the identities of the people with whom 'Madeleine' had been sent out to work, and the structure of the network. Operating in Paris and the Loire valley, it was the most important of the networks in France, a kind of super network, to which others became tributary. The big chief was an Englishman, 'Prosper'. His second-in-command and principal radio operator was 'Archambaud', also English. She believed their real names were Suttill and Norman, but they always called them Francois and Gilbert, their Christian names in real life. Courier to them was a French girl, 'Denise'. 'Madeleine' had met and started to assist 'Archambaud' when, in the early hours of 24 June 1943, 'Archambaud' and 'Denise', and then 'Prosper' were arrested. Within a few weeks, a wave of arrests spread wide. Estimates differed. Hers, which included secondary consequences, was

19

1,500. The agents dropped from London had been told they should remain silent for forty-eight hours, which would give their comrades time to get away. That was all very fine for them. They had no roots. It was no use to the people living in France whom they recruited. The farmer who had helped bury parachutes could not leave his beasts and land. The farmers were always arrested. Her husband's arrest was on 1 July. How had the disaster occurred? The Tambour sisters, letterbox to 'Prosper', had been arrested in April. A Swiss had paid over a vast sum of money to the Abwehr to release them. The prison van stopped, but two prostitutes were given out. London ordered a second attempt. A second payment was made. This time men jumped out of the van, with cameras with which they photographed the waiting 'Prosper' and 'Archambaud'. Mme Balachowsky had been waiting with the Doctoresse Helmer, to whose home the Tambour sisters were to have been brought, had the rescue succeeded. 'Prosper' and 'Archambaud' came in, crying, 'They photographed us!' She could not give me the date, but it was before 'Prosper' left for London in May. He parachuted back in the early hours of 20 June, just before the blow fell. She suggested I see the Tourets, who had a restaurant in Paris in the rue Troy on. I found them on the defensive. 'Il y a des choses que les Anglais ne veulent pas comprendre,' said Mme Touret darkly. One night a man came asking for 'Gilbert'. There was a Gilbert in the group that lunched there almost every day. She told the caller that at that hour Gilbert would be playing poker at the Square Clignancourt, 'right in the north'. She stretched up her arm as if to indicate on one of the giant metro maps of Paris that it was tight on the northern perimeter of the city. 'I never dreamed of a German speaking French like that!'

So Mme Touret had directed a German to 'Archambaud'.

On 15 February I saw Miss Atkins again, and told her I thought of asking the French if they would allow me to see Vogt. She reacted against this, saying it would not be worth my while. He was not sufficiently high in the German service to know anything of importance. 'He might make a list of the clothing of a prisoner who was brought in,' but that would be about all. Then she said she saw no point in my 'trying to establish the incidents of her life in the field'. Surprised, I said they were an important part of my friend's life. She retorted sharply, 'Your readers will find that much the least interesting part of your book.'

Since my researches were not welcomed, I resolved not to trouble her for a further meeting.

I went to Paris again at Easter, saw Starr and told him I was hoping the French might permit me to visit Vogt in the prison in which they were holding him. He thought it would only be the DST that could give permission. He telephoned to an Inspecteur Coupaye of the DST and invited him to meet us for morning coffee at the Café Kléber on 19 April. Coupaye came accompanied by a very senior officer, Stanislav Mangin. They wore military uniforms though they had police ranks. Starr explained to them that I was writing a biography of 'Madeleine', and that brought the conversation to the recent trial of Renée Garry, about which they made some strange remarks.

'Does Colonel Buckmaster exist?' asked Coupaye suddenly.

As though I had misheard, I said I had seen him for a few minutes only.

'It is more than we have done!' they chorused. 'We've never seen him.' Nor had they ever received a letter from him. Renée Garry's advocate had shown the court a letter signed 'Maurice

Buckmaster', but they had had no model with which to compare the signature.

I supposed it could do no harm to tell them Miss Atkins said that if Garry was an agent, his wife and sister were not, though they would have been party to much that was going on. She supposed Buckmaster received letters from a vast number of people after the war who told him what services they had rendered his organisation and he probably wrote back polite thank-you letters without thinking of them as consequential. I reported that I had told Miss Atkins on 8 November that Renée Garry was coming up for trial on the 17th, and thought she would have told Buckmaster.

'We notified him officially!' they said. At the time when they had Renée Garry charged. Whenever they were bringing proceedings against a former member of his organisation, they notified Buckmaster, in formal manner, at once. This they did as a courtesy, and to give him the opportunity of rallying to his agent's support. The formal notification was then complemented by a personal letter, in more human terms, inviting him to tell them anything he might like with regard to the case. They had never yet received a reply; not even an acknowledgement. They told me the address to which they had sent their communications over the years. Nothing had come back from the dead letter office, but did I know if it was correct? I did not know Buckmaster's residential address, but said I felt sure anything they sent to him care of the London office of the Ford Motor Company would reach him.

Coupaye spoke about 'Archambaud', and said he was certain he had been confused, to his detriment, with another man. It was a pity the British had hanged Kieffer without making him available to the French for questioning, and had also greatly delayed handing over to them two of his staff officers, Placke and Vogt. If they had had Vogt when a certain case was brought to trial, 'it would have made all the difference'. I know, now, that he was speaking of the Déricourt trial.

My request for permission to visit Vogt in prison came too late. They had released him — as they had now released all the Germans. As I would be seeing Captain Mercier, they suggested I should ask him for Vogt's address. This Mercier gave me.

I wrote to Vogt, explaining I belonged to no official service but had been a friend of 'Madeleine' and would like to see him. He replied (I translate from his German):

> 4 May, 1950
>
> Of Miss N. Inayat Khan... alias 'Madeleine' I have only good to say. She made a very good impression on me, was very brave during her captivity and during her short stay at 84 Avenue Foch conducted herself as a good brave Englishwoman.

He had questioned her daily for about five weeks, and if I came to Germany he would be pleased to see me.

Because I was the posthumous child of a regular officer killed in the First World War, Germany had always been the enemy; not a matter of hate, just of fact. I always try to meet a human being just as such, without prejudice, but I had never been to Germany, and as the train crossed the frontier, in the early morning of 17 June, it was an unsettling moment.

At a small town in the Black Forest Vogt's aunt met me and conducted me to my hotel. Vogt himself called later. He was tall, with grey eyes behind spectacles, so thin it shocked me. I asked him about his experiences in Allied hands. He said the last eleven months had been in a cell of the Prison du Cherche-

23

Midi, alone, except when led out for interrogation, He still felt dazed, out of practice in normal conversation as in crossing roads. He opened his wallet and showed me his certificates — one from the French, saying they had completed examination of him and did not want him for war crimes, earlier certificates from the American and British, a combined one from the three governments, and one from the West German Denazification Authority, that he had not held membership of the Party.

He had assumed I would wish to hold our conversation in the English Institute, so that is where we went. When I took a chair by a table he said, 'Under a table can be a microphone,' and when I pulled it away, he said 'Now we are under a light. In the bulb can be a microphone.' I moved away from that too. He began to feel under the seat of his chair and said, 'Impossible to tell if there is a microphone without turning it upside down or getting down on my knees to look. Either would attract attention.' I said, 'I think you would feel more at your ease if we walked in the open air.'

We climbed to a bench with a view over the town and the sweeping green of the Black Forest. 'Do you believe 'Madeleine' is dead?' he asked. He saw her so vividly before him he felt she was alive, and that if she survived death then so did we all. He would like to think she was with us. 'She was the best human being I have known.' She would not reproach him her death. She knew she would be shot. 'He [Kieffer] promised her nothing, because she did nothing for us.' He would not be ashamed to meet 'Madeleine' again. He would be ashamed if, when he too was dead, he met 'Prosper'. Kieffer promised 'Prosper' that his life and the lives of all members of his network would be spared if he would disclose the addresses at which the arms and munitions parachuted from London were stored, before they had been used to kill Germans. 'Prosper' asked Vogt, 'Can I trust your chief?' Vogt had said, 'Yes.' The pact was obtained from Berlin, 'stamped with the seal of the Reichssicherheitshauptamt', and given to 'Prosper'. He was sure Kieffer believed in its worth. 'After they passed from Kieffer's hands, they were all killed. It is the most shaming thing with which I have been associated.'

Back at the hotel he gave me at dictation speed his account of how he had arrested 'Madeleine', and of his interrogation of her during five weeks. In a drawer in the room in which he arrested her, he found a notebook in which were all her past messages to London, in cipher and in clear, showing the security check, so there was no need to interrogate her about that. What he tried to obtain, during his long conversations with her, was some impression of her personality, which he could pass over to Goetz, because she did not relax with Goetz, as to some extent she did with him, perhaps because, as a civil auxiliary, he was not in uniform. Uniforms for civil auxiliaries arrived only in June or July 1944, after the Normandy landings. He showed her a photostat of a letter she had written to her mother. That made her cry. 'She loved her mother.' But she would not talk of her family, or of her work. On topics she thought could not help the Germans, she let herself be drawn out, particularly music. 'If someone gave me a ticket for a concert of classical music, I would go and I would enjoy it, but I would not afterwards be able to speak knowledgeably of the performance or the composer's work. She could. I thought she had perhaps been a student at a school of music.' This was true.

Vogt told me — something I had failed to get from Miss Atkins or Buckmaster — the names and locations of the schools attended by the agents, Wanborough Manor in Surrey, Arisaig in Scotland for tough physical training, Beaulieu in

Hampshire for security, and Ringway, Manchester, for parachuting. He even told me that Buckmaster's office was on the corner of Portman Square and Orchard Street, Orchard Court.

'Did 'Madeleine' know the Germans were playing her radio-set back to London?'

'It was not to the interest of our service she should know. I did not tell her. She would not have believed it possible.'

'How do you want to call me?' He suggested Ernest — with a second 'e'. It was the only name by which his prisoners knew him. He wanted to keep Vogt out of it for his family's sake. The French had put him aboard a train, with a ticket for Laufenburg, where he had father, brother and an uncle living. When he came to this town to look for employment, another uncle and the aunt who had met me took him in (I was invited to coffee with them at their home). They had lent him money, because he had not yet drawn his first month's salary from the bank, but they were disgusted with him for having got himself into what they called 'that dreadful service'.

He was German on his father's side, Swiss on his mother's, born on 28 June 1904, in Laufenburg, 'where the Rhine is so narrow one can shout to relations on the Swiss side'. At twenty he left to look for work in Paris, and found it as a clerk, first in a bank, then in a patent attorney's office. His French naturalisation was to have come through in a few days when war was declared. He asked if it could be expedited but naturalisations were cancelled for the duration. Interned at Paris, when the Germans occupied France in 1940 he was directed to report to SS Sturmbannführer Kieffer, as interpreter.

He was very distressed by the hanging of Kieffer. Only after the execution had he learned Kieffer was even on trial. He would have wished to give evidence. Probably it would have made no difference, but, 'I would have liked him to see me *there*, and doing my best for him.' He had heard that the order for the shooting of those commandos was given Kieffer from Berlin. I told him Starr had given evidence for Kieffer.

How had he begun interrogating? It was after a first, unrewarding morning questioning 'Archambaud' that he told Kieffer he believed he would learn more if he might question him alone. During three weeks au pair in Tunbridge Wells he had learned to make tea and thought it would make an English prisoner feel at home. After that he interrogated all the major agents of the French Section, except that the radio operators were interrogated on the technical side of their work by Goetz. A man called Erich Otto, regular SS, was formal head of the radio department, but it was Goetz who conducted the radio-game. (Joseph Goetz had been a schoolmaster, was called up when war began, was Oberleutnant in the German army, detached for service with the Sicherheitspolizei and placed at Kieffer's disposal.)

Goetz asked 'Archambaud' for his code and for his distinctive security check. Using these, he sent a radio message to London as from 'Archambaud'. The reply from London included the words 'You forgot your double security check — Be more careful.' Goetz showed the reply to 'Archambaud', who was bowled over by London's ineptitude and exploded to everybody about it. The radio operators had been told before they were sent out that it was permissible to give their code. It was the security check — in 'Archambaud's' case, double security check — that was the real key: its absence would signify 'Am in German hands'.

Kieffer's direct chief was Oberststurmbannführer Karl Boemelburg, of the Gestapo proper, at 82 Avenue Foch, though there were some matters where Kieffer took instructions from Helmut Kopkov, head of the Reichssicherheitshauptamt in Berlin. Kieffer had his quarters on the fourth floor of no. 84, the radio department was on the second floor, and he, Vogt, had his office on the fifth, where the French Section (Buckmaster) prisoners were kept. There was also no. 86, under a Dr Schmidt, to which were taken the de Gaulle prisoners.

On 18 November 1943 Vogt was told to go with August Scherer, his best friend there, to arrest 'a terrorist, as I am afraid we called them'. When they entered the room of 'Hercule' he was transmitting. He whipped out a pistol and killed Scherer with the first shot. Vogt drew his own, and they each fired the entire contents of their pistols into the other, 'Hercule' having one fewer. When Vogt regained consciousness he was in the Hôpital de la Pitié and 'Hercule' was in the next ward. Kieffer came to visit him there, and told him 'Madeleine', Faye and Starr had got out of their cells and nearly escaped. Starr never betrayed anyone or anything.

When Vogt returned to work in January, his first case was a Swiss. The Swiss asked if he might see 'Archambaud'. 'Archambaud' was in the Hôpital de la Pitié. It was because, after five months, when he was being transferred from the Avenue Foch to Fresnes, he tried to run away and was shot in the leg. Kieffer gave Vogt permission to take the Swiss to 'Archambaud's' bedside. The Swiss said he had informed London of 'Archambaud's' arrest and received a reply: 'Impossible, Archambaud is still transmitting.' He had then ordered his radio to send a further message saying that if 'Archambaud' was still transmitting he was a traitor, for he was in German hands. Now that the Swiss was himself in German hands, he realised it was not actually 'Archambaud' who was operating the set — and wished to apologise.

Then there was a South African major, 'Antoine', who had worked with 'Prosper' and 'Madeleine', returned to London, then was reparachuted into German hands. He was in a towering rage, and seemed to think the people in London had done it deliberately, for he called them 'murderers'.

'Do you believe that?'

'I do not know. If it had been the Japanese, they invented a torpedo that has to be ridden by a man, who is killed when it hits its target. But the English?'

Could 'Antoine' have been told in England that if he was captured he should use such words?

Vogt could not think of a reason for such an instruction.

'Perhaps as a prelude to planting misleading information on you,' I suggested. 'Did he tell you anything which subsequently you found untrue?'

'No.' 'Antoine', after regaining his self-control, had simply closed his mouth.

We discussed how I could present in a book the betrayal of 'Madeleine', in view of the acquittal of the person against whom he had given evidence. He suggested I could just call her 'Renée', for, he said, 'Nobody doubts that the woman with whom I dealt called herself Renée.' The question of her identity had not come up until after the arrest of 'Madeleine', when the woman telephoned again and asked that he should meet her again, at the same place — the gardens of the Trocadero — to pay her the 50,000 francs she had been promised. He went out to meet her, but said he was not authorised to pay in the street. 'You can walk away now, and no one will follow you. But if you want the payment, you will have to come back with me to our office, show your identity card and sign a receipt.' This had not pleased her; she had hesitated; but she had come. The identity card which he saw her produce from her bag was made out in the name Renée Garry. 'My evidence stands challenged only upon the point of my claim to recognise her.'

'How were 'Prosper' and 'Archambaud' arrested?' I asked.

'Through the mail. The mail they sent to England was routed through our office, for photocopying.'

'How did that come about?'

'I cannot say.'

I had become so used to his answering questions in a straight manner, I did not notice the ambiguity in the phrase.

2: THE STARR AFFAIR

Madeleine was published on 29 September 1952. I had said in it nothing about her set being played back, nothing about the radio-game. It was my first book, and I did not want to jeopardise its chance of publication. Now that it was safely out, the BBC had made me an offer for the right to produce a television play based on it, to be written by Duncan Ross. I accepted, subject to the script's being submitted to my approval. This I owed to all those who had given me their witness. I was particularly concerned Vogt should not be made into a typical Gestapo villain. Ross thought he should see the scenes in Paris, and I said I would take him round to meet all the characters.

Mercier, to whom I had written that I was coming, collected me from my hotel and took me out to lunch. He was overcast and silent as he savaged his chop.

'I saw three of my countrymen executed this morning,' he said suddenly. He said they had a rule that if one passed the death sentence one had to see it carried out. He had gone to the prison at dawn. The guard had unlocked the three cells.

'I say "Bonjour", and it sounds ironic, because for them it is the worst morning. I offer them each a cigarette. It would be unforgivable to come to an execution without cigarettes. There is no talk. It has all been heard before you in court. You know what they have done, they know what they have done; it only remains to go through with the execution of the penalty the law prescribes. There is no hate, only cooperation. You pray that each one will walk to the wall where he has to stand to be shot without making too awful a scene. He wants to cut a last figure as a man. So you want the same thing. There is an identity.'

'An identity?'

'I have never passed sentence without identifying with the man on whom I passed it.' The causes of treason, 'in the kind of cases I have to try', though superficially various and complex, were in essence few and simple. 'With a woman, jealousy. He betrayed her with another woman, so she betrayed him to the Gestapo. That has been seen several times. With a man, greed for money or fear for his life, or moral fear, because some situation presses on him. These germs are in all of us. Have I never coveted luxury and ostentation? Have I never feared, physically and morally? I get very Jansenist. I think we were born with an inbuilt tendency to do wrong, simply because we are men and descend from Adam, from which we are only redeemed by Grace. When I appear before my Maker at the Last Judgement, I am not going to plead my works. I am going to say, "Lord, have mercy on me, a sinner." In this case, there were no mitigating circumstances. At any rate, none that I could see. But how does one know what springs and promptings are in another man's heart, unspoken, unformulated, even to himself? I believe in a Justice above, which rectifies ours. If I didn't, I could not do my job.'

These words would remain long with me.

On the next day I saw Starr. I was considering the possibility to ask him what he thought of a book on him. He was tempted, but uncertain. When Ross arrived, he told him his story, trying it out on him, including the awkward bits.

Ross said, 'Write a brave book, Starr, and it will go round the world.'

Ross told us he believed their organisation was called SOE. It surprised him Starr did not know this. 'What did you and the other recruits call it between yourselves?'

'We never knew it had a name. We called it the organisation, "The Thing".'

Ross had also ferreted out, as he believed, that the head of it was a General Gubbins. Starr had heard of no one higher than Buckmaster. 'We were told the head of it was Churchill, but of course there must have been people in between.'

On 17 December I flew back to London. Starr had given the green light, and on Christmas Eve I walked to Her Majesty's Stationery Office and — just before it closed for the holiday — bought myself a copy of the Official Secrets Act.

On 9 February 1953 I flew back to Paris, met Mercier for coffee at the Palais de Chaillot, where he was briefly assigned, and told him it was settled. *The Starr Affair* was written during the ensuing four weeks. I stayed at my usual little Hôtel Confort in the rue de Casablanca, and went to the Starrs' every evening. I took down practically at his dictation, and during each following day typed the text out, organising it into chapters.

I flew back to London on 12 March and gave it to Gollancz almost immediately. Their reaction was one of near disbelief, that the Germans should have been playing back the radio sets, luring agents to be dropped straight into their hands, and that we should be the only people to know about it. They felt almost overwhelmed by the responsibility of giving this out, upon one man's word, against the official silence. There was nothing about it in Colonel Buckmaster's book, *Specially Employed* (Batchworth, 1952), which was a success story. I had interviews with their lawyer, Harold Rubinstein, who showed me a letter from Victor Gollancz, saying he was not worried about libel in the ordinary sense, only that we should all find ourselves in the Tower.

The typescript was submitted, not to Buckmaster or Miss Atkins, but to the regular authorities, for official clearance, and reappeared with a wrapper saying, 'The War Office, in consultation with the Foreign Office, have held that no security objection can be taken to the publication of this book. They add that the departments concerned in no way vouch for its accuracy or otherwise.'

The book's serialisation in the *Sunday Empire News* brought a letter from Colonel Buckmaster, occupying a column, right down the front page, saying it must have been German bragging which deceived Starr into mistaking the penetration of one network for the collapse of all:

> To say the French Section deliberately sent men and materials into the hands of the German security police is monstrously and libellously untrue.

I had not said it as from myself, though I had, in a footnote, quoted the words which Vogt had told me 'Antoine' spoke to him. I replied cautiously that more than one network had been penetrated.

I was feeling myself to be under heavy fire when, on 20 August, I received a telegram from Colonel Frank Spooner, inviting me to spend some days with him and his wife at their home in Guernsey. I knew that Spooner had been head of the Security School at Beaulieu and felt sure I was being summoned to be told my book constituted a gross breach of security. I flew to Guernsey on 25 August. Colonel Spooner was on the tiny airfield to meet me, and drove me away in a small bumpy car. 'If I had had my way your little friend would be alive today. That is the first thing I wanted to say.' He had recommended against her being sent to France, as having 'too little security sense — and not hard enough'. Buckmaster had preferred the opinion of Miss Atkins.

He was Indian Army, like my father, growing daffodils in his retirement. Outwardly stiff, his mind was nimble.

We had hardly entered the house, at St Martin's, when the telephone rang. It was for me, from the *Sunday Empire News*, to read me a further letter they had received from Buckmaster and would print in their next issue:

> ... Miss Fuller has no knowledge whatever of the chain of command. She states that not one but a number of our networks became German controlled. I know it was only one and consider I am in a better position to know than she is.

I told Spooner. He said, 'If even *one* became German controlled that is something I never knew. I learned it from your book. Now Buckmaster has confirmed it.' And he added, 'Chalk that up to yourself.'

It dawned on me he was on my side.

After lunch I got out pencil and paper and his wife Marjorie left us to work. SOE, the Special Operations Executive, he said, was 'Churchill's baby', responsible to the Cabinet neither through the War Office nor the Foreign Office but through a temporary Ministry of Economic Warfare. The first head was Hugh Dalton, succeeded by Lord Selborne. Then came Major-General Sir Colin Gubbins, then Henry Nathan Sporborg, of the City solicitors Slaughter and May; then came the heads of country sections, including Buckmaster, as head of F Section. Its sister service, RF (Repubhque Franchise), often called the de Gaulle or Free French Section, under James Hutchinson, a Glasgow shipowner, also depended from Gubbins, though not through Sporborg. A number of big firms, notably Courtaulds, had donated funds to SOE. The only real brain — and certainly the most powerful personality — in SOE seemed to Spooner to be Miss Atkins, of Rumanian nationality, with whom he had several clashes. 'Not having a rank helped her. If she had been a major in the ATS, I would have outranked her, but one can't outrank a Miss.' She was made squadron-leader in the WAAF later, probably after her British naturalisation, in 1944 — very likely to give her authority in the war crimes trials, in which she represented the Section.

Spooner himself had retired from the Army before the war began, when he wrote to ask if he could still be useful. One of the first jobs he was given was to train the agents to assassinate Heidrich. He had no compunction in regard to Heidrich, who was an odious human being, but in reprisal all the people of Lidice were massacred. 'That had nothing to do with Buckmaster, that came to me through a different channel.' Nevertheless, he thought that right through SOE there was too little regard for the civilian population and the reprisals it was likely to suffer for SOE operations.

I told him Vogt had told me the locations and functions of the training schools, as he had them from Kieffer. 'Are they correct?'

'Yes. I wish he had told you how they knew!' He recalled that he had reported for careless talk a conducting officer, André Simon, who took trainee agents from one school to another.

Marjorie, who had brought in tea, said, 'The security was appalling.' It was in SOE she had met Frank, and whenever she took a taxi to Orchard Court, the driver responded with 'Spy HQ!'

There had appeared three German books. *London Calling North Pole*, by Colonel H. J. Giskes, former Chief of German

Intelligence (Abwehr) for Holland, Belgium and Northern France, disclosed that from March 1941 every one of the British agents parachuted into Holland had been captured, each one's radio being played back so that further ones were dropped into German hands. That the entire organisation in Holland was in German hands was realised only when Pieter Dourlein and J. B. Ubbink escaped on 30 August 1943, and on arrival in Switzerland disclosed the radio-game.

The others, *La Chatte* and *Monsieur Jean*, were both by Erich Borchers, from Adolf Sponholtz, 1950 and 1951 (German text despite titles). The first told of a drama of 1941, of which more later. The second told how Sergeant Hugo Bleicher of the Abwehr, after his capture of 'La Chatte', arrested in March 1943 one Marsac, whom he bamboozled into giving away people — among them Roger Bardet. Bardet, to save his life, became Bleicher's agent and introduced him to his chief, Henri Frager, 'Paul', who thus became German-controlled without knowing it. The rivalry between the Abwehr and the SD extended to their respective French agents, and Bardet was in rivalry with 'Gilbert'. Frager loved Bardet as a son, but suspected 'Gilbert', whom Bleicher told him worked for the SD. When 'Gilbert' boarded Frager on a plane for London, he tried to make Bardet board it too. Bleicher commented (I translate from the German):

> 'Gilbert' was the most important double-agent of Sturmbannführer Kieffer He worked for him and for London. He was a quite unscrupulous man and was lacking in that inner sense of right conduct which characterised every other agent I have known. 'Gilbert' was wholly selfish. He worked for his own profit. For that, he was capable of anything, even treason. He was what soldiers call a swine.

Now there appeared an English edition, entitled (with reference to one of Bleicher's pseudonyms) *Colonel Henri's Story*, translated and annotated by Ian Colvin (Kimber, 1954). Colvin wrote (p. 127):

> In the involved mind of Bleicher one can trace only one prevailing thought in this intrigue with Roger Bardet, to defame 'Gilbert'... Colonel Buckmaster has identified 'Gilbert' to the Editor as the code-name for his Air Movements Officer in France... The assertion of Bleicher is that this important man was in the same role of subservience towards the SD Chief Kieffer as Roger Bardet was to Bleicher... 'Gilbert', a Frenchman, is at liberty today....

It was suggested I should meet Louis Burdet, Manager of the Stafford Hotel in St James's Place. He received me in his office at the Stafford and said he had been DMR (Délégué Militaire Régional) — that is chief — for RF of the whole of the region from Marseilles to the Italian border. The DMRs had geometrical names and he was 'Circonferance'. He knew nothing of 'Gilbert'. What burnt in his memory was that he had been told a series of messages with the names of colours — Plan Red, Plan Blue, or Plan Black — which would be broadcast over the BBC (BBC messages not to be confused with radio messages). On hearing them he was to order his people to do different things, such as to cut railway lines and blow up bridges. The last, Plan Black, meant emerge from cover and engage the enemy openly, and was to be broadcast on the eve of the invasion of the South of France from the Mediterranean. Plan Black was broadcast on the evening of 5 June 1944, and he brought his people out immediately. When he learned in the morning there had been a landing in Normandy he was not at first disconcerted, for he thought it had been planned to invade from the Channel and the Mediterranean on the same day; so his men fought on, in the confidence of a landing in the south to support them before the evening. It did not arrive, and they were badly mown down by the German troops. When he realised the support was not coming, he tried to get his people back under cover, but it was too late. They had been much weakened. The Communist networks had received the same set of signals but had not budged. How had they known the 5 June signals were best disregarded? If they had private intelligence, they did not tip him, and how did they have it? The landings in the south did not materialise until 15 August, when the Communists at once rose, and were able to make a much better showing for not having been prematurely exposed.

This suggested a line of thought different from, or additional to, that I had been pursuing.

Immediately on my return to London, I had written to Vogt, asking him if he knew anything of 'Gilbert'. His reply electrified me:

> I know 'Gilbert' and his affair very well and I gave all the details to the Tribunal Militaire Permanante de Paris in 1948. 'Gilbert', whose real name is known to the British authorities, had obtained an acquittal before my arrival in Paris. It is the most distressing case I have known, far graver than that of Renée.... I could only tell you about it verbally, not in writing. Know only that I consider 'Gilbert' responsible for the great disaster of the French Section in 1943, at the moment of the arrest of Suttill, alias 'Prosper' and Norman, alias 'Archambaud' and their colleagues.
>
> 'Archambaud' had Gilbert for cover-name, and it was under that name his colleagues in the Resistance knew him. He had nothing to do with the other 'Gilbert', but I fear many have confused them....
>
> Ernest

Meanwhile, Wing-Commander Yeo-Thomas, GC, the 'White Rabbit' of RF, had offered me an appointment for the 18th, at The Friend at Hand, Bloomsbury. Tough as a pugilist, he was accompanied by Barbara, refined, fair and elegant. He had come over for an operation — legacy of a Gestapo beating over the kidneys at 82 Avenue Foch (RF and F Section prisoners had different interrogators). He had been brought in hospital, a copy of *The Starr Affair*. He suggested I see André Simon, the wine merchant, an F Section man.

3: A NEW QUEST

André Simon poured me champagne. Had I heard of Déricourt?

'No.'

He was surprised I had not heard of Déricourt. He had been very much discussed. He received British aircraft and boarded on them agents leaving France for England. After the war he had been charged with intelligence with the enemy. He had been acquitted, but Vera Atkins remained convinced of his guilt. 'I have proof,' she had said. But Simon had not seen the proof. The agents who landed on his fields were mostly not arrested. 'But they were trailed,' she said. Simon maintained it was impossible to trail a man for months. Before becoming a conducting officer, Simon had been parachuted into the South of France in 1942, and he made a point. Between the times when one had to do something, there was seemingly endless time during which — having no normal job — one had nothing to do. 'Nobody tells you how *boring* it is.' Either one sat in one's room by oneself, or one sat in the bar, drinking. Nobody could follow a man through months of this sort of thing. 'Déricourt was a rascal, of course.' He always said he only served for the money. 'There was no hypocrisy about him.' Yet Simon did not think he would have sent people to their deaths for money. 'I would drink a glass of wine with him any day. I've been tight as a tick in his company more times than I can remember.'

I realised then that Déricourt must be the real name of 'Gilbert'.

On 18 October I lunched at the Stafford with George Whitehead, of RF, and he asked if I would see Maurice Norman, the father of Gilbert Norman, 'Archambaud'. The old man, who was President of the British Chamber of Commerce in Paris, had been fighting a long battle to clear his son's name.

On 21 October Norman came to see me, bent and decrepit, bearing five files of correspondence on the case of his son, who had been shot at Mauthausen on 6 September 1944. An Abbé Paul Guillaume, historian of the Resistance, had written of him as a traitor, and he had been trying to obtain from our government material to refute these charges. He himself thought the big traitor was Pierre Culioli, a *Résistant* already tried and acquitted. In one of his letters to a British government department he said he wished his son *had* given 'the lethal pill' to Culioli. The reply did not include an allusion to this mysterious phrase.

I told him I did not think it was Culioli. I told him what Vogt had told me. He then wrote and gave me a letter to Vogt, which I forwarded.

Vogt sent me a copy of his reply. After saying he had been touched by receiving Norman's letter and was infinitely sorry his son was dead, he continued (I translate from his French):

> I was for a few weeks in daily contact with your son and able to appreciate his superior intelligence, his loyal character and his sweetness [*gentillesse*]. I took my meals with him at the same table, and had conversations with him on all kinds of subjects unconnected with his service, and hoped to see him after the war.
>
> The affair of your son is rather complicated ... I never considered either 'Prosper' or 'Archambaud' as having betrayed their country.

At first reading, I thought this was a clearance; then as I re-read it, I became less and less sure. He had written a full page, yet nowhere said categorically 'He gave us no information.' It was not like Vogt to expand, yet miss the point. There were trap sentences... conversations 'on subjects unconnected with the service' did not preclude on subjects connected with it as well. *He* did not think of him as a traitor, therefore other people might do. And in the circumstances, I would have preferred a stronger word than '*gentillesse*'.

In his covering letter, he said he would explain when we met. I took the train from Liverpool Street at 7.30 p.m. on n November 1954; the journey took over twenty-four hours. Vogt was on the platform to meet me. With him was his wife, a Frenchwoman, who had still been held by the French when I saw him before. I had dined on the train, but they had bought a bottle of wine for me and in my honour he served tea, which he made as he made it at Avenue Foch.

It was impossible to speak of 'Gilbert' except in private because he had been acquitted. His real name was d'Héricourt or Déricourt. The spelling by French magistrates was not uniform. Until he heard this name from them, Vogt had thought he was English.

He told me the whole story that night. In the morning I wrote it out in my hotel, before bringing it over to their flat for checking. Vogt read it, then suddenly said he would write it out himself, 'so that I know that any nuances that are in it are those I have put in it myself. He wrote in pencil, on thin sheets of foolscap (I translate from his French):

It was not until the arrest of 'Prosper', 'Archambaud' and their colleagues that Kieffer gave me for the first time photostats of documents bearing the reference BOE 48 and it was not until some time after that I learned from him that

BOE 48 (Agent 48 of Boemelburg) was one 'Gilbert', responsible for the landing of British aircraft in the occupied zone of France. 'Gilbert' was charged by the French Section with the duty of selecting landing-grounds, organising the landing of aircraft, receiving the agents who landed by these aircraft, putting those due to return to London aboard homebound aircraft and forwarding by the same aircraft the mail of the agents of the French Section.

To the end of 1943, 'Gilbert' was the agent of Boemelburg, chief of the Gestapo in France, and came directly under him. At the time of Boemelburg's departure for Vichy, towards the end of 1943 or early in 1944, he became the agent of Kieffer and worked immediately under him. However, I never met 'Gilbert' in our office at Avenue Foch. It was Goetz who made the liaison between Kieffer and 'Gilbert', and their meetings took place outside our office.

In fact I only saw him once, shortly before his return to London in February, 1944. Kieffer had never entirely trusted him and told me to accompany Goetz to a meeting with him as a precaution since he was afraid 'Gilbert' might have Goetz kidnapped and carried to London. The meeting took place in an empty apartment not far from the Arc de Triomphe. Goetz had a key to it. 'Gilbert' came alone and confirmed that he was going to London. He said he thought he was under suspicion. He gave Goetz the BBC code message that would announce his arrival there. A few days afterwards we heard this message broadcast by the BBC.

Later we arrested Robert Benoist, alias 'Lionel', a French officer of the French Section, who told me that he had travelled back to London in the same aircraft as 'Gilbert', and that in London he had been questioned about him by the British Security Service, which suspected 'Gilbert' of being a traitor. Robert Benoist told me he had testified in favour of 'Gilbert' as he had no reason to suppose he was a traitor. He asked me if 'Gilbert' was really in relation with us. I did not answer. 'Gilbert' had a letter-box in Paris where he or his courier, 'Claire', received agents and the mail for agents of the French Section for the whole of the occupied zone of France. The letter-box and the meetings in a café in Paris became known to Kieffer, though I presume that meetings must also have been held in places we did not know about.

We came to know of 'Gilbert's' landing-ground near Angers and Kieffer was from time to time aware of BBC messages which gave warning of forthcoming landings. 'Gilbert' passed on to Kieffer some of the mail and information about the arrival of aircraft. In return, he obtained a promise that the Germans would never shoot down or capture any of the aircraft landing on his landing-grounds. Thus he could receive and despatch aircraft in all tranquillity. The British agents' mail for London, which 'Gilbert' passed on to London, was photographed by our service and then returned to 'Gilbert', who sent it on to London. I do not suppose that he passed over the entire mail to Kieffer.

'Prosper', 'Archambaud' and their colleagues were arrested as the result of reports intended for London, which 'Gilbert' had passed over to Boemelburg. After their arrest, Kieffer handed to me photographic copies of the reports that 'Prosper' and 'Archambaud' sent to London. They contained almost complete information about their activities, together with addresses and names. It was these reports which enabled us to bring off our big sweep of the 'Prosper' network.

There was, Vogt said, something else, which he had not put in this statement. There was an occasion when three agents were arrested in Paris after being trailed from 'Gilbert's' field. The proceedings of that night differed from the usual, but he could not remember in what respect, or perhaps had never understood. Perhaps the trailing gang had gone on to the field or else there had been a second gang...

He had never been present at any of 'Gilbert's' operations, so did not know how close the trailing gang came. He had once visited his field near Angers, not in his company but in that of a French prisoner who said that might have been where he left his radio — they did not find it.

Benoist was not parachuted back until after 'Gilbert's' recall, and his arrest was not 'Gilbert's' fault.

When he referred to an empty apartment, did he mean literally empty?

Yes. Bare floorboards. Nobody lived there.

Why did they let 'Gilbert' return to London?

He did not know. Probably they reasoned that if they detained him London would stop sending aircraft to his fields, whereas if they let him go he might return. He told Goetz 'Marc' would carry on. 'Marc' was his assistant, but was never in intelligence with their service.

It was obvious Goetz would know much more, being 'Gilbert's' direct, regular contact. But where was Goetz, and would he talk?

'What was "Gilbert" like?' I asked.

Vogt smiled with slight irony. 'He made what in any other circumstances would have been a good impression.' His clothes were of good quality. He had a good presence. 'Agreeable face, even.' Tall, for a Frenchman. His bearing had in it no sense of shame. 'One would have said, a gentleman.'

'What happened at "Gilbert's" trial?'

He did not know. Vogt had been first arrested by the Americans, who passed him to the British, who sent him back to the Americans, who having once finished with him, greeted him with 'What have you been sent back to us for?' It was, he learned later, just at that moment the French asked for him, and they had sent him to the Americans instead. When eventually he arrived in Paris, he was asked to make statements regarding a number of persons, including 'Gilbert'. A few days later, one of the officers said to him, 'It is a pity we did not have you earlier. He has been tried and acquitted. If we had had you, the verdict might have been different.'

We spoke of 'Archambaud'. 'Did you notice my letter to Mr Norman was written in a certain way?' Vogt asked.

'Yes.'

He had made and destroyed a number of earlier attempts. His aim had been to write something that would give the greatest possible comfort to a grieving father, short of telling a lie. He wanted to discourage him from pursuing details; they would not make him happier. He had referred to his son's 'loyal character', because he felt sure 'Archambaud's' natural character had been one of loyalty to Britain; that having been said, his confidence in his chiefs in London had gone to nothing. Certainly not thinking of himself as having become a German agent, he yet threw himself on the mercy of the Avenue Foch staff. He said he was going to go to London after the war and ask for an inquiry. In the meantime, he advised all other prisoners to cooperate with their captors, and did so himself. 'What was unfortunate was he had such a good memory. He gave me so many names and addresses without hesitation. If he had said sometimes he could not remember, I might have believed it, and he could have kept some back.' A complicated false story could often be broken, but a simple 'Can't remember' is impossible to prove false. 'It would have been worth trying on me!'

Vogt did not know why both 'Prosper' and 'Archambaud' had it in their minds it was from London they had been given away. He never told them there was a traitor in London. He showed them photostats of the mail they had sent to London, so they must have realised it had been betrayed by 'Gilbert'.

They seemed convinced, however, they had been betrayed from far higher up.

'Do you really intend to publish all I have told you about 'Gilbert'?' He was afraid that 'Gilbert' would sue me.

On 15 November I caught the sleeper to Paris, and on the 16th Major Mercier (as he had now become) collected me from my hotel and took me out to dinner. When I told him I had a statement from Vogt, he seemed at first disinclined to look at a new exhibit for the prosecution after the acquittal. Yet, as we sat side by side in the restaurant, and I put the thin pencilled sheets into his hand, he read them. 'Even if *we* believe Ernest,' he said (he was always amused by my faith in Vogt, though not actually saying it was misplaced), 'I do not know whether a panel of my colleagues would have done so, or if they had done so, whether they would have convicted. I didn't sit on this case.'

Some experienced French officers, he said, thought that Vogt tried to give his evidence honestly, but as Kieffer's former adjutant he might have felt obliged to maintain certain reserves and make some dissimulations, from motives not necessarily discreditable. His statement contained a lot of 'Kieffer told me', that is to say, 'reported speech'. (Mercier meant what English lawyers call 'hearsay'.) Reported speech was not evidence. If they could have had Kieffer go into the box, it would have been a different matter. Vogt had not the capacity to affirm what Kieffer told him was true, or stand cross-examination on it. There were two possibilities to bear in mind. Vogt might not have understood what Kieffer told him quite correctly; and even if he had understood it correctly and it was true as far as it went, it might not be the whole truth. There might be things within Kieffer's knowledge, relevant to the case, which he did not impart to Vogt. So Vogt, taking the little truth he had been told to be the whole, could draw invalid conclusions, which could even colour his way of remembering.

The statement, Mercier pointed out, fell into two parts. Vogt saw photocopied mail with BOE 48 on the back. That is evidence. He went with Goetz to an empty flat where they met a man who told them certain things. That is evidence. But the link between these two pieces of evidence was hearsay and deduction. How did he know BOE 48 was 'Gilbert', that the man he and Goetz met was this 'Gilbert', or that he was Colonel Buckmaster's Air Movements Officer? Behind each of these connecting links there was a silent, 'Kieffer told me'. Mercier said, 'These are all points which, if I had been acting in my function, I would have had to draw to the attention of my colleagues.' If Vogt had given this evidence from the box, these were points at which he would have stopped him. The last paragraph he would have directed his colleagues (the panel of military *juges*) to disregard altogether. That it was 'as a result' of the photostatting of their mail that 'Prosper' and 'Archambaud' were arrested was 'a supposition of Vogt'. Kieffer could have had sources of information about them he did not disclose to Vogt, which are still unknown to Vogt. 'Before one can take a man out to be shot, one has to be so terribly, terribly sure, almost surer than it is possible for man to be.'

'I'm not trying to get him shot,' I said.

On the following day, 17 November 1954, I called on Starr and the door was opened to me by his elder brother, Colonel George Starr, DSO, MC, 'Hilaire'. In Gascony, he had been Organiser of one of the few successful networks that survived to engage the Germans after the invasion. But, he said to me over the lunch at which I was invited to join the family, in a

49

wild, forested region, what he was organising was a Maquis, hardly liable to penetration by double agents. It would be false to make comparison between a network such as his and those I was investigating, based on Paris. But he said an odd thing. At one moment he warned London through his radio operator that the radio of a neighbouring network was German-controlled. The reply he received was: 'Mind your own business, we know what we are doing.'

There must be reports of Déricourt's trial in French newspapers. I flew back to Paris on 6 January 1955, and on the same day called on Yeo-Thomas at the Federation of British Industries. His window was squashed up against the blue-green dome of the Opera. He had been talking with Michel Pichard, who for a while received and despatched aircraft for RF, which gave me the cue to ask if he knew anything about the man who did it for the Buckmaster Section.

'Déricourt. Yes. He was a German agent.' Pichard told him Buckmaster's pick-up man could be in liaison with the Germans. Just after that he had to return to England, in November 1943, so he told his own chiefs and asked them to tell Buckmaster.

He could not remember the date of the trial, but suggested I see Roger Hérissé, 'Dutêrtre', who had also done some receiving and despatching of aircraft for RF until arrested and sent to concentration camp. He rang him and made an appointment for us to meet at his office on the 13th.

When I returned to Yeo-Thomases on the 13th, the sky behind the blue-green of the Opera was turning the peculiar yellow of threatened snow. Hérissé rang to say he was not well enough to come out. Yeo-Thomas said I would visit him at his home. He put me in a taxi.

By the time we arrived at a small house in the outer suburb of Puteaux, the snow was falling fast. Hérissé told me he had gone to England, because although he was a pilot himself it was considered necessary he take the special Lysander course at Tempsford. On entering the pilots' mess, he saw propped against a wall a propeller with its nose bashed in. He asked how it had happened. James McCairns said he had been flying it, and the chief of operations on the ground, Déricourt, had set one of the lights too near a tree. Nevertheless, when Hérissé went to England for a reunion on 11 November 1954, he heard Déricourt spoken of as 'always careful with the aircraft'.

He would give me a piece of information of which he was not at liberty to disclose the source. Déricourt had been arrested at a very early stage of the war, and when he went to England, in 1942, it was in the German interest.

'I cannot use it like that,' I said. It was the gravest accusation made yet, without evidence and upon anonymous denunciation. 'Of what nationality is your informant?'

'French. A person of weight and consequence.'

Yeo-Thomas suggested I should see Gaston Cohen, MC, 'Justin' of F Section. I called at Cohen's office and he took me out to lunch. He had worked in the Marne area, as radio to a Swiss, a self-constituted *Résistant*, but liaised with 'Prosper'. (This must have been the Swiss that both Mme Balachowsky and Vogt had mentioned.) 'I had an appointment with 'Archambaud' at 9.30 in the morning on 24 June.' Archambaud had been arrested in the small hours, and had he instantly turned traitor would have brought the Germans to the rendezvous. 'Madeleine' was not the only one to signal to London that 'Archambaud' had been arrested. Cohen did. The replies he kept getting were 'Impossible' and 'Check'.

Apparently, they were still receiving transmissions over 'Archambaud's' circuit. Cohen's Swiss chief told him to signal that if so 'Archambaud' must be a traitor, for certainly he had been arrested.

This was the story Vogt had told me, but Vogt had been unable to remember the name of the Swiss.

'What was the name of your Swiss chief?'

'Jacques... How silly, I have forgotten.'

4: DÉRICOURT ON TRIAL

There was an index to the files at *France-Soir*, but it was behind the counter. I did not like to ask the assistant to find the Déricourt trial, in case it got around an inquiry was being made. So I just went on turning the pages, year by year. On 19 January 1955, at last, I found myself looking at a photograph of 'Le Capitaine Gilbert', over an account of his acquittal. The issue was dated 8 June 1948. I was able to buy a copy. Then I went round to the offices of *Figaro, Le Monde, Paris-Presse, Le Parisien Libéré, Franc-Tireur, Libération, Combat* and *L'Aurore*, and bought their issues of the same date. Putting the accounts together, it was possible to form a picture of what had happened.

At 10 a.m. Henri Déricourt, thirty-eight, dressed in a dark blue suit with a discreet white stripe, had entered the box at the Caserne de Reuille of the Tribunal Militaire de Paris. His gaze was direct and his personality commanded instant sympathy, said *Libération*. The President of the court, Dejean de la Batie, asked him if he denied having been in contact with the enemy.

'Not at all,' he replied, and *Le Parisien Libéré* told its readers his sincerity showed. On 2 June two Germans called at his flat at 1 rue Colonel Moll. He had known them at Le Bourget when they were pilots for Lufthansa. Now they were in Luftwaffe uniform. But they asked him out for an aperitif, and he went with them. When he got into their car, he found three Germans in civilian clothes already in it. At the Porte Maillot the two pilots got out. He was about to follow them, but was detained and driven on round the Bois de Boulogne. One of the civilians told him that he knew he had left France via

Gibraltar in 1942, gone to England, engaged in the RAF and been parachuted back to receive and despatch aircraft. 'He knew my whole life. I did not know what to do. I am an airman, not a spy.'

'I could have you shot as a spy,' this person had said to him. 'But you are intelligent and I hope you will work for us.'

'And what did you reply?' asked the President of the court.

'I accepted, naturally. Not for money, as some newspapers have alleged. Not from fear of death; for a pilot, it is classic. But because I wished to continue my work and save the lives of the agents of the Intelligence Service dependent on me.'

He was 'a prisoner at liberty', but thought best 'to feign to work for them, so as to keep the contacts for future exploitation'. Not to arouse Boemelburg's suspicion he might play them double, he had given the location of eight out of fourteen airfields he had found in Touraine. 'The information I gave them was not of consequence. I threw sand in their eyes. The eight airfields I disclosed to them had not been homologated by London, so I knew no aircraft would land on them. The Resistance would not suffer.'

The President asked if he had informed his chiefs in London.

'I did not trust the discretion of the intermediaries. I gave nothing to Boemelburg but promises. If I talked with him, it was to sound him, not inform him.'

'What a dangerous game!' exclaimed the President.

'The greater, then, my merit!'

Major Guyon, observed that he had received Bodington and Agazarian when they landed in July, he had known Norman, with whom they had a rendezvous in the rue de Rome, was in German hands, yet failed to warn them. Agazarian had been arrested.

'I said, "Don't go there. He has been arrested. His concièrge told me."'

'Did you say it was from the Germans you knew it?'

'It would have been no use. To convince a senior British officer he is mistaken is impossible.'

The German witnesses, Colonel Dr Knocken, Dr Goetz, Joseph Placke, all of the SD, and Bleicher of the Abwehr, provided the prosecution with little support. Cross-examined by Maître Moro-Giafferi (celebrating his seventieth birthday) for the defence, they agreed that very likely Déricourt had only pretended to work for them. According to Goetz, he interested them only in as much as they hoped he might one day be able to tell them the date and place of the invasion.

Le Parisien Libéré observed:

> One would have found it difficult to believe the Abwehr [sic] asked nothing further than fields that had not been homologated, had not the German witnesses come to testify that the accused interested them only in so much as he might be able to tell them the date and place of the Invasion.

That closed the morning's session. When the hearing was resumed in the afternoon the whole ground was taken from under the prosecution when 'the very mysterious Major Bodington of the Intelligence Service' went into the box. He said, 'Déricourt told me of his contacts with the Germans within hours of my arrival on his airfield in July 1943.'

'What did you say?' asked Maître Moro-Giafferi.

'I advised him not to break them. It was the natural thing.'

Bodington said he had remained in France for a month, and must have been arrested if Déricourt, who knew his address, had told the Germans. 'If I had to start all over again, I would start with Déricourt.'

People who had passed from France to England through Déricourt's hands included General Zeller, who wished to shake his hand, General Ely (later Commander-in-Chief French Armed Forces), M. Mitterand, Mimstre des Anciens Combattants (later a President of France), Mme Féliz Gouin, wife of the Prime Minister, who sent a written testimony that Déricourt had fetched her from a clinic near Istres where she was under surveillance, Mme Pierre Block, wife of the Minister, M. Roualt, Director-Adjutant of the Préfecture de Police, Major Gerson, M. Lucien Rachet, M. Didier-Daurat, M. Fille-Lambie and M. Wuyard, an assistant of Déricourt's team.

Major Guyon, seeking to delay the acquittal, asked the President for permission to put supplementary questions. Maître Moro-Giafferi, riding the tide of victory, would have none of it. 'If he is guilty, there is still death and the firing-squad for traitors. If he is innocent, give him back his honour.'

The nine military judges were out for only a few minutes. When they returned, it was with a unanimous verdict of 'not guilty'.

I was puzzled. If Déricourt had told Bodington of his relations with the Germans, then Bodington was in honour bound to come forward and say so. He might have advised him to play along with them until it could be decided what to do, but then he would have had to inform Buckmaster. If he did so, it seemed extraordinary Buckmaster should sanction his continuing to receive British agents landing in France for a further six months, until Yeo-Thomas's warning was received. Had Bodington kept it to himself? And what would that mean?

It occurred to me there should be an account of Déricourt's arrest 'Eighteen months is a long time in the life of a man,' said *Libération*. 'What can compensate him for the eighteen months in Fresnes and the calumnies heaped on his head?' I turned back through the pages of *France-Soir* for eighteen months, and found in its issue of 29 November 1946: DOUBLE AGENT CAPTAIN GILBERT ARRESTED. I bought copies of that date's issue of all the other papers too. Déricourt, it appeared, had before the war flown for a civil airline, Air Bleu, and at an early stage in the war was a test pilot, till he went to England. He was accused of having during the period of his mission entered into relations with Boemelburg, Goetz, Placke and the Bony-Lafont gang of the rue Lauriston. (Pierre Bony was the French police inspector in the prewar Stavinsky scandal.) *Combat* cited an unnamed one of the Germans as saying, 'It was through Captain 'Gilbert' we achieved our great masterpiece of the war; he frequently received payments of several millions of francs.' Déricourt had told the same story as at his trial, but had named the man in the car who trapped him with menaces as Dr Goetz. In the box, at his trial, he had not named him. It was presumably upon the statement of the German witness that the prosecution had been brought. Why had they changed the tenor of their evidence at the trial?

It was mentioned that Déricourt had earlier faced a smuggling charge, at Croydon, on 15 April 1946. So on my return to London I went to the Newspaper Library of the British Museum and applied for the files of the *Croydon Times* and *Croydon Advertiser* for April 1946. In these the case was big news. I found also a small paragraph in the *Daily Telegraph*. Putting the accounts together, Déricourt, thirty-six, had brought in an airliner from Paris on the evening of 10 April, and was to take off again at eight the next morning. He passed through the customs, but one of the customs officers, happening to walk down the passage which led to the aircraft, five minutes before it was to take off, noticed him closing up a bag. He asked him what he had put into it. 'A box of cigars,' said Déricourt. He was invited to return to the customs.

Beneath a pair of pyjamas were found fifteen pieces of platinum and a nugget of gold. In his canvas bag were 139 pieces of gold bullion, in nuggets and in strips, and £1,320 in £1 notes. The platinum weighed 20lb 1oz, the gold 14lb 10oz, and was valued at £1,500. The fines leviable were £9,474 on the platinum, £4,500 on the gold and £426 on the notes, a total of £18,000. Smuggling was punishable by imprisonment. Déricourt produced £100 which he said had been paid him to carry the metal to France.

The aircraft was waiting for its pilot. Déricourt was allowed to fly it to France, and return to England to face the charges. On 12 April he appeared in the Croydon Borough Court and was remanded in custody. On 23 April he reappeared, defended by Derek Curtis Bennett KC and two junior counsels. Déricourt told the magistrates that two weeks before he had met a man in Paris whom he had known in 1944 when they both belonged to SOE and who bore the code-name 'Ignace'.

'Ignace' told him he was building up a new underground movement and needed funds, invited him to bring them over from England and, on his consenting, instructed him to contact a Mr Robert Marshal at the Savoy Hotel, London, and to give him a lady's white handkerchief. 'I was to give him the handkerchief so that he would know I was the right one.' Having brought in his aircraft on the evening of the 10th, he telephoned Mr Marshal at the hotel and a meeting was arranged. He gave Marshal the handkerchief and Marshal gave him a parcel, which he told him contained £10,000 worth of gold. It was the contents of this parcel which he had attempted to smuggle.

Curtis Bennett, defending, told the bench that Déricourt had escaped from France in 1942 by way of Spain, come to England and joined the RAF, and that in 1943 he had been parachuted back as an agent of SOE. He had been sent on secret missions; he had been trusted and his word had been accepted. He was traced by the Gestapo, escaped to England and was parachuted into France for the second time 'on important work for the underground in preparation for the invasion'. For that work he had been recommended for the DSO and held the Croix de Guerre 'with three bars'. Later he rejoined the Air Force, had been seriously wounded when his aircraft was shot down and had spent some time in bed.

'I suppose that during his work in France he would think nothing of carrying two dozen fictitious passports,' said Curtis Bennett. 'He has spent most of his life doing unorthodox things, for which he has had credit.' The French Resistance movement was still in being 'to protect democracy should it again become necessary and Déricourt was doing a job for it. As a result of his action, he had already lost his employment with Air France.'

The magistrates noted that he had lost his career; they appreciated also that he had willingly returned to face the charges, and while the offence was serious they recognised 'the seriousness of the defence'. They imposed a fine of £300 on the platinum and £200 on the gold and notes, and recommended Déricourt for deportation.

He had got off with a fine of £500 out of a possible £1,800. His having, as a French citizen, come back to this country of his own accord to face the charges had understandably made a favourable impression. What I did wonder was what was meant by the Resistance being still in being in 1946. As a skeletal structure in case of another war?

I had sent Vogt copies of *France-Soir* and *Libération*, which carried photographs of Déricourt. This crossed with a letter I received from him about Bodington and Agazarian (I translate from his French):

> 4 February, 1955
>
> Our department knew of Bodington's stay in Paris in 1943. Kieffer knew some days before his arrival in Paris. We gave him a rendezvous at one of the letterboxes in Paris controlled by Kieffer. But instead of coming himself, Bodington sent the radio who had come with him from London. While the radio went to keep the appointment, Bodington remained in the vicinity of the house to wait for him to come out. The radio was arrested at that address and Bodington fled ... It was the radio himself who recounted this to me while being interrogated by me. He was not pleased with Bodington. Obviously Bodington feared a trap had been set for him and preferred to get his radio arrested than enter it himself.
>
> I cannot do otherwise than advise you to be very prudent what you publish about *Gilbert*. I fear you may have enormous troubles....
>
> Ernest

In a PS he added that the papers I had sent him had just arrived. 'I recognise him.' He thought the defence adroit but did not believe a word of it. He suspected it had been preconcerted.

5: PIECES IN THE JIGSAW

On 23 January I had lunched with Yeo-Thomas and Barbara at their flat near the Passy steps, and told them Bodington's evidence. Barbara, who had been in the London office of RF, said she had sat next to Bodington at a dinner, at which he talked of stocks and shares and the influence of money on politics. 'He was a friend of André Simon.'

Yeo-Thomas said, since I was investigating mysteries, there was another. A man called Gilbert Turck was suspected by the de Vomécourt brothers and others of having given a lot of people away. A *jurie d'honneur* had sat on his case but never delivered its verdict. Yeo-Thomas, who had been asked by Turck whether he could hurry it up, suspected Turck's real offence lay in his having refused to share with Pierre de Vomécourt a sum of money which had been parachuted but not used. Turck had after the war handed it in to the British Embassy ('The British Embassy must have fainted!' put in Barbara). Yeo-Thomas said the practice of sharing out unused funds privately had become almost general, yet even a rancour over that did not explain the malevolence with which the de Vomécourts hounded Turck. He felt there must be something more at the bottom of it. Whether it would link up in any way with what I was investigating he did not know, but he would like my impression of Turck. He rang him, and Turck agreed to receive me the next day.

From the eagerness with which he did so, I feared he hoped I was somebody who, if satisfied, could do something. It was a long and complex story which I took down at dictation. In brief, he had gone to England in 1940 and enlisted under

Brigadier Leslie Humphreys, the head of D Section (Escapes). He had been given the code-name 'Christophe' and was parachuted on 6 August 1941 with Jacques de Guélis. His mission from Humphreys was to organise an escape line from the Occupied to the Unoccupied Zone of France. He also gave Georges Bégué of F Section some help in organising arms dumps, and through him came to know the brothers Philippe and Pierre de Vomécourt. As a safe-house, he rented the Villa des Bois in Marseilles. In Paris, in the Café Colisée, he had a meeting with Philippe de Vomécourt. The latter was sitting with his back to a mirror, and as he opened his wallet, Turck saw in the mirror his German pass between the zones. 'I saw the eagle.' It gave him a shock, which he was unable to dissimulate. Afterwards, he reflected that a fake pass might be a useful thing, and perhaps he should try to get one made for himself. Yet he never convinced himself Philippe de Vomécourt's was fake, never trusted him again.

Returning from Paris, he broke his journey at Lyon, where a Commandant Zundel warned him the Villa des Bois was occupied by Vichy police. He therefore did not return to it; then, soon afterwards, he was arrested and sent to concentration camp. When he returned after the war, he learned that a number of people had been arrested in or near the Villa des Bois. He showed me a summary of the affair by Wybot, head of the DST. According to this, the address had been found on Francis Garel, a recruit of de Guélis, arrested on 9 October 1941. The Vichy police installed themselves. C. Jumeaux and Pierre Bloch were arrested when they arrived at the Villa des Bois on 17 and 20 October. So, when he called, was the tenant of the nearby Villa Bernadette. There, or near it, were arrested Robert Lyon (another recruit of de Guélis), J. B. Hayes and de Harivel. Finally, on 24 October, Georges Bégué was arrested at the Villa des Bois. All these people had later escaped, but Turck now found they believed he had been inside the villa, opening the door and saying, 'Come in', to them as they arrived to be arrested.

He was summoned to face a *jurie d'honneur*, consisting almost entirely of those caught in the trap. Only Bégué claimed to have recognised him. What cut more ice was that Philippe de Vomécourt claimed to have telephoned to the Villa des Bois and recognised Turck's voice. He could only say he was not there.

The President of the *jurie* was Roger Hérissé, but the proceedings were absolutely dominated by Philippe de Vomécourt. Philippe de Vomécourt was a baron, the owner of great lands, a person of weight and consequence.

Hérissé I had seen to be a person of modest circumstance.

On 10 February 1955 I received a letter from the House of Commons. It was from Irene Ward, the Conservative MP for Tynemouth. She was writing a history of the FANY Corps. Might she quote a passage from *Madeleine*, and would I dine with her at the House of Commons?

We dined at the Commons on 21 February. She was fair, with blue eyes that looked at one very straight, a full, melodious voice and clear articulation (she had when young studied singing, and was a Trustee of the Carl Rosa Opera Company). She pronounced the 'o' long in 'soft' (sawft), 'frost' (frawst) and 'often' (awfn), as one used to hear it in aristocratic pronunciations but rarely does today. We talked mainly about the FANY girls who had served in SOE. It was only at the end of the evening I mentioned *The Starr Affair*. Her eyes opened wide. 'I didn't know you wrote *The Starr Affair*. We shall have to meet again.'

She came to dinner with me at my flat, on 8 March. She had been abroad when *The Starr Affair* had been published. The first she heard of it was when she was refused the FANY girls' SOE files. She expressed surprise, as Jerrard Tickell, the author of *Odette*, had been allowed to see her file. She had been told a decision had been taken in the Foreign Office after *The Starr Affair* that SOE files were to be closed — the book had provoked intense pressure to open them. She had not disclosed her ignorance as to what *The Starr Affair* might be. I told her Yeo-Thomas had told me that at the British Embassy in Paris he had been asked to 'play it down'.

'I think they were in a flap,' she said. Her guess was they did not know the radio-game had been played on SOE from France until they read it in *The Starr Affair*. They did not know who I was, did not know whether what I wrote was true, and knew no quick way to find out. After the war, just before all the files of SOE French Section had to be handed to the Foreign Office, there had been a fire where they were kept, and the telegrams and papers that would have made it possible to check had perished.

She first became aware of SOE through her friendship with Jacques de Guélis and his wife. In 1941 he returned from a brief visit to France perturbed by the manner in which a lot of people had been arrested in a house. He asked her if she knew Anthony Eden well enough to put a letter into his hands. She said, 'Yes.' A few days later he gave her a letter in a sealed envelope. 'I gave it to Anthony.' Later, Eden told her he would receive her friend. Although SOE was not under the Foreign Office, she understood from de Guélis that the relationship was maintained.

Eden was 'irritated' by SOE. He felt it impinged on the Foreign Office. She believed he had made persistent efforts to get it under Foreign Office control. He resented not being informed of decisions taken in it. She believed that in introducing de Guélis to him, she had set up, unawares, something of long consequence. When de Guélis left for Algiers in November 1942 he told her he had arranged to have a successor.

There was also an unfortunate sequel. In the early spring of 1944, about March, a woman friend of hers who was in the London office of SOE had asked her if she could hand an envelope to Eden. It seemed like the de Guélis approach all over again. It had 'gone off all right that time', and she had said certainly she could give something to Anthony. She gave Anthony the bulging envelope which the friend then committed to her. About five the next morning men arrived at her door asking for the envelope and asking questions. She went to Eden and told him what had happened. He said he was most awfully sorry. The important thing had seemed to her simply that he should get on the telephone and tell MI5, SOE, Scotland Yard and whoever else, that it was to him the envelope had been given and he still had it, and would give it back. The envelope had contained letters from French nationals serving in the British French Section of SOE, Jerry Morel and others, expressing concern as to what their position would be after the war, because the de Gaulle 'government' was taking an extraordinary attitude to them, as though they had entered the service of a foreign power; it looked as though they would get no pensions, but only troubles. They wanted some high-level British intervention with the Free French government in London. They thought their complaints were being neglected though, in fact, Eden had already made some representation to the Free French in precisely the sense Morel wished.

Irene did not think it would be Eden who had ordered the files to be closed. He had no reason. She suggested taking him into confidence, but later... 'when he has succeeded Churchill as Prime Minister'. Just after he had become Prime Minister I was dining with her at the House, saying 'Antoine' had been dropped to the Germans, and she kicked me. Eden had sat down at the next table, unaccompanied, so must have heard; and she had changed her mind about taking him into our confidence.

Bodington was Buckmaster's second-in-command. What could have been the link between Bodington and Déricourt? In Guernsey on 17 March 1955 I asked Spooner. He paced up and down. 'Dirt-track racing! I'll bet it all goes back to dirt-track racing!' It had been a favourite sport of Bodington, before the war, when he was Reuter's correspondent in Paris. 'What you want to find out is whether Déricourt went in for dirt-track racing.'

His guess was they had been partners in something illegal. The financial structure of SOE was an open invitation. Salaries were paid not by banker's draft but in banknotes, never of higher denominations than £5, so that people had to come with suitcases. Requests for expenses were met with hand-outs without apparent record. 'If Déricourt found a way to diddle Buckmaster I wouldn't hold it against him.'

As to Bodington's having sent Agazarian in his stead to a risky rendezvous, 'Militarily, he was right.' In his view Bodington should never have entered the field at all. He knew the composition of every network, and if he had been captured and broken under interrogation, it would have meant the arrest of all our agents in France.

But, I protested, why should anybody have gone to that flat? Cohen and Inayat Khan had both told London 'Archambaud' had been arrested. If it was felt someone should view him, to see if he was free or guarded, why not in a more open place? I would have suggested the middle of a large field — so that if there were people with him they could be seen from sufficient distance to make a getaway possible.

'Yes, of course,' he said, 'if it had been possible to arrange that. But supposing that for some reason someone had to go into that flat, it was better it should be the less important man.'

On my return to London, I found a letter from the Abbé Guillaume, Norman's enemy. He had read *Madeleine* and enclosed a long extract from the deposition to the DST of Joseph Placke, dated 1 April 1946. This said that 'Prosper' had after forty-eight hours of interrogation given the address of Darling, with whom arms were stored, near Gisors. 'He wrote Darling a letter, telling him to give the arms to bearer.' Placke had charge of the party which went to the house, Triechâteau. Darling, on seeing 'Prosper's handwriting, led the way on his motorcycle, to the cache in the woods, and helped load them on to a lorry. Then he was told to put his hands up. He tried to ride off, but was shot in the liver and died in the hospital at Gisors next day. During the week, expeditions to collect arms and make arrests were made to Meru, Creux, Evreux... Kieffer later instructed Placke and Karl Holdorf to substitute themselves for two captured Canadians, 'Berttand' (Pickersgill) and 'Valentin' (Macalister) and go, as instructed by London over the latter's radio-circuit, to the Café Colisée, to an appointment with 'Madeleine'. They had a talk with her, and she, without suspecting anything, introduced them to some of her colleagues.

Now, at last, I understood that story Gieules had told me. The Abbé was correspondent for the Loiret to the

Commission d'Histoire de l'Occupation et de la Libération de la France. He would put further documentation at my disposal if I came to see him.

I flew to Paris on 12 May 1955, breaking my journey to see the Tourets again. The restaurant had changed hands, but I traced them to their new flat. They were happier now. Some months ago they had been honoured by a visit from Colonel Buckmaster, who had talked with them until late. What he had wished to hear about was the visit of the German and how they had directed him to the Square Clignancourt. They had always felt they had made a bad blunder, were relieved he was so nice about it and overjoyed when a few months afterwards M. Touret had been invited to the British Embassy to be decorated with the King's Medal for Courage. Now they felt they should not talk about what had happened any more. 'We have the impression it is something the Intelligence Service prefers to keep between itself and us.'

On the 16th I took the train to Orleans. From the station the way by taxi lay across the Loire and then about fifteen kilometres over flattish country, with heath, birch and ponds. I had a theory I wanted to try out on the Abbé. It had come into my mind during my first meeting with Burdet, when he told me of how his network had been prematurely exposed to the German panzers, the Communist networks not. The seed of suspicion had been unexpectedly watered when, just afterwards, on 14 October 1954, Burdet invited me and Jacques Robert to dine with him at the Stafford Hotel. Robert had been an important member of a network that worked in the Creuse area (Midi). He said several times that Buckmaster was a very nice man. But afterwards, while driving me back to my flat in his car, he admitted that it was only since recent meetings with him he had realised how nice he was; during the war, he had been pretty cross with him. Whenever he asked for arms, the deliveries were late and insufficient. When the Communists asked for them, they got them on time, and in the quantity they had asked for. Yeo-Thomas had also said, 'The Buckmaster Section was dropping a lot of arms to the Communists.' Before I decided the extent to which I would confide in the Abbé, I would let him talk first, to sense how the land lay.

The Abbé, small and dark, had on his desk in his little house a copy of his books, *La Sologne* and *l'Abbé Pasty*, which he gave me, and a typescript copy of a memoir written by 'La Chatte', one of the only two in existence, which I could borrow, as also his big pile of enemy testimonies. These were made to the DST, which did not expose its files to the public but had to disclose to the lawyer of an accused person papers affecting his case, including those suggesting others might have done that of which he was accused. Culioli was a friend of his, and after his acquittal had given him his lawyer's file. He showed me Vogt's deposition of 1949, which was to the same effect as that he had made to me, though he referred to Déricourt as 'Gilbert' alias 'Claude'. The Abbé also had a signed statement from a person invited to give evidence for the defence, that the signatory had asked permission of the War Office and been advised not to, as Déricourt was believed guilty. He could not show me without permission of the signatory, with whom he did not know how to make contact. From clues he let drop, I worked out it must be Agazarian's widow.

Déricourt (who, he believed, was alive and in Indo-China) had been appointed when London wanted to bring back agents. Culioli had for four months previously been receiving the parachuted agents. It had been Raymond Flower who had been sent to receive *parachutages*, but on the night of 24/5

September 1942, when Lise de Baissac and 'Denise' sailed down, Flower was not on the field and it was Culioli, a local man, who received them. 'Jacqueline' (Yvonne Rudellat), intended as courier to Flower, transferred her allegiance to Culioli, and it was Culioli and 'Jacqueline' who, on 1/2 October, received 'Prosper'. Flower complained to London about having been displaced and asked for something with which to kill Culioli. When 'Archambaud' arrived, on 1/2 November, it was with a sealed envelope he had to give to Flower. He was horrified when told by Flower it contained a lethal pill to be administered to Culioli (who had helped him out of his harness), and refused to cooperate in finding a way to make him swallow it. London now accepted that for the future it was Culioli and not Flower who would be their parachute reception man. He received *parachutages* in the Loir-et-Cher south of Loire.

As to the demise of the 'Prosper' network, the Abbé thought one should go back to the arrest in March 1943, by Bleicher, of Marsac, who gave away not only Bardet, who became Bleicher's agent, but probably the Tambour sisters, arrested at Easter. Not only did 'Prosper' and 'Archambaud', in their attempts to rescue them, get themselves photographed, they had to find a new letterbox. They found a Mme Bossard, at Avaray. But in May there arrived 'Bastien' (Marcel Clech), the radio operator of a new team, sent to work with Frager, Bardet's chief. Bardet now suggested to the newcomers that in place of the fake identity card with which they had been provided in London, he could, if they would let him have photographs of themselves, procure them authentic ones. He did. They were provided by the Abwehr, at the Hotel Lutetia, copies being of course kept on the Abwehr files. 'Bastien' was further persuaded to disclose his wavelength and so on to

Bardet so that the Germans were able to monitor all the messages he transmitted to and received from London. His radio work he did from Bossard's villa at Aulnay-sous-Bois.

'Denise' lodged at 51 rue des Petits Ecuries, over a café frequented by French employees of the Avenue Foch, Mario Bay and Michel Bouillon, the latter a member of Placke's fake 'Canadian' network. According to a deposition of the landlord, they took an interest in her movements.

Then there was the encounter between Christmann of the Abwehr with 'Archambaud' and 'Denise', of which I would read in the enemy depositions. And, as I said, there was Déricourt submitting the team's mail. Which if any of these leaks was the cause of the arrests?

On 13 June, between Neury and Meun-sur-Beuvron, when Culioli, M. Bulher and the Comte and Comtesse de Bernard were waiting to receive a parachute cargo, the Halifax which flew over dropped a bomb. This not only exploded itself, but detonated the explosives in the containers that came down with it, causing two explosions, the second much louder than the first. This brought to the scene the police, Feldgendarmerie and Gestapo of Blois. The area seethed with investigators, examining the parachutes, which there had not been time to remove, and the remains of the containers. On the night of the 15/16, the two Canadians, 'Bertrand' and 'Valentin' (Pickersgill and Macalister) were parachuted to reception by Culioli, who took them to his home. On the night of the 19/20 'Prosper' was parachuted to Culioli.

Here I interposed a question, whether 'Prosper' had said anything of significance? No, said the Abbé, Culioli just helped him out of his parachute harness and handed him the bicycle on which he made for the railway station. There was a lot of other activity that night, four other parachute deliveries to

71

different fields in Culioli's area, and the team which had loaded one of them on to a lorry was made prisoner.

On the fatal morning of 21 June Culioli and 'Jacqueline' set out in his Citroen, carrying in the back the two Canadians, whom he was to take to 'Prosper' and Armel Guerne, in Paris. On the road there was soon evidence of abnormal police activity. One should remember that the 21 June was also the morning of the biggest blow ever to fall upon the Free French. As Culioli's party was setting out, the Gestapo of Lyon was closing in upon the chiefs of the CNR from all parts of France as they arrived for their conference at Caluire at midday. Therefore there may have been an idea of blocking escape routes, apart from the agitation caused by the parachute operations in Culioli's area. As they approached Dhuison from Vernon, the village appeared to be in a state of siege. The Feldgendarmerie were stopping all cars and making the persons in them go into the *mairie*, to answer questions. Culioli and 'Jacqueline' were merely asked what business caused them to be out so early in the morning, and, giving plausible answers, were issued with passes. They returned to their car, and could have driven away, but that they waited for the Canadians. 'Valentin's' French was so bad that it excited suspicion. His person was searched and papers tucked under his belt seized. Culioli could not see what these were. The Canadians were not brought back to the car... Too late, Culioli tried to drive off. He and 'Jacqueline' were both heavily wounded. In the car was found the Canadians' radio set, with the crystals for it, and, separately wrapped, a new set of crystals, marked 'for 'Archambaud'', intended to change his wavelength, and handwritten notes addressed to 'Prosper', 'Archambaud' and 'Marie-Louise' (the last named being a member of de Baissac's network in Bordeaux).

Not knowing what had happened, 'Prosper' went that morning to the Gare d'Austerlitz, where he expected Culioli to step off the train with the two Canadians. Of course, they did not come. Déricourt, however, came, to take off his hands a shot down airman, Taylor, in need of a passage back to England. It was obviously 'Prosper' who had asked Déricourt to meet him and take charge of Taylor.

On 24 June, between midnight and 0.15 a.m., a M. Laurant, with whom 'Archambaud' lodged, was awakened by a ring at his back door, on the Boulevard Lannes. A man asked for Gilbert — on behalf of 'Archambaud'. Laurant fetched 'Archambaud' (whom he knew only as Gilbert), who came downstairs and was seized by about fifteen men, who had poured out from two cars. Then they went upstairs and arrested 'Denise', who was spending that night at 'Archambaud's' lodgings. 'Prosper' had been arrested later that morning — at about ten o'clock at the Hôtel Mazagran, according to the proprietress, though there was a deposition from Déricourt saying that at nine 'Antoine' told him he had just seen him arrested at the Gare St Lazare.

When Culioli was told of the pact that lives would be spared in exchange for certain information he asked if he might see 'Prosper'. He was told it was impossible, but 'Archambaud' was brought to him and said, 'It is true.' Then Culioli fell in with the terms. He gave the addresses of four people on whose premises arms were stored and wrote each of them a letter saying he was sorry to be obliged to give them away. After the war Culioli was charged with having betrayed 'Prosper'. A woman agent of the Gestapo of Blois, Mona Reimeringer, declared he had led the Gestapo to the Hôtel Mazagran. Wounded as he was, this was impossible. The court was closed at one moment for Armel Guerne to give evidence in camera.

Culioli was found guilty of acts prejudicial to the Resistance, and discharged. He demanded a retrial, and obtained not guilty.

The woman who 'did' for M. l'Abbé brought in steaming plates of asparagus from his garden. The question of Norman had so far lain silent between us, but now in the lantern-light, he said, 'I suppose Mr Norman thinks very bad things of me?'

'Yes,' I said. He felt charity should spare the names of the dead.

'There is historic truth,' said the Abbé. When we had finished our supper he got out his papers against 'Archambaud'. He had given away M. and Mme Flamencourt, Jean and Guy Dutems, M. Bulher, Robert Arend, Mme Dr Helmer and the Comte and Comtesse de Bernard. The Comte had been surprised when his interrogator told him what they had had for dinner last time Norman ('Archambaud') came. Edouard Flamencourt did not return from captivity but had told Richard Mounet, who did, that at the Avenue Foch Gilbert had told him, 'It's not worth hiding anything. They know all. The best thing is to tell them all you know. They have promised everyone's lives will be spared.' The Abbé believed 'Prosper' would have kept strictly within the terms of the pact, whereas 'Archambaud' went beyond them. Mme Flamencourt had testified that in a cell of the rue des Saussaies Germaine Tambour had told her that at the Avenue Foch she had seen Gilbert serving tea and showing the Germans the parachute fields on a map. In front of them, he said, 'But Germaine, you haven't told them this... haven't told them that,' compromising new groups and defeating her endeavours to save any persons.

Commandant Braun had testified that on 9 September 1943 he had been for a few moments put in a cell with 'Robin', chief of the Juggler network, and 'Ernest' (Marcel Fox, not to be confused with Vogt). 'Robin' had warned, 'We are watched,' but Fox had whispered, 'It was Gilbert who betrayed us all. He even gave the code.' Georges Brault of Romorantin had deposed that in the second half of July 1943, during his interrogation at Orleans, in a passage of Boulevard Alexandre Martin, he had passed Gilbert-'Archambaud' and Denise. 'Whereas I was escorted by an SD with a revolver, they were unguarded, talking to each other, at ease.' M. Gouju of Evreux had deposed: 'I do not think I have known a more painful moment in my life than when, on 4 July, Gilbert Norman came towards me and said with the most beautiful poise, "You can tell them everything. They are stronger than we are."'

The Abbé inclined to blame 'Archambaud' for the arrest of Agazarian, as it was through Goetz the appointment at the rue de Rome had been made. At Compiègne, on the way to concentration camp, a P. Philbée had been told by Agazarian it was four days after his arrival with Bodington that he had been arrested, and that 'Archambaud' and 'Denise' had told all.

However, Marcel Charbonnier of Pontoise reported 'Prosper' as having said, before the blow fell, 'There are hard blows coming, and it is from London they will come.'

M. Mounet had been told by 'Archambaud' at Avenue Foch, 'It all came about through London, perhaps from a fault in the coding. I know I was under surveillance before I was arrested.'

A Jacques Bureau, who had worked with the old 'Carte' network before joining 'Prosper', deposed that after his arrest 'Archambaud' had told him, in the Germans' presence to 'shed some light'. In French, the phrase 'faire de la lumière' is not usual, and Bureau thought there might have been an intention to advise him to tell something but not everything.

'Now,' the Abbé reminded me, 'you said in your letter you had something confidential you wanted to say to me.'

I voiced my notion that one might not have to think only of pro-German treason but double-dealing in favour of the Communists, who probably hoped to dominate Europe after the war.

'I had dealings with the Communist networks,' he said. He believed they had been straightforward with him. He had never felt he was being used, in any sense other than that to which he had given his consent. 'Obviously, there was an ideological difference. That they were probably atheists did not appeal to me, and that I was a priest probably did not appeal to them. But the thing was, to get the Nazis out.' He did not know whence they received their orders and funds — he supposed from Moscow; that is, if Moscow had a way of transmitting these to France. 'They were very mysterious. I never knew who they were. Their man would walk up to this house, neither so slowly nor so fast as to attract suspicion, knock, step inside, hand me a packet and receive one from me without a word, and depart. I several times offered coffee or a cognac, but it was always refused, as was any conversation. I was really very impressed with them.' Now, if it had been the 'Prosper' network! The 'Prosper' people were always having great luncheon parties, dining and wining with their hosts and telling everybody their real names and a great deal about themselves. The 'Prosper' network could have fallen apart simply from the indiscretion of its members.'

I did not tell him a story Mme Balachowsky had told me. A friend of hers had seen 'Antoine', his arms round the waists of two girls, walking up the Champs Elysées singing 'Rule Britannia'!

As soon as I got back to Paris, on 17 May 1955, I called at the Tribunal and found Mercier. It was the first time I had seen him since finding the Déricourt trial. He congratulated me wryly. 'I think our people understood the British wished Déricourt acquitted,' he said. It was awkward for him to comment on a case in which French Justice had played 'un rôle involuntaire'. To have convicted Déricourt after Bodington gave his evidence would have been a hostile act against Britain.

I said there were those who did not believe Bodington came officially.

That did not impress him. Déricourt was a British agent-perhaps still. He could have been briefed to pretend to work for the Germans, and to mislead them as to the date and place of the invasion. A brief to do that would have had to come from far higher than Buckmaster.

'Is that what you believe?' I asked.

'I know only that Déricourt is a person whom a profound mystery surrounds.' Then he added, unexpectedly, 'Of all the people you know — whose names you have told me — there is only one you can be sure is not a spy. Me. It is forbidden to *juges militaires*.'

I read the memoir of 'La Chatte', Mathilde Carré. She and a Pole, Roman Czerniavsky, had founded the Interallié, Marseilles and Paris, which worked to the Intelligence Service. Bleicher arrested Raoul Kiffer, who became his agent and betrayed them. 'La Chatte' was arrested on 18 November 1941 and was forced to use the telephone to offer her friends appointments in cafés where the Germans were sitting round waiting to arrest them. On 26 December she was licensed to contact Pierre de Vomécourt — 'Lucas' of SOE — but confided to him she was under German control. She then persuaded the Abwehr to let them and Ben Cowburn escape by boat from the Breton coast, by promising to work for them

77

in London. In London, however, she confessed. Her memoir was dated, London, 6 April 1942.

I was dreading seeing Norman again, yet called on him on 18 May and told him I had visited the Abbé Guillaume. He asked wryly whether I found in him 'any disposition to withdraw his allegations against my son?'

'No.'

He told me his son had set in splints the broken leg of a sparrow.

Then he gave me a slip he had obtained from a credit investigation agency. Dated 2 December 1954, it stated that H. Déricourt rented a flat at 58 rue Pergolèse for 40,000 francs a month, plus service charges.[2] His earnings were between 100,000 and 180,000 francs monthly. 'Good morality, solvency not in doubt, pays his bills... One can have business dealings with him.'

Mme Balachowsky had invited me to take an aperitif with her at Auteuil that afternoon. 'Prosper', she assured me, was a most upright man. She saw him for the last time on the morning of 20 June — in the early hours of which he had parachuted. Since he left for England a month before, he had aged ten years. 'He told me he hardly dared to talk with his wife in a corridor of the War Office [sir].' I asked what she understood by that. She hesitated; she supposed he thought information was getting back from the top office to the Germans. He told her he had returned to France solely in order to protect the French whom he had involved in his network. It was to protect the French he made that pact, she said. It was 'Archambaud' who had gone beyond its terms.

---

[2] The franc then stood at just over 977 to the pound and should be multiplied by approximately ten to bring it to 1987 values

Her last conversation with 'Prosper' had ended on the steps of the Gare Montparnasse. She did not know that he had left his usual rooms in the rue Hautefeuille for a hotel in the rue Mazagran.

I did not have to rush back from Paris as before. During the previous year, an artist friend, Marie Steward, had died, leaving me her stocks and shares and her house in Tintagel. Although it was rich in associations for me, the journey down to the north Cornish coast occupied too many hours for living in it to be compatible with my frequent need to hop over the Channel. Reluctantly, I sold it. The half-sad cheque had come through, and, in the café at Auteuil, I worked out that I could give up teaching.

I felt I should see Armel Guerne, to ask if he would tell me what it was that, at Culioli's trial, he had told the court in camera. The Abbé sent me an address, but when I called at it, on 3 June, I found only his wife, 'Pérégrine', who said he was living with another woman. She would not tell me where.

On the following day, 4 June, I was invited to tea with Marie-Madeleine Fourcade, OBE. She had written to me because my books mentioned her colleague Léon Faye, 'Aigle' in L'Alliance, and she would like to discuss some points. I found her, slight and fair, in a handsome drawing-room, in which some of the furniture was Chinese in ornamental, dark wood, and some upholstered in blue silk. She showed me crinkled slips of paper, found behind the radiator of the cell he had occupied in Bruchsal. They told of his days as a prisoner, and I was relieved to find his account of the attempted escape across the roofs from 84 Avenue Foch tallied with that I had received from Starr.

When it took place she had been in England, and had woken in the night with a tremendous feeling of elation, followed by one of black depression. It must have corresponded to the escape and the recapture.

She had been head of L'Alliance, her code-name 'Hérisson'. 'We had nothing to do with the Buckmaster organisation [SOE]. We worked to the British Secret Intelligence Service.' She had always worked to it through the British Consulate in Madrid, but in July 1943 she had been fetched to London to confer with her chief, from whom all her orders had come, whom she now met for the first time. 'Colonel Dansey.' Had I met him?

'No.' I had not even heard of him. So unguarded and chatty was her manner, I did not realise she had given me, without warning, as it were, the name of the *éminence grise* of our own Secret Service, the one that is really secret, and that her claim to have worked for SIS (MI6) was true.

She had found him pleasant and understanding. And Commander Cohen, had I met him?

No. The only names I knew were of SOE people.

They abstained from contact with SOE, she said, because its functions were so different. It went in for sabotage. Her people restricted themselves to the collection of information. Her greatest problem was to restrict numbers.

'It is not like an army. In an army, the more men it has, the stronger it is. In espionage, the ideal number for the accomplishment of a task is one. Two may be needed, but two are weaker than one. If three are needed, three are weaker than two. In a railway station, I find one, who will note the German troop movements by train. I don't want to come back in a little while to find he has recruited six. Each addition is one more *who can betray all the rest.*'

Had she ever heard of a double agent, Déricourt, alias 'Gilbert'?

No. Unless she saw something about his trial in the papers, after the war, but they had not had to do with him and she did not read the case.

The only double agent she had to deal with was called Blanchet, 'Bia'. Back in 1942. Dansey's order to her was to kill him. She did not have to do it herself, but had to give the instructions. They had taken him prisoner and she instructed her people to give him some of the lethal pills supplied by London, dissolved in his soup, coffee or tea. Perhaps because of the dilution, the cyanide failed to cause death. She told 'Loup' to get him on to a boat and drown him, but the moon was too bright. In the end she ordered Faye and another to take him out and shoot him. 'We offered to bring a priest to him first, but he refused.'

My interviews were yielding nothing about Déricourt, but the Abbé posted me a statement made by Déricourt on 5 June 1948, that is while a prisoner, three days before his trial (I translate from the French):

> In November, 1942, I was witness to the statement of Wing-Commander Pickard, then commander of the British squadron charged with special parachute missions.
>
> Two months previously, therefore about September, 1942, Wing-Commander Pickard had gone out with a team in a Whitley bi-motor, to parachute containers and agents. The aircraft reached the target, but the lights were ill laid out, and the signals ill made. The lights were set in a line along the edge of a wood, at about 20 metres from it. The conditions being such, the security of the operation was ml, and doubt was felt as to the quality of the agent who had set the lights out in such a manner. Wing-Commander Pickard therefore decided not to complete the operation but to return to base.

I was astonished. Déricourt must have been serving with the RAF before his transfer to SOE — and by November 1942.

The Abbé wrote that Déricourt had, besides his Paris flat, after his trial taken a flat in the *château* at Vitry-aux-Loges, Loiret, then taken a *château* at Vimory, near Montargis. There he reared poultry, and had a permanent guest, Claude Jouffret, a former lover of 'La Chatte'. The Abbé sent me a cutting from *L'Aurore* of 7 December 1949, reporting the trial of Bleicher's agents, Roger Bardet, Raoul Kiffer and Claude Jouffret. Of Jouffret it said: 'One has only to look at this young man, tall, blond, with big pouches under his eyes, to see that he was merely weak.' He had been only eighteen when 'La Chatte' identified him to Bleicher by kissing him. It was this that broke his morale. Perhaps the judge was of the reporter's opinion, for he sentenced Bardet and Kiffer to death, Jouffret only to four years.

But why had Déricourt, who had been acquitted, taken him in? Had they met in prison while both were awaiting trial, or had Déricourt had some connection with the altogether earlier drama with which Jouffret had been involved, a drama which took place before Déricourt came to England and joined SOE, and which had an entirely different cast? This puzzled me more than anything.

In the meantime I was working through the file of German statements the Abbé had lent me. I read the deposition of Richard Christmann, of the Abwehr (I translate from the French):

> It was towards the end of May, 1943 that Colonel Blunt of the Dutch Section in London informed us it was essential we should get in touch with the French Section in Paris... Our network was registered in London and I myself was entrusted with arranging the withdrawal of English and Dutch agents

parachuted to us... London insisted we should send back the head of our sabotage network, 'Anton'... It was agreed the French Section should take charge of him in Paris and be responsible for his journey. I was to play the part of 'Arnaud', the Belgian head of Nordpol circuit, and an adjutant of the Abwehr was to play the part of 'Anton'. London gave us the password which enabled us to meet 'Gilbert' of the French Section, who was to take charge of 'Anton'. The meeting was to take place in a flat on the third floor of 6 or 8 [sic] rue de Clignancourt, and the son of the tenant Alain, was to act as intermediary. Everything in Paris went according to plan, except that instead of our meeting 'Gilbert', Alain put us into touch by mistake with Gilbert-'Archambaud'. Several meetings were needed to clear up the misunderstanding but in the end 'Marcel' of the French Section took charge of 'Anton'. After the last meeting of 'Marcel', Alain, 'Anton' and me, 'Anton' alone was arrested by the SD at the Restaurant Capucines, so that he would not have to go to London.

During the meetings between ourselves and members of the French Section we were always encircled by a cordon of the SD. They had orders not to arrest anybody lest it should cause our Nordpol operation in Holland to be suspected in London. This activity in Paris must have lasted till the end of June. Through the SD surveillance, Untersturmführer Gutgesell of Section 4E sinned by excess of zeal and arrested Gilbert — 'Archambaud' and Alain....

The Abbé told me Alain's name was Bussoz, and I went to Square Clignancourt, inquired at every house and eventually found at no. 10 what had been the family flat. Yes, Alain Bussoz has been arrested there as a result of a Resistance meeting and died in Germany. I knew I must find Christmann, but in the meantime called on Mme Aigrain, who wrote me in my presence a letter (I translate from the French):

9 June, 1955

Mademoiselle,

I remember very clearly that in November 1943, in the course of my interrogation at Avenue Foch, the German who arrested me showed me a photocopy of a report made me by one of my friends, Monsieur Andrès, since deceased.

This report was given to 'Madeleine' after the bombing of Boulogne and Courbevoie, and 'Madeleine' told me she gave it to 'Gilbert'.

It is unfortunately impossible for me to be sure of the date.

Assuring you of my best wishes,

G. Aigrain

The 'Gilbert' to whom she referred was Déricourt. I was leaving that day, and she shared a taxi with me part of the way. She said I should see the Tourets, who were positive 'Gilbert' betrayed everyone. I said the man they meant was Gilbert Norman, 'Archambaud', who ate at their restaurant and who seemed too much at ease at Avenue Foch. That 'Gilbert' died in Germany. The one she meant, whom she identified with the man put on trial, and with whom she had been confronted, she said, in the office of the *juge d'instruction*, was a different man.

She was shaken. She and Madame Touret had always agreed the great traitor was 'Gilbert'. It never occurred to her they were not talking about the same man.

I re-read Giskes's book, *London Calling North Pole*. On page in was a passage that must relate to the incident Christmann had described. Giskes said London had asked for one of its agents back. He had sent 'Bo' to impersonate the London agent, and sent with him, as guide, 'Arnaud', who ran the Allied escape routes that were under Giskes's control:

'Arnaud' conveyed this 'chief to Paris and introduced him into the organisation by means of a password which had been arranged through London. But as the result of a 'random' raid by the German Secret Field Police on a café in the Boulevard des Italiens the 'chief' fell into the hands of the Germans before leaving for Spain. 'Arnaud' and the English operator, 'Marcel', who were present at the time, 'escaped', and 'Marcel' at once gave London an accurate report of the incident...

'Spain' puzzled me. If the 'escape' was to be through Spain, Christmann would not have needed to contact 'Gilbert', who arranged passages by air to England; but Giskes said he had written the book without memoranda and I thought his memory had slipped. I wrote to him care of his publisher, explaining that I was trying to understand the case of 'Gilbert' and the 'Prosper' disaster. Could he put me in touch with Christmann, or even see me himself? He replied, saying the missions of the two men were not to make arrests in France, and if arrests had followed their intervention it was perhaps because the mock arrest of the bogus Dutchman caused alarm, such that Kieffer feared the 'Prosper' group would scatter if not rounded up. 'This is only a hypothesis, but my guesses have sometimes had the good luck to come near the truth.' He would see me if I came to Hamburg.

I flew to Hamburg on 21 August 1955. He was at the barrier to meet me, with his sister. They escorted me to a hotel they had found for me near the River Alster and his own flat, in the Uhlenhorst district. He was busy for the next two days, so my formal interview with him was not until 23 August. He had with him Herr Huntermann, who had been his radio expert.

Giskes began by asking whether I had acquainted the official people of my own country with my researches and the fact I was here. I thought he wanted to be sure I was not part of some Communist conspiracy, so I said I was nobody's agent, but people who knew I had come included (now Dame) Irene Ward, Colonel Spooner, Field-Marshal Sir Claude Auchinleck (under whom Spooner had served) and le Commandant Mercier of the TMP, Paris.

He asked: 'Were the services rendered to the Germans by 'Gilbert', alias Déricourt, paid?'

'According to the newspapers.'

'It is not sufficient. Have you proof — a receipt signed by him?'

I had not. 'Is it important?'

'It is important.' Without that, we could go no further. He would have liked to speak to Kieffer. As he was dead, to Goetz.

I did not know where to find Goetz. I had heard he was a Hamburg man.

He told Hunterman to look through the telephone directory, and whatever else he could think of, but Goetz was not found.

'But you mentioned that you knew Vogt, Kieffer's interpreter!'

Unfortunately Vogt had not known if he was paid. He had, however, quoted Kieffer as saying, 'He betrays the British and his own compatriots to us. He would betray us to them the day it suited him better.'

'I will write you a letter to a Herr Bodens in Bonn.' Bodens would give me the address of Christmann. He said Bodens might not tell me much, but what he said I could believe. Christmann was an exaggerated talker.

'He is our enemy,' said Huntermann.

This was so unexpected I looked at Giskes. He did not dissent. He referred to the house in which the meeting with the Résistants took place. The story of its being encircled by the

SD was fiction, he said. If Christmann and 'Anton' had felt they needed protection, they could, when they reported to the Lutetia (the Abwehr headquarters), have asked for a couple of men to be posted near. 'But our *own* men, not the SD.'

I was just leaving when Huntermann said it had come back to him that the radio message from London said that in Paris 'Arnaud' and 'Anton' were to meet 'Marcel' and 'Gilbert'.

Next morning, Giskes came to my hotel and gave me the letter he had written Bodens. He said, 'It would be better not to tell Christmann you have seen me.'

This worried me as I sat in the train for Bonn.

Bodens had pink cheeks, and was a little plump. He spoke neither French nor English, so I had to try to speak German. 'I did not meet 'Gilbert',' he said.

It was only then I realised Bodens was 'Bo', the bogus 'Anton'. He had stayed outside the house, while Christmann went in. I said I thought the arrest had to be visible — '*sichtbar*'.

'It was visible,' he said, with a peculiar laugh. 'You will tell Christmann you have seen Giskes?'

'Giskes asked me not to tell him.'

I could see this troubled him. He wrote a letter, put it in an envelope, sealed it and gave it to me. 'Give him that.'

The address was in Frankfurt, but when I reached Frankfurt I could not find it. After hours*of despair I gave up and took the train on to see Vogt and Lilli.

Vogt did not like the sound of it at all. 'Did you see the letter before he put it in the envelope?'

'No. Do you think it says, "Do not tell her anything"?'

He smiled faintly. 'I could steam it open for you, if you like, and seal it again so that it would hardly be noticed.'

I did not like to have it tampered with.

He held it up to the light, but could make out nothing.

Reluctantly, he telephoned Bodens and was able to explain to me it was Christmann's fiancée for whom I should have asked.

I asked whether he remembered Andrès' report on the bombing of Boulogne, Billancourt and Courbevoue.

Yes, Vogt replied. It was he who had shown the photocopy to Mme Aigrain. But the Andrès report did not have BOE 48 on the back.

On my return to Frankfurt I found Christmann, on 29 August at 5 p.m. His fiancée, Eva, let me in. In a bed was a blond, youngish man. He explained he had been knocked down by a car. My immediate impression was that he had been an actor.

'When you say 'Gilbert', whom do you mean?' he asked.

'Both of them.'

His eyes narrowed, and I faced a barrage of questions. What was my interest? Not wanting to say too much, I mentioned knowing Norman's father, and he thought I wanted the son cleared. But, he said, it was Bodens alone who had entered the house at Square Clignancourt. 'I waited outside.'

It was the other way round from what Bodens had said.

Bodens, he said, came out with 'Archambaud', 'Marcel' and Alain. 'Archambaud' said, 'I am Gilbert but not the 'Gilbert' you want.' He would try to contact the 'Gilbert' who arranged the Lysander passages. In the afternoon they met again. 'Archambaud' said he had met 'Gilbert', who could not come for a day or two. 'I have a nose and I smelled something.' It came to him 'Gilbert' might be a German agent. A few days later he had to call at the Avenue Foch, he said to Kieffer, 'So you have an agent called 'Gilbert'!' Kieffer said this must not be known.

'So you never met 'Gilbert'?'

'Not really...' After the war he had been confronted with him at the DST but denied knowledge of him. Afterwards a little present was delivered to him in his cell, with a scrap of paper on which was a single word — 'Merci'.

'But you have a letter for me!' he exclaimed.

I handed it over, he broke the seal, began to read, and suddenly started, 'You have seen Giskes!'

So that was what Bodens had done. Giskes thought of Bodens as his friend, against Christmann, but Bodens and Christmann had a secret against Giskes. It worried me, as I lay sleepless in the sleeper on my way back to Hamburg.

Giskes invited me to lunch at an open-air restaurant, on a lawn running down to the Alster. He asked my impression of Christmann and said he had never known what to make of him. He had 'a flair for deception work that involved impersonation'. To have reprimanded him for the lies in his reports might have killed it. Nevertheless, when I mentioned the Avenue Foch, he started.

'The Lutetia! Surely he said the Lutetia! Abwehr HQ!'

No, he had not mentioned the Lutetia and he had mentioned Avenue Foch.

'He had no business to go to Avenue Foch. Did he say why he went?'

'No.'

Giskes said their sole business in Paris was to go to the Lutetia and ask for men to make a mock arrest of 'Anton'.

I said it was not the Abwehr who mock-arrested him. It was the SD.

Giskes was shocked and puzzled.

I mentioned that Christmann had said that in November 1943 he had thought to go to England by Lysander to meet a gem-smuggling contact. When I saw the expression on

Giskes's face, I added hastily that I was sure he meant to come back.

'He had no mission to go to England,' said Giskes heavily. 'If he had done it, and come back, and I had found out, I would have had him brought before court-martial.'

He had never telephoned to the Lutetia to ask them to confirm that Christmann and Bodens had reported there....

Christmann wrote to me (I translate from his French):

> Frankfurt, 13 September 1955
>
> ... When I was interrogated at the DST at the end of May 1946 about Gilbert Déricourt I was not confronted with him but a dozen photographs were set in front of me to see if I could pick out 'Gilbert'. I was at that time half blind following prolonged interrogation under 'sunlights' and it was only with difficulty I recognised one as being that of a man I had seen two or three times on the premises of the SD, Avenue Foch. The Commissaire of the DST told me it was the photograph of Gilbert Déricourt.
>
> On Wednesday 29 October at 10.30 I was summoned before the *juge d'instruction* Captain Trossin, who interrogated me concerning Gilbert Déricourt ... It was only on Tuesday 4 November 1947 that I was confronted with Gilbert Déricourt in the office of the *juge d'instruction* Captain Trossin. When confronted I then recognised in Gilbert Déricourt a) a man whom I had seen several times at liberty at the Avenue Foch; b) the person whom I had recognised in May 1946 in the photo...
>
> I said nothing about this to Captain Trossin and pretended I was setting eyes on 'Gilbert' for the first time.
>
> I have explained to you why I then charged poor Gilbert Norman, because I knew him to be dead....

I asked him whether, as a smuggler himself, he knew if 'Gilbert' smuggled during the war. He replied, on the 29th, that he did not know, but 'Marcel' was conducting a black market in gold and diamonds.

Then from the Abbé Guillaume came a worrying letter (I translate from his French)

> Ardon, 8 October 1955
>
> ... officers of the Abwehr... have now re-grouped and reconstructed their service... and they have decided... that they should cover collaborators who worked with them from ideology... but abandon those whose services were remunerated, deposing against them if need be, even to the length not only of handing over compromising documents but fabricating them...

This explained why Giskes had had to know whether Déricourt was paid; however, I had made plain I wanted not fabricated evidence against him but the truth.

I found letters from a Mme Renée Guépin, Liquidatrice of the 'Prosper' network, on the files Norman had left with me. I wrote asking if he could fix an interview with her.

On arriving back in Paris, I met Mercier on 23 November 1955 for an aperitif I showed him Christmann's statement, saying I hoped the French would not make trouble for him for having avowed the statement he made for them was false. No, he said, but asked what made me suppose the one he had made for me was true? 'All you can say is he has now made another one, which is different.'

On the 24th Norman accompanied me from the Gare St Lazare to Colombes. He had not been to see Mme Guépin before: 'In case she, too, told me my son was a traitor. I funked it.'

She explained to us that in 1940 she had had a house, Triechâteau, near Gisors in Normandy. A Captain George Darling, left behind in the BEF retreat of 1940, had made his home with her and been recruited for the 'Prosper' network. 'Prosper' and his team used to stay with her when in that district. Norman talked about his son, then asked her who she thought betrayed the 'Prosper' network. For a moment she looked acutely embarrassed. She said that just before he left for London in May 1940, 'Prosper' had told them Gilbert was not to be trusted. 'Denise' exclaimed, 'That's what I have been telling you for months!' Mme Guépin had not been arrested until months after the others. Then, in Fresnes, she had glimpsed 'Denise', who whispered to her, 'C'est Gilbert qui nous a tous vendu.' At the time, she had thought 'Denise' meant Gilbert Norman. But after the war she learned that 'Denise' had smuggled a note out to her sister, in which she said, 'Gilbert me protégé'; also that there was another 'Gilbert', of whom she had never heard before — Déricourt. Therefore she now thought the Gilbert who protected 'Denise' must be Norman's son and the one who sold them must be Déricourt.

Reverting to 'Prosper', she said that when he returned from London he came to Triechâteau on 23 June. 'I hardly recognised him, he looked so grey and strained.' She asked if he was ill. He seemed to have a presentiment this was the end, for having said goodbye, he came back twice to say goodbye again.

He caught the 7 a.m. train to Paris. She did not know he was staying at the Hôtel Mazagran.

She said: 'At a certain moment we were all convinced the betrayal came from the top office.'

Mme Guépin gave me the address of Mme Laure Lebras, whom I found the next day, white-haired and gentle. She had been recruited by Germaine Tambour. Two days before she and her sister Anette were arrested, on 22 April 1943, Mlle Tambour had said to Mme Lebras, 'The treason comes from the base', meaning the base in London.

From Marjorie Spooner I received a letter suggesting I call on the Baron Henri de Malval. I called on the 29th. He was a big, sunny man. It was his Villa d'Isabella, in Cannes, which had in 1942 been the safe house for the Buckmaster agents arriving on the Riviera. He knew nothing of Déricourt.

'If the name were spelled d'Héricourt, what would that mean?'

That he was one of *les deux cents familles*, one of the two hundred old aristocratic families of France.

'And spelled Déricourt?'

'That does not exist. It is invented.'

'It is somebody's legal name.'

'A bastard, perhaps.'

He gave me two addresses, Mme Odette Fabius and Francis Basin.

Mme Fabius I found in her office on 1 December. She was the holder of a Croix de Guerre, and a Ravensbrück survivor. 'I believe I was the only woman who escaped from Ravensbrück — over the walls, at least.' She had been recaptured when she dropped down the other side, and given a considerable number of strokes with a leather lash of several tails. 'My scars can be seen by anybody.' She was a pretty woman, with small gold hoop earrings and a crisp white blouse. 'As I am Jewish and as I was a spy for the Intelligence Service, I am lucky to have survived,' she said laconically. She had been 'Biche' in the Centurie network of L'Alliance, under

Mme Fourcade. She knew, of course, nothing of Déricourt, but she had known 'Carte'. I had received a letter from New York from 'Carte', André Girard, warning Starr and myself that we were up against more than we knew; for (in his English): 'From higher authorities it was welcomed that the French Resistance could not be too strong at the end — even at the cost of many lives.' This cryptic passage I had almost by heart. I asked Mme Fabius whether she could make anything of it.

'Something to do with Communism,' she said. 'He tried to create a network without Communists in it, or he feared that Communists would take over Europe after the war.'

On the following day, 2 December, I saw Basin, 'Olive', now crippled and in a wheelchair.

'My position is delicate,' he said. 'I owe my life to Déricourt.' He had been arrested on 8 August 1942 and had later escaped. Claudette Menessier (who had helped him escape) and he were put in contact with 'Gilbert', who boarded them on a plane for London. Had he not done so, they must have been captured. In retrospect, Basin realised Déricourt could not have run a service of that kind without the complicity of the Germans. 'But I was one who benefited.'

Mme Guépin had dropped the name of a Swiss, Jacques Weil, who must be Vogt's and Cohen's Swiss. I asked her for his address, which she sent me after my return to London. I wrote to him, saying I had first heard of him, 'from Ernst Vogt, the German who was your interrogator while you were a prisoner at Avenue Foch....'

He replied, offering me an interview in Paris, which he cancelled with a telegram saying he would come to London. On 20 April 1956 he arrived, bringing a friend. Almost as soon as I brought them in, I told him I had written to Vogt to tell him his Swiss was alive, and he had replied with a message. 'He thought you would have been hanged at Buchenwald, but he asks me to tell you he is happy you are alive, and to give you his regards.'

Weil made no comment on this, except that he could easily have been hanged. I made them coffee. We talked, I forget of what. I went out to the kitchen, made more coffee. It was as I was bringing back their second cups, he said, 'I was never arrested.'

This was obviously a lie — I was astounded. 'You never knew Ernst Vogt, then?'

He did not answer. Vogt had told me nothing against him but how had he talked them into letting him go? He admitted to having been Cohen's chief and to having instructed him to radio London that 'Archambaud' was in German hands — but not to having denounced him to London as a traitor and having apologised to him for so doing in the Hôpital de la Pitié, which would have involved admission of having been taken prisoner. He did show himself still exercised over the question of 'Archambaud's' loyalty. It was he who tried to obtain the release of the Tambour sisters.

He mentioned Déricourt in a vague way as a double-agent, but without antagonism. He thought Déricourt might have been doing something similar to himself... This he did not explain.

Someone told me of Arthur Watt. I went to Paris to see him on 23 April 1956. He said he had been 'Geoffroi', sent in October 1943, to join Déricourt as his radio operator. He should, therefore, have been able to tell me a lot, but was too wary. When I asked him what he thought of Déricourt, he said, 'Déricourt is a controversial personage. Some people are against him and others for him.'

'Did you like him?'

For the first time he was forthright. 'Yes. I liked him.' Whereas some people were prey to nerves, Déricourt was cheerful and inspired confidence. 'He was very strict about security. None of his team was arrested.'

'Did he tell you he was in contact with the Germans?'

'No. He did not say that.'

He heard he was in Indo-China in the mid–1950s.

I was getting no further. Georges Adam, of the *Figaro Littéraire*, who had translated *The Starr Affair* and hoped to translate my new book, thought it was essential I confront Déricourt, if he had returned from Indo-China. While we were discussing how to approach him, he hit the headlines again. A large Armagnac, said *France-Soir*, had on 29 January 1957 crash-landed at Orly, in four pieces and in flames, with twenty-one persons aboard, of whom only one was killed. The pilot was Henri Déricourt.

We knew now where he was — in hospital with head injuries. I was terrified he would die. In any case we had to leave an interval before charging him with matters fourteen years old. While we were waiting, Adam learned Bodington was in Paris and on 25 March telephoned him, saying he expected to be translating a book in which Bodington's name was mentioned.

'What is it about?' Bodington asked.

Adam said it was about the fall of the 'Prosper' network.

'Oh, I don't like that at all,' said Bodington. Nevertheless, he agreed to call at Adam's house at six the following evening. He neither came, nor rang nor wrote to excuse himself.

I authorised Adam to initiate contact with Déricourt. He replied that he had dialled the number in the telephone directory and found himself speaking to Déricourt. Déricourt had come to his house on 4 April. He had read *Madeleine*.

Adam lent him *The Starr Affair* and told him my new book involved him critically. Déricourt said he had been tried and acquitted, and if anybody attempted to reopen the case he would sue for defamation.

In France or in England, asked Adam?

Déricourt said if the publication was in England only, he would shrug his shoulders; if in France, he would react violently. He was never without a revolver, and could put a bullet through a jam-jar at thirty paces. All he wanted was not to have his name involved in a way that could upset his social and business relations; he would rather not be obliged to bring an action for libel and suggested I should refer to him simply as 'Gilbert'.

Alan replied that it would be a case of identifying him by his activities and suggested it would be best for us to meet. Déricourt agreed.

I flew to Paris on 6 May 1957. Adam drove me to the Terrass-Hotel, Montmartre.[3] The Adams had asked me to dinner, and when I had deposited my case, we pursued a steepening climb past the black hulk of the windmill into the cobbled 'village' of Montmartre, to the Adams cottage in the *impasse* called Villa Léander. There, the next day, I should meet the shadowy figure I had trailed so long.

---

[3] This was a rather grand hotel, which no longer exists From an elevated corner of the rue Joseph le Maistre, it commanded a view across the cemetery over the roofs and domes of the city of Paris With Déricourt

6: WITH DÉRICOURT

It was 7 May 1957. The appointment with Déricourt had been made for 2.30 p.m. Adam had asked me to come half an hour early, so that we could have a prior chat, but as I approached I saw there was a man walking before me, in a good suit, in brown, on the other side of the Villa Léandre, and felt he was heading like myself for the end house. I quickened my pace, and overtook him, so that it was he who walked up the steps and stood behind me as we waited for Adam to answer my ring at the door. 'He has followed me up, I think,' I said, looking over my shoulder.

'Oh no, I haven't followed you,' Déricourt said. 'Don't get me wrong already.'

He was of medium height, broad-shouldered and muscular. His hair was medium fair, strongly growing, tending upwards into curls. The soul is in the eyes. His eyes were blue, bold and guarded.

Although Adam introduced us, we at first addressed our remarks to him putting off a direct encounter by taking up Adam's comment on the recent redecoration of his sitting-room. It was Déricourt who came to the point. 'But you didn't ask me here for my opinion of your colour scheme.' He said he had read my books. 'I knew Boemelburg before the war, when he was at the Embassy here.'

I had suspected he knew Boemelburg before 1943, but by declaring it himself, in this easy manner, he had denied me the possibility of accusing him of it. No one had told me Boemelburg was at the Embassy.

Déricourt was recalling the early months of the Occupation, the vexation of having the Germans comporting themselves as masters. I was letting him do all the talking. I must tackle him.

'Monsieur,' I said, 'I know.'

'Know what?' he asked.

'The real character of your relations with the Germans.'

'Are you an agent, or only a writer?'

I said I was not an agent, but I had made researches and established some facts.

'Don't let's be vague. Give me some details. Give me a precise fact.'

'You were BOE 48.'

'Certainly not.' The question had been examined and he had been cleared of it. 'Everybody knows that except you.'

I offered him a cigarette, but he did not smoke.

He said, 'I don't know who BOE 48 was but I can swear it wasn't me. It was the number of a German agent. For Heaven's sake, I haven't ever been a German agent.' It had been examined for eighteen months. He had been promoted since his acquittal to a higher rank, major, on the reserve list.

I doubted that. I told him I knew he had submitted the mail of the 'Prosper' network, which was photostatted. The photostats were kept in Kieffer's department at Avenue Foch.

'I never went to the Avenue Foch and I never met Kieffer.'

'That may be ... It was Goetz who acted as liaison between you and Kieffer.'

'I never met Goetz... except in the office of the *juge d'instruction...*'

'Ernest was present at your last interview with Goetz, at an empty apartment near the Arc de Triomphe.'

He said he had never met either Goetz or Ernest. Perhaps this was 'suggested' to Ernest?

'No. He said it to me and I certainly didn't suggest it to him. He recognised your photograph as that of the man he had met in the empty flat.'

'You put the photograph in front of him and asked, "That's 'Gilbert', isn't it?"'

'No!' I told him I had posted Ernest a newspaper cutting and he had written back that he recognised the photograph.

Déricourt said it was too easy to 'recognise' people that way...

I accepted his point about the insufficiency of identification from a photograph, but said it was the quality of Ernest's testimony that impressed me. I felt his seriousness.

'Don't feel too much. And don't accept the fable of the good, poor German lamb, officer of the Gestapo.'

Although we were sparring, the atmosphere had improved.

I told him of Christmann's statement, from which it appeared he must have been in touch with the Germans before 2 June, the date he told the court.

'Didn't I say 2 May?'

'No, you didn't, you said 2 June.'

He said the story was made up that he had told the court about the two pilots who had asked him to go with them for a drive, on which he was trapped. The date on which it happened could only be fictitious since it never happened at all. It was useless to cross-examine him on the details of what had been 'a conventional presentation', made to conform to a pattern of such stories, simplified for the panel of military judges. They expected traps. 'C'était du théâtre!' 'I was in the face of the enemy — I looked on the judges as my enemies... Il fallait les vaincre. You don't expect the truth-literal truth — in a court-room.' Nevertheless, the story he had told the court was true in spirit, if not in fact, and some details in it were true.

He *had* known two German pilots before the war and they had really called on him, though all had not followed in exactly the way he told the court. It had been necessary to present something short and easily comprehensible. 'The truth was not important. The important thing was to be acquitted.'

I was amazed by his frankness. Yet the robust vigour with which he declared the whole a fiction gave me more confidence that I might ultimately get at the truth than if he had weakly tried to cling to his story.

Adam left us to fetch beer. Alone with Déricourt, I asked, 'Why did Bodington do as he did?'

'Didn't he say he had been present in the room of the War Office when I was briefed to approach the Germans on my return to France?'

'No, he didn't. He supported the story you had told the court.... If your story was partly untrue, why did Bodington go into the box to confirm it?'

'He thought it was the truth. I didn't suggest it to him and I didn't press him. He did it spontaneously, at least as far as I was concerned. Bodington wasn't questioned in court about the way I got into contact with the Germans or they with me.'

He would rather not say anything about Bodington.

'But that is the knot of the problem.'

'Yes,' he said simply. 'That is the knot of the problem.'

I felt that there was in his reply a kind of complicity with myself. He knew very well there was a problem, and agreed with me as to where it lay, but for obvious reasons could not speak of Bodington. He said I must not press him concerning Bodington. I realised that he had a debt of honour towards him, since it was to Bodington he owed his life. I must respect that and not try to make him break it.

Whereas earlier he had been maintaining his contact with the Germans was authorised, now he said, 'I wasn't authorised.'

I thought I had won a confession.

'Not by the French Section but by another organisation in London.' I believed he had meant the first statement to stand alone, and that by the addition he was deliberately teasing me, as well as giving himself a cover I was meant to see through.

Adam came back with the beer. I said, 'We have made some progress while you have been out.'

Déricourt instantly covered himself. 'I expressed myself badly … I was not really authorised for a moment, because the whole thing had got too big and too desperate. For a time I had to carry on without being really authorised, but I succeeded and then everybody was on my side.'

I listened with scepticism. Yet I noticed it was questions touching Bodington he refused to answer. At least there was a loyalty there, to someone who had done something for him.

Adam said, 'I have some consideration for you — you've come here. But I'm under no obligation to him.'

I said to Déricourt, 'If you're concerned about him, it is for you to contact him and bring him here.'

He shook his head. He had not been in communication with Bodington for years.

'Can't you write a story about Tarzan or Jumbo instead of putting your nose into this stinking business? It is too recent to tell the whole truth. Some people are still alive, or even on duty. Come back in fifty years and I'll tell you the truth.'

'I know it already.'

'What?'

'You were BOE 48.'

'Encore?' He insisted BOE 48 was another man.

Adam kept pressing him to identify this other man, stamped, and said, 'It's all your honour, or all his.'

I said to Adam, 'There isn't any other.'

'But I want to believe there is. If he can convince me.'

Déricourt said, 'I can say nothing. I'm a prisoner of the job I did. I have sworn not to reveal secret matters, and I keep my oath.'

'You're an eel,' I said.

The expression does not exist in French, and I had to explain. 'You are sinuous and slippery. One cannot grasp you.'

When he understood, it was with delight. 'Thanks for the compliment. Don't forget I have been an agent. A good agent... Orders are orders.'

I said I did not believe he was still on duty.

'Certainly not. Now I am *brûlé* in every country. That keeps me out of trouble and prevents me from dying young. I am only forty-seven. I can't even look at a second-hand car without a policeman saying, "Move on, sir."' As regards the past, he was bound.

'You know all the ways of getting yourself out of things.'

'I have an interest,' he said with a disarming smile.

'Look,' I said, 'you have been acquitted and nobody can do anything to you.'

He agreed with that.

'So it can't hurt you to tell the truth and admit it was you.'

Adam said to me, 'He can't if perhaps it wasn't.'

'It was he,' I said.

Déricourt made the point that the 'Prosper' network had been penetrated from a very early date, indeed from the beginning, in the sense that it was created partly out of the ruins of earlier, contaminated networks. He insisted one must go back to 'La Chatte'. Kiffer (Kiki) was not the only member of her ruined network to go over to the Germans, or at any rate to be trailed by them, and some of these went into the 'Carte' network of 1942. In the 'Carte' network, too, was Marsac, who went to sleep in a train and woke to find his briefcase missing, in which were names and addresses....

'Prosper' picked agents from 'Carte' and from Noble I where 'La Chatte' was, and in all these networks there were already German agents.'

I did not at the time know what Noble I was, but it was to become significant later.

He spoke of the stupidity of London in having given 'Prosper' for letterbox the Tambour sisters, who were letterbox to 'Carte'. By that his network was contaminated from the beginning. He spoke of the arrest of Marsac, of the Tambour sisters, of Bardet, through whom Frager was controlled, of the stupidity of attempting to bribe the Abwehr to release the Tambour sisters; in attempting that, 'Prosper' exposed himself to trailing...

I knew all these points were legitimate. Both Mme Balachowsky and the Abbé had made them. Yet it was only the betrayal of the mail which Vogt mentioned.

Déricourt began to speak of the pact.

I said, 'The pact was an epiphenomenon. They concluded it because they knew they had been betrayed, and it is not for you to speak of that.'

'It is not an excuse,' he said sharply. 'And I have my idea, which is different.'

'Prosper' had endeavoured to take him under his command. He had asked London what to do, and been told, 'Cut at once. You are your own chief in the field.'

'Did you warn him of the German infiltration?'

'Not really.'

'Did you tell him you were in contact with the Germans?'

'No,' he said simply.

I told him that in May 'Prosper' expressed suspicion of him. He retorted that 'Prosper' had returned to London through his hands. I said there was no other way he could go.

'Nuts!' he said in English. 'There were MTBs and the route through Spain.'

He spoke with extreme violence of the behaviour of some of the members of the 'Prosper' network. I said it was not for him to blacken them.

'But I don't blacken them. Spying is not a business for angels. It is only to people who don't understand that that some of these things could look black. "Madeleine" lacked security sense.' (Mme Balachowsky had said the same.)

I said he was not in a position to criticise anybody.

He replied, 'Listen, Miss Fuller. 'Prosper' was magnificent — strong, young, courageous and decisive, a kind of Ivanhoe; but he should have been a cavalry officer, not a spy. He was not sufficiently trained in these things. In Britain we learned how to jump by parachute, use all kinds of arms, open any lock, write in code, use wireless. But nobody can teach reckless people to be calm and weigh things carefully.' It was no more possible than to teach audacity and decisiveness to the over-prudent.

'That may be, but we are getting away from the subject. It's you we've come here to discuss, not 'Prosper'.'

'Well then?'

'I should like to tell you what I honestly believe — that you knew something against the people in London, and that they were therefore in your hands and were obliged to protect you for fear you would tell what you knew about them.'

105

With the most radiant smile, he exclaimed, 'But of course! That's exactly it! But not in the bad sense. In the sense of discretion only, not complicity. A tacit accord. It's elementary.'

I told him I had seen him as a pointing arrow.

'Do you mean you saw me as something pointing to something else?'

'Yes. You are guilty, and London protected you knowing you to be guilty.'

He reacted with a flash of anger. 'I am not guilty. I have proved it, and I can still prove it, even after the deposition from Ernest.'

'Yes, you are guilty.'

'No, I am not guilty.'

'Yes.'

'No.'

'Yes.'

'If you believe it,' he said with an odd hint of accord.

'I do.'

He shrugged slightly, smiling. 'You must never believe me further than you wish, Mademoiselle, for I can't always tell the whole truth.'

I repeated to him again the points of Ernest's statement. '... He went with Goetz to the empty apartment of which Goetz had the key, and there you met them. You confirmed you were leaving and gave them the BBC message that would announce your arrival. You were recalled in February.'

'The fourth of February,' he said. Morel had tried to take him back on the 1st. He had declined to go without being given time to make proper arrangements. He had said he would be willing to come on the 4th, and on the 4th he did. After his release from SOE he enlisted in the Free French Air Force...

'I haven't accused you of being a coward.'

'Nobody could.' He had been shot down on 9 September 1944.

I held to Vogt's testimony.

He said it did not hang together. He was neither BOE 48 nor the man in the empty apartment.

Long ago, Mercier had pointed out to me there was no proof the two parts of the statement referred to the same individual, and that one Déricourt, but I felt that he was the person meant, in both parts of the statement. 'I *know* it's true.'

He looked me very deeply in the eyes, and said, 'It's true for you, if you believe it.' I had the oddest feeling, that he spoke to me as in the confidence of the temple of which we were both initiates. He was telling me I was right, and had earned the right to be assured I was right, which he could not without breaking that confidence deny me, though it was something the profane must not know. Adam was not meant to catch it.

But if what I was right about was his having done such a shaming thing, was there some justifying reason for it, that could not be told either? I felt in that moment that a kind of bond had been made, though there was a mystery I could not fathom.

He told me it was he who had received 'Madeleine' when she had been landed by Lysander, and he wondered I had not come to see him when I was writing my book about her.

'I did not know you existed.' Neither Miss Atkins nor Colonel Buckmaster had mentioned his name to me. He was not mentioned in Buckmaster's book. 'I think you are the skeleton in the cupboard.'

This expression, like eel, was new to him, and entertained him greatly. I gave him also 'a dead rat'.

'You are not trying to accuse me of having betrayed 'Madeleine'?' he asked suddenly.

'No, a woman did that.' But, I said, there was a problem concerning 'Madeleine' of which I would like to tell him. When I began my researches, one of the first people I met was Mme Garry, the widow. When 'Madeleine' arrived, she stayed at first in the Garry's flat, together with Renée Garry and 'Antoine'. After a Gestapo raid on that flat, they all left it, and 'Madeleine' and 'Antoine' went for a while to Mme Aigrain. He left during the summer; she stayed on, but in the autumn was expecting to be fetched to London. Mme Garry told me 'Madeleine' was expecting a radio message which would tell her where and when she had to meet the man who would conduct her to the incoming aircraft. The Garrys were expecting to go to London as well, perhaps by an aircraft following hers. The aircraft to collect them should have come by the October moon, but they were arrested, 'Madeleine' on the 13th, the Garrys on the 18th.

The man to meet them and conduct them to the aircraft would have been himself, said Déricourt, if such an instruction had really come from London. However, he received none. More than one aircraft left by the October moon, but he had no instruction to board 'Madeleine' or the Garrys.

I told him Miss Atkins told me no arrangement had been made to bring my friend back to England. She was impatient with the story. Yet I was sure it was true. Mme Aigrain told me that on 10 October 'Madeleine' had called in briefly to thank her for her earlier hospitality and say goodbye, as she was being fetched to England on the 14th. Ray monde Lacours, a childhood friend of 'Madeleine', had told me 'Madeleine' brought her a gold powder compact as a parting gift, because her mission was terminated and she was being fetched to England. The Inayat Khans' family doctor, Dr Jourdan and his wife were other private associates of 'Madeleine'. They knew that something had happened at the end of September that caused her to feel the danger of capture too extreme for her to continue working. Mme Jourdan was with her when she received and deciphered, at their home, the last radio message from London. It was, unexpectedly, 'May God keep you.' She burst into tears. She had been expecting an operational instruction, and suddenly to be addressed as a soul undid her. The Jourdans urged her to keep in their flat until the man she expected came to conduct her to the aircraft. She said there was something outside she had to do, but then she would return and take sanctuary with them until the 14th. They never saw or heard from her again. So that made three households in which Mme Garry's memory was confirmed. She and Garry had been to say goodbye to her sister. Both Mme Aigrain and the Jourdans mentioned a specific date, the same date, the 14th. Moreover, Vogt told me that when he arrested her, she burst out in a passion: 'This would happen on my very last day! Tomorrow I would have been on my way to England!'

'London let her down,' was Déricourt's interpretation. It had been Mercier's also. Déricourt said he did not like the sound of that last radio message, 'May God keep you'. He thought it meant, 'because we are throwing you away'. I had always assumed, as 'Madeleine' had apparently assumed, that it meant 'until our man comes to fetch you'. Mme Jourdan was sure she was still expecting there must come a further message, an operational message, giving her the exact appointment, but I had a sinking feeling that the words could bear the interpretation Déricourt placed on them. 'But why? Why?'

Perhaps, he suggested, it suited the London game better to have her still running around Paris, in contact with Germans and with German agents without knowing it.

I did not like to think that, yet if the plan had been changed, a further message from London — received of course by Dr

Goetz — would have had to contain an apology or explanation of why the pick-up was not arranged. The telegrams would have revealed all, and their destruction was forever unfortunate.

The aircraft that left by the October moon, said Déricourt, had a full complement of passengers. No spaces for three more. And London did not reproach him with boarding three too few. He had wondered why she did not return to London in the summer, with 'Antoine' and so many others. He did not see her after that.

I was sorry he had added that, because I had to say that in September Mme Aigrain had given a report to 'Madeleine', who later told her she had given it to 'Gilbert'. After Mme Aigrain had been arrested, Vogt showed her a photocopy of it.

He said it was false. He had ceased to see 'Madeleine' by that date.

I thought he lied from prudence. There was nothing in the report that mattered. It was only about the effects of an RAF bombing.

I told him what Christmann had told me. When I came to his having seen him at Avenue Foch, Déricourt said, 'Christmann lies on that point. I was never at Avenue Foch.'

I accorded that Vogt had never seen him at Avenue Foch, or heard of his coming there; yet I could not think why Christmann should have made this up. 'He thinks he sees in you something of the same kind of man that he is himself.'

Déricourt made a slight movement of impatience. He did not deny having been in contact with the Germans. 'The Germans in Paris had higher orders to respect me. If I had betrayed 'Prosper' to them they would not have liked that. They would not have thought well of me, and they did.'

'I can tell you one who didn't.'

'Who?'

'Kieffer.'

'Kieffer's dead.'

'I have his words from Ernest. Do you want to know what he said about you. It's not nice. Do you want to hear it?'

He hesitated just for a moment, then said, 'Yes,' looking me in the eyes.

'He betrays the English and his own compatriots to us; he would betray us to them the day it suited him better.'

He was silent for a moment, then said, 'Ah well.' The silence continued. Then he said, 'Kieffer did not know me. Perhaps if he had known me he would not have said that.'

He said sometimes he had to carry on without instructions, make decisions on his own responsibility. One could be blamed afterwards.

'Are you saying you were authorised but went too far?'

'I hardly know what answer I can make to that. I never sacrificed anybody. All my agents are still alive.'

He said one should distinguish between those who betrayed their colleagues from interest, and those who did so only to save their lives.

'You have told us you were not under duress, so I can only suppose it was from interest.'

For the second time he showed anger. 'I didn't take money.' He added, roguishly, 'Not much. Not what I call substantial.'

He said that money had not been the motive. 'It was not dirty money. First, as I was not a German agent, I didn't receive a monthly salary. It is well known, because we have the pay-lists of both the Gestapo and Abwehr agents. Secondly, as I never gave people or anything to the German service, I was not in a position to claim a reward for it. Thirdly, it would have been stupid to take any, as it could have caused me to be

111

distrusted. But I had the chance to make some personal profit on some international business in which German as well as British businessmen were involved. And they took the best part, leaving me only the crumbs.' He added, 'As Christmann told you, smuggling and spying are cousins.'

He referred to the rumour that there were German agents in London. 'We agents working in occupied countries were open to tales. Some thought only, some had what they called proofs, some knew. For those, tales were not tales. For those it was worst. All of us had the weight of this on the chest like a stone. We avoided reporting to London because of this. I took "my own measures" without knowing at the beginning they were in line with what London wished; but it took time before my chiefs in London realised I had puzzled the Germans in Paris, and what is more, the Germans in London, too.' Without being a prisoner, one could be the prisoner of a situation.

I said, 'You must realise I have been nice with you.'

'Yes,' he said. 'But for my part, I could have reacted to this in a very much nastier way.'

All that concerned him really was that his real name should not appear in print. He had his present job, a house in the country, and did not want his life turned upside down. I should call him 'Gilbert', 'and say all the bad things you like'.

We spoke of the radio-game, and he said he was certain London knew of 'Archambaud's arrest. 'Madeleine' and Cohen were not the only ones to transmit the information. He, too, had had a radio message sent. Nevertheless, he had nothing against London. 'Can't we, agents between ourselves, keep a secret? That is not blackmail.'

I told him Starr's theory, that the radio-game had been kept up deliberately in order to feed misinformation. Against that, I had never learned of any misinformation the Germans received through it.

He said, 'It was rather to keep the Germans occupied. To distract their attention, I think.'

That, also, was a theory Starr had voiced — that the French Section was used as a blind, and the real thing entrusted to some other group of people.

Déricourt said, 'My theory — I won't tell it to you — is not so crude as yours. I knew, and I reported to London at Easter 1943, that the French Section was penetrated from a very early stage — from before 'Prosper' was even parachuted into the field. I suppose 'Prosper's' chief knew that, and they handled it in their own way.'

I wondered if that was what 'Prosper' had sensed during his visit to London just after, from which he returned so overcast. 'But if the French Section was used in this way, do you think Buckmaster knew?'

'I don't think so,' he said. 'As for me, I reported to an officer of much higher rank, and I believe that Buckmaster did not know at that time.'

Out of a silence that fell, he asked, 'Have you seen Gubbins?'

'No.'

'It's a pity.' I cannot remember exactly what words he used, but my impression was that for Gubbins he had respect.

However, he did not believe it was within SOE the game was played. In some other quarter.

'And the people in this other quarter, were their motives honest or dishonest?'

'Honest!' he said, and his eyes blazed. It was as though I had struck a vein of pro-British patriotism.

He believed there had been a high-level strategic decision to sacrifice the Section. He came to a personal conviction about that in the course of his visit to England at Easter 1943, and on his return to France had 'taken his own measures'.

What did he mean by 'own measures'?

'I managed to get myself solicited by a German agent — on my own initiative in the first place, but soon I informed my chiefs of the steps I had taken. I went secretly once more to London. There I received the order to carry on my mission as Air Movements Officer and "other" orders, also.'

I said this was impossible to check, and he said he could not help that.

I said that, according to the French papers, he was on his recall to London in February 1944 placed under arrest.

'I was not under arrest, I was distrusted,' he said. He was ordered first to the Swan, Stratford-on-Avon — he was able to walk about amongst the whitewashed cottages with the black beams, but not to put to the test whether he could follow a play of Shakespeare in English, because the Memorial Theatre was not yet opened for the season — then to the Savoy Hotel, London.

I was surprised, because Dourlein and Ubbink, when they escaped from captivity in Holland and returned to London, to unveil Nordpol, were accommodated in Brixton Prison for their pains.

He said he had to undertake not to go out on his own, or to speak to French people, but could look out on to the river through the window and see Waterloo Bridge and the barges passing. As time went on, restrictions were eased. He walked about London, went to the Tower, as a tourist, not an inmate, saw the ravens and shivered suitably at Traitors' Gate. There was sometimes a man from Scotland Yard who escorted or tailed him, but less so with time. He went sometimes to a cinema, found stage plays too difficult to understand in

English... He had to go to Northumberland Avenue to answer questions. 'Have you been in there?'

'No.' I supposed he was speaking of the hotel in which potential recruits were interviewed.

He thought there might have been an activity more exciting and interesting than that going on there.

He was released soon after D Day, and it was a relief to be flying again, fighting a clean war. As though it came over him as a wave, he spoke with intense bitterness of everyone in SOE.

I said he was not doing himself any good with me by being unpleasant about other people.

'For hours you have been saying the most disagreeable things to me,' he said.

It was true.

We were all tired. We had talked for six hours. I said I would write out a *compte rendu* of our conversations, and show it to him. 'I don't want your head,' I said.

'You couldn't get it!' he retorted, but we were smiling as we shook hands. 'It's too recent,' he said. 'If we were all dead, it would be different.'

And he was gone down the garden path. Almost cheerily.

Back in my hotel bedroom, I spent most of the night writing out all I could remember of our conversation, while exchanges and phrases were still fresh. In the morning I went to ask Adam if I could borrow his typewriter on which to type it, at the same time making a carbon I could give to Déricourt.

'What do you think of him?' he asked.

'The dreadful thing is — I like him.'

'So do I. But he told us a magnificent cover story.'

I could not understand why I had not an adverse reaction, as from a foul personality.

115

'Amoral,' said Adam. Not a bad conscience because no conscience.

I was sure he was guilty, but I did not feel he was evil. Unconvinced 'amoral' was true, either. I remembered how the eyes had blazed when he said, 'Honest!'

Adam telephoned him and told him I had made the *compte rendu*, if he would like to see it.

Déricourt said he would be free tomorrow morning.

Adam would not, but 'Miss Fuller is. You are grown up enough now to meet without me.' It was arranged he should come to the Terrass-Hotel at 10 a.m.

I had now a feeling that, on my own, I might get further with him.

Déricourt was punctual the next morning at ten. I made towards a table in a secluded corner of the lounge, where we could talk in confidence over our coffee.

'But we have nothing secret to talk about!' he exclaimed, and found us chairs by the window. While we talked, he repeatedly looked out of it at the people coming in.

'When I was told you wished to see me I thought it was blackmail,' he opened. 'I didn't believe there was a book.' He had come, apparently, expecting to be asked for compensation for putting a (non-existent) book aside. 'I get a lot of people trying to blackmail me,' he said chattily. 'I get it from people who haven't a tithe of what you have on me.' A trace of admiration showed in his voice. 'With the little they have, they try it on. I have a method for getting rid of blackmailers.'

'I thought it was supposed to be difficult. What is your method?'

'I tell them I will kill them.'

'And they believe you?'

'Yes.'

I told him I had been warned not to walk on the outside of the pavement...

'It's elementary. I could think of subtler things. A crane could drop its load on you, and it would never be brought back to me.'

'You would have to get me to walk under a crane.'

'Believe me, my fertile brain is capable of devising accidents I won't tell you...'

He was smiling, and I did not feel he meant me any harm.

Yet I said, 'For me, it is not excluded that you were a German agent, purely and simply, from the time you first knew Boemelburg before the war, and that you were sent to England in 1942 by Boemelburg.'

'You're wrong,' he said. 'I was in espionage before the war but I have never been a German agent.'

'But you knew Boemelburg.'

'Say rather the son of Boemelburg. It is truer. I knew one of his sons, the one who limps.' It all went back to aerobatics and dirt-track racing. Watching dirt-track racing, he met Bodington (so Spooner was right!) and at aerobatics he met the son of Boemelburg, and also the two Luftwaffe pilots. After the displays, they would all repair to a nearby café. Later, the son of Boemelburg took them all back to his parents' villa at Neuilly, and they met Boemelburg, who treated him as a friend of his son. His attitude never really changed, 'even after I did things for him. I can truly say I never met Boemelburg clandestinely. At all times I went openly to his house, pressed the bell and entered by the front door. Sometimes I would have a meal with the family — which from spy to spymaster, in that relationship, is unheard of.'

This acquaintance had not rendered him politically sympathetic to Germany. Mobilised on his birthday, 2 September 1939, he had served with the French Air Force as a transport pilot. Later test pilot. After the Armistice he flew backwards and forwards between Marseilles, where he was then living, and Paris, Toulouse and other towns. On 13 December 1941 he married, in Marseilles. But he felt depressed by the German dominance, and decided to escape to England. 'My escape was arranged by the British Intelligence Service.' I did not believe him. 'It's true,' he said. 'It was all arranged through the American Consulate, which was in collusion with London. A message came from London, all was arranged.' He had to take the train to Narbonne, then make his way to a small port, where he was to travel by the 'Pat' line. 'You have heard of 'Pat'?' Of course I had heard of 'Pat'. 'Pat O'Leary' was the code-name of a Belgian (not Irishman), Dr Albert Guérisse GC. The 'Pat' line was the best known of all the escape lines, and Déricourt could have heard of it without having been a passenger by it.

'It's true,' he maintained. 'Pat' received me, boarded me himself.' It was on a trawler flying a Portuguese flag, but really commissioned by the British Intelligence Service. It took him to Gibraltar, where he landed, and he had some days to wait for a ship that would take him onwards to the United Kingdom. He arrived in Greenock, Glasgow, about midnight on 7 September 1942. He was met by Dewavrin and took the train from Glasgow to Euston and saw London for the first time from under the black Euston Arch. He declared contact with German Intelligence, not wishing to be shot as a spy, but nobody took any notice. After clearance, he found his way to the Air Ministry, enlisted and was posted to Newquay, Cornwall.

'Do you know Newquay?' he asked.

'I have been there, but only on a visit from Tintagel on the same coast.' Tintagel I knew very well. 'Did you see Tintagel Head? A great cape or headland?'

He was not sure if he saw it. He saw a coast much slashed by capes and inlets, but from the air.

But why was he on a coast not facing enemy-occupied territory?

It was not for operational flights. For training flights. Although he was an experienced pilot, he still had to learn to fly a type of aircraft new to him, understand instructions given in English and work with the RAF. It would not have been any use to go to a school of languages, as the teachers would not have known aeronautical terms. 'The problem wouldn't have arisen if I had gone with the Free French Air Force, but I had a fancy to fly for the RAF.'

He said that while he was in Newquay there was a fire in the town and he rescued a woman from a burning house.

I was suspicious of an unverifiable claim to heroism, and invited him to describe Newquay.

He gave a fair description; in any case I did not think most Frenchmen would have heard of so small a place and he pronounced 'Newquay' correctly. But, he said he was stationed just outside and behind the town. 'At St Morgan? Do you know it?' I could not for a moment think of a saint of that name. When later I checked with a map, I realised he must have been saying St Mawgan. Moreover, I must have passed it in the bus between Newquay and Wadebridge.

By about November he was with 161 Squadron, on the border of Bedfordshire and Huntingdonshire. I am not sure that I correctly followed his account of how this transfer occurred. He was at the Air Ministry. He met André Simon, who told him there was something more exciting to do than flying, and gave him the address at Orchard Court. He met Buckmaster and the others briefly, and so he found himself in Bedfordshire, doing a Lysander training course. On 23 January 1943 he was parachuted back to a field near Prithivier, in the Loiret.

We went through my *compte rendu* of the first interview. He found my reporting fair, but asked for the deletion of some phrases he had used, and for paraphrasing in more discreet terms. To say of the testimony he had given in court that it was 'theatre' was not exactly to say it was false. Imagine a dramatist writing a play about Charles I. He wondered, incidentally, what happened to the head of Charles I, after it had been cut off? The dramatist would probably take some liberties with scenes and dates, transferring events from one time and place to another, to make his presentation more dramatic and simple. The grand lines of the story had to stand out, without clutter. Things that happened in different places, over years, would be brought together in a single scene. It was that sort of liberty he had taken in giving his evidence, yet in spirit it was true to what really happened. 'Even though you only call me 'Gilbert', people are going to recognise me from this, and I don't want to look a fool.' The pseudonym 'Gilbert' would protect him from the curiosity of local tradespeople, the people in the baker's where he bought his bread, the people with whom he worked, at Orly, to whom this name was unknown. That was the most important to him. Yet all people in the world that had to do with these operations, or trials would know he was meant....

'You have been acquitted, and no matter what I publish, you cannot be re-tried.'

'True,' he said. 'But I can be assassinated.'

'By people you have betrayed, or their relatives?'

'No.' By people who feared he might talk about them. 'There are some people with whom I have a *quid pro quo*. They know some bad things about me — not the same bad things you have collected — a different set of bad things you don't know about. Belonging to an anterior epoch. I know bad things about them, of about the same weight. That is balance.'

I was not quite sure I understood his drift. He would give me a parallel from the present. After his recent air accident an inquiry was started. An investigator asked him if the Met had given the altitude correctly. He had replied, 'Certainly. The Met was correct.' That would have got back to the Met. Later they asked the Met if the pilot had approached the ground correctly. The Met replied, 'The approach was perfect.'

'These people with whom you have a *quid pro quo*. Are they French? Do they live in France?'

He nodded, almost imperceptibly.

'Do you see them?'

'No.' He did not wish to see them, and felt very sure they did not wish to see him. They might pass each other in a club, but would not engage in conversation. 'There is equilibrium. It is the surest of all relationships.'

'You are very cynical.'

'Not really.'

His fear was that if they heard he was holding conversations with a writer, they might think he was talking about them, and take measures to stop him. 'If there is a rupture of equilibrium, they have to do something.'

'You don't think they would murder you?'

'In peacetime … I doubt if they would be bold enough.'

We returned to the *compte rendu*. I asked him why he had chosen 2 June as the date for his fictitious arrest.

121

He did not know why it had been made 2 June. His *juge d'instruction* read him, as he was bound to do, the statement that had come concerning him, and 2 June was in it. The *juge* asked him if it was true. Naturally he said 'Yes'. What else should he have said? 'No, May'? He pulled the glum face of someone answering stupidly. I laughed, and it was as though there was a moment of complicity.

I asked him about his trial at Croydon. 'How much of the story you told the Croydon magistrates was true?'

'Nothing.'

'There was no Ignace?'

'No.'

'No Mr Marshal?'

'No.'

'No white handkerchief?'

'No. It was all fiction.'

'Then you must have deceived Derek Curtis Bennett.'

'Of course. One must always deceive one's advocate.' If he told him the thesis on which he wanted him to defend him was untrue he would be insulted, and perhaps refuse. 'In such a relationship deception corresponds to respect.'

'Would you like to tell me the truth?'

'No!' he exclaimed, with amused petulance.

'Who paid Curtis Bennett? And the two junior counsel and the solicitors?

He had never thought about it. Nevertheless, he supposed they must have been paid, for no bill ever came to him. All had been arranged for him. He had been told the address to which he should go to meet his legal representative. The war with Germany was no sooner ended than organisation of resistance against Russian espionage began...

I did not believe that if our government needed to transfer funds to the Continent it would have done so in a way that laid a carrier open to a smuggling charge, though he was implying heavily that it was the same people who had looked after him at his trials both in Croydon and in Paris. When I said I would put in my book that he said that, he said, 'If you put that, I'll have trouble. Put that I said that — that I said I'll have trouble. That way, I won't have trouble.'

I said I felt there was something wrong in London, and the proof of it was they were susceptible to blackmail by him.

He said, 'You are crediting me with more power than I have ever had. Blackmail is an awful word. In any Secret Service the man who talks too much is disliked, and the one who knows how to keep his mouth closed is appreciated. If I had tried to blackmail the Foreign Office, I should be either very rich or very dead. I am rich of a quiet life.'

He had let it be known in London that he found himself in an embarrassing situation and there had been a response. That did not mean he could not have got an acquittal otherwise. 'I don't care a fig for truth — literal truth — and I don't mind if you quote me for that.'

I must have said something about his not being an honourable person, for he touched his lapel, drawing my attention to what I had not noticed, that he was wearing the thin red ribbon of the Légion d'Honneur.

'You have no right to it!'

'I have a right. The President of France pinned it on me.'

'On you it is a mockery!'

He said it was worn by people who had done things as bad as he had done. Indeed, worse.

He added, 'I was recommended for the DSO.'

As I began to react, he smiled reassuringly. 'I was recommended for it, but then somebody thought "No, not the DSO".' The award had been stopped. Even his Médaille de la Résistance had been stopped. He had no medals. The Légion d'Honneur was his only decoration.

Did he really think the chapter I had written on our conversations would harm him?

He was a bit worried about 'Wybot'. When he was first arrested in November 1946, he was in the hands of the DST and had the unenviable distinction of being interrogated by its head — 'Wybot', real name, Roger Warin. Déricourt described him as 'a Machiavellian and terribly intelligent being, the modern Fouché'. But 'Wybot' had once said that in dealing with a fool he lost half his power. If an intelligent person found himself confuted, he broke down; the woolly-minded did not see when they had been confuted. Déricourt had played upon this need of 'Wybot' for mental coherence in the person he was interrogating. 'I changed my story at every hearing, at every minute, contradicting myself within a sentence, driving 'Wybot' mad.' Only if one's story is set, rigid, could one be confuted. He kept all the elements fluid and changing. His advocate, Moro-Giaffery, at first told him he must not keep changing his ground. 'But after a time, I fancy Moro perceived I had a method,' he said slyly.

Again, there was that tacit assumption we both knew. He added, 'to have beaten 'Wybot' is a dangerous feat. *Il doit m'en vouloir.* He must have it in for me.' 'Wybot' could read English, and when my book came out might be provoked to make trouble for him.

'Wybot', he said, found fault with everything British in order to glorify everything French. 'Like de Gaulle, only worse.' He had it in for those of the French who had joined the British or

Buckmaster Section instead of the de Gaulle one. 'I gave myself more pains to get out of having been a British agent than out of being a German one! I started by denying I was an agent of the IS. That was before I knew I was going to have Bodington. From the moment I knew I was going to have Bodington, I made a right-about turn.'

'How did you explain it?'

'Easy. I had not known they would sustain me. I had been discreet.' Also, he was no longer in the hands of 'Wybot'. 'I was out from between those tongs.' He was by now transferred to examination at the Tribunal Militaire, where he had for *juge d'instruction* first Captain Trossin, then Captain de Résseguier.

In the way he had said, 'Easy' was, I felt, an acknowledgement that this, too, was a fiction. What he was telling me was frankly the tale of how he had got out of a scrape.

We passed to more general topics, and I asked for his comments on some episodes of which I knew only from Bleicher's book. Was 'Elie' another name for 'Prosper'? No, he said, 'Elie' was Sidney Jones. He arrived with his radio, 'Bastien' (Marcel Clech), and his courier, 'Simone' (Vera Leigh). 'It was I who received them, at Azay-sur-Cher.' 'Elie' confided to him that he had a very delicate mission. Ostensibly, he was sent out as liaison officer to Frager, he was an independent Resistance chief, not an officer of the Buckmaster Section, though he accepted money from it. Actually, 'Elie', being a British officer, was supposed to try to take over the control of Frager's network, which made him unwelcome to Frager. When Bodington visited the field, part of his mission was to contact Frager, and only by using 'Simone' as cut-out was he able to do so without Bardet's learning where Déricourt had lodged him. Even so, it must have been through Bardet Bleicher learned Bodington was in France.

I told him that in his memoirs Bleicher claimed he could have arrested Bodington if he had wished.

'No,' said Déricourt. 'Remember La Fontaine's fable about the fox who said the grapes were sour, because he could not get them.'

Then, I said, in Bleicher's book was a story about 'Gilbert' having tried to force Bardet aboard a departing aircraft.

He would give me the background of that. The love of Frager for Bardet was by convention represented as avuncular. It was not. 'Cet amour était un amour péderaste.' It was because Frager was in love with Bardet that through Bardet Bleicher could control him.

I said it was, in fact, apparent from Bleicher's book that the arrest of 'Elie's' girl courier when she kept a rendezvous with Bardet was through betrayal by the latter.

Bardet, said Déricourt, had even got one man arrested who had nothing to do with the Resistance at all, for personal convenience.

That, too, I said, was in Bleicher's book. Bleicher said Bardet was having an affair with the wife, and asked Bleicher to have the husband arrested so that he should cease to be in the way.

It was not for the wife, Déricourt declared. 'For the woman, that would have been fine, wouldn't it? But it was for the flat!'

He reproached me that I considered him as low, whereas there were others lower than he. 'The Curé de Saint Maur confessed the *Résistants* and betrayed the confessions to the Gestapo. That's lower than me, isn't it? Et lui était prêtre!'

I ought to have told Déricourt it is not a matter of whom one is less low than, and quoted him Krishnamurti on the uselessness of comparisons. But I was thinking, this was a character I could not place.

Later, I found in the Abbé's book a brief reference to this brother of the cloth (p.56) as having been tried and condemned in 1948 and shot by firing-squad on 2 February 1949. Code-named 'Alesh', he had been an associate of Kléber and Jouffret — so must have become Bleicher's agent back in the days of the Interallié.

In October, Déricourt said, he received by radio from London as usual the number of passengers to be boarded and the pass-phrase by which he and they would identify themselves to each other. One of them turned out to be Bardet. Déricourt was delighted that they were going to be rid of him. Bardet was of the party that travelled together in the train from Paris to Angers. They got out. As they were crossing the road from the station, Déricourt noticed that Bardet was lagging behind. Not trusting him, he looked behind to see why. Then he saw Frager was following them, and it was for him Bardet was waiting. 'I was very angry, and I walked back and asked Frager how he dared to trail me and spy on one of my operations.' Frager then said he was one of the party to go to England, and Bardet had merely stood in for him until the time came. 'I was furious. Bardet had given me the pass-phrase. The person who gave me the pass-phrase was the person to go.' Frager said the pass-phrase had been given to him, and he had given it to Bardet, so he could stand in for him. Déricourt said this was totally irregular, two persons knowing one pass-phrase; it made them in a sense one person. He could not know to which of them it was that London had given it. Since they both knew it, they would both have to go. Frager would not have Bardet board the plane. 'I said, "Why don't you want him with you? You are friends."' Bardet slipped away and

Frager held out his hand. 'I refused to shake the hand of such a fool.'

'Elie', 'Bastien' and 'Simone' were afterwards arrested. He would not say Frager took that way to be rid of them — Frager was in London telling everybody 'Gilbert' was a German agent — but when he came back and found them gone, he might have wondered what had happened to them; he might have seen where the betrayal was coming from. 'He did not see because he did not want to see.' And one must understand the relationship to understand that.

He said the sexual relationships in SOE were important: Marsac arrested through Hélène, 'Madeleine' through jealousy over 'Antoine'. 'You need a *Who's Who of the Bed*, with the names cross-referenced. I should make you one if I had leisure.'

We had coffee; he talked in a more relaxed manner. He spoke more of his recent air accident. Crash-landing in fog, he had used his hands to beat out the flames before they spread to the 8,000 litres of fuel aboard, and the injuries with which he had been taken to hospital were mainly burns. He showed me his hands on which the burns still showed.

The one passenger killed had been a Tunisian general. 'Now if it had been a French general it wouldn't have mattered so much. France has several. But the Tunisians only had one. And I killed him.' I wish I could reproduce the comico-rueful tones in which he said it.

He now had to prepare himself to face a court of inquiry into the causes of the accident, which was the chief reason he did not want, just now, adverse publicity which could put the commissioners against him. If they found the fault to be his, he could lose his flying licence; that meant his livelihood.

He was also concerned about the effect on his wife. She had suffered very much already, because of him. In February 1944, if he had climbed into the aircraft beside Morel, as ordered, it would have meant abandoning her to arrest by the Gestapo, either for revenge or to hold as a hostage against information from England. By gaining the few days' delay, he had been able to take her to England with him. She had stood by him at his trial, but the strain on her had been considerable, and he did not know how she could bear any recrudescence of trouble.

'Would it be of help if I came to see her?'

The idea horrified him. He had not mentioned to her the interviews with Adam and myself. He was going to tell her nothing about my book, and hope she never saw it.

'Have you any children?'

'I had two. They died. I would have liked to have had children, if the circumstances of my life had been different. As things have turned out, I am glad to have none.'

At another moment he said spontaneously, 'I had a Chinese woman during the two years I lived in Indo-China. If I go back there, I'll find another.' He had learned to speak Chinese a little, and had a feeling for the Chinese way of living.

When we met the following afternoon at five *chez* Adam, Déricourt had brought not only the copy of my *compte rendu* I had left with him, annotated, but a handwritten document of many pages, his own *compte rendu*. It started as a replica of mine, then diverged. I objected. 'That's not what you said... that's not what I said...'

Disarmingly, he said, 'I didn't expect you to accept it as a substitute; but I thought it could provide a talking point.'

I agreed to some modifications. At seven Adam's wife obviously wanted to serve dinner and Déricourt and I left, together. As we descended the steps from the Avenue Junot to the rue Caulincourt, we were talking of T. E. Lawrence. Déricourt had read *The Seven Pillars of Wisdom* and *The Mint*, and said, 'Glandular trouble, don't you think?' We went into the café of Le Terrass, where we had a light supper ourselves. Déricourt said he had to fly an aircraft to Algiers that night. He flew between Paris and most places in North Africa and the Near East: Tangier, Algiers, Tunis, Beirut, Jeddah (Arabia) and Baghdad. We could meet in four days' time, on Tuesday the 14th.

We must have talked until late, for though it was May it was dark when we parted in front of my hotel, where he had parked his car. I mentioned that I had seen Watt.

It was the only time I saw fear on Déricourt's face. His eyes seemed to grow dark. 'You've seen Titch? The small man?'

'Yes.'

He swallowed, and with hardly another word got into his car. I feared he would not return.

On the 11th I was invited to the Yeo-Thomases'. 'He has taken it very well,' said Barbara. She would have expected a traitor, taxed with his treason, to be violently nasty. 'I can't get over his being so nice about it.' She worried for him. When my book appeared, 'He won't be able to show his face in a club.'

Yeo-Thomas paced up and down. He thought 'Wybot' was not going to like it.

I assured him Déricourt did not claim to have deceived 'Wybot'. He was sure 'Wybot' knew he was being told stories though he had not been able to box him in. He said, 'I lied and lied and lied to 'Wybot'.'

Barbara said, 'In a way, it's a pity he's so frank about it.' It made it difficult for Tommy to soften 'Wybot' down. 'He is the most dreaded man in France. People here dread him as if he were Robespierre.' Nevertheless, they knew him, and could put it nicely for Déricourt. They both agreed with his description of 'Wybot's' character.

'Is there any danger the British will ask the French to have him extradited for trial in England?' I asked Yeo-Thomas.

'I shouldn't think so. More likely the French will bring a charge of perjury.'

I was alarmed. Did he really think that?

'It entirely depends on 'Wybot',' he said. 'If 'Wybot' wants him prosecuted for perjury, he will be prosecuted for perjury. If 'Wybot' wants no action taken, none will be taken. I think it best I talk to him. If the matter is *confided* to him, by me, he may be nice about it. If he is left to find out about it, he has no reason to be nice.'

He felt some responsibility, with regard to the case of Déricourt, since it was he who had denounced him to London as an agent of the Gestapo and was in that sense the start of his troubles. 'Wybot' was notoriously anti-British. Déricourt's phrase, 'Like de Gaulle, only worse', was only too true. 'Because I had served in RF, I'm the only Englishman he will endure.' That made him the obvious intercessor.

Barbara said, 'Wybot' has come here to dinner. The best thing is, to ask him to dinner again. Tommy can tell him it's because he has a story to tell him.'

Yeo-Thomas said he would like Déricourt to tell him, himself, if he wanted him to do this. 'I don't want to be accused of meddling in his affair, for a second time.' In case it turned badly, it might look as though he were persecuting Déricourt.

To relieve the tension of the intervening days, I wrote to Mercier, who had been posted to Algeria. I also went to the headquarters of the Légion d'Honneur and checked that Déricourt was on its roll.

Punctually at 5 p.m. on the 14th — Déricourt was always punctual — he was at Adam's to meet me. We worked until seven. Then, as before, Déricourt and I walked back to the Terrass and had a snack supper in its café. I was adding to the *compte rendu* something he had just said when he stopped me from mentioning a third meeting. He would have preferred me to put everything as though it had happened at one single meeting, our first one. I had wanted to mention the second meeting, at the hotel, and he had agreed. He could not admit to there having been this third interview.

I did not understand.

He tried to explain. 'One can give one interview — perhaps under protest — and say very little. But it's obvious one cannot give three interviews without talking about something. It is almost a collaboration!'

Obviously he did not want to be thought to be talking more than he should.

I told him I had seen the fear in his eyes when I mentioned having seen Watt.

'I thought of something which he might have seen,' he said slyly, 'and which he might have misinterpreted.' I knew he meant me to understand, 'interpreted correctly'. I assured him that whatever Watt had seen he had not told me.

We were sitting side by side, eating our omelettes, when he touched his lapel. He was not wearing the red ribbon of the Légion d'Honneur. 'I removed it, specially for you. I thought it would make a better atmosphere for our conversations.'

It certainly did, though I had not noticed. I was touched by the gesture.

Joking, he said, 'If we keep on meeting it will run me into buying second suit.' He had had to leave home wearing the ribbon as usual, as if his wife noticed he had taken it down she would wonder why, and become uneasy. He had had to carry small scissors in his pocket and retire into a *toilette* in a metro station to unpick it. He would have to find a convenient place to sew it on again during the return journey, so that his wife would not see him come home without it. It would be less trouble to have two suits, 'one without Légion d'Honneur sewn in, and one with, and change twice a day'. But then, he reflected, 'She would wonder why I was always carrying a case or parcel, and perhaps find the suit without, and that would be worse.' He would just have to unpick it, every time he came to see me, 'since you don't like me to wear it'.

It was distinctive in Déricourt that he could take a situation other men would have found shaming, and refer to it with a frankness that made it irresistibly comic.

'But', he added, suddenly serious again, he would normally have to continue to wear it — 'because I have to keep my head up'. If certain people saw he had taken it down, they would think he had been cowed and he would not give them that satisfaction. 'They wear theirs, though they have done things as bad as I have, so I have to wear mine.'

I asked if he was speaking of the people with whom he had a *quid pro quo*. Yes, he said.

Had he been serious when he said they might assassinate him?

Now that it was peacetime, he did not really think they would have the nerve. The danger was that if they came to know of his meetings with me, they might think he had told me more than he had. If it was reported he had been seen no longer wearing his Légion d'Honneur, they might draw the conclusion that he had made, or was about to make, a confession that included them, and take measures to prevent it. Those measures might be disagreeable not only to him but to me.

Would he trust me with their names?

After some hesitation, he said, 'De Vomécourt. The brothers Philippe and Pierre de Vomécourt.'

I was surprised he should have known them at all. He was never identified with that early period of the Resistance. They were not in the 'Prosper' network. When had he known them? Before he came to England?

It was in an 'anterior epoch'. In 1941. Before he himself belonged to the French Section or knew that it existed, something had happened. He must ask me never to research that. It was deeply dangerous. If he were to tell me what had happened then, he would place me in the same danger in which he stood himself. It made for my safety that I did not know — genuinely did not know. He counselled me not to let the name de Vomécourt come anywhere in my book. Even if I said nothing bad at all about them, to see their names could make them suspicious he had told them something bad.

He was very serious. I felt that he was thinking for me, not trying to frighten me out of publishing my book. As it was to accuse him that I had come, I was touched by his care.

I assured him I would not mention the de Vomécourts. Were they the people he did not wish should learn how many meetings we had had? I had thought he was worried about the Intelligence Service.

'Oh I don't worry about the Intelligence Service, or any official people. Only about the de Vomécourts.'

I told him I had told something of our conversations to Yeo-Thomas, who knew 'Wybot'.

He started. 'Wybot' was, of all official people, his worst foe. 'I told him so many lies, he must have it in for me.'

'Listen,' I said. 'It's to do you good, not to do you harm. You're not worried by having committed perjury, but Yeo-Thomas says that when it becomes obvious, from the publication of my book, "Wybot" can have you prosecuted for it.' Plainly, that disturbed him. I outlined the plan. 'Wybot' was to be invited to dinner and the admission *confided* to him, nicely, with the suggestion the matter might now be let rest. 'Yeo-Thomas stands well with "Wybot". It's the best offer you'll ever get. I've got you a friend at court. But it's risky, and he won't do it unless you tell him you wish it.'

He wavered for some moments, then said, 'Yes. Thank him for me. Does he wish me to call on him?'

If he was to call, he would like to be given an appointment. 'Because he might not like it if he was out when I called and the door was opened to me by Mme Yeo-Thomas.' When he announced his identity, if she were alone, it could give her a fright.

I thought I should mention that I had, also, written something of our conversations to a friend of mine who was one of the *juges* at Tribunal Militaire.

He showed neither alarm nor resentment, but said quickly that the officers of the Tribunal Militaire were men the most total integrity, and 'of the most refined judgement imaginable'. He felt sure that they must have known how to read between the lines of the evidence he had given in court, and so arrived at the right verdict without having the naivete to suppose the evidence was factually true.

He had had the option of being tried by the Cour de la Seine or the Tribunal Militaire. He felt that if he were tried before a lay jury, composed of the grocer, the baker, the middle-class family man, people who knew nothing of espionage, to whom the double game would be incomprehensible, he would be found guilty. His only hope lay in the trained judgement of the officers of the Tribunal Militaire. They were 'extraordinarily scrupulous'.

He claimed that before the war he had done a little work for the Intelligence Service. One had to provide, every fortnight, a list of all the people one had met, even passingly. 'So that they can warn you if any of them is an agent. You get a reply, "So and so believed an agent of a foreign power." They don't tell you which one.'

I pointed out there was no way I could check this.

'To anyone who knows, mention the fortnightly lists, and he will know that you know.'

This frightened me a little in case it could be true. But yet, he could be bluffing, or teasing.

Out the blue, he asked, 'What do you think about Haig?'

I did not know if he meant the Field-Marshal or the whisky.

'In the First World War,' he went on. 'Passchendaele. He killed 240,000 of his own men, and 240,000 of the Germans, the same number. And all to gain a ridge! Lost again in a short time. 480,000 were killed for nothing.' He spoke with intense passion. 'How many is it you charge me with having killed?'

'Ernest mentioned three.'

'Three! Let us make it four, or six — a round half-dozen, in case there are one or two more that you don't know, or that I don't know. What is it, in a war? I was getting out of France a vast number, including two generals and a minister.'

'I don't know that one can look at it in numbers...' I knew the military thought in numbers, but it became nasty when the safety of some was paid for by the sacrifice of others. Humanly, I would prefer all took their chance together.

He said, 'I want to put something to you in a way that may seem to you childish, but which is one in which I have often put it to myself. Suppose that all the people who have ever lived since the world began are, on the Day of Judgement, arranged on a great staircase, leading from lowest Hell to highest Heaven, in order of their real wickedness or virtue, as seen in the eyes of God. Which of us stands above the other, me or Haig?'

I could only say, 'I don't know.'

'I don't know either. But I am not eager to change places with him.'

I said, 'Haig wasn't making money out of it...'

'He had the pay according to his rank.'

'So did you, but you know what I mean.'

'All right, Haig was an honest man and I am a dishonest one. As they died in the mud of Passchendaele, do you imagine it consoled them to know it was because of the orders of an honest man?' He was almost crying, with anger. 'A field-marshal is at the back. He does it coolly. Anything I have done, I have done to save my life.'

I said I thought what was dreadful in what he had done was the personality of the betrayal. A field-marshal, though he knows the divisions he is sending into action, and therefore some of the officers, does not hand-pick the casualties. Giving the time and place at which an aircraft would set down passengers came very close to that.

'You met those three who landed on your field at Angers. You opened the hatch and helped them down, saw their faces in the moonlight, spoke with them, handed them their bicycles and showed them the way to the station, knowing you had told the Gestapo they would be coming.'

For the first time he refused to look at me. 'They knew when they came out it was dangerous. Anybody who opted for that job bargained for being arrested.'

'They didn't bargain for being handed straight to the Gestapo by the Air Movements Officer of the Section.' To avoid catching my eye, though we were sitting side by side, he was staring fixedly straight forward, assuming an attitude of insensibility. I felt it was so bad for him to seal off his humanity in this way that I hammered on his moral sense, assailing his emotions. 'Don't you feel anything for them?'

'Poor men, I am sorry for them. What else can I say?'

I realised it cost him a lot to say that.

Suddenly he went into reverse completely. 'But we have been talking as if Ernest's story is true, when of course it's fantasy.' If the Germans knew of arrivals on his field at Angers, it was only because they had set microphones round it. 'I detected one and cut the wire; there may have been others hidden in the grass.'

I declared this was an absurdity.

Serious again, he said, 'You must never believe me further than you think you should.' In most of his utterances, he said, truth and falsity were mixed. 'I leave to you to make the discrimination.'

To help me, he would give me a key, he said. 'Diamonds.' He did not want to be more explicit, but I was puzzling over certain mysteries and an element in the complex was missing to me. 'Remember what Christmann told you. Smuggling and spying are cousins. Where you find one, look for the other.'

Was he associated with Christmann in diamond smuggling?

'No.' He was not associated with Christmann in anything. He had certainly done smuggling of diamonds — not for putting in my book. During the war, the smuggling of diamonds was even more profitable than in peace-time. He began to speak very rapidly, and because I was unfamiliar, alike with diamonds and with smuggling, I missed the sense of the innumerable particulars he must have given me within the minute. What I saw was the extraordinary vitality with which he was suddenly possessed and the way his eyes gleamed. At one moment, as he exclaimed, 'Dix fois le prix!', it was as though his whole body were animated by a powerful spring.

Carried away by his own momentum, he declared the Yard took its cut, and mimicked an English police voice saying, 'Quick, have you diamonds? What, no diamonds? Then what have you come for?' As I eyed him sceptically, he sallied, 'Ask Interpol about me! Try getting Interpol to do anything against me!' For a moment I was dismayed, wondering if he was deeper in crime than I had suspected. Then I realised he was teasing me.

I said, 'You are just trying to impress me! You can't make an impression as a virtuous character so you are pretending to be a great crook!'

'What do you think I am?'

'A little crook!'

Now we were both laughing, but he protested he had made disbursements to the police of more than one country.

It was always difficult to know when he was making up a story and when telling the truth. His address was 58 rue Pergolèse. He said Bleicher lived during the war next door, at no. 56. This I disregarded as a fantasy. Later I learned it was true.

We met again the next morning, 16 May, in the coffee lounge. Working from nine until twelve, we finalised the *compte rendu* as a chapter to be printed. He asked if I held anything else against him.

I told him Hérissé's story about the light and the tree.

'Oh no!' he laughed. Surely nobody could think anything bad about that. 'It was the pilot's fault for not putting on his landing light.' When he returned to England at Easter it was for a refresher course at the RAF station at Tempsford. His commanding officer, Hugh Verity, talked with him about the operations to date and they discussed particularly that one, because it had gone wrong. All that was in a friendly spirit, and he was sure he enjoyed Verity's confidence. 'And that is all the testimonies you have against me?'

'Yes.'

He asked because at his trial there was a last-minute witness. The prosecution cannot produce something that has not been submitted at the *instruction*, except by leave of the accused. The President of the court asked him, 'You permit it?' He said, 'Yes.' It proved to be a Mme Artus, in whose flat 'Bastien' had been arrested. As 'Bastien' had given Bardet his wavelength and the Abwehr had been monitoring his transmissions ... 'I permitted her, because I knew I was going to be acquitted and I did not want anyone going around saying if she had been heard it would have made a difference.' It was in that spirit he asked me if I had now produced all my witnesses.

'Yes,' I said. 'If I get anything else against you I'll let you know.'

But when was it he reported his suspicions to London?

At Easter, also. He did not spend the whole of his time at Tempsford.

He said that he went again to London, for one night only, in July. He spent that night in André Simon's flat. His chiefs in the French Section did not know he was in London that night.

I wondered if it was from André Simon he obtained diamonds. Barbara had said André Simon and Bodington were friends. I wondered if Déricourt, Bodington and Simon formed a smuggling ring. Or was he trying to tell me he had gone to see somebody in the Intelligence Service proper? I could not make him explain the one-night trip, and had of course no means to check that he had made it.

In the agreed account of our conversations, designed to form a chapter in my book, naturally much was suppressed.

'If I were dead,' he said, 'it would be different. Then you could write it in quite a different way. It could make a nice little study. Your problem is that I am alive.'

Seeing where his logic appeared to lead, he added, 'Don't kill me to solve that one!'

He made a comment on the Sufi background of 'Madeleine's' childhood, of which he had learned from my book. He was interested in Islam because he often flew to Jeddah, which was so near Mecca he had made a visit. He also spoke some Arabic.

'I have ideas on religion,' he said.

'You have a religion?'

'Yes.'

'May I ask what it is?'

'Christian Science,' he said shyly.

I was a student of Krishnamurti's teachings, also of *The Secret Doctrine* of Blavatsky. Christian Science, however, made a talking point. It seemed to me he had not read Mary Baker Eddy's *Science and Health*, but took the term Christian Science to mean understanding the fundamental truths of spirit and physics must be one and the same. Science and religion appeared so far apart that either one must have gone far off the rails or the other. But the law of physics and spiritual law must be one. I was amazed — and yet not amazed — to hear him make the point as finely as a trained metaphysical thinker. Our relationship had found its basis on a different plane.

'Do you believe in reincarnation?'

'I don't see the need for it.' He was ready to face the Last Judgement at the end of this life.

Considering the way he had lived it, I was surprised.

'I detest all churches, priests and their superstitions,' he said. He would answer for himself at the Last Judgement. He did not want 'an intercessor or mediator'. (Something almost Quaker here, I thought. No sacraments and no ministry.)

He said that when he was seventeen he had a gipsy girl-friend of the same age. She took him to meet her mother, who asked to see his palm. He showed it, and she exclaimed in horror that he would die when he was thirty, or it would be better if he did.

He thought of this on his thirtieth birthday, 2 September, 1939. In the morning, while driving, his little car was crushed by a lorry and he was lucky not to have been killed. At dinner, in a restaurant, a bullet went through his hair. It had not been meant for him, but again he had been lucky. During the night General Mobilisation posters were posted up everywhere, so that in the morning he and all his fellow pilots woke up as servicemen. France was at war with Germany, and he thought he might be killed in the war.

I asked him to give me the hour and place of his birth, so that I could cast his horoscope.

'About one in the morning. In a tiny little hamlet. You would never have heard of it … in the Aisne, near Soissons.' He hesitated for a moment, then said, 'Château Thierry.' My first thought was that Château Thierry was not a village but a town, but perhaps he meant near it. After a pause, he went on, 'I

142

assure you it was there, only — as I know you're likely to check — my name is not in the register.'

In France births are registered only at the *mairie*. Was his registered in a name he did not want to tell me, perhaps the maiden name of his mother? My mind went back to de Malval's suggestion that he could be a bastard of the house of d'Héricourt.

As I had watched him walk up to the reception to ask for some coffee for us, on the first morning, I had felt confident he was used to asking for things in good hotels. But for our last few meetings he had been wearing not his good suit but old corduroys in which he might have been mending the underneath of a car. Probably it was his solution of the problem of his Légion d'Honneur, as his wife would not expect him to wear it in working clothes. But in working clothes he could have been working class.

I took from my bag the ephemeris for 1909 which I had brought with me, as I knew the year of his birth, and roughed out on a piece of typing paper a circle divided into twelve segments, in which I inserted the position of the Sun, Moon and planets. 'These two, Neptune and Uranus, facing each other at 180 degrees, across the horizon, where the ecliptic cuts the equator, from east to west, are practically at right angles to those two groups, facing each other from the Midheaven to the Nadir. It's across and across, in the sky, a double cross. The term is not pejorative, but geometric.'

'Can you give me spiritual counsels starting from that basis?'

I said that with Mars in Aries on the Midheaven, he would not lack courage, boldness... nor, with Venus in Libra at the foot of the map, a foundation of kindness, sweetness. That Uranus in the western angle provided the unexpected turns of fortune, but the key to the map lay in the rising Neptune. That was a call to adventure into the unknown, into the uncharted, into mystery. But at what level? Sacred or profane? 'You have to raise the level of that Neptune.'

I talked with him in some detail. His acquaintance with Greek and Roman myth helped him to fill out the symbols intuitively. Egyptian also. At one moment he referred to 'Anubis, the dog who leads the souls of the dead...' He was not stranger to that tableau in the papyrus of Am which shows the heart being weighed against the feather of truth.

'What I lack is stability,' he said.

In fact, he had nothing in fixed signs. I suggested more use of the mutable, to balance the cardinal, and said I would type him out a proper delineation and post it to him from London.

I would have liked to invite him to call on me in England, but remembered he had been recommended for deportation. 'Does that mean you are *persona non grata*?' I asked.

'I can come,' he said, 'but there are difficulties. I have to notify that I want to come and explain the reason.' Then he had to report at Scotland Yard each day, just to say he was still at the address he had said. He would like to accept my invitation to tea, if he had a reason to satisfy the Special Branch.

He gave me the name of his airline, Sageta, care of which, at Orly, I should write to him.

7: THE JANUS FACE

For lunch that same day, 16 May 1957, I was invited to the Yeo-Thomases, and from saying goodbye to Déricourt went straight to their flat, carrying the finalised *compte rendu*. Naturally, it recounted only the conversations of our first two interviews; the 'Haig' conversation did not figure, in which he had conceded he had given the Germans advance particulars of the operation at Angers, at which, according to Ernest, three men were arrested. That was between ourselves. Nevertheless, Yeo-Thomas was staggered by the admissions he had authorised — chiefly the admission that the evidence he had given at his trial was concocted.

I said he agreed the 'Wybot' plan, and I told Yeo-Thomas about the appointment suggestion — 'as you would not like him to arrive when you are out and perhaps give Barbara a fright'.

Yeo-Thomas said he would take it from me that Déricourt wished his intercession. 'Unless he wants to see me, in which case he can write or let me know through you.'

I had a third appointment that day, at 5 p.m. with Armel Guerne. It was he who had given evidence in camera at Culioli's trial, and I had at last traced him to a winding street in the Quartier Latin.

He and the lady with whom he shared a flat received me kindly. He was dark, pale, thin and fervent. He had, he said, been recruited by 'Prosper' in a café in Montmartre; 'Prosper' and 'Denise' were showing people how to use Sten guns. It sounded rather indiscreet. Guerne became 'Prosper's' right hand man, he told me. He and his legal wife, Marguerite,

'Pérégrine', from whom he was now separated, had been arrested at the restaurant in the rue Troyon on 1 July. At Avenue Foch he had asked to speak to Gilbert Norman, because he had known him before the war. Norman told him the pact 'Prosper' and he had concluded with the Germans provided the lives of the French members of their network — not their own — should be spared.

I did not think this could be so. Vogt, Starr and Culioli had all understood that the lives of 'Prosper' and 'Archambaud' were to be spared as well as those of their French collaborators. Guerne had mentioned he was a poet, and is seemed to me he was a romantic, perhaps with creative imagination.

As he said they made the pact because they knew themselves betrayed, I asked him where he thought the betrayal came from.

'From London,' he said, 'from the top office.' He referred to 'Prosper's' return from London on 20 June 1943. On the 21st and 22nd 'Prosper' had gone to the gare d'Austerlitz to await Culioli and the two Canadians. When they had still failed to appear, he had come with 'Denise' to lunch with Guerne, at 1 p.m. on the 22nd. He said that he had threatened London that unless the invasion was mounted that summer he would, on his return to France, bring the whole of the Resistance out — all over France. If the 'Prosper' network came out and engaged the Germans, so would all the others. Either the High Command would have to order an immediate invasion or let the whole of the Resistance in France be massacred. To stop him, London gave him away to the Germans on his return.

'But why did they not just keep him in London?' I asked.

'He had said if he was kept in London, 'Archambaud' would bring the network out.' But, said Guerne, 'Prosper' assured him that after his threat the British had guaranteed him the invasion would be mounted before 1 July. When he was arrested, on 24 June, he was expecting the invasion within days. As the invasion had in fact materialised almost exactly one year 'late', and it appeared from all that had been published that there never was any intention — or indeed much practical possibility — of mounting it before 1944, he supposed that the promises had been given to 'Prosper' in perfect bad faith, because it was known that before 1 July he would be arrested. Why? Because they would give the Germans the means to arrest him. 'Not treason, collusion — to prevent a massacre.'

But how did he suppose London told the Germans, I asked.

'By the radio.' His voice rang out. 'Le courier n'était qu'accessoire.' By one of the German-controlled circuits.

They had not got one working as early as that, I said. The Canadians had been captured with their radio on the 21st, but I did not think the play-back had started in time to be used in that way.

'Then by Déricourt,' he said. On order from the High Command, from the Cabinet, from Churchill even.

I was physically shocked. Could I all this time have been following Winston Churchill's own agent?

My brain was running round. Mme Balachowsky had been told by 'Prosper' only that something seemed to be wrong in London, but perhaps he had not told her all that was on his mind. Buckmaster had said in *Specially Employed* that 'Prosper' was sent back to tell the Resistance the invasion would not be that year. Could that be what Buckmaster had come after the war to think — a post-war rationalisation? 'Prosper's' own address, in any case, could never have been in the mail, for none had gone back since his return. He had gone to the Hôtel Mazagran instead of to his rooms in the rue Hautefeuille.

'Is this what you told the court, in camera?'

'Yes.' His evidence, of course, was for Culioli, and he had asked for the public to be excluded from the court while he gave it.

He would also tell me another story. After the war, he had been told by a Czech that when the Russians entered Berlin they captured the papers of the Reichssicherheitshauptamt, among them the Déricourt file, 'the Gestapo's own file on Déricourt'. It was now at the Soviet Embassy in Paris. Not for action to be taken on it. Just kept, as a dormant document.

I felt weak as I walked out. I wanted now to see Déricourt again, but I had not the money to remain in Paris until his return in about a week. I wrote to him before leaving. We had parted such good friends I was sorry the first news I should have to send him was of a new attack. Of all my subsequent letters to Déricourt, I have carbons taken on the typewriter, but of that first letter, written in a Paris café, I have only my memory. I did not mention Guerne by name, nor Winston Churchill. I merely told Déricourt that my '5 o'clock appointment' had suggested to me he was ordered by London to give 'Prosper' to the Avenue Foch and had also said the Gestapo file on him was alleged to be at the Soviet Embassy. Déricourt had known I was to see Guerne, so would assume it was he. I posted the letter to him care of Sageta, and caught the plane to London.

As soon as I got back I wrote to Irene. She asked me to dine with her at the House of Commons on 23 May, and I told her everything. She was rather overwhelmed. During the next few days we were in constant contact by letter and telephone. On 8 June she came to see me. She said, 'Will you let me tell Harold?'

She meant the Prime Minister. Harold Macmillan had succeeded Eden as Prime Minister on 19 January. Macmillan would not know if what Guerne had said was true, as he had been out of England at the time, but he would know how to inform himself. If he found it to be fact, he would not be able to tell us — it would be a secret of state — but Irene felt that from his response she would be able to make her own judgement. 'Certainly he would be able to tell us if we are doing an injustice to Déricourt.' It was unsatisfactory to have a situation in which Déricourt hinted to me that he had acted under orders of a British government department while maintaining he could not say which one, because of his oath. 'Harold can absolve him from his oath. As Prime Minister he can call for the files of any Ministry. If Déricourt is bluffing, it would be the means of calling his bluff.'

I said that if she went to the Prime Minister, and what we understood from him was positive, I would give up my book. But before she went to the Prime Minister I should like to ask Déricourt if he wished her to do it. I had not yet had a reply to my letter.

Irene thought his reply would test the issue. If he showed any sign of grasping at the line thrown to him, that he had betrayed under orders, then the next thing would be for me to ask him if he would like her to inquire of the Prime Minister. If he said 'Yes', or if I wanted her to, she would do it.

At last I received my first letter from Déricourt. Predictably, he supposed the person I had talked to was Guerne. Then he asked (I translate from his French):

A. How can he know the 'Gilbert' file was seized by the Russians when they entered Berlin?
Has he seen it with his own eyes?
In that case —

— when, how and why was he in Berlin...?

— why did the Russians, the NKVD, show it to him...?

B. Supposing the NKVD to have the document, and to have given it to the Allies... when? How? Where? and then —

1. Why did these services tell Guerne? Where? When? How?

2. If they only spoke of it in an evasive manner — When? Where? How? Why?

3. Why have these services never used it against me?

4. Why did Mr Wybot, so marvellously well informed, not mention it to me? He did not make me presents.

You see, Miss Jean, how many questions the mere assertion unleashes, which have to be answered on pain of disbelief ... he said it 'of his own accord' you say — I understand that by that you mean you did not suggest it to him — I am sure of that... you ... do not know enough to understand...

Example, how can you understand the effort of swimming if you do not swim? How can you understand the pleasure of resolving a problem of higher mathematics if you know nothing of algebra?

I am hard because, if you are sympathetic to me, I hate people who spit gratuitously ... I do not hate their digestive tract, their locomotive or reproductive systems, but I condemn without appeal the iniquitous, illogical, persistent ill which pervades their atrophied spirituality — atrophied to the point of its disappearance. It leaves in its place an empty negation which is the embodiment of evil. They are neither truth nor love ...

I do not wish to follow you along the path you suggest to me, that London knew of the Lysander and mail leaks and, I would add, the German agents of SOE in London. All that holds together-it seems to go with the 'vexatious' message about the double security check of 'Archambaud', the escape of 'Madeleine' (not over the roofs), the trailing of her from before her arrest ... I do not honestly think the War Office deliberately sacrificed people who could not be saved; nor that they sacrificed new arrivals in the field. Would they do that just to make their intoxication of the German services a little more profound?

I read and re-read, and while I admired the polemic style, it seemed to me that the last passage could stand two opposite meanings. It was my first example of what I was to come to think of as the Janus-faced paragraph of Déricourt. Irene pored over it with me. At any rate there was no 'climbing on the waggon', so she did not feel it necessary at this stage to go to the Prime Minister. It might be better, she said, to let the book go forward. She would, however, go to Macmillan at once if at any time I felt I was getting into too deep water.

It occurred to me that Mme Balachowsky might be able to shed some light. Without mentioning Guerne's name, I wrote to her and told her what I had been told. She replied:

'Prosper' (for us Francois) was very disquiet at the beginning of June '43, fearing that the invasion would not take place in '43 and that *we should be all taken* [arrested], those were his own words. He wanted Paris to be taken by an encirclement of parachute troops, by gliders transporting parachute troops and armaments; he looked for landing-grounds for gliders, and I went with him in the region of Grignon (Seine et Oise); he thought an encirclement would avoid the destruction of Paris.

On his return from London, 'Prosper' was very depressed, having learned that the invasion had been put back. He told us London understood nothing of the situation in occupied France, which I could tell for myself...

Beware of a half-mad person called Guerne ... I cannot think of anybody but he who could have told you a story so *rocambulesque.*

I showed Irene the draft chapter, 'Gilbert'. She was struck by the regard in which Déricourt appeared to hold Gubbins. She thought Déricourt must have been Gubbins's man.

Indeed, how had Déricourt known the name of Gubbins? When I wrote *Madeleine*, the name Gubbins and the title of the organisation, SOE — Special Operations Executive, were unknown to me. They were unknown to Starr. 'We were told we were all under Churchill,' he said, but between Buckmaster and Churchill was a void.

I had spent the summer writing the book, and now wrote to Déricourt that it was completed. When he returned to Paris I would bring him the typescript so that he could read it as a whole. He replied from the Far East on 1 August to say he would be in Toulouse 'for a short training, (I'll be training when I'm 90)'. Then from Toulouse, on 6 August, came a pathetic lie; 'I'll probably soon be permitted to speak of my job past — thing is on examination at the War Office.' He continued (in English which I will not spoil by correcting):

I never said I never went to the Germans on instructions from London. On Easter 1943 I knew already enough things to understand what was the German game. I managed to be solicited but I could not ask the authorities of SOE or it would have spoiled everything. When I found the adequate service to London to report I had made a long way on my own.

The feelings and nuances about amoral and immoral are amusing but I am not the monster Adam makes of me — no — I have a self-control many British people could envy. As I told you, I am Christian Scientist. I have a very [good] sense of morality — this morality is not that of what I call 'concièrges' or peasant — for usual readers of newspapers — you betrayed, you are blak; you have not, you are white. That is the common sense of good and bad — like for peasant —

in spying business — which is not at the beginning so good than that, you have to consider all the nuances of grey, from dark grey to nearly white. What do you think of 'Prosper' having contacts with Abwehr officers — not authorised — on the purpose of rescuing T sisters, was he not a little grey — he gave, in doing that, willingly or not — information to the enemy — I don't criticise, it is like that, I 'constate'. What manner of grey is it — very light? Any way, it is not the pure peasant white.

That is what I want you to understand, because in saying others are grey I don't charge them. I am not white, I don't admit to be black.

That is not amoral. I don't show my feelings, that's all...

Amorally I think of you as a good girl,

H. Déricourt

He accepted my invitation to write a paragraph of his own which could go at the end of the book, and enclosed one:

I read the whole script of Miss J. O. F. and for the part of the events I have been mixed up I put my signature on. I lived them as it is said. But seen now from another point of view, from other sides, by people knowing facts I ignore they can look different. Me, like any British, German or French agent have to recognise that they could have been abused. We were blinds fighting in darkness. To succeed in the mission we were responsibles we had often to get out of our way what could have been a nuisance — We used to risk our lives three times a day, every day, without any rest or 'encouragement'. We were rich of what we had in our hart and our mind. Today I am rich of the friendship of the people who knew what I did.

I can't and won't say more. I prefer to let the pointing arrow of Miss J. O. F. make its way, on her own riding and her own responsibilities.

That a man who had lived his life in the world of duplicity and treachery should sign, blind, his approval of a book he had not read and which threatened to incriminate him, I would not have believed, and I was deeply touched by the trust he reposed in me.

He wrote that he would call me, and on 24 August I received a continental telephone call. 'C'est Déricourt.' It was my welcome *persona non grata*. Could I get up early enough tomorrow morning to take a plane which would get me in to Orly at 11 a. m.?

'Yes.'

In the plane, going over, it was impossible not to think of the people who had made this flight in the war — to reception by Déricourt, the Gestapo lying in wait. For me to have come out on a flight proposed to me by Déricourt was perhaps asking for trouble.

He was at Orly to meet me, in workaday corduroys, in which he might have been doing a mechanic's job; and I felt it a dubious honour to be shepherded through the Customs by an ex-smuggler. He introduced to me a girl — 'My secretary'. She was tired-looking, without make-up. 'I am writing a book in rivalry to yours,' he explained. 'She will type it. I will give you the English translation rights.' I thought she had been brought as a witness, and felt it a recession in our relations yet as we got into his small car, he was as friendly as ever. Was the paragraph he had written all right, he asked?

'It's wonderful,' I said. 'But you wrote it without having read what you were signing for.'

'I thought it would help the book — that it would give authenticity if I said I had read it,' he said, missing my point about his trustfulness.

I asked him if he would accept a share of the royalties.

He replied almost loftily, 'No. It would mean nothing to me. I am broke now, but I have had big money.'

The enquiry into his accident had turned out well for him. Now that was over, he did not mind so much what appeared.

We came to be talking about 'Denise'. He was not sure she was the girl-friend of 'Archambaud' in quite the way I thought. She spent weekends out of Paris sometimes with 'Archambaud' but sometimes with 'Prosper'. They did not appear to fight over her. He thought there was an accord. There was 'a great sense of corporal liberty', and the British officers preferred to keep with a girl who had dropped from the sky with them rather than to look for one amongst the population who might betray them.

He set me down at the Terrass-Hotel, left me while I settled in, and we reassembled below in about an hour. He sat between me and the girl, and told me about his own book. It was to be a novel, and was going to begin, 'Je sais que tu sais que je sais' ('I know that you know that I know'): it was of course one double-agent speaking to another. The theme was going to be, 'On mange l'orange et jette l'écorce' ('The orange eaten, the peel is thrown away'), which referred to the attitude of intelligence services to their agents.

He wrote, he said, while piloting his plane. The pilot's attention was only required during take-off and landing; during the main part of the flight the automatic pilot left the human one with nothing to do. When there was good visibility he liked to look down, watching the fields, capes and bays below; it gave him the same delight as when he flew for the first time. But if there was cloud he read or wrote. On the ground, in cafés or at home, he found it difficult to compose, but in the air there was no likelihood of being interrupted.

At first the presence of the girl disturbed me, but she made no attempt to take part in our conversation, and, obviously having been brought as guardian, evidently considered her protection needless when she saw how we teased each other in a friendly way.

I opened my typescript on the table and we worked until 8 p.m. when he had to leave, saying that on the morrow we could work from as early as I liked until n p.m. He had to fly a plane from Orly at midnight to Jeddah. I said he should come at 9 a.m., which would give us fourteen hours.

He arrived at nine in the morning punctually, and he was alone. We continued to work through my typescript. In order not to mark it, Déricourt made his own notes on separate sheets of paper. He interested himself not only in the matter but the grammar and syntax. In English, could a pronoun refer to a person other than the last named? 'Take a sentence, "John said goodbye to Paul, then he left the town." Who left the town? In French it is Paul, because he is the last named.' He surprised me by saying he had started to take a teacher's training course. Though he had given it up, in order to learn to fly, his feeling for the French language remained.

At one moment he lamented that in my book he came out 'black, black'. Yet in other respects he liked it, because it made points about the inefficiency and worse of SOE. He approved a point about its overblown size, but added, 'It was the fault of giving the agents military ranks.' I too had thought this silly, because, not being in uniform, most of them seemed to have given their ranks out to be higher than they were — thus 'Major Agazarian' and 'Colonel Bodington'. Yes, he said, but as soon as one did it, his companion had to do it too, in order not to be downgraded; and so it spread right through. Everyone gave himself out a grade higher than he was. But that was not his point. In the army, the ranks went up with the number of men commanded. 'A captain commands a greater number than a lieutenant, a major commands a greater number than a captain, a colonel must command more than a major... that is how it goes all the way.' That, said Déricourt, gave to the officers of SOE a terrible motive for increasing the numbers they recruited. They wanted more, so that they could say 'I have so many', and hope to be promoted. That might be appropriate in the case of a *maquis*, an armed group camped in the mountains or woods of the wild parts where numbers might correspond to strength, but it was dead against security for the networks in the streets of Paris. For espionage, numbers must be kept low. (It was the point Mme Fourcade had made.)

'They should not have given military ranks,' he said, thoughtfully. 'Increase in seniority and appreciation should have been marked in some other way. That is, if they wanted security. At a certain moment, I rather thought it was insecurity they wanted.' I caught his nuance.

I apologised to him for having taken the account of his trial from newspapers, but I had been told at the Tribunal Militaire no transcript had been made. 'But,' he said, 'there were the depositions of Goetz, Placke, Bleicher and the rest, made during the *instruction*.'

I said I had been refused permission to see them as I had not a judicial reason.

'I am probably the only person who could get them for you,' he replied. He thought that, as the person who had been accused, he might be able to obtain sight of them again. 'Or perhaps Moro still has them, because of course copies of them were supplied to the defence.' If not, he would write to the

Tribunal Militaire — 'not call'. Even to pass there still gave him an uneasy feeling.

In the newspaper reports of his trial, it amused him to read he had had the 'good taste' to remove the Légion d'Honneur from his buttonhole. 'It was not left to my good taste. There is an official who picks it off with scissors before you go into the courtroom. You don't stand in the dock wearing that. Afterwards, it is handed back to you — if you have been acquitted... C'est tout de meme impressionant.'

When we came in the typescript to Ernest's testimony, I said, 'But that is only my typed translation. I have brought the original for you.' I opened my bag, and produced Ernest's thin pencilled sheets.

Very gently, he pushed back the papers I was holding out to him, as though he could not bring himself to look at them.

But it was in French, I said. He ought to read the original, and check it line by line with my typed translation.

'No,' he said. 'I know you have done it honestly.'

When he had finished reading it, I asked if there was any comment he would like to make.

'No,' he said, very low. 'There is nothing to say about a statement like this.'

At midday he asked if he should leave me, so that I could lunch.

'What are you going to do?' I asked.

'Walk around.' He had left his wallet in his locker at Orly, and could not go back to his flat or he would encounter his wife. So as to have the whole day free, he had told her he would be flying from Orly in the morning.

'You'd better have lunch with me,' I said. 'But not in this hotel, it would cost too much.' What I had left now would be stretched by having to pay for lunch for two, unless we could find somewhere very inexpensive.

He took me in his car, to 'a place you would never find for yourself.' It was a restaurant on an upstairs floor with which he seemed familiar, obviously for eating at modest cost. The waiter handed him the menu, but he motioned him to pass it to me, saying, 'Madame paye.'

We obtained a curious dish, consisting of a flat, circular slice of batter, with capers on it. I ordered us a half-bottle of red *vin ordinaire*. It was the first time I had seen him take anything stronger than tea or coffee, and he poured himself only a small glass. He said that he valued a clear brain and his eyesight above everything else.

Gently, I told him I did not believe he had been authorised by London to enter into relations with the Germans.

Across the table, slowly and timidly, he held out his hand to me, palm upwards. I felt a confession was coming, and advanced my own, until the tips of our middle fingers touched.

'I was not authorised,' he said.

He snatched back his hand. 'Not at the time, but later I understood it was what they wanted.' He was withdrawing the confession, but I had shared the moment of truth. It was always like that with him, one step forward would be followed by a step or two backward.

Now he was back in the moment of truth. 'It doesn't prevent me from sleeping. It is in the mornings, when I shave and I have to look at myself. I say to myself, "Think of the things you have done."' He said it as though they suffocated him.

I must have questioned him about some detail in a way that irritated him, for he reacted sharply. 'Never try to box me in, catch me out, confute me! The Intelligence Service couldn't do it. 'Wybot' couldn't do it. You won't be able to do it. If I tell you things, it will be voluntarily.' Now I would have to wait and see whether he found himself in the mood again.

When the waiter brought me the bill, it was so small I thought there must have been a mistake.

He wanted to drive me to another restaurant, not to eat but to speak with the proprietor, Tutulle. He did not believe the Abwehr had been given an appointment with 'Gilbert' by radio. He believed Christmann had picked up that name in the course of previous visits to Paris and had called chez Tutulle asking for 'Gilbert', and so was directed to 'Archambaud', at Square Clignancourt. I felt this was the story I had been told by the Tourets very early in my researches, when I was hardly able to appreciate its significance. When we reached the restaurant, where Déricourt asked for Tutulle and was told it had changed hands, I had a feeling of *déjà vu*. 'Never mind,' Déricourt said, 'I have a deposition from him, but I would have liked you to hear it directly from him.'

We were about to step from the pavement, when I asked him, 'How did you get into spying?'

'In Spain, in the civil war.' He was flying from a town in the zone occupied by one side into the other zone. As he was walking to the door through which the pilots went out to the aircraft, a man approached and asked him to carry a letter to an address written on it, which was in the town for which he was bound. Together with the letter, the man held out a wad of banknotes, and told him when he delivered the letter the recipient would very likely give him something further. 'I thought nothing of it, except that it was a way to earn some money.' The envelope was sealed, so he had no idea of the contents. 'I found the address, but when I presented the letter, what happened was not what I expected. I had to do something else. And then something else, and something else. I was the prisoner of a situation. Il y avait des suites.' The *suites* had lasted for years. 'One doesn't get into espionage gradually. Not in my case. It all happened within twenty-four hours. I began the day a simple airman. Before the day ended, I was in espionage so deep I never could get out — all my life.'

We were still standing on the kerb.

'Sometimes I transpose the location and the date,' he said, 'but the story is true.' When he told the court-martial he was the prisoner of a situation, that was true. He had transposed to Paris in the summer of 1943 something that had its setting elsewhere, earlier. Though not in the way he had told the court, he had in fact been trapped, and was the prisoner of a situation.

'It can never end,' he said. 'It has become less acute since the war, and particularly since my trial and acquittal. But if anything rakes it up again, the situation is still the same. I am a prisoner of that situation all my life.'

I felt he was telling me the truth, as nearly as he dared. Yet I found it difficult to understand. French policy, like British, had in the Spanish Civil War been non-interventionist. He might have been seized by one side or the other. Whichever side that it was by which he had been seized — for obviously he meant that when he went to that address and pressed the bell, he was seized and dragged inside, a prisoner — and made to do things against the other side. That would not make him traitor to France, and the experience, though unpleasant, would have given his captors no leverage over him, once he eluded their hands. Was this how he had come into contact with Boemelburg — through this blunder in Spain, and not through getting to know his son?

We got back to his car. Our way lay through the Etoile. As we circled the Unknown Warrior's flame, Déricourt said, 'Each time I pass, it constricts my throat.'

I felt, oddly, that he was a patriot, notwithstanding everything.

'My feelings are for the small people of France,' he said, '*les petits gens*. The concièrge, the postman, the cleaner. Wars come and wars go, Germans come and Germans go. But they are always at the bottom. Nobody worries about them.' The British officers from London regarded them as expendable. When a train was derailed, the French driver was sacrificed.

I remembered Cohen's telling me with admiration that 'Denise' would derail a train in the night and meet one in the morning for coffee. I remembered Vogt's telling me, 'Garry derailed a train. Many people were killed. I have often wondered whether his wife knew, and if she knew, if she approved. She was so gentle.' The Abbé's book contained a diagram showing the emplacements of derailments effected by Culioli and 'Jacqueline'. All these agents were French, though directed by London. The Abbé showed also a photograph of a gasometer wrecked by 'Prosper's' people.

Déricourt was looking for a space in which to park his car near the Terrass. 'When I was arrested,' he said, 'I thought I'd be shot. It was morning when they came for me. I was dressed to go out. I never thought I'd come through.' As he reviewed his case, it seemed impossible he could be acquitted.

We went walking back to the hotel when he said, suddenly jocular again, 'If I'm BOE 48, who were the other 47?'

'I don't know.'

'But just think of what it means! Forty-seven turned traitor before me. Try naming the first forty-seven.'

'I couldn't.'

'Then it isn't fair to me. Why does only the poor forty-eighth one interest you?'

We re-entered the hotel, and sat down to resume our reading of the typescript. Regarding Ernest's testimony, he said we should have to evolve a formula to enable us to talk about it — between ourselves.

'Can we say that what Ernest writes is absolutely true, except that it relates to a man who is not me, who bore my name and occupied my function — *seemed* to occupy my function — and resembled me extraordinarily?' The word 'seemed' was stressed with a deliberate spice of humour, and the last phrase, 'qui m'a resemblé extraordinairement' with a smile that invited my complicity.

'We can say it,' I said, feeling that it was, in part, a plea to be allowed to put the past behind him. The atmosphere was such that I suddenly felt we understood each other, without possibility of misunderstanding. He was so easy and disarming about it, it was hard for me to believe that he had actually done what he admitted.

'The only thing for which I slightly reproach him is that he told you,' he said. 'I would have preferred he kept it to himself.' Then, 'Couldn't Ernest have noticed that at the trial all the other Germans took back the allegations they had made at the *instruction*?'

'Thanks for reminding me,' I said, 'I had been meaning to ask you why they did that.'

'Perhaps they thought the Intelligence Service wanted it,' he suggested mischievously. It had done him no end of good with the French. It convinced them he must be very highly protected in Britain. 'If ever I find out who did it for me,' he said, laughing, 'I'll tell him he didn't do it properly, because he left one out!'

Picking over the long statement again, he chuckled over Kieffer's fear he would try to kidnap Goetz. 'No, I wouldn't have tried to kidnap Goetz. He is a big man, bigger than me. Did Kieffer think I would come with a gang?'

'I suppose Kieffer did think that.'

'I know what gave him the idea. I suggested to Goetz, once, that he should come with me to London.'

'What?'

'I suggested to him he should board one of my Lysanders, and spend a few days in England. Just to look round.'

I was incredulous. What had he in his mind when he made such a suggestion?

'It was a joke, really. Just to see his reaction. I didn't expect my invitation to be accepted.'

At our first interview he had denied having met Goetz. I had not believed him. Now I did not believe he had invited Goetz to England.

'What happened to Boemelburg?' I asked.

'He is supposed to be dead.'

'Supposed to be?'

'He is said to have been killed in an air raid in Holland. I should think he has gone under.'

He spoke almost with a trace of affection of 'Boem'. It struck me he had never referred to Buckmaster as 'Buck'. Probably he knew Boemelburg better than he knew Buckmaster. I never heard that Buckmaster invited him to dinner.

'The family don't believe he is dead,' he said.

'You have met the family since the war?'

No answer.

'It's not treason, after the war,' I said.

He resisted my pressure to answer.

'Have they any reason to think he is alive?'

'I shan't be the one to go looking for him!'

He rejected the last paragraph of Ernest's statement. 'Prosper' and his colleagues were not arrested through the mail.

Long ago, Mercier had told me if he had been acting in his function he would have had to direct the jury to disregard the last paragraph, because it was supposition by Ernest.

'Ernest is a simpleton,' said Déricourt. Christmann, on the other hand, was very far from being a simpleton.

'He is as big a liar as I am!' he declared. 'You can tell him I said that. That way, I don't moralise.' Laughing, he went on, 'I always thought I was the biggest liar in the world. Now, I find I have a rival. I have to look to my lying laurels.'

Christmann's lies, he said, were worse than his, for Christmann intended his to be believed. 'There are two kinds of lying. There is lying to be believed, and lying so as not to be believed. When I lie to you, I intend you to know that I am lying. I employ an exaggerated tone and absurdities. I tell myself it is impossible you should believe me. That way, I don't he.'

I said I understood. 'I know I'm not to believe all you say.'

'You have only yourself to blame if you do. But there are nuggets of truth in my lies. You have to spot which they are.'

Really, he sighed, it was a pity Christmann and he had not been able to talk before they had to make their depositions before the French magistrates. 'We should have brought our lies into accord. If he had told me what points he wanted to hide, I could have adapted my statement, and perhaps he would have done the same for me. It would have been more dignified.'

'Dignified?'

'Yes. As I see it. Since there was not the slightest possibility of either of us telling the truth, to have made our lies tally would have been more dignified than our telling opposing sets of lies, at each other, across Captain Trossin. That wasn't dignified.'

'For the first time, I pity the *juges*.'

He contemplated Christmann's statement, and said, 'I know why I lie — obviously. What I don't know is why he lies. Let's go through it, line by line, and see if we can't guess the reason.'

He did not know why Christmann claimed to have seen him at Avenue Foch. 'I can say categorically that I was never at Avenue Foch.' More important was that Christmann himself had no business to be at Avenue Foch. Agazarian, when he came to tell Déricourt of the visitation at Square Clignancourt, spoke of one 'Dutchman' only, not two, 'Antonio, not Anton; we will keep the distinction.' Déricourt thought 'Antonio' must have been Christmann, both at Square Clignancourt and at the Capucines restaurant. If the man arrested at the Capucines, by the SD as we knew, was in fact Christmann, that would explain how he came to be inside SD headquarters, Avenue Foch, explaining himself to Kieffer.

There was a deeper mystery. Déricourt was positive Christmann got to Square Clignancourt by calling at the restaurant Chez Tutulle and being told by Tutulle he would find Gilbert (Norman) at Square Clignancourt. Then why had he pretended that it was London which directed him to Square Clignancourt by radio, with London confusing the two 'Gilberts'? Déricourt maintained that this was absolutely and totally impossible. 'Archambaud' and I had the same handler — it is the term used. It was Morel. He knew us both.'

'But,' I protested, 'Huntermann told me the name 'Gilbert' was radioed from London after "Marcel"...'

'Did Huntermann really say "Marcel"?' asked Déricourt, very perplexed.

I assured him he did, and that 'Marcel', though not 'Gilbert', was mentioned by Colonel Giskes in his book *London Calling North Pole*.

Déricourt said that if the name 'Marcel' was really transmitted by London it must mean Agazarian, whose code-name was 'Marcel'.

It was the first time that I heard Agazarian's code-name. Déricourt more usually called him Jacques — from his cover-name, 'Jacques Chevalier', or as French pronunciation of his real Christian name, Jack — or just 'Aga' for short. The Abbé Guillaume had identified Marcel to me as Marcel Charbonnier, and I had never questioned that identification.

Déricourt said London would not know even the existence of Marcel Charbonnier of Pontoise; he was not an agent, neither trained nor registered in London. At the most, they might know that 'Prosper' had a sub-agent of that name, but they would never refer to him as 'Marcel'. If people like Tutulle or the Abbé Guillaume, French sub-agents of the 'Prosper' network who were not registered agents, spoke of 'Gilbert' and 'Marcel', then of course they meant Gilbert Norman and Marcel Charbonnier; but if London sent over the air an enciphered radio message referring to 'Gilbert' and 'Marcel' then they meant Déricourt and Agazarian.

When I first read Shakespeare's *Comedy of Errors*, in which a complicated plot was woven around the circumstance that two persons called Antipholus each had for attendant a person called Dromio, I thought it ludicrous and improbable. I saw now that life had caught up on Shakespeare; only it was a tragedy of errors that had embroiled the destinies of the two 'Gilberts' and the two 'Marcels'.

167

It remained to consider why London should have radioed its Dutch network (as it thought) that the agent they wanted back should contact Agazarian in Paris. Déricourt said that when he was first parachuted he was told Agazarian would be his radio operator. 'Then "Prosper" stole him from me, although he already had "Archambaud".' For a long time he had to make do with a share of Agazarian and a share of Grover Williams, the radio operator of another network, until at last he was sent Watt. In principle the French Section networks were supposed to be separate from Escapes Section ones, but only if Agazarian had been acting also for Escapes Section — perhaps because of shortage of radio operators — could it be understood why London should order a man they wanted back from Holland to contact Agazarian in Paris.

Déricourt was certain, however, that he had never received a radio message from London telling him to board a Dutchman called 'Anton', nor had he been given a rendezvous at which to meet such a person. It was obvious Christmann had no proper rendezvous with 'Gilbert' given by radio from London or he would not have been to the restaurant to ask where he could find someone of that name — and so been put on to Gilbert Norman by mistake. Déricourt did not believe that a radio message was received in Holland in which the name of 'Gilbert' was mentioned; besides, London expected 'Anton' to escape through Spain. He suggested Huntermann and Christmann might have been in league to trick Giskes.

I remembered Huntermann's saying of Christmann, 'He is our enemy.' It had been apparent to me then that Giskes trusted Huntermann to be on his side, though they both distrusted Christmann.

Then, said Déricourt, Christmann tricked them both — that is, if Huntermann really believed a message from London mentioned 'Gilbert'. Could Christmann have transmitted from the Continent so that Huntermann thought it came from London? Or slipped a false 'transcribed' message in amongst those received? 'I don't know how he did it. But he did it.' Unless, of course, Huntermann was making it up. If I knew Giskes well enough, could not I write to ask him why one or more of his officers should take pains to mislead him.

Perhaps Christmann had an interest in meeting the Air Movements Officer, which he did not disclose to Colonel Giskes and was very anxious to keep from him?

'But how would he know such a person existed?' I asked.

Christmann, Déricourt pointed out, had been through Paris a number of times, as escort on the escape routes (I recalled Giskes's book said Christmann escorted parties bound for Spain or Switzerland, which must have gone through France). On one of these previous journeys he could have picked up the name 'Gilbert'. Déricourt's guess was that it was Hélène, the mistress of Massuy, an Abwehr agent, from whom Christmann learned of the restaurant Chez Tutulle as being a place where he could pick up information about *Résistants*. The nationality of the mysterious woman was given in some depositions as Belgian, in others as Dutch; her surname, James, was English. Her husband was, Déricourt believed, a diamond merchant in London; he hazarded a guess it was she who introduced Christmann to diamond smuggling.

When Agazanan had come to tell him about 'Antonio', Déricourt had asked who was at the Square Clignancourt when he arrived. Agazanan said that besides himself there were 'Archambaud', Marcel Charbonnier, Alain Bussoz, 'Denise' and a woman he did not know. Who was the other woman? If I ever found that out, would I tell him? Was she a FANY girl? Hélène? Or just the girl-friend of one of the men? It was important to be clear about who was present at Square Clignancourt when the rendezvous for the Capucines was convened, because only someone who knew of it could have betrayed it. But, he went on, if Hélène betrayed, it would have been to the Abwehr. The betrayal was to the SD. So who betrayed? 'There is only "Archambaud", Agazarian, Charbonnier, Bussoz, "Denise", a woman unknown — and me, because I knew of it, as Agazarian told me.' He invited me to think of it as an Agatha Christie 'Who-done-it?' There were seven suspects. Eliminate one by one. 'Not Bussoz; he died of it. Not "Denise"; it is against all we know of her. Not Agazarian; transparently loyal. Charbonnier? Nothing known against him. So three suspects only. "Archambaud" — very suspect because he turned traitor later; unknown woman; or me. Only *I* know it was not me; though I had the capacity to do it.' He was, he reminded me, in contact with the SD at the material time. That made him suspect No. 1. That was why he had been anxious to keep back the fact he was by then already in contact with the SD. 'Find the informer and I'll avow — even openly.'

He said the truth about this whole affair had been masked by the assumption that the arrest at the Capucines was that laid on by Colonel Giskes, which would have been by the Abwehr. From the SD's point of view, a mysterious 'Antonio' who was probably a German agent yet not known to Boemelburg, was just a nuisance. Probably Boemelburg's idea was to give him a fright and get him out of the way. Déricourt was interested by the caution in Bodens's letter to Christmann not to go 'jaywalking'. It interested me too, as I had felt so strongly about the element of complicity between Bodens and Christmann. Déricourt wondered what had been the literal expression used in the German. In French, the phrase was 'to go out from between the nailed lines'. If it was the same in German, Bodens could have meant to warn Christmann not only to get run over again but not to go out from between some agreed lines.

A lot had been made of the demoralisation of 'Prosper' and 'Archambaud' by the sight of photocopies of the mail, alleged to have been betrayed by Déricourt. 'But what about the demoralisation of me, by them?' After the happening at Square Clignancourt, he had felt there was little he could add to the damage.

He criticised the poker parties at Square Clignancourt. Why did 'Archambaud' and the others have to meet in the evenings to play poker? Agents would be better advised to sit in their own rooms when not operationally employed. Why did they congregate?

I said probably they derived a feeling of comfort from keeping together.

But it increased the risk of arrest, he said; for it meant that if one was detected, all were. It was he who had first found the restaurant in the rue Troyon. He had introduced Jean Worms to it. The next time he went, he saw, 'at one table, "Prosper", "Archambaud", "Denise" and Worms. After that I did not go again,' he said, and added, breaking into his broken English, 'I did not want a so unconscious people in my hereabouts.'

'Denise', he said, was better than her chiefs; not before capture but after it. 'We do not hear that she talked.' He would also like to say a good word for Worms — 'small, slight, dark, gesticulating, more like a gipsy than a Jew'. They were parachuted together, blind, on 23 January 1943, near Prithivier, in the Loiret. Worms was carried by the wind, his parachute harness caught in a tree, and he was dragged and his leg was injured. Déricourt helped him out of his harness, with assistance from the farm people — still alive. Worms did not know how to take his bearings from the Pole star. Déricourt knew, as an airman, but was surprised it had not been taught to agents who were going to be parachuted blind. In the fields there were no obvious landmarks. Worms was not specially secure. That he was arrested, on 1 July, in the restaurant Chez Tutulle, was his own fault, for he should never have gone back there after the arrest of 'Prosper', 'Archambaud' and 'Denise'. But it was after his arrest that he showed his quality. 'Worms never spoke. In spite of being badly beaten. The beating was not so much because he did not speak as because of his arrogant manner towards the Germans, insulting them.' (I did not ask him how he knew this, and supposed Boemelburg told him.)

One point, Déricourt said, worried him, because he did not understand it. When 'Prosper' was arrested, the first person he gave away was Darling, Why? 'Darling was another Englishman. It was Darling who should have succeeded him and carried on.' If 'Prosper' had made his first disclosures less important ones, Darling would have had time to learn of his arrest and go into hiding. 'But he was given no time to escape.'

He went on, seriously, 'When one starts to betray, there are two ways in which one can do it — carefully, so as to do the least harm, or diabolically, so as to do all the harm possible. I tried to do the least harm. 'La Chatte' appeared to have been taken with a fit of diabolism and given away all she could. And, sorry to say, so did 'Prosper'.' Déricourt thought it was because 'Prosper' had become megalomaniac. He was the big chief, he had made his network the greatest, so when he was arrested he did not want anyone else to carry on in his place, step into his shoes. 'Have you seen Wagner's *Crépuscule des Dieux* — *Götterdämmerung?*'

I have, since, seen *The Twilight of the Gods*, but had not then, and he described to me how the curtain went up to disclose an enormous tree — 'It is very impressive' — round the base of which, in the gloaming, one discerned three weird figures, huddled. They were the Norns, weaving the Fates, but what they were enmeshing the tree in seemed to be sinister. 'To understand the fall of the "Prosper" Network you must see Wagner's *Twilight of the Gods*. The tree is "Prosper". The weird figures he felt to be gnawing his roots are the double agents, amongst whom he probably saw me. When he fell, he brought the world down with him.'

Once, when he was present, 'Prosper' had talked about the end of the world. He pictured the whole world devastated by war. From that devastation, he said, 'will rise a small blue flower, and that will be truth.' Déricourt said, 'Don't put into your book about small blue flower. There is only my witness and I don't want to say bad things about him.'

'Oh come, you have said much worse things. Blue flower is not bad.' 'But it is,' he said, 'given his position. If it had been peace-time and he had been a poet, such an idea could have been made into a nice little poem. But there was in that image a sense of impending doom. Even of looking forward to it.' A man with the idea of doom could draw it on to himself, and on to others. When he was arrested, it was Ragnarok. Gnawed through, he fell, taking his world with him. He took care to see it all washed up. Déricourt was furious with the whole idea of the pact. Any sort of contract or agreement supposed the parties to it both to be free. Between prisoner and captors it could have no reality: 'It didn't even deserve to be called a game. I played a game, but I was at liberty. It was a limited liberty, but yet within the limits I had room to manoeuvre. For a prisoner to attempt a game is to sit down to a game of chess without chessmen. For a prisoner, it is better to be silent.'

That, I said, did not come well from him. He had betrayed the 'Prosper' mail and had not the right to criticise 'Prosper'.

'Yes, I have the right!' he exclaimed angrily. Then, as if trying to meet me half-way, he said, 'I will try to put myself into "Prosper's" shoes. He has been arrested. Although he had expected it, yet the falling of the blow is a shock. Then he is shown photocopies of the mail he and "Archambaud" sent to London. He sees that the mail was betrayed. Does that excuse him for betraying Darling, and everybody else?' With increasing passion, he spoke of the 'hundreds of small French people he recruited, stirred up into assisting him in action against the Germans and then gave into German hands. C'était immonde, ça! It was filthy. I will not be made responsible for that carnage! Not even in the capacity of a demoralising example. It is not an excuse. He saved nothing. He gave everything. Everything.'

The primary demoralisation, he said, came from London.

'You did not respect your chiefs?' I said.

'How could I?' he asked.

He felt, naturally, an immense warmth towards Bodington. Nevertheless, he said, as a high staff officer Bodington should not have come into the field. He knew the whole of the organisation and every agent sent to France. If the Gestapo caught him, he would have been under great pressure to talk, and if he had done so it would have meant a bloodbath compared to which the 'Prosper' one would be a drop. 'Now Nic is a brave man, so I suppose he would not have talked if he had been torn limb from limb. But it wasn't fair to him or to anybody.'

'Did the Germans know how high up Bodington was?'

'The prisoners at Avenue Foch knew and probably told,' he said. And agents in the field knew it. With intense anger, he demanded, 'Did they send him to me to deliver to the Gestapo?'

He thought Bodington had been sent to France to kill him. In the early morning of 23 July, he and 'Marc' had received Bodington and Agazarian (returning from a trip to London after the Capucines incident) on a field at Soucelles, near Angers. As soon as he was alone with Bodington he said, 'Tu es venu pour moi, n'est-ce-pas, Nic?' — 'You have come to kill me, haven't you, Nic?'

'No,' Bodington replied, je ne suis pas venu pour toi.'

He determined to save Bodington. He told him he was in great danger but would not be arrested while they were together, nor while he was at the lodgings Déricourt would find him. 'That could only mean I was a Gestapo agent.' It was not necessary to be more plain. 'He was intelligent enough to work it out.'

He put Bodington into 'Claire's' flat, Place des Ternes. Agazarian he put into another flat, nearby.

Later that morning 'Aga was arrested'. He said it with heavy fatality, as though the circumstances had been painful and undiscussable. I remembered Vogt's telling me it was Bodington who sent Agazarian into the trap. Yes, but Déricourt had known 'Archambaud' was not at liberty, and must have warned Bodington, which was why Bodington had sent Agazarian to keep the appointment in his stead. But why need anybody have kept it? Perhaps because if nobody walked into the trap, Boemelburg would have known Déricourt had warned Bodington and they would neither of them have got out with their lives. I did not press Déricourt about this, for I felt it sat heavily on him that Agazarian had been sacrificed, and he could not explain without showing the responsibility of Bodington, which he would not.

According to the Abbé's papers, Agazarian was arrested four days after they landed, but that it was later on the same morning, as Déricourt said, seemed more logical.

During the first fortnight of his stay, Bodington lodged sometimes at 'Claire's' flat, on the Place des Ternes, sometimes at Déricourt's own, 58 rue Pergolèse. Déricourt could not have him constantly at rue Pergolèse because Bleicher — or more exactly Bleicher's mistress, Suzanne Laurent — had a flat in the house next door. Only when they appeared to be away could Bodington's coming to the rue Pergolèse be risked.

Nevertheless, the Gestapo hunt for Bodington was becoming too pressing. Déricourt felt it was not safe for him to be in Paris at all, and moved him out to a rented house of 'Claire's' at Yerres, in the Seine-et-Marne. It was really Jean Besnard, whom she afterwards married, who rented for 'Claire' both the flat and the house. At Yerres, Déricourt stayed with Besnard, 'Claire' and Bodington. It was mainly there that he and Bodington talked, in the kitchen, while peeling potatoes and the like. I should not exaggerate the intimacy between them. 'I did not tell him all my secrets, and he did not tell me his.' However, he talked to Bodington in such a way as to assure himself that Bodington had grasped the nature of the situation. 'I tried to tell him in such a way that he could have it both ways — that he had been told, or that he had not been told — as he wanted it. If I told him plainly, then he had to tell Buckmaster. I told him in such a way, he knew for himself, yet was not obliged to tell Buckmaster.'

As I puzzled, he explained, 'Buckmaster was not then colonel. He and Bodington were both majors. He was the chief, but I thought Nic could take over from him.'

This, he said, had been an important factor in his way of thinking at that time. Nic was more astute than Buckmaster. 'I was giving him information he could keep for himself and use in his own way.' Nic, if he could become chief, could run him as a double agent knowingly, feeding misinformation to the Germans through him.

As it happened, Nic was forced out of the Section almost as soon as he returned to England, so that hope collapsed. Déricourt saw him off, from a field at Pont-de-Braye, in the Sarthe, on 16 August and when he himself returned to England he found Nic was gone.

Although the way in which his fate had been entwined with Bodington's had been strange, leading to 'an incredible situation', what had happened was, in essence, simple. 'I saved his life. By testifying to it, he saved mine.' The skin whitened over his knuckles, so tightly were his fingers digging into his palms, as he said, almost to himself, 'We are level. We are both free. One could say that neither of us owes the other anything any more...' Then, with a rush of warmth, 'But I shall always be grateful to him. Because he came forward. He might not have done. He had to do something, certainly, but might have done something a great deal less agreeable to me.'

When did he enter into contact with the Gestapo, I asked?

When he returned to England at Easter, it was because Verity wished to speak with him about the accident in which the aircraft hit the tree, as he had told me. But he did not spend all his time at Tempsford. There had been a situation that had been weighing on his mind, from very soon after he was parachuted into France, and he thought he should take the occasion of being in England to warn somebody of something that was grave for the security of the Section. No notice was taken. He supposed they knew already, and let the situation continue. Perhaps in aid of a plan in which the agents were sacrificial pawns. 'It was because of that I took my own measures.'

Meaning he decided to go to the Gestapo? I had always, till now, imagined it was in France, while in some kind of tight corner, he had done it. 'Were you in London when you made the decision?'

'I knew what I would do when I returned.'

Meaning, I suggested, that he remembered he had known Boemelburg, so went to him and threw himself on his mercy, confessing he had got mixed up with this dreadful, amateurish organisation which had parachuted him from London and asking what he should do to put himself in the clear.

He said nothing. The silence lasted for so long, that I asked again, 'When did you do it?'

'I don't keep a diary,' he said, looking off into space. 'You have given an interpretation to my words, on which I don't have to comment.'

'Did you go to Boemelburg as soon as you got back?'

'It would have been a few days after I parachuted back.' He did not walk straight in on him. He made a telephone call, to test the ground. There were circumstances to be arranged. 'I arranged to be solicited.' The story he had told the court was not entirely fiction, for two pilots had really called on him. (Did he mean he had asked for them to call, so that in case of trouble arising he could tell the very story that he had told the court?)

But why did he return to France? If it was while in London he had come to this dreadful suspicion as to the way in which the agents were being used, why did he not just stay there?

'My wife was in France. I could not abandon my wife. Or 'Marc' whom I had drawn into it.' If he had not taken measures to prevent it, he himself would have been arrested, on his return, and so would all those who depended on him.

'I took my own measures to save my own life and also the lives of my wife, "Marc" and all the members of my team.'

'What were the terms of your pact with Boemelburg?'

'Oh, please, don't say "pact". It makes me think of "Prosper"!'

'But when you went to see Boemelburg, it wasn't just to get a cup of coffee.'

There had been 'an accord', he said.

'What were the terms of your accord with Boemelburg?'

'I would rather not say,' he said, simply.

We had worked all through the afternoon, with only pots of weak French tea. It was dark again. I said, 'You cannot fly to Arabia on an empty stomach. You'd better have supper with me.'

We moved to a table and I ordered two omelettes.

While we were waiting for them, he asked, 'Would you prefer that I had been shot?'

'No. I'm glad you're alive. I'm glad they made a mistake.'

'If I had told the truth to the court martial, c'eut été la balle. They would have sent me to the firing-squad.'

'Necessarily?' I asked, ever so gently.

'What? Extenuating circumstances? I couldn't think of any. I racked my brains, but I couldn't see an extenuating circumstance.'

Appreciating that he seemed to have condemned himself, he added, 'I know what *I* think of as extenuating circumstances, *bien sur.*' They were, however, not of a kind the court could accept. 'They can only judge within a very narrow framework. I would have given them no option but to have me shot.' In a faint voice he said that perhaps, if he had told them what really

179

happened, they might have had the understanding... but no, it was too big a risk to have taken. 'As I saw it, my only chance was to deny everything, lie, lie and lie, and hold my head up! And hope for a lucky break.'

He would never admit fault while the de Vomécourts, who had done things as bad as he, walked about wearing the Légion d'Honneur — 'because they've not been found out.' He would not give them the satisfaction of seeing him cowed or pleading. That had been a powerful motive for his holding his head very high in court, and had been behind the pride, almost arrogance, of some of his retorts from the box.

As to his having got off, apart from having a disinclination to be led out and riddled with bullets, 'It would not have made me feel any cleaner. Anyone who sought purification through that, I would suspect of masochism.'

I thought of the end of Dostoievsky's *Crime and Punishment*, in which Raskolnikof confesses his crime and is thereby purified; but my feelings were in line with Déricourt's. I said I did not favour capital punishment. It denied time in which to do anything good and useful, whereby to improve the balance-sheet of one's deeds.

He agreed eagerly, and said, 'There are two things necessary. Repentance and reparation. I should try, now, to make some reparation, I should try to live better.'

There remained the Last Judgement, 'Before that, there is no dissembling of the evidence. At that bar, in that court, one can only answer truly. But there, I have no fear. Because there, all is known. There I am sure of my acquittal, or at any rate, of a grace.'

He never went to Confession. He did not need a priest, an intercessor. As he spoke, it struck me he was Protestant with the force of the early Huguenots, who had just discovered priests could lie. He would, he said, answer for himself. 'The real confession is the internal confession. When the confession is sincere, the absolution is assured.'

It was spoken like an initiate.

He smiled a little, and said, 'St Peter, when he sees me coming, will let me creep in and find myself a very low seat. I shall sit on the floor, at the feet of the virtuous. I shall listen to the virtuous in their conversations. Listening, I shall learn. Perhaps I shall even become virtuous — if we are permitted a continuing evolution....'

'Of course,' I encouraged him. It was, I reflected, Blavatsky's view at the time when she wrote *Isis Unveiled* — that we went, on death, straight into an evolution eternally to be continued upon higher planes — before she received the more detailed and exact teaching she later put into *The Secret Doctrine*, which included, before that stage was reached, a great many returns into the human incarnation here. In any case, the end idea was the same, from matter to spirit, a continuing purification, and evolution in understanding. Why should I seek to improve on something he had won through to, a truth he had found for himself?

'But,' he said, 'it's difficult to be a Christian Scientist and a spy.'

I begged him, if he was still in espionage, to give it up.

'It's rare for a spy to retire,' he said.

'I know it's supposed to be difficult to get out of, but you can get yourself out of anything. Get yourself out of spying! If you are out of it, stay out. If you are still in it, get out.'

He thought I meant because it was dangerous.

I said, because it was loss of purity. Apart from becoming a double agent, any sort of intelligence work was based on dissimulation. It was all getting people's confidence in order to betray it. 'It's the falsification of all relationships, and gets you involved with impure people. You're worth more than the people with whom you got yourself mixed up.'

'Don't begin to flatter me now, or I'll be confused!' For a moment, he really did look confused.

What won my regard, and caused my concern for him, was his capacity for naked honesty underneath what had been the superficial bluff. It was an honesty such as few 'respectable' people would be capable of.

Speaking very quickly, as though making an unwise disclosure, he said, 'I don't do spying any more, I do something else. You'll have to make what you can of that.'

I urged him to live within the law.

In a faint voice he said, wistfully, 'I'm an old leopard for changing my spots.'

Then he said, 'I have a moral problem. I want to go back to China, but my wife doesn't want me to go. There are other possibilities. The Emir of Kuwait has confidence in me.' Yet it was China that drew him.

As he had earlier said that if he returned to China he would take a Chinese mistress, I wondered if the question was really, should he take a Chinese mistress? Obviously that would do nothing for his marriage, but I did know the quality of the marriage. 'I would like your counsel,' he said.

I cut the Gordian knot. '*I* shall be sorry if you go so far away. I've grown attached to our conversations, and shall miss you.'

He said we could write to each other, and he would come back sometimes.

I told him he had done me some good. Since our meeting in May, I had stopped smoking. I had started it, in my 'teens, as something one had to do in order to appear sophisticated and move in the world. I had thought, if he could go through without it, so could I.

'You'll be better without it,' he said, like an ordinary friend.

I asked him if he thought it was wise to keep from his wife the fact that a book about him was in preparation. When I had suggested I see her, it was not because I wanted a second person to deal with, but because she would be upset if she discovered a *fait accompli*.

He said he had declined to introduce us because nothing contrary to his honour would be listened to. Having now read my manuscript, he was resolved she must never see it. 'If she read Ernest's testimony, I don't think she could bear it. Or the whole array of testimonies you have collected. She wouldn't be able to get over my having given my consent to the publication of all this. She would think I had gone out of my senses.' Had he told her anything about this, he knew what she would have said; that he had been acquitted and did not have to discuss the matter, and that if anything contrary to his honour appeared he should sue for defamation. The kind of relationship which had grown up between us during these hours was something he could never explain. We were sitting almost shoulder to shoulder, and he looked sideways at me, as if to say what he could never explain was that we had become friends. 'How do you pronounce your first name?' he asked.

'Jean.'

'My wife's name is Jeanne. It is the same...'

She could read English, but seldom read English books or papers. So long as his real name was not in the book, he did not see why she should learn of it. If Déricourt appeared in reviews, people would tell her, 'There's something about your husband in the paper.' But to the people she knew, 'Gilbert' would mean nothing. He did not think she would read reviews of it and so find 'Gilbert' in the small print. But he would ask me not to let even 'Gilbert' appear on the jacket, 'In case it should catch her eye in a shop-window.'

I gave him my word. I would keep 'Gilbert' off the jacket, and do nothing that could alert her to the book's existence. He said it was the very paraphernalia of security which produced catastrophes in espionage; the codes, pass-phrases, signs for recognition. 'I don't sit on a park bench to wait for a man who will be dressed in a certain way, carrying *The Times* or *The Canary Fancier's Gazette.*' If he was to work with somebody he must know his name, where he lived and all about him. 'Don't mistake me. It is not "I know Jean-Pierre and know him brave and true". Much more likely it is "I know Jean-Pierre and know he is a louse". But I know what sort of louse. What I need to know about a man is what he will betray me for. To save his wife, to save his friend, for money, or just to save himself. When I have that clear, I'm settled. Why should I expect anyone else to be better than I am?'

We received our omelettes and began to eat them. Déricourt said, 'I am sitting with my back to the door. I can't see who is coming in. I take it on trust that you haven't arranged for someone to come in and shoot me in the back.' Only then did I realise why, when we first met at the hotel, he had insisted on sitting by the window, from which he could see the people entering the hotel, as well as the lounge door.

'There is a disease that comes to old spies,' he said. 'It is called *espionitis*, the disease of thinking everybody is a spy. You have been to Germany. How did you find Ernest? I'll warrant Ernest suffers from *espionitis* worse than I do.'

I had to laugh, for while I liked Vogt, it was true.

I remembered to ask him about Claude Jouffret. 'Why, when you had been acquitted, did you take into your home the ex-lover of "La Chatte"?'

He was put out, vexed that I knew. 'Can't I start a chicken farm with whom I like?'

But it was a strange association, I persisted. According to *L'Aurore*, it was in Marseilles Jouffret entered the Interallié. 'Was it in Fresnes, while you were both awaiting trial, you made friends, or in Marseilles, back in the days of the Interallié?'

He would not answer.

He recovered his humour, however, and later, perhaps while we were waiting for the waiter to bring us something further, he suddenly began to speak again about the 'anterior epoch'.

'There was a *souricier*. I don't know how you say that in English.'

'A mousetrap.'

'A mousetrap house, in which a number of agents were arrested, one after another, in Marseilles, in 1941.'

I remembered that Turck had told me of such a house, but I did not know how many agents SOE had in France in those days. There could be agents I had never heard of who had entered a different mouse-trap house in Marseilles.

I took from my bag a piece of paper, laid it on the table and was about to write on it 'Marseilles', when he stopped my hand.

'Too dangerous. In case that piece of paper should ever get into certain people's hands.'

I said I would not have written down anything compromising. Marseilles was a big city and the name of it, by itself, could not mean anything to anybody, I protested.

'In the context of conversation between me and you, to certain people, it could only mean one thing,' he said. They would be afraid that he had told me everything. That would be dangerous for me, too.

It seemed to me he was referring again to the de Vomécourts, and to avoid using their name, I asked, 'The people with whom you have the *quid pro quo*?'

'Yes.' He was so tense that he was quivering as I had never seen him.

'Write nothing,' he said. 'Listen. Engrave what I am going to say on your memory. What I am going to say now is the most dangerous thing I have ever said.' He came to a stop, and I did not know whether he was going to continue. Then he said, all I needed to know was that everything went back to the mouse-trap house. From what had happened there a situation ensued which in '43 became very serious for the French Section.

Did he mean, I asked, that a person who had been arrested in the mouse-trap house in 1941 became a German agent, which became serious for the French Section in 1943?

'Yes,' he said. It was needless to enter into details, I just had to understand that what happened in Paris and the Loire Valley in '43 was the consequence of what happened in the mousetrap house in '41.

'This is within your certain knowledge?'

'Yes.'

He had attempted to warn London. Not Buckmaster. What he had to say was so serious that he felt it should be to somebody higher. He managed to get the ear of somebody who was much higher. But in the presence of this person he did not blurt out what he had to say. He had to sound the ground first, to test how it would be received. So he put things obliquely at a tangent to what he really wanted to say, to see

186

the reaction. He said one thing which should have caused this person to react very visibly and positively, because it was a thing that should have been very startling to him. But he showed no alarm, no anger, nor any strong reaction or keen interest. 'My interpretation was that he knew it already, or that it was in line with what he wanted, and so he pretended not to understand.'

'Perhaps he really didn't understand,' I said. 'Your hints can be very subtle, and in London they "are not very clever".'

'Then they had no business to be in spying,' he replied. Then, with a laugh, he said, 'If it was that, it wasn't any better. It was still a reason for taking my own measures.'

I felt I should not withhold my suspicion that it was because of the money he was drawing from the Germans.

That was the only time Déricourt really shrank, as if he had been hit. 'Celà me ferrait vil,' he said.

I said I did not believe he had not accepted money.

He had to laugh, despite his distress. 'If I had refused it, that really would have made them suspect something peculiar about me. A spy should not step out of character.' But it was, he said, money made on the side, not related to operations. 'Je ne vendais pas des têtes!' he cried, facing me. 'Je ne vendais pas mes camarades.' Angry tears were standing in his eyes.

'I'm not a monster,' he said; and he asked, as if really enquiring, 'Do you think I'm a monster?'

I was abashed, before his agony. 'I did think you were a monster, before I knew you. I don't now.'

He relaxed. The money, he said, was the rake-off on some financial business.

What happened, I asked, to the vast amount he made? 'What did it go on?'

'The costs of my defence.' After his trial, he said, he walked out from the prison — for he had to go back there from the Tribunal Militaire to sign the register — 'Alive, but with nothing'.

As we finished eating, he said he had a small complaint against me. 'You give me bad marks for the bad things I have done, but you give me no good marks for the bad things I haven't done. I think one should receive good marks for the bad things one did not do.' He had not defended himself by accusing anybody else.

'Prosper' and 'Archambaud'...

Ah, that was different, he said. They were dead, so no trouble could be made for them, and he only referred to the pact, which was common knowledge. He had not sought to refute the charges brought against himself by telling lies that might get another person charged, and perhaps shot, in his place. 'Culioli was under *instruction*, awaiting trial, at the same time as I was,' he said. 'His trial was the day after mine.'

It would have been very easy for him to shuffle certain things off on to Culioli. 'I didn't do it.' Both of them were fighting for their lives. He had abstained from making things worse for the other one. 'My defence was clean. I got myself out of it — lied myself out of it — in such a way as not to charge someone else.'

I realised it was a spiritual achievement.

He drew up the notes he had been making during the reading of my typescript. In one or two I felt he was up to his monkey tricks, but as he had been on the whole so good over the book, which charged him heavily, I did not make difficulty over allowing his notes. I asked him if he would like me to print them in his exact English, which was sometimes unintentionally a little comic, or to correct the grammar. He said he thought it preferable the English should be correct, so I corrected it with him.

I also showed him a typed copy, in corrected English, which I had made of the paragraph he had written for printing at the end of the book. He made some additions by hand, referring to Ernest, Christmann and Mme Aigrain. 'I want to create an order,' he said; and I understood that he was placing Ernest first in order of respect. He also added by hand that he was not responsible for the arrest of 'Prosper', 'Archambaud' or 'Madeleine'. I stopped him.

'Don't put 'Madeleine'. Everybody knows her arrest was nothing to do with you.'

'I thought some people might think I betrayed her too...'

'No,' I said firmly. 'It is known who betrayed her. They know it at the Tribunal Militaire. I assure you, absolutely.'

He looked at me, as though inquiring whether I was advising him for his own good.

'You don't want to put ideas into people's minds,' I said.

He struck through 'Madeleine' and substituted 'any others'.

Thus amended, his text for publication read:

GILBERT'S PARAGRAPH

I have read the whole script of Miss Jean Overton Fuller, and to the parts treating of events in which I was concerned I can put my signature. Nevertheless, I do not agree with Ernest as regards the whole of his statement, or with Christmann on some small points, and I do not agree with Madame Aigrain. I can sleep in peace because I know I was not responsible for the arrest of 'Prosper', 'Archambaud' or any others. But seeing things now through the eyes of different people, I realise they can look different from what they were in truth.

I, like any other British, German or French agent, have to recognise we could have been abused. We were blind, fighting in darkness. To be successful in our missions we had often to clear from our way causes of nuisance. We used to risk our lives every day, three times a day, with no rest or encouragement. We were rich in what we had in our hearts and in our minds. Today, I am rich in the friendship of the people who know what I did.

I can't and won't say more. I prefer to let Miss Jean Overton Fuller's book make its way on her own responsibility.

We had worked for fourteen hours and were both tired. In fact we had sat together past midnight, the time by which he had said he must go. 'The captain can't keep the aircraft waiting,' he said.

'I don't like the idea of your flying an aircraft after all this,' I said. I thought we must both be emotionally exhausted.

'I shall be all right,' he said. The spy had disappeared behind the aircraft's captain.

'Don't have a motor accident on the way,' I said, 'rushing to get to Orly in time to take off on schedule.'

'I won't,' he said, reassuringly and firmly. 'Take off will be a few minutes late.'

As it was the end of our conversations, and he was rising from his chair, I said, 'I don't think you were the worst kind of traitor.'

For a moment, he was speechless. The colour came into his face and neck. Then he said, very deeply, 'Thank you.'

As we parted, I gave him my hand. 'Send me a postcard to let me know you have arrived safely.'

8: LETTERS FROM THE FAR EAST

That he had survived the flight I learned from a long letter from him (twelve pages of foolscap, closely written), full of afterthoughts on the text and all that we had been discussing. The best parts were those intimating psychological atmospheres. I translate from his French:

Club QBG,[4]

6, rue des Italiens, Paris 9

13.9.57

Dear friend,

... What I wanted you to understand when I spoke of professionals: the professionals are not patriots, or if they are they hide it to the best of their ability. To be a spy one must doubt everything and everyone. All motivations are possible — all the filths and all the heroisms — the refinements of the game are infinite — no one is black or white — but grey or at least tinted....

I am leaving the aviation company with which I have been employed to take up a far mission — I shall not see you again for a long time, at least a year — but write to me.

I insist that my real name be nowhere mentioned, and Gilbert not on the outside of the book, cover or jacket, uniquely so that it will not catch the eye of my wife in a shop-window.

I do not ask you to believe me in everything. Even my being nice was self-interested...

A percentage! My poor friend, you are probably more broke than I am. I wonder even whether your book will sell. You

---

[4] The great airmen's club in Paris QBG is a code instruction, 'Fly above the clouds'

should write something more sexual and tormented in spirit
— that always sells — see Franchise Sagan or St Laurant —
that's business. But our turpitudes do not interest people any
longer.

With sympathy,
HENRY

I replied (I translate from my French):

18 September 1957

Dear Henri,

    I address you for the first time by your real name, as you
have signed it. Indeed, the pseudo, 'Gilbert' did not have very
happy associations, and I make the change gladly.

JEAN

His next letter replied to Christmann's replies to questions I
had asked him:

QBG
11 Oct, '57

Dear Jean,

    ... Morel could not confuse me with 'Archambaud'. RAF
Sq. 161 would *never* have sent an aircraft to 'Archambaud'...
Neither Morel nor Buck nor Gubbins could have made a
mistake... therefore it all happened extra-service.

    For my own book, don't worry ... it will make enough
noise for the English translation to be easy to place. I will
send you in due course — for this moment I am up to my
eyes in Chinese and am not in the mood to write except to
you.

    As for the post, the people at the QBG put all my mail in
the diplomatic bag and it goes without stamps or trace of
having been forwarded.

On Christmas Eve I received a picture postcard from Déricourt, without address but posted from Hong Kong (in English):

19.12.57

Sorry to let you down so long but I was in bed with fever and so on. Fit now, I'll whrite [*sic*] you — Happy New Year.

The next letter I received from him had been begun earlier, put by, and continued in the new year. In French, it bore the address that was to be his for a long time:

Air Laos,
Vientiane,
Laos
8.11.57

Dear friend,

.. I have not written to you sooner because I have been in bed following an injury. I have got up this morning for the first time...

I continue 7 January from Vientiane... With regard to myself, I had to leave again brusquely, my wound not being completely cured. I was nursed in Hong Kong. Now here I am in a little rat hole absolutely unlike the Dorchester. I hope to leave in 3 months for Paris ... I hope to see you in the spring in Paris or London. I have a mass of stories to tell you, of which you will not believe half.

I found Vientiane on the map. It was on the Mekong, and was the capital of Laos, a new country, created out of part of what had been French Indo-China before the fall of Dien Bien Phu.

Yeo-Thomas had written a letter to Putnam's describing my book as 'a masterpiece', and a contract had been signed, 1

December brought a shock; they could not accept legal risk of publication. I wrote to Déricourt: 'They fear Buckmaster will take action against them.' I told him they were still willing to publish the book if I re-shaped it so as to concentrate upon Ernest and 'Gilbert', and leave London out of it as much as possible. This, as I told Déricourt, was a hard condition. It had never been my intention to pillory him, and I had used his case in order to raise a question which I thought should be of national concern. But it seemed I had no choice. Admittedly, he and Ernest were the most humanly interesting and sympathetic characters, and Irene undertook to raise in Parliament, and in a letter to the Prime Minister, the questions I had been obliged to take out of my book.

On 25 January I sent Déricourt an article in *John Bull*, 'They Spied over England' by Charles Wighton (it appeared in November but I had only just seen it), saying that on 31 January 1943, two Abwehr (Belgian) agents had left by Lysander from a field at Fleurines and entered England, to be followed by others. This was said to be from a 'Lahousen' diary. I had just received a telephone call from Wighton, who said he was writing a book on SOE and that both Hugo Bleicher and Miss Atkins were friends of his (not the most endearing self-recommendation) and he wished to see me to ask who I thought betrayed the 'Prosper' network. I had replied that I was writing a book on this question myself and therefore could not give material to him. As he pressed for an interview, I had given him an appointment for Tuesday next, not in my flat but in the lounge of the Bonnington Hotel in Southampton Row. However, I was determined to give away nothing.

I also mentioned to Déricourt that Ernest and I were having trouble with a German magazine, *Quick*, which had lifted material from my earlier books but represented 'Madeleine' as having been arrested and interrogated by Bleicher. She had been uniquely Vogt's case. We both protested. The proprietors offered me a cheque and him a series of articles, remunerated, on condition of his consenting to appear as having taken over her case from Bleicher. As all we wanted them to do was retract their historical untruth, which they refused to do, we both refused their offers.

From Déricourt I received a large envelope, bulging with thirteen pages of foolscap. He had written in English.

28.1.58

Dear Jean,

... As I let you know, I have been slightly hurt. While crossing a river the boat turned upside down because of the current and the rocks. Nobody drown by chance but we lost a lot of things. My wounds were not dangerous but due to the lack of medicines (in water) they turned badly — When I reached an hospital it was really time to go to bed with fever. I was sent to Paris and as soon as I recovered came back here ... I am still flying, not ready to retire yet. I hope to go back to Paris in April — I'll send you details...

I am sorry for you that the editor did so — and sorry you can't shake the Buckmaster old tree — but I warned you.... Bleicher, really sorry for you of all that trouble but as it is printed already you should have taken the money.

(cont.) 31.1.58

I read the Wighton tale. It could be dangerous for you, but you have been very careful in not giving any information — No he have not contact me yet. I never heard of him I won't give any information to him and I don't give you permission to speak... ask me first — that will help you to stand firm.

... No Fleurines was not one of my fields. I never operated north of Paris... I should like to bet anything against Wighton that this story is another tale of Hugo Bleicher. H. B. begins to turn mad … I never heard of Lahousen…

So I have to leave you for I have to sleep a little — wake up at 4.0 a.m.

… I have completely recover — fit and ready for any emergency. I am a bit slimmer that's all.…

He suggested the passage in my book about his horoscope might be used 'to make your hero a little more interesting, more attractive.' This was harmless fun.

My interview with Wighton had by now taken place. He said it was Jacques Weil of whom he was writing a biography. I kept quiet on that subject.

Putnam had accepted the book again but did not like the title, *The Pointing Arrow*. I asked Déricourt if he could think of any other titles. He sent me a picture postcard from Hong Kong:

10.2.58

I'll send some titles tomorrow. What a nuisance for you.

This was followed by (in English):

29.2.58

… Some titles I thought of: *Road without Signposts, Short Cut for Nowhere, Slippery Road for Beginners* (and, as air navigator) *Driving Blind, Point of No Return*…

For my book, I will change the title once more … I thought of *Psychology de l'Espion*. What do you think of it?

I liked his aeronautical titles, but they would have assumed the story to be told from his point of view, and on 7 March, my birthday, I wrote to him I had decided upon *Double Webs*:

... spider webs have the quality that they are sticky and difficult to get off, and I think this is true of the 'webs' of espionage; also, a network is another kind of web....

He wrote again on 4 March from Saigon, and on 11 March in an envelope postmarked 'Poste aux Armes T.O.E.' Within this letter, which puzzled me as it seemed to prove he could indeed use an address of the French Armed Forces on active service, he enclosed his idea of a design for the jacket — title *Double Webs* and my name enclosed between spider webs, radiating from the four corners and slightly overlapping. On the webs were four spiders, with very prominent eyes. There were markings on their backs, such as common or garden spiders bear — but when one looked more closely, one saw that one had on his back a Union Jack, one a Croix de Lorraine, one a Swastika and one a question mark. I have always regretted the publishers did not use Déricourt's own design on the jacket.

Always interested by the hypothesis of his possible noble bastardy, I had asked him, on 5 March, 'I have noticed that many people write your name as d'Héricourt instead of Déricourt. Is there any significance to this? You need not tell me if you do not want to.' In his TOE letter, of 11 March, he replied with a tease, showing he understood but refused to be drawn out:

> If people write my name with a d'H it is only a phonetical deformation, that's all. Anyway, why shouldn't I have a King in my ancestors like anybody?
>
> ERIC LE ROUGE

I smiled, because the son of Eric the Red was Leif the Lucky, and he was always saying he was lucky.

Largely, however, the letters of this month were taken up with Ernest's testimony. Déricourt wrote that in the beginning,

'I did not mind if I was to be the rascal of the SOE', but now, on the file of his case he had obtained from his lawyer, he found two depositions of Ernest which had been made prior to his trial, so he 'lied' when he said the prosecution did not have his evidence.

I wrote to Ernest, enclosing copies which I typed from Déricourt's transcript, asking if it was authentic. He replied that someone had been sent to interrogate him for the French while he was still in American hands, at Dachau, and he had completely forgotten having it. He had no copies from which to check the transcripts, but, yes, they looked to him like authentic transcripts of what he must then have deposed.

Déricourt was somewhat ungracious about the admission wrung from Ernest and talked of 'lies' to make his later statement more important. I said I felt sure Ernest's having forgotten was genuine, and Déricourt half-apologised for being ungracious, saying he tended to attribute the worst motivation to people who made mistakes which went against himself. He did, however, light-heartedly pick on Vogt's description of him in the deposition to the DST: 'Gilbert was about 30, tall, fair, sportsmanlike in figure, pretty good-looking, well dressed...' This, he said, could not possibly describe *him*.

About this time I read *The Way Back: The Story of Lieutenant-Commander Pat O'Leary, GC, MBE*, by Vincent Brome (Cassell, 1957), in the hope of finding in it confirmation of the story Déricourt had told me that it was Pat who had arranged his escape from France in August 1942, meeting him at Narbonne and boarding him on a trawler flying a Portuguese flag in reality commissioned by the British Intelligence Services. To my dismay I could find nothing about it there — neither Déricourt's name nor any episode that could be the one he described. I concluded therefore that he had made it up and —

not to expose him to exposure — omitted it from *Double Webs*. I sent Déricourt a copy of Pat's book, as he had asked me, but without comment.

In his letter of 14 March 1958 Déricourt said he had earlier written that there was 'a second mysterious man, Christian.' He now continued: '*Christian* — I have a statement on him. I give you only an extract and not the origin — sorry.'

I recognised at once the passage which he copied out for me. It was from the deposition of Pierre Bony, who assisted by Henri Lafont, trailed people on behalf of the SD. Bony said Kieffer's department used 'a double agent, Christian', whom he referred to thereafter as 'the informer', who received parachuted agents, whom they trailed from the nearest railway station to Paris. In truth, I had always had a heavy suspicion Christian was Déricourt, although he did not receive parachuted agents (Culioli's job), but only agents from aircraft that actually landed. He had always said Culioli was innocent, so whom did that leave? Was he playing a game with me, inviting me to speculate as to the identity of a person who was himself, or could there really be some third person unknown who received arrivals? Bony mentioned that the agents followed were sometimes arrested, sometimes left free (on orders). The sole name he gave of an agent who had been arrested was Bonoteaux. As this was a name unknown to me from any other context, it did not enable me to identify the informer as Déricourt, or anyone else.

He went on to quote another passage, which I recognised as from the same deposition. It concerned an occasion when Bony and Lafont were standing in front of a metro station when they saw a taxi arrive from which stepped a girl in a blue coat with red belt, and two men:

> She had been followed since leaving the café Colisée … in the company of [word which I reserve] and another.

The word he had held back, as I checked with my photostat of the complete deposition, was 'informer'. Why had he bothered to make a mystery of that?

He said he felt 95% sure that the girl was 'Madeleine'. That was the reason why he had asked me earlier to ask all the people who knew her at that time whether they had ever seen her in a blue coat or dress with red belt or trimming of any sort.

What I thought of was that 'Madeleine' had been sent to the Cate, Colisée to meet two Canadians, 'Bertrand' and 'Valentin', (Pickersgill and Macalister). As the two Canadians had been arrested after parachuting, at the same time as Culioli, it was the Germans, Placke and Holdorf, who had replaced them, and through their operation of the radio circuit kept up the game with London. It was therefore Packe and Holdorf whom 'Madeleine' had met at the Colisée, on radio order from London. I wrote back to Déricourt suggesting that in this passage the informer (I knew the word he had left out) was Placke or Holdorf.

At least one thing was good. He had copied out, without changing the words, two passages highly detrimental to himself, in the suspicion they cast on him, unaware I had access to authentic copies from which I could check his transcription.

In any case, the eventual arrest of 'Madeleine' did not proceed from that imbroglio. The Germans must have lost her again, since they later needed a woman informer to sell them her address.

As to the wretched mail, which Déricourt kept trying to get out of, I wrote to him:

... For nearly a year I have searched my mind (since I cannot think of you as an evil being) for mitigating circumstances; I have thought you knew the 'Prosper' network was already penetrated from many sides and that you supposed the Germans could arrest 'Prosper', 'Archambaud' and the others at any moment if they wished and that the mail could not make much difference... This was my attempt to make the crime less ... If in fact you did *not* give them the mail I should be very happy... But the esteem I have for you is for the man *now*, the man I know *today*, and is not based upon proof of what happened or did not happen in the past ... If you did do it you do not have to avow it, but you do not have to try to make me believe you did not do it (unless *really* you did not do it) in order to retain the regard which I have come to feel for you... You do not have to convince me in order to have my good will... Whatever is proved, I will not withdraw my friendship; for my relationship is with you *now*, not with you *past* Can you understand that? Try to understand.

I received from him a mammoth letter, twenty-seven pages of his large, closely written sheets, halfway through re-dated, after receiving mine, He wrote in English.

25.4.58

Sorry to let you down but we lost a plane. I was in the rescue party (as usual) — I found all dead — too bad — and yesterday evening some people very north of here met some MIG 15 in flight — from me to you (strictly) some of our friends here are playing a very hot game — that will end badly...

Thanks for the esteem. I quite appreciate. If in appearance it looks like it was me who gave the mail — with or without the excuse of the penetrating of the 'Prosper' network by the Germans — the War Office people would not have let me go like that — and would not have help me at my trial and at

Croydon — It is really because I did a lot of good (St Bernard's dog) and because of my carefulness that I am still alive...

An informer is somebody who gives informations like a sneak — he could be an enemy agent or a doorkeeper. It could not be Placke or Holdorf.

But then, the 'sneak' must have been him. He had certainly chosen an unattractive appellation for what seemed to have been his role.

Nor did I really think that it was the War Office that had helped him at his trial, or at Croydon. He knew I did not accept that. After a time it came to me that it was his way of telling me, gently, for myself, that *although* he had given the mail with or without excuse — he had been careful in his selection from it of what he handed over, so as to avoid doing the utmost damage, and had done good to be weighed in the balance against that. I remembered it was on his own responsibility he had taken Basin under his wing, when on the run from the Gestapo, having just escaped from prison, and, despite that this name was not on the list he had received from London, boarded him, along with other agents, on an aircraft leaving for England. In saving Basin from what would otherwise have been the probability of recapture and death, he had indeed played the role of a St Bernard dog.

I wrote to tell him Buckmaster had a book coming out on 28 April. In his reply he commented (2.5.58): 'Poor Buckmaster, he did his best which was nearly nothing.' There followed lines whose violence and bitterness render them unpublishable. As to people knowing his identity:

You can tell them that the last you heard of me was that I was on 'duty' in the Far East... After your book is on sale — you can say that you got my address and that you will transmit me any letters — I will ask you to *open them* — to *read them* and to give me your *critics* about the text and about the people — I can't give you better proof of confidence...

This morning we have a tremendous thunderstorm — the first one of the rainy season — Lightnings — Ram as in monsoon — temperature has fallen only 84 at 10 p.m. What is curious is the sudden apparition of toads — hundreds of toads — the ram makes them get out of their hiding place — they are the kind of the black toad what we call buffalo toad because of their shout which is like the buffalo — deep and loud.

I have good news. I can expect to be in Paris from the 1st July.

He wrote next (in English):

Sunday 18 May, 58

Dear Jean,

Just coming back once more from very north I find your letters waiting — and the Buck book too — too bad that my letter was not in time to save you money...

Yes there are many mistakes — at first I see a dozen at least — he is boasting all the time ... he does not speak of Bodington, very few of Morel — not of Gubbins!

The letter contained the only nice thing he said about Norman:

'Archambaud' — I don't really think he did something wrong — He was not a man like Roger Bardet, R. Kiffer, Henri Frager, 'Bastien'... and so many others. Although he was very self-contained, he never tried to make me caught — and I quite appreciate the way he opposed in the case of the Culioli pill.

He affirmed SOE was much too ready to kill upon suspicion. Then, after acknowledging my news that my galley proofs had arrived ('Good show for your book! It is just in time.'), he ended with a reference to the recent take over in Algeria by de Gaulle:

> For the troubles in North Africa they did at last what they ought to have done already — For inside France I hope they will sack that Government and change the ungovernable constitution — the worst is that when I'll come back everything will be over — and without me.
>
> Good luck,
HENRY

I had sent him the books of Bleicher, Giskes and Buckmaster; but he asked me once for spiritual counsel, and these were hardly food for the soul. Now I saw that *Winged Pharoah*, by Joan Grant, had appeared in paperback, and it came to me as a happy thought to buy it for him. Written as a novel, in the first person, it told the story of a life in ancient Egypt, brought over an atmosphere of calm and order, and conveyed more accessibly than in Blavatsky the idea that in our long journey towards illumination we are born as a human being many times, learning a little more of wisdom at each incarnation, and, over the centuries, correcting and redeeming our faults, however bad.

I wrote to him at Air Laos:

22 May 1958

Dear Henry,

    ... When I first read the book, in 1940, it made a deep impression on me... it opened quite a new perspective and seemed to show a deep and beautiful spiritual philosophy... All the books I have sent you have been about espionage and

204

secret agents and operations; it is because we met in the first place to speak of these things. But our relationship has evolved since then; in that sense this little gift is symbolic because it relates to a different plane.

JEAN

His letter of 18 May contained a curious reproach:

> I understand that if your father and grandfather travelled, you don't — You ought to — living with books and in the same place with the same friends is not good at all. You see others' life through your personal optic-subjectively...Instead of me, always ready to go anywhere, I meet different peoples, Chinese, Spanish, Russians and from the coolie to the banker ... I do not crystallise ... You ought to make a tour hereabout — I should introduce you to the most amazing people!

I took this a little hard, as it seemed to me I had done little else for a long while than trek about meeting and trying to understand people of backgrounds very different from my own — including him. I knew his suggestion I should tour the Far East was only meant as a joke, yet there was one sense in which what he said was right. Studying statements about SOE all the time was narrowing; it had been a long time since I had been abroad other than to interview somebody and take a statement. I replied saying he could treat me to a Chinese meal when next we met in Paris. China was out of the question. I had worked out I could just about afford to treat myself to a trip to Istanbul. I had always wanted to see (next to Karnak and the Potala) St Sophia. He replied:

14.6.58

Dear Jean,

I am sorry to have annoyed you with my theory about travelling... but I was trying to explain why sometimes you seem to not understand me. Istanbul is a good idea — I know quite well Turkey — and mostly the Iranian-Syrian-Turkey border. I understand Armenian too.

Was he thinking of a link up? He ended:

> Here the rain has come — not the European rain — but monsoon — All the country is a lake — roads are cut — planes take off heavily — visibility comes to nothing — Everything becomes mouldy — shoes in one night are completely white with patches of green — and at midnight the thermometer is over 82 farenheit.

As he was coming home, I asked him to bring me as a souvenir the seed of a plant that grew in Laos, which I could plant in a pot and try to grow in my flat.

The Tourets had come up in our correspondence. I told him of my two visits to them, during the first of which they seemed to me much on the defensive, at the second (after receiving a visit from Buckmaster and a medal) much happier but less communicative. He replied (in English):

> ... Your letter delights me very much. Mme Touret did not know anything about me during the war. The quiproquo [sic] started after the war... we met... She asked me about Gilbert. I told her I was Gilbert. She reacted very curiously. She was afraid (of what?)... why Buck came there, closed her mouth with a medal (surely very late)...
>
> Between Mme Touret and me there is a quiproquo — in that time I told her that I knew her questioning by the Germans ... so that placed me Av Foch with the Germans... She believes I was on German side (she believe I told her myself)...

Plants — no plants from here grow only in damp wet heat — you can't grow them in England. I'll bring you something else...

We lost a plane yesterday — I hope that will not affect my departure! That makes five planes in two months.

He was careful to explain that it was in the Cinquième Bureau, with which he was working after the war, that he had seen the interrogation of Mme Touret at the Avenue Foch. This I discarded as I was sure I was meant to discard it. He gave me kernels of truth within shells of fiction that I was meant to throw away. It was, I believed I was meant to understand, really the Germans who had told him what questions they had asked Mme Touret, and her replies.

On 30 June I received a telephone call from Mme Guépin to say she was in England, at the Special Forces Club. Would I join her there for a drink that evening? When I arrived, she introduced to me Baron de Vomécourt. They were over here for the annual dinner, being this year's two guests invited from France at the club's expense. My reactions to Philippe de Vomécourt may have been jaundiced by what I had heard of him, first from Turck, then from Déricourt, but he struck me as assertive, fussy and waspish. He was President of the Libre Resistance, the *amicale* of the Buckmaster Section in France. Elizabeth Nicholas, who was writing on SOE girls, had been in touch with him; he expressed vexation she had not shown him what she was writing. I did not give away that I had met either Turck or Déricourt, still less that I was writing a book on the latter, and was as wary in my conversation as though I were in the face of the enemy. On getting home, I telephoned Elizabeth to warn her, and she said she had not mentioned the name of de Vomécourt in her book. I sent Déricourt an account of the encounter.

Apart from a picture postcard from him postmarked Hong Kong, I received nothing for nearly a month. I continued to write to him at Air Laos: page-proofs had come, the proof of the jacket. This sported the Croix de Lorraine, which was the emblem not of the Buckmaster but the de Gaulle (RF) Section. I asked the publishers if they could remove it, but they said it was too late to change the design. To Déricourt I explained how many people were involved in the production, and that it was difficult to keep control of every aspect of it. In the event of a film, where control would be even more difficult to maintain, I suggested he should figure on the contract as co-author, share the proceeds with me 50/50 and sign his name after mine to make any agreement complete. That would strengthen both our hands in preventing distortion. At last I heard from him again, in English, on the headed paper of

> Golden Gate Hotel,
> Kowloon, Hong Kong
> 4 August 58

Dear Jean,

Just receiving a lot of letters from Vientiane I find yours... still on leave — I have been in Macao — and around — I expect to stay 15 days here — the weather is lovely — beach — swimming — gamble ... I expect not to go to France but in Middle East. I met someone here who told me S. Sophia is biggest monument of pure beauty... send letters to my previous address...

I quite understand what happens to you (and me)... To put the de Gaulle Cross on the jacket is a pity! By chance my name is not printed!... you make the game more difficult. Buck will laugh.

I strictly forbid you to print a word in French without my permission from the string and the wrapping paper around the book to the signature. Tell that to Adam and the possible editor [of any French edition] and — no question of any film, even in G.B. — in case of any — no rights without my permission — not because I will ask for any money — no, because I probably have more than you — but because I don't want any mistake in your name about me.

But then, in a letter from Hong Kong dated 19 August 1958:

... But there is a good thing — you are going to have your book — That's the best — I don't know if I'll be in France — but I'll be happy for you.

Considering how hard on him it was, and the trouble for him it was likely to cause, I found that generous beyond belief. For himself, he added: 'I did what I did — a lot of good with some spots.'

I received from him, on 5 September, a thin, oblong package. With a box was a tightly folded letter in which he reproached me for having tried to raise a kind of new trial. But it ended (in English):

You should read La Fontaine fable about the story of the bear — Strictly in good friendship I should spank you. Thanks for birthday — 49 — I send you a gift — Cambodian dancers — in prove of non-aggression mind.

HENRY

Within the box was a beautiful bracelet in silver, with white enamel plates on which were the dancers. I wore it incessantly.

I received my author's copies on 9 September, inscribed the first of them to Déricourt and posted it care of Air Laos by air mail. He replied from Hong Kong (in English):

Dear Jean,

I read your book already twice — he begins to be covered with remarks. It seems to me to be good — although it is not Gilbert opinion — Much better than *Madeleine* and *Starr*. Next one will be your very success.... You could have shown your being perplexed with the blackmailing traitor or silent hero — or skillfull double agent or even triple agent....

You will receive a lot of letters about me — promise me to send me a copy (full copy) of *all* of them, even the worst — I promise you not to start any prosecution on their account and to keep them secret.

Enclosed was a letter to André Simon (I translate from his French, which employs the familiar 'tu'):

My dear André,

I have just finished reading Miss J. O. F.'s *Double Webs...* I am disagreeably surprised by the opinion of me you expressed to her ... I know well the words transcribed by her represent those you used... 'Rascal — money' and so on...1 think you must have been in one of your days of euphoria and joyous pleasantry. I do not intend to take you to court. I want to say it to you, that's all.

... I permit myself to recall to you that on the eve of my departure at Easter 1943 I confided to you £70 sterling and asked you to put the notes in my kit-bag or credit the sum to my account... This you omitted to do. I reminded you, and one day leaving the office near Oxford Street you gave me back £30...You still owe me £40. It was my personal money, not money of the service... To justify the opinion of me which you expressed to Miss J. O. F. that I 'served SOE for money', I will ask you to give it back.

It has been hard to swallow. However, I hope your repugnance does not extend to refusing my handshake, which I offer you,

In a P.S. to his letter to me, he said:

> I have an awful idea about the money A. Simon kept back
> from me. Did he know I was to be 'rubbed of'? So that I
> never should have asked him for the £70?

I sent the letter on to Simon, but there was no reply.

Publication was to be on Monday, 6 October, and I wrote to
Déricourt to say there would be a little celebration party at my
flat on the evening of the 5th. We should probably drink to the
book:

> ... After this is all over, it would be nice if we could talk about
> quite different things. Tell me some time about your family
> and early years. But only if you would like to, not if you do
> not wish. And tell me when and how you became a Christian
> Scientist. There are some things happier than espionage.

My letter crossed with one from him from Bangkok (in
French):

> Still at a loose end. I fled the typhoon sweeping Hongkong.
> The water is cold. One can no longer bathe. I long to speak
> French — and to drink red wine.
>
> Your accursed book is never out of my hand. I am at the
> 3rd reading. I find it each time better, which is annoying. I
> have filled two note-books with criticisms. Prepare to be
> stunned. Buy yourself a rugby-helmet.
>
> So, suddenly my book is out... Ah! I would like to make a
> few retouches for the French edition — very few, changing
> the sense not at all and the lines very little. Do not forget to
> tell me how the sales go.

He enclosed a letter for Christmann, and said letters to Bodington, and perhaps 'Carte', the Abbé and Yeo-Thomas would follow ('I will send them *all* through you, so that you will not be ignorant of my way of thinking … ').

That to Christmann read (I translate from the French):

22.9.58

Mr Christmann,

I have read Miss J. O. F's book *Double Webs* and find in it numerous details about myself of which you are the source. I will say straight away that I do not intend to take you to court. I do not know whether the comparison Miss Fuller makes between us is valid but I entertain towards you neither resentment nor friendship.

I found in you an adroit adversary and I am very proud of having detected and countered you within minutes of your appearance in my neighbourhood, in May 1943. There are witnesses living who can certify some small inexactitudes in your account, to wit:

— omission of any mention of the restaurant from which you obtained the address of Gilbert 'Archambaud', which you did not know, and of your having obtained the address of the restaurant from a certain Hélène, whom you know very well...

— the fact that Kieffer forbade you even to think about 'Gilbert' but that you spoke all the same to the Abwehr in Paris (perhaps to von Feldmann).

— the fact that you did not know for certain which Gilbert Kieffer was talking about.

What is more grave is your claim to have seen me at the Avenue Foch … I was never there in my life...

Still worse, you say that to clear 'Archambaud', whom you charged by error, you played a role before the Judge Trossin... but you did not play a role... You do not have to charge 'Archambaud' in order to cover me. It is unnecessary. You really had never seen me before, but only heard of me, and in saying that you were spontaneous and natural...

And then, when you speak of the present I must have given you [*je vous aurais fait*], if that can impress a journalist, or even Miss Fuller... for me as I *know*, that lamentably diminishes you. How can a man of your experience dare to speak in a police matter (I employ the word as more technically precise than an espionage matter) of a thing that cannot be verified?

I tell you all that without hatred, though with a little bitterness. I am disappointed that a man of your class should have fallen into inexactitudes... During the war I did what I thought I had to do and am very proud of it — we were not on the same side of the barricade and mine was more dangerous than yours. Today I do not think there is a barricade any more, at any rate one should try for there being none, that is why I permit myself to express to you some reproaches, as to a friend ... I reproach you just a little for having talked so much to Miss Fuller without my permission. You could have found me... through my lawyer...

If nevertheless you will accept this letter as an absolutely peaceful attempt to straighten things out... perhaps you will answer these questions:

1) What password did you have to give to 'Gilbert' and what was the reply? Weigh each word of your reply: each omission, each uncertainty, each thing forgotten can have a value, a significance.

2) Did the message from London really mention 'Marcel' in addition to 'Gilbert'? Or is that a later addition? Memory can mix what one knew on the 28 and 29.

I know what it is to suffer anxiety, menaces, soreness of heart [*écoeurement*], and so pardon you and hope to hear from you,

H. Déricourt

It was, I thought, a letter not lacking in dignity, indeed surprisingly nice — though oddly worded about the present. He had omitted to say he did not send one. Each omission...

I sent it on, a copy of the book also.

The unexpected letter to 'Carte' was also enclosed. 'Carte' (André Girard) was in 1942 the big chief of the French Resistance, then centred on Cannes. It splintered when Frager broke away from under his direction, taking with him Roger Bardet, Peter Churchill and Odette — all destined to entanglement with Bleicher. Girard was fetched to London on 20 October 1942 and prevented from returning. He had got on the wrong side of de Gaulle, but also conceived a revulsion against the direction of SOE in London, which, in his letters to me from New York, he expressed in terms of unpublishable violence. All this was before Déricourt joined SOE and I did not think he could have met him, but Déricourt wrote (I translate from his French):

25.9.58

Dear Monsieur Girard,

I have until now put off a decision to write to you, but Miss J. O. F. in her book in which she sets out my faults and doings mentions your name and permits me to write to you.

... I know certain things concerning you, but have avoided forming an opinion. I knew your adversaries very well — if that interests you I will speak of it to you.

I had totally forgotten the war. Miss J. O. F. came to reawaken my memories and revivify my curiosity. For me, all that now seems so far away that I feel as though I am bringing back to life persons totally strange to me.

Excuse this intervention....

Yours sincerely,
H. Déricourt

Now, which adversaries did he mean? Probably just Frager and Bardet.

From Déricourt I received a further letter about Christmann and the Square Clignancourt affair, from Hong Kong (in English):

... About the message from 'London' giving to 'Arnaud' and 'Anton' [Christmann and Bodens] rendezvous in Bussoz' flat with Gilbert and Marcel, *I don't give up* — that telegramme was not been sent by Morel. Although Morel and me are not friends I knew him enough to say that he did not make that mistake — and as he was in charge of 'Archambaud' and me at that time with operations every day for both — he could not have made that mistake — no — there is something else.

Could it be possible to Huntermann to have been double-crossed by Christmann? Christmann as Bleicher says he was willing to go to G.B. — For Bleicher we know that it was not sincere and that his chiefs were informed (Schaeffer, von Feldmann) but for Christmann? We have the tendency to think it was the same thing for him — but if it was not? Suppose Christmann introduce a fake message in the radio circuit between the coding of CW department and Huntermann — to send Arnaud and Anton — if Arnaud was really trying to go to London that could be an explanation — and more, as Christmann heard of 'Archambaud' (and Marcel??) through Hélène on the name of Gilbert — and probably heard, too, some arrested agent speak of 'Gilbert' (Air Mov. Off) he wrote himself the telegramme and introduced it in the Funkabwehr circuit, mixed involuntarily the two Gilberts. He could have done that with the idea to go to London... Then he came to the Capucines with the idea to meet me — to go to London — he was disappointed — then he was arrested by the SD — and he had to deal with a cascade of lies and the fear to be discovered — and he was angry about the Gilbert who — in his opinion — had given

215

the SD the Capucines appointment — (in his mind it was me).

That argument would suppose it was Christmann and not Bodens who had been arrested at the Capucines — though even the arrest of Bodens could have knocked the plan back — but it was the last part that interested me.

> I sent you a letter from Bangkok not so kind... But how could you have written and think that the answer from the Foreign Office could be 'amusing'... for me it could be not — please don't kill me...
>
> Deepest hearty sympathy, Miss Catastrophe,
HENRY

By now the review copies had gone out, and on 1 October I received a visit from Richard Findlater, of the *Sunday Dispatch*, with their photographer. I wore Déricourt's bracelet. (I did not tell them.)

'What was 'Gilbert' *like*?' asked Findlater. 'I can't place him. I've been trying to say to myself "He's like so-and-so", but I can't.'

'You probably don't know anyone who is like him. He isn't a type.'

'What class does he come from?'

'You couldn't have asked me a question I find more difficult to answer. I have often wondered. Not being English, there isn't a class accent, just a French accent.' The French, in any case, go less by accent than manner and deportment. A Frenchman, Adam, took him first for *petit artisanat*, and was really startled when he made a reference to an archaeological work on Arabia, not a popular one, but one which Adam had attempted to read and found required a good deal of knowledge on the part of the reader. He could criticise T. E.

Lawrence — *Seven Pillars*, was bored and disappointed by *The Mint*. Enjoyed Graham Greene. His English, I thought, was picked up by ear, not learned at school. His French, in so far as I could judge it, was faultless. He would never confuse the parts of speech — 'Hors' and 'Or', as one sees it in the letters of less educated French people. Had even a pedant's stickling for syntax, and had done part of the training to be a schoolmaster. Yet I thought, as regards higher education, self-educated. Manner without ostentation, therefore good. With waiters and people like that, very good. Asks for what he wants simply and quietly. Relaxed. Never embarrassed in any situation. To a greater extent than with most people, however, the social silhouette that he cut altered with what he was wearing. In a quiet, good suit, he was of the upper classes, in workman's clothes, a workman.

'I don't want "Gilbert" pilloried,' I said. In a sense, he had never been the subject of my inquiry. When I began it, it was not so much because it seemed important to know whether or not he was a traitor — all the occupied countries were full of traitors — as why, supposing that he was one, he had been covered up for. I did not want Bodington pilloried either. I wanted to know where responsibility lay. All my real questions I had been made to cut out from my book, as the condition of getting it published. My concern was less with SOE's past than with its present, for despite its dissolution, by Attlee as soon as he took office, it survived as an old-boy network, with its many members in many influential places. It was Spooner who had first drawn my attention to its representation in big business, and when I had remarked to Yeo-Thomas on the number of people who had started to come forward, in a spontaneous manner, then drawn in their horns like stunned snails, his rejoinder was that a newspaper could be threatened with the loss of full-page advertisements. That made me appreciate that although my own financial means were very small, they were not such as anybody could cut off. That made me independent in a way that people in positions were not. Secret organisations were easier to create than get rid of. I was not sure Churchill's baby had been a good idea.

As Findlater left, I said, 'No "Gilbert" in the headline.' The headline, on the front page of the *Sunday Dispatch* of 5 October was: MISS FULLER RAISES CLOAK AND DAGGER STORM.

9: REVERBERATIONS

My party that evening was small: my mother, Irene, Elizabeth Nicholas, Whitehead, and a friend unconnected with these operations, Dr Patricia Thomson, the Wyatt scholar. We were un-corking the champagne when the telephone rang. It was Yeo-Thomas, from Paris, to wish the book good luck.

It would be Elizabeth's turn in ten days. We had not read each other's books until we exchanged signed copies. Hers to me was dedicated, 'To Jean, a comrade in arms!...' *Death Be Not Proud* (Cresset, 1958) was, like my book, the record of an inquiry, but concerning certain of the women. Elizabeth had unearthed the fact that Diana Rowden ('Paulette') and John Young ('Gabriel') had carried on for over four months after the arrest of John Starr, but were betrayed by A. Maugenet ('Benoit'), a Canadian sent out to them but arrested before establishment of contact. The French Government had after the war asked Canada for his extradition but he had gone to South America.

Later that month I received a sixteen-page letter from Déricourt, going back yet once more over the Christmann affair:

Saigon,
10.10.58

... Christmann went alone to the restaurant ... at the Royal Capucine; who was arrested, Bodens or Christmann? For me it is Christmann.... Giskes don't even suspect he could have been double crossed by Christmann. But why Christmann did that?...

219

He went on to speak with bitterness of what seemed to him the levity with which London sent out unsuitable people and sent them to their deaths: 'We were in a mad house... madhouse, slaughterhouse...' He would not judge 'Prosper', 'Archambaud' or any: 'They did what they did — like me — What would *you* have done in the same place?'

I asked myself. I had spent the whole of the war in London. All I had seen of the Germans was the array of their missiles — bombs, oil-bombs, land-mines, V1s, V2s. One just ducked when something was coming. There was nothing to test one's morality.

He enclosed a letter for Bodington (in French, employing the familiar

Hong Kong
15.10.58

Mon bien cher Nic,

It is so long since I have had news of you, and I should so like to have it — I do not even know an address at which to write to you. I hope you are not angry with me

I have been obliged to return to the Far East. The modest little life I had made for myself has been completely overturned...

With my best friendship,
HENRI

It was a touching letter, yet the last paragraph upset me. Was it I who had sent him into exile? I wrote asking if it was by me and my book his life had been overturned.

I could not send the letter on as I had not Bodington's address. But indeed I would have felt some reluctance to be the instrument of bringing together again two whose partnership I felt had been ill-starred. I would not keep harmless friends apart, yet still did not know how far I trusted Bodington.

On the 23rd I was Irene's guest to dinner and a theatre, and she said she would like to give a party for Elizabeth and me — after tabling her motion — and invite the press to meet the authors of the two books. Before tabling the motion, she was writing a personal letter to Selwyn Lloyd, asking whether 'Gilbert' was just a German agent or a Foreign Office agent in SOE.

On the 30th she telephoned to tell me Selwyn Lloyd had asked her to delay tabling her motion touching these questions until he had had time to read the two books. She would therefore put it off till 12 November.

It was on the morning of 12 November I received, by registered post, the only frantic letter I ever had from Déricourt (in French):

6.11.58

Dear Jean,

... I ask you, I pray you, I supplicate you, if you wish me any good, not to bring the Foreign Office into it... That could damage me so much in my present job that I could be obliged to resign. I do not suppose that is what you want...

I wrote to Nic that you had overturned my quiet little life. Yes, I meant you...

There is a story of La Fontaine called *The Two Friends* about a bear that made friends with a man. One day the man, asleep beneath a tree, was troubled by a fly walking over his face. The bear, to crush the fly, picked up an enormous stone and brought it down, killing his friend. Please, dear bear, do not use your stone...

I am too young to die!

With my friendship,
HENRY

P S. Your *official* opinion of me is still, 'I do not know — I still do not know — G. is an eel — G. is strongly protected — There is a skeleton in the cupboard.' Thank you.

I was afraid Irene's motion would already have been handed in, but took a taxi to the House of Commons, and was lucky to encounter Irene in St Stephen's Hall. We sat down on a cold slab of stone. The motion, she said, had been delayed, because first John Profumo, yesterday evening, then Selwyn Lloyd, this morning, had asked her to take out the reference to the Foreign Office. 'I have been standing firm,' she said. I opened out Déricourt's blotted letter, and she read it with me. It was obviously worse for him to be designated a Foreign Office agent than a German one. The fable from La Fontaine reached her heart. 'I'll do for him what I wouldn't do for them. I have compassion for this one,' she said.

She recovered the text from the Parliamentary Clerk and, still sitting on the slab, she re-drafted it so as to leave only the suggestion he had been a German agent. She thought his fear was the French Government would be upset by the suggestion he was an agent of the Foreign Office. I thought that, too, but I also thought, privately, he was afraid of his bluff being called if in fact he was not — for it was his great legend in France.

Irene suggested his anxiety came in part from ignorance of parliamentary procedure. What she had drafted was not a question and there would not be an answer. On Intelligence matters neither questions nor debates were permitted. This was a motion, which would not be called. He probably imagined a lot of people who did not know anything about it getting up and speaking. I should assure him there would be no debate. This motion was a purely silent gesture. It would simply lie upon the Order Table until she picked it up, which she would do when she had received some kind of satisfaction, in the form of a letter from the Prime Minister or Foreign Secretary. It would, however, be seen by the parliamentary representatives of the press and something might appear in the papers.

I went out and sent a very long telegram to Bangkok, followed by a letter, to explain this to him.

The motion, tabled on 13 November 1958, read:

> That this house is of the opinion that the recent publication of *Double Webs* by Jean Overton Fuller (Putnam) and *Death Be Not Proud*, by Elizabeth Nicholas (Cresset Press) demands an investigation into the effectiveness of the Special Operations Executive and the operation of the Official Secrets Act;
>
> that the success stories of Special Operations Executive written by Colonel Buckmaster, Head of the French Section, and others, have led the public to believe that an amateur organisation, bravely manned and devotedly served by both British and French agents, was a match for the German Intelligence Services;
>
> that had the Official Secrets Act been adequately enforced by authority and proper care taken to protect in Britain and France the reputation of those who became the unwilling victims of Nazi German success, much painful recrimination would have been avoided, but that under the circumstances the question of whether the Air Movements Officer of the Special Operations Executive and central figure of the book *Double Webs* was a German agent working in a British organisation must be cleared up;
>
> that although the disclosure of German penetration of the Dutch Section of Special Operations Executive was the subject of an International Enquiry, the fact that this penetration extended to a vitally important area in France, causing the arrest of many men and women, has been deliberately concealed, has led to disclosures damaging to our security and to our relationship with those close friends in

France in the years of danger going unchallenged and without official comment;

    this House, therefore, urges Her Majesty's Government to publish a book giving an authoritative account of the successes and failures of the Special Operations Executive.

Within minutes of this becoming public, at 2.0 p.m., the first newspaperman was on the telephone to me, at my flat, asking for the real name of the Air Movements Officer. Pressure to reveal it kept up for hour after hour. My saying I had given my word of honour not to reveal it made not the slightest impression. They went over to Irene, and to Elizabeth, and, failing to get it from either of them, to Yeo-Thomas in Paris, and Mr Norman. Thank God both of them held fast. I think there must have been every newspaper in London on the line. Two of the biggest dailies were racing each other. 'What can it possibly matter?' I said to one. 'Of course it matters!' he gasped. I realised that none of the reporters ringing up had read the book, so they did not understand anything. It was difficult to explain over the telephone that what was important was not the Air Movements Officer in himself but why he had been covered up for. I did not want to throw Bodington's name to the wolves... 'You should read the book,' I said to one. 'No time,' he said. They had, however, obtained a number of copies and distributed them among the staff, each one being detailed to start reading it at a different chapter and make a summary of what was in it, which summaries, when put together, should give some idea. Of course the newsmen had no contact with the papers' book-reviewers. I was becoming really desperate, for if his name appeared in a newspaper, I would feel I had betrayed Déricourt.

Just before midnight I rang the office of one of the biggest dailies, managed to speak to the Editor, and told him the Air

Movements Officer had authorised my treatment of his case in my book on condition of not being named. If his name appeared in a newspaper, he could still sue the newspaper for libel. He said, 'If it's brought in, you can rely on me to stop it.' After that, I slept.

In the morning the name was in none of the papers. Accounts were pretty garbled, but that did not matter. I thought that was the end of it, but then the telephone calls started again. They were still trying to get the name. One did. Summoning all my strength, somehow I managed to talk him out of using it, chiefly by refusing to confirm it was the right one.

The reviewers, like the reporters, were somewhat at sea, but there were intelligent reviews in the *Daily Telegraph* and *Tribune* (Rivers Scott and Richard Cléments). I sent Déricourt a complete set of the press cuttings.

Irene brought me a letter she had received from the Prime Minister thanking her for a copy of my book — 'I look forward to reading it.' This she gave me, to keep. Shortly afterwards she allowed me to see a letter he had written after reading it. In this, he said, 'I share your concern.' He was considering seriously the suggestion she had made, that the government should publish a history.

Irene invited the press to meet the authors of the two books at the House of Commons, Room C, on 19 November. I assumed the men from the Press who thronged the room would have read the books, so used the occasion to complement mine with some additional points, and to read them a letter I had just received from Ernest Vogt, which had made me very happy:

I have now read your book in its entirety. After reading all the statements you have published I am no longer so sure of the

225

guilt of 'Gilbert'... it was only a supposition of my own that... the arrest of 'Prosper' and his colleagues must have been a consequence of the photostatted reports which Kieffer gave me.

Having read your book and the statements by Christmann, Huntermann and the others, I realise that Kieffer... and also the agents of the Abwehr already had relation with certain members of the 'Prosper' group ... I have now to suppose that the arrest of 'Prosper', 'Archambaud' and their colleagues was above all things the consequence of the intervention of Christmann, Anton etc. of the Abwehr ... I begin to think that 'Gilbert' rendered greater service to London than he did harm. He was able to carry on with the reception and despatch of British aircraft while giving the Germans only what he thought good to give them, avoiding doing the greatest damage possible.

Yours sincerely,
ERNEST

I sent copies of Ernest's letter to Déricourt, Mercier, Yeo-Thomas, the Abbé and Adam. Adam wrote back that it spoilt the interest of the book. This reaction shocked me. Déricourt's next letter, however, put it into perspective:

> In France people like the worst traitor... with blood and sadism... not chess play... In G.B. people prefer intricate stories like Agatha Christie's.

At his trial, he said, the reporter on *Franc-Tireur* had walked out saying, 'It is no longer interesting', when it became obvious there was going to be an acquittal. He thought my book, with the twist, whereby 'the villain turns out to be — may be — a good villain' might be better understood in England.

Everything was slewed in an unexpected direction when, on 21

November, the *Sunday Dispatch* carried on its front page a challenge by six French *Résistants* to Peter and Odette Churchill to prove 'one single effective act of sabotage' performed by either of them during the period they spent in Cannes in 1942. This did not take me entirely by surprise, as when I had called on the Baron de Malval in 1956 he told me he had lodged all the men sent to the Riviera coast at that period, including Peter Churchill, in his Villa Isabelle at Cannes, and — having no woman in his house to look after them — arranged with his friend, Marie-Lou Blanc, 'Suzanne', who ran a beauty parlour, to have stay with her all the women, including Odette, at her home nearby. He was vexed to exasperation by the way in which the media concentrated publicity on just 'those two', giving to the public the idea they must have been the most brilliant and important, whereas they were just agents among so many, and the greater achievements of others were unsung. He had attempted to mount a protest when the film *Odette* was shown in France, but had been silenced on the ground that what he said could offend the British. Now he had rung me up from Paris, so early in the morning that the bell woke me from my sleep, to read me a text he had composed and delivered to the *Sunday Dispatch*. He could retrieve it if I thought it would distract attention from my own book. I thought it probably would, but that as the newspaper already had it, it would be a mistake to stop it.

So there it was. Only the names of Basin and de Malval were printed, which left me, like everyone else, guessing as to the identities of the other four signatories. What staggered me was Odette's answer to the Press, in which she launched the speculation that one of the signatories whose name had not been printed was the man referred to by Dame Irene Ward in the House of Commons as a traitor. She claimed to know him very well, and to know that he must have instigated de Malval and the others in order to divert attention from himself. I knew it was impossible, as they did not serve in the same place at the same time. From Déricourt I received a letter saying he did not know de Malval and did not know Odette, and could not think why she claimed acquaintance with him. It was Elizabeth who guessed at the explanation: 'She hasn't read your book and thinks Irene's motion referred to Roger Bardet, whom of course she did know.' I implored de Malval, for Déricourt's sake, mine and his own, to publish the complete list of the signatories. He did, in an article published in the French L'Expres, though not until February. By then, Girard ('Carte'), having seen the Dispatch piece quoted in an American paper, had written from New York to de Malval, asking for his name to be added to the signatories, and, as he had been the big chief, Basin and de Malval had placed his name before theirs. Others, also, had asked to be added, and the list now swelled to fifteen. One could say it was the Cannes Resistance.

In the meantime, I felt as though I were living through weeks of Bedlam, all the papers, French and British, publishing their conflicting misunderstandings of what was going on. In a French paper Irene Ward, a Conservative from birth, was referred to as an MP 'of the extreme Left'. Elizabeth and I were not helped by mistranslations of our titles. *Death Be Not Proud* was everywhere rendered *Mort sans Fierté, Death Without Pride*. For the benefit of readers whose acquaintance with English does not extend to Donne's verse, it is the Angel of Death who is admonished by the poet not to be proud, because there are some whose glory can never die. *Double Webs* was rendered *Reseaux Doubles, Double Networks*.

I had no idea Buckmaster was going to appear on television, so was out on the evening of 1 December 1958. As soon as I came in, my mother was on the telephone to tell me Buckmaster had been questioned by John Freeman on 'Panorama' about my book. I wrote to the BBC, asking if I might have a transcript of the interview, and was sent one. I read:

> *Freeman*:.... the widespread allegation against 'Gilbert'... is that he was either a traitor or a double agent... he was honourably acquitted and I don't want to call that verdict into question... Major X [Bodington] said that when he went to France in July 1943 he was met by 'Gilbert', who then told him he was doing some work for the Germans, and Major X told 'Gilbert' that he should continue his work with the Germans. That... does seem to establish 'Gilbert' as an authorised double agent... When Major X returned to London in August 1943, did he tell you what he'd found out about 'Gilbert' and what he'd told 'Gilbert'?
> *Buckmaster*: Yes, he told me Gilbert had contacts with the Germans, that was regarded as possibly a useful thing.
> *Freeman*: Did you know... that before the war Gilbert had been on terms of personal friendship with a man called Karl Boemelburg?
> *Buckmaster*: I didn't know that, no.

Asked if he had authorised Major X to give evidence at 'Gilbert's' trial, or known he was going to do it, he said no.

I was very much surprised, but pleased, Buckmaster claimed to have known Déricourt was in contact with the Germans yet let him carry on, and sent Déricourt a photostat of the transcript.

The Prime Minister had fixed 4 December as the date for Irene to be received at the Foreign Office by Lord Lansdowne. I waited by the telephone, and she rang me as soon as she came out.

She had been received not only by Lord Lansdowne — Joint Parliamentary Under-Secretary to the Foreign Office — but Robin Hooper, 'head of the permanent Foreign Office staff', or head of the Permanent Undersecretary's Department — PUS. It is often said that this is the formal title of the head of the Foreign Office Secret Service, Secret Intelligence Service or MI6 — which by whatever name it is called everyone knows 'does not exist'. That does not mean he directs it, but the person who does direct it is under him and ultimately responsible to him. Now there was a most extraordinary coincidence. Robin Hooper had served in the Foreign Office before the war, but during the war in the RAF. He had been a pilot in 161 Squadron, which was Déricourt's squadron. He had known Déricourt. But he swore to her that never, by word or by wink, had he suggested to Déricourt he should work for the Foreign Office. They were both under the command of Hugh Verity, and knew each other as one airman knows another. Déricourt was a good pilot and a perfectly agreeable colleague with whom to work, generally liked at Tempsford and Tangmere. Hooper, after the war, went back to the Foreign Office, and had no further occasion to think of Déricourt until she tabled her motion about the Air Movements Officer and he read *Double Webs* — a copy of which was open on the desk, with numerous pages flagged and passages marked. Since studying this, he had got out the old Foreign Office pay-lists and searched through them year by year, but did not find the name of Déricourt. He had never been on a Foreign Office pay-list, before, during or after the war. He appeared, therefore, to have had no clandestine duties, other than his known duty for SOE (not under the Foreign Office) as Air Movements Officer, and his more mysterious sayings to me, inasmuch as they might seem intended to imply he worked for the Foreign Office, were, Hooper was sure, fictitious.

Lord Lansdowne, however, said it did result from his inquiries that before being sent on his mission for SOE Déricourt had declared contacts with German Intelligence. This, indeed, might have suggested his greater suitability to be employed as a double agent, which was perhaps his idea when he declared it, but this possibility did not appear to have been exploited. He had, apparently, been sent over as a straight agent only, and it was the belief of both of them that if he had, during the period of his mission, renewed his contacts with German Intelligence, it had been on his own initiative and his own responsibility.

Irene was struck that they spoke of this, and of him, with no ill will. 'We don't bear him any rancour.' They had no intention of trying to punish or in any way harm him, and did not mind if I told him that. They would just appreciate it if he would stop pretending to have worked for them, the Foreign Office. They spoke of him — with perfect good humour — as 'an international personage'.

The answer to all the questions Irene had asked Selwyn Lloyd in her letter to him which had been passed to them was 'No'. No, the Foreign Office had not paid Déricourt's fine and legal costs at Croydon. No, the Foreign Office did not suggest to Déricourt the lines of his defence, when charged by the French, or send or authorise Bodington to give evidence for him. And no, the Foreign Office did not authorise Buckmaster to appear in the BBC TV programme, 'Panorama'. It had not been submitted for their approval, neither of them had chanced to be watching television and they did not know what had been said. It was emphasised that Buckmaster, Bodington and Miss Atkins had, since their demobilisation, returned to ordinary civilian life, and anything and everything they did was on their own responsibilities as private persons.

I was really very relieved. I had felt sure Déricourt's bluff was going to be called, and was surprised they had been so nice about it. Indeed, their being so nice left the impression they did not regard him as a traitor, in the worst sense. I felt it lent colour to his own assertion that he had by his double dealing done for the British more good than harm.

Irene had not been asked to keep secret anything they said, and I wrote to Déricourt immediately, giving him both the good and the bad news: that they said he was not one of theirs but substantiated his claim to have declared his contacts with German Intelligence (though it seemed to me strange he had apparently not been asked in what these consisted). This letter crossed with one from him (in English):

4.12.58

... Don't take my part — not too much — it could bring suspicion on you...

There is some trouble between Thailand and Cambodia and Vietnam Sud which has interest in it... Ambassadors taken back — fighters patrolling over enemy territories — and prisoners — 32 for the moment, nobody killed yet — so probably nobody will be killed — no war yet — but it is in the air and I have to stay — The big point is that Cambodia has now a port — an harbour — which is really a good one — instead of Bangkok is muddy on the river Menan and Saigon is still the same further on inside the land — so Cambodia — pro-Communist — threaten both Thai and Vietnam Sud trade Any way. I'll be back for Christmas. I'll let you know.

From Dorset came a letter about my book from an old colleague of Yeo-Thomas called Thackthwaite:

Déricourt was getting out of France the highest and most influential Frenchmen through the Buckmaster organisation... reading the courier might have been of small importance. Much of it was confirmation of cables. If Déricourt could make a selection, little harm could have been done. I think no one could foresee the complete demoralisation that could be caused by showing the courier to the agents and the subsequent use the Germans would make of them... The later catastrophies were due entirely to the incompetence and negligence of H Q in London.

From Brazil came a letter from L. A. Latimer, formerly of SOE Belgian Section, expressing his gratitude to 'Gilbert' and his assistant 'Marc' for boarding him and two of his colleagues on an aircraft that took off from near Angers on 21 July 1943 for England.

In December I received a series of letters from Mme Balachowsky. She now disclosed that after her husband's arrest, she had met Hélène Leduc, Placke's mistress, and later Placke himself. They wanted her, if neither of them survived the war, to look after a child. In reciprocity, he smuggled to her husband in Buchenwald books from which he was able to learn to give anti-typhus injections, and so to get transferred to the block working on anti-typhus vaccine. Placke told her he was in radio communication with London, and she sent a warning of the radio-game to London on 5 August 1943 by a Madame Monier-Vinard, who arranged the return of shot-down airmen by boat. She was told of the attempted escape of 'Madeleine', Starr and Faye three days after it had taken place, and notified London by the same lady, and through Switzerland and through Vichy. She could not conceive this information — particularly that 'Madeleine' was in German hands — did not reach Buckmaster.

She referred to Déricourt as 'the only lucid person in this affair'.

> You have pursued in your book an aim of innocenting 'Archambaud' and accusing 'Gilbert'... One has not the right to accuse a man who has certainly obeyed an order. You should now try to find out by whom 'Gilbert' was directed.

This reproach was painfully ironic to me. Since Déricourt and I had become friends, I had felt on my honour not to over-represent his point of view to the detriment of Norman's son. Now it seemed I had overdone it and become unfair to a friend who meant a lot to me. All the same, I did not believe he had obeyed an order or been directed by anybody.

From Déricourt I received a card post-marked not from the Far East but from the Lebanon, with a picture of Beirut on the front.

> 18.12.1958
>
> On my way back to Paris but not straight to Paris — unfortunately.
>
> HENRY

10: WASPS' NEST

I had received on 8 December 1958, a note, typed, unsigned, on unheaded paper:

> I consider it my duty to let you know the following:
>
> The people here of LIBRE RÉSISTANCE and their AMICALE... are very upset and they intend to send a 'communiqué' to the British Embassy in Paris... asking the British Government to stop all those journalistic' quarrels about French Resistance and if necessary to provoke another MP [to table] another motion against Dame Irene Ward's motion. It seems to me ridiculous but perhaps all the better for us who only want the truth to be known... All this is very funny indeed... but I only wish Dame Irene W to be informed.
>
> I must also tell you our friend Mme LEBRAS is frightened to death... she was told by the peoples of LIBRE RÉSISTANCE to keep quiet and she does not even dare to see me now.

I thought it was from de Malval, and sure enough I received from him a letter dated 24 December, in which he referred to his of the 6th, conveying a warning — to which he now added a paragraph marked most secret, giving an outline of the attack to be mounted against Dame Irene.

In a further letter, he wrote: 'LIBRE RÉSISTANCE: DE VOMÉCOURTS... I hate them.' Apparently they had tried to induce him to add his signature to the ill-intentioned document, which was how he knew about it.

Naturally, I showed the warnings to Irene, who mentioned to John Profumo, as Secretary of State for the Foreign Office, that if anything of the sort was received she would like to see it. But time went on, and all that arrived — through my publisher — was a series of letters from the London solicitors of the de Vomécourts. They wanted me to write a letter undertaking to remove from page 194 of my book the phrase, 'Noble I where "La Chatte" was', which they could exhibit in a German court of law where Pierre de Vomécourt was suing Graf Soltikow for libel. If I refused to do this and he lost his case, they would have to hold me responsible for his costs. The words that worried them came in an utterance from Déricourt. I ought to have asked him to clarify 'Noble I', and did so now. He replied:

> QBG
> 14.1.59
>
> Philippe de Vomécourt is a lawyer, a big personality here. You have to be careful. His brother did a lot of mischief here about but he recover with the weight of his brother. It is impossible to say anything about him.

There followed a very long explanation of his idea that in the mind of SOE "Noble" was to take command of the [Interallié] network in 1941. It was fortunate that Thomas Cadett, a major figure in the London office in those days, rang me from Paris. He told me Noble was Georges Bégué, the first agent dropped, one of a large group of agents arrested one after another in a house in Marseilles in October 1941. Déricourt's idea that he was meant to take over the Interallié was therefore incorrect. Déricourt had not realised the Interallié did not work to Buckmaster but to the Intelligence Service (to Dansey, as I know today), whereas Noble was one of the French Section agents caught like mice in a trap. All the same, his letter showed knowledge of minor characters involved with that affair — Mireille Lejeune, concièrge of 'La Chatte', 'a man called Kléber, long, thin, long neck'. I remembered Déricourt's friendship with Jouffret, who had been the lover of 'La Chatte'. Jouffret could have told him about the other members of that network. I had learned from the Abbé that it was for complicity in the arrest of Pierre de Vomécourt, on the latter's return to France in April 1942, that Jouffret had been sentenced to his four years. There might lie something under that. On the other hand, Déricourt had told me it was in 1941 there had arisen the situation giving rise to the *quid pro quo* between himself and the de Vomécourts; he knew something bad they had done, but they knew something bad he had done, so both were immobilised, unable to tell on each other.

Déricourt warned me, now, that in no circumstances could he help me in a war with the de Vomécourts. I understood that. However, I was not affected by the *quid pro quo,* and the best protection, not only for myself but for him, lay in my appearing to know nothing about it, which could best be demonstrated by my being uncooperative. Therefore, although I thought, privately, that Déricourt's phrase 'Noble I where "La Chatte" was' resulted from confusion, I composed a letter to the de Vomécourts' solicitors, which my solicitor copied on to his own paper and signed, saying the phrase was not defamatory of their client and I had not to alter a phrase in my book to oblige one of the parties to a lawsuit with which I had no concern.

Next I received a letter from the Abbé Guillaume, dated 20 January 1959, that was worrying. He recalled to me that he had once suggested another person had retracted a statement under pressure. 'I never thought it would be my own case.' Unable to read English, he had been told his name was frequently cited in the 'unleashed frenzy' of the British press, and that the British Embassy was about to intervene. He was being reproached for having lent me his typescript of 'La Chatte's' memoirs, in which 'Lucas' (Pierre de Vomécourt) was mentioned. He was enclosing the draft of a formal letter to myself, complaining of the way in which his name had been used in my book and demanding the suppression of pages 95–6, where I mentioned the '*La Chatte*' typescript and briefly said what it was about. This complaint was not made by him voluntarily. It had been imposed on him. He had been told to copy it out, sign it and return it to a third person. It had been 'brought by a third person'. Across the top of the unsigned draft was written (in French):

> The Abbé must write the attached letter to Overton Fuller and return it, signed, to me As soon as I have it, I will transmit it to my solicitor in London so that he may pursue the matter with the publisher of *Double Webs*.

I supposed the 'third person', author of these lines, to be Philippe de Vomécourt.

I wrote back to the Abbé, assuring him that although my press-cutting agency had sent me seventy-five reviews and other notices of my book, in not one of them was there reference to his name, or even to an Abbé. I also told him I had read the story of 'La Chatte' in Erich Borchers's book of that title, published in Germany in 1950, and that 'Lucas' was in that called Pierre de Vomécourt.

Whilst I did not think Pierre de Vomécourt could sue me, as the Abbé seemed to fear, I was relieved to receive a further letter from the Abbé (I translate from his French):

21 January 1959

Dear Mademoiselle,
    Since yesterday I have reflected concerning your trouble with 'Lucas'.

I have not the intention of returning to him the signed copy of the letter addressed to yourself, for him to give to his English solicitors, so that they may institute a judicial action again you, which seems to be his intention...

On 26 January he sent me a copy of a letter he had sent on that date to 'the brother of Lucas', Philippe de Vomécourt, he who had brought him the unsigned draft to be copied and signed, declining to oblige. I realised this was a brave action on his part, for people in France seemed to be terrified of Philippe de Vomécourt.

Shortly after that, Irene told me, John Profumo had come up to her in the House of Commons and handed her a letter. She noticed the envelope was marked *Foreign Office Secret*, and asked, 'Ought I to read a Foreign Office secret?'

'It isn't one,' he said. 'I just put it into that to bring it over.' It had come to his desk at the Foreign Office from the British Embassy in Paris, to which it had been brought by a deputation consisting of the persons who had signed it, and it concerned her. He did not want it back. It was not of interest to the Foreign Office. He could have destroyed it, but had thought she would like to see it and perhaps show it to her two friends, whose names and books were mentioned in it. She could do what she liked with it.

She had brought it to my flat. So far as I can remember, for I did not take a copy, it called upon the British Government to suppress the books *Double Webs* by Jean Overton Fuller and *Death Be Not Proud* by Elizabeth Nicholas, to stop newspapers publishing articles showing SOE in a bad light, to put up an MP to table a motion contrary to Dame Irene Ward's motion and take some punitive action against Dame Irene Ward for 'advertising' in Parliament a book for which she had written a foreword (*Double Webs*). It was signed Philippe de Vomécourt,

239

Pierre de Vomécourt and a few others. Not de Malval. This was the paper they had endeavoured to persuade him to sign, of which he had warned us.

Irene said she would write to de Malval to thank him, and invite him to dinner at the House of Commons.

On 21 January 1959 I slept late and was woken by the telephone. It was Elizabeth, saying she had received a letter that was all about 'Gilbert'. It was from Mme Arend, the sister of 'Denise', one of the women featured in her book. Mme Arend had now written to say she had gathered from a French newspaper that my book said 'Gilbert' was a traitor. She was writing to tell Elizabeth she quite agreed. Her sister had written her letters from Fresnes, smuggled out by the wardress, Rosy Scherer. In these letters, Andree ('Denise') said, 'Gilbert sold us all... Gilbert took part in the interrogations...'

I cried out, 'That's not my Gilbert!' I remembered the depositions of the Flamencourt couple — reproduced on page 8 of the Abbé's book, *La Sologne* — that Gilbert Norman denounced them and helped the Germans interrogate Germaine Tambour.

Elizabeth stopped short, for she had started reading the letter to me before finishing reading it to herself. I went on to re-tell her a story Mme Arend had told her at their interview, and which she had put in her book. Gilbert Norman, whom her sister sometimes brought home, arrived one day in an open car with three Germans at the home of her husband's parents, with whom she and her husband were then staying, and asked for the wireless he had left there. So natural was his manner they thought the Germans must be 'tame' ones who had in some way been brought or bought over to our side, and gave them drinks and cigarettes while her father-in-law looked for the crystal. Not being able to find it, he said he would fetch his son, who would know where it was. It still had not dawned on them Gilbert Norman was under the escort of his captors, but a few days later both father and son were arrested. During the interrogation of the younger Arend at the Avenue Foch, Gilbert Norman was brought in... Then Arend realised the situation. Both father and son had returned from Buchenwald to tell the tale.

Mme Arend and her husband were not registered agents, neither was the elder Arend. They understood that Andree had become an agent for the British, but did not know her code-name 'Denise' until after the war and did not know the colleague she introduced to them as Gilbert had the code-name 'Archambaud'. They had no idea there existed another agent, whose code-name was 'Gilbert'.

Mme Guépin had spoke of 'Denise's' whisper to her when they passed each other in Fresnes, 'It was Gilbert who sold us all'. What hit me now was that she had been right in the way she understood 'Denise' at the time, to mean Gilbert Norman, wrong when after the war she revised her opinion after learning there was a 'Gilbert' whose real name was Déricourt. It was unfortunate I had gone to see Mme Guépin in company with Mr Norman.

I had done Déricourt a wrong. I was anguished yet immensely happy to have discovered it. I wrote to him about it at once, but briefly: I was hoping to see him in Paris and tell him in detail. But whatever was I going to do about Maurice Norman? In the beginning I had given him a hope that the confusion between the two Gilberts could have affected his son's reputation adversely. Now I found it to be the other way round. For Déricourt's sake I would have to put this straight. I had tried once, gently, to explain to Maurice Norman that because of the pact his son had been obliged to give away... He had stopped me, saying, 'Don't tell me my son was a traitor! I couldn't take that.' I had lacked the strength to go on. Now, finally, I wrote and told Yeo-Thomas that I was leaving it to him to tell Norman, if he thought fit.

Mme Arend had lent the letters from 'Denise' — as she thought, for copying — to a Major Hazeldine, who had called on behalf of the British Government after the war. They had never been returned. Elizabeth and I both wrote to Irene about this, and she took the matter up with the Foreign Office at once. Major Hazeldine was traced and questioned, but said he could not remember having been given any letters.

Déricourt, because of his geographical dodging about — he had, since arriving in Paris, been to North Africa and back — had received my letters about the de Vomécourts' pressure, Buckmaster's TV broadcast and the 'Denise' letters all at the same time. It was not the best moment to meet. He had found his wife seriously ill; at the root of it was a nervous depression. Naturally he was giving her most of his time, but he hastened to answer my letters, especially about the de Vomécourt intervention and the pressure on the Abbé:

24.1.59

... That story is curious — I find it very dangerous — one could say the Abbé was trying to lure you on to a terrain where you would be vulnerable to an action for defamation ... I do not believe in the 'intimidation', I would say 'complicity' and Philippe de Vomécourt is powerful on this side of the Channel — nothing on your side.

No, I did not think the Abbé was trying to lure me into anything — by the time I received this he had already found the courage to resist the de Vomécourts' pressure. Yet, as Déricourt seemed to think, were they hoping my reaction would be to write something to the Abbé, about them, which would give them cause to sue me for libel? Was I on the receiving end of an action *agent provocateur*? It sounded a bit over-convoluted, to me. However, he knew them, and since plainly he thought them sinister people, I made a mental note to be specially careful not to expose myself to an action for libel.

Referring to Buckmaster's assertion on television that Bodington told him of Déricourt's contact with German Intelligence, Déricourt wrote:

> TV thanks. t is very important for me, for it is a completely new fact — a completely new taking of position — it reveals a curious side of the question and it is really a pity I can neither say nor write it — for you would laugh till your sides split. In any case I need an authentic document … I might have to produce it officially. I count on you.
>
> The letter of 'Denise' interests me very much. I should like a copy and perhaps to see the sister — but I should like to see the letter — where 'Denise' speaks of Gilbert — first — quick a copy — please.

He said he was hoping to find a job in Paris. I was delighted, though he obviously thought it a possibility that the hubbub over my book might give a prospective employer pause. I sent him a photocopy of the BBC transcript, as something he could show around as evidence that Colonel Buckmaster had accepted responsibility for him in a very public way.

As I would not now be seeing him immediately, I wrote to him in greater detail about the 'Denise' letters, explaining confidentially my appalling embarrassment over Maurice Norman:

28.1.59

... But now, for the next edition (that is when there is a paperback edition in 1960), I must change something on p. 170. I can't let it go on record for history that 'Denise' accused Déricourt when I know she accused Norman. Without mentioning a name, if the father is still alive, I can put a footnote saying that further information convinces me that 'Denise' referred not to 'Gilbert' the Air Movements Officer but to another person... That I must do, for your sake and for truth's sake.

Déricourt replied with great understanding concerning my embarrassment with regard to the father and the difficulty of charging a dead man. 'At the same time it is not agreeable to be living and to bear the blame for a dead one.' He would appreciate a footnote in the sense I suggested. 'I am agreed that it is not necessary to name Norman.'

He thanked us for trying to get the 'Denise' letters, but he was prepared to bet a princely sum the Foreign Office would not produce them. I was ashamed to have to tell him Irene had been told by Robin Hooper that the Foreign Office did not appear to possess the 'Denise' letters. He assured her they would not have been destroyed because they caused embarrassment, and thought they could not have been received. Déricourt took the disappointment philosophically: 'I win! No letters!'

Unexpectedly, the next letter I received from him was dated from Laos. He had been called back suddenly.

… I found here an horrible mess… but what is amazing is that instead of forwarding my mail they kept it here, as if they knew I was due to come back. Nothing could make anybody suppose that…

Amongst it he had found a copy of Elizabeth's book I had sent him. He had read it, and enclosed a letter to her plus seven pages of comments. 'You can transmit to her or keep them as you like.'

I sent them on. The letter to her said (in English):

Thanks to you and to Miss Fuller to have noticed and to have had the courage to speak of the 'Denise' letters — and of the different ways to understand Gilbert — which Gilbert — I knew already that, but should I have had told that to anybody it would have become sullied…

The most interesting part of his comments I found the passages concerning the network to which one of the women, Vera Leigh ('Simone'), was sent out, as courier to Sidney Jones ('Elie'). Their radio operator was Marcel Clech ('Bastien') and they had to work with Frager:

The reason why 'Elie', 'Simone' and 'Bastien' were arrested… 'Elie' had been through all the training courses, Frager not — 'Elie' was a British officer, Frager not — So, as it was the [SOE] rule to put in a regular… 'Elie' was sent to take command of the network… with his staff, 'Simone' and 'Bastien'… But Frager took the arms, received the money… but did not agree to be under a British HQ and much more not under 'Elie'. He would have lost his prestige — and the money…

I don't say Frager gave them away to the Germans — No — But he could not ignore that Bardet had done so… You

245

can retort that Frager, although abused by Bleicher, trusted him to be a friend, anti-Nazi... yes, that could be, but Frager too knew he was a German *contre-espionnage* officer, that if he had British contacts he was forced to give to his superiors something to bargain with, that is the principle of the double game ... so 'Elie's' arrest suited perfectly everybody except ['Elie'] himself...

I wish — I would like — that you could understand that when I criticise somebody dead or alive I quite appreciate the good side of what he did. Nobody is perfect and me less than any of those I have spoken about. But they were as they were — I am not resentful — I don't try to blacken anybody — It is not because somebody is dead he is pure gold — as Beaumarchais said, 'Sans liberté de critiquer il n'y pas de louange sincère' [Without freedom to criticise there is no sincerity in praise].

11: SHIVERY CORNER

From Paris I received a letter signed 'Robert Lyon'. He said he had some material with which he would like to acquaint me. Something in the phraseology caused me foreboding. He arrived at my flat on 27 March. His code-name, he said, had been 'Adnan', and he showed me papers made out to himself in his cover-name of 'Gilbert Calvaire'. He had been flown out in company with a Colonel Bonoteaux, who was not of the French Section but the French Regular Army — not one of those who had come over to serve under de Gaulle, but (as he learned later) one of the Vichy army. Bonoteaux had paid England a clandestine visit and was being given a lift back. The Lysander in which they were passengers was piloted by Hugh Verity. Their flight was on the night of the 2 3/24 June 1943, and it was about 2.30 in the morning of the 24th that they landed in a field at Pocé-sur-Cisse, near Amboise. 'Gilbert' and 'Marc' were on the field to meet them, gave them bicycles and told them to make themselves comfortable until about 8 or 8.30, when there would be a train from Amboise to Paris. Then 'Gilbert' and 'Marc' left them.

Bonoteaux and Lyon sheltered against a hedge until the daylight came and they judged it time to cycle into Amboise. Shortly before the train came in, they saw 'Gilbert' and 'Marc' stroll on to the platform. Naturally, they avoided showing any sign of recognition. In the train, Bonoteaux and Lyon sat in the same compartment. From time to time they saw 'Gilbert' and 'Marc' pass along the corridor. At the Gare d'Austerlitz they all got out, and negotiated the barrier safely. That was about 11 a.m. Lyon parted from Bonoteaux, and went, first, to an address near the Porte de la Villette and afterwards to the Gare de Lyon, where he took the train to Lyons. He was never arrested. The network 'Acolyte', of which he became the Organiser, could claim to be one of the fortunate ones, for it endured to the end. He was telling me this story because it gave the lie to Déricourt's statement to the DST, cited in *Double Webs*, page 243, that at 9.0 a.m. on the morning of 24June 1943, at the Gare St Lazare, he met 'Antoine', who told him he had just seen 'Prosper' arrested there.

I had always felt uneasy about that, because it also contradicted the evidence of Mme Fèvre, of the Hôtel Mazagran. However, I defended Déricourt, saying it did not seem to be to his advantage to associate himself with the time and place of 'Prosper's' arrest, if he had a true alibi.

But, suggested Lyon, supposing that he was genuinely innocent of complicity in the arrest of 'Prosper', might he not have associated himself with that and the Gare St Lazare in order to give himself a fictitious alibi with regard to another person, for whose arrest he *had* been responsible? 'Bonoteaux!'

Some years after the war, Lyon said, he had seen a statement by a General Olleris (Vichy army), who had been a prisoner of war in the same camp as Bonoteaux. Bonoteaux had been shot at Dachau, but before his execution had told his story to General Olleris. On leaving the train at the Gare d'Austerlitz, he had taken the metro to Auteuil, and gone to the address of his sister, in the Auteuil district. She was out. He took the metro back from Auteuil to the Gare d'Austerlitz, where he was arrested. That this was Déricourt's doing Lyon could not prove, but that Déricourt was not at the St Lazare at 9 a.m. he could confirm. 'That is a lie. It's your word against his,' I said.

He said he could prove the date of his own landing, and asked me whether there would be a second edition of my

248

book, and if so would I include a mention of his visit and what he had told me confuting Déricourt. I said I would write to Déricourt to give him the possibility of reply to this new accusation, and make my decision about any revisions after hearing from him.

Lyon said he had not been called to give evidence at Déricourt's trial. At that time his evidence would have been for him. He himself had not been arrested, and only later learned what had happened to Bonoteaux. It was particularly regrettable as in Bonoteaux's cases were found not only two radio transmitters but papers relating to the work he was to do with a General Fèvre whom he was to contact, and who had been arrested a fortnight earlier. All these generals and colonels were, he believed, Vichy. (I could see there was a political story here, concerning the collaboration of Vichy with London, but was too much concerned over Déricourt to have interest to spare for it.)

Lyon spoke of Déricourt as a braggart, who boasted a false DSO. I rescued what I could of Déricourt's honour by testifying that what he had said to me was that he had been put up for a DSO but it had not gone through. 'The Legion of Honour he does have.'

Lyon said Morel had told him that when he flew out in February 1944, his orders were to shoot Déricourt if he refused to come back with him; but that he had abstained because he had been so convinced of Déricourt's sincerity in asking for a few days' delay within which to make needful arrangements.

The next question Lyon wanted to raise with me was what was intended exactly by a phrase in my book, 'Noble I, where "La Chatte" was'. I said Déricourt had explained to me that the intention of London had been that Noble should take over the control of the Interallié, which he therefore called Noble I, to distinguish it from a later phase of that network which he called Noble II. It was really a terminology of his own. Lyon seemed somewhat mollified by this. Interestingly, he let drop a phrase which had been used by my publishers in their reply to the de Vomécourts' solicitors. He had not said he had been in contact with the de Vomécourts, but it seemed obvious he had been in consultation with them before coming.

Having come to the end of what he had come to say about Déricourt, Lyon produced from his briefcase a bundle of papers. Since I had a taste for mysteries, would I like to write a book about an earlier one, for which he would give me the information? During his own first mission he had been in Marseilles in October 1941. Two other Buckmaster agents, Hayes and Jumeaux, came to see him, saying they had instructions to go to the Villa des Bois, to meet a Mr Turck, 'Christophe', but could not find it. Could Lyon find the Villa des Bois? Lyon walked around the streets, with Hayes, looking for it. They had parted from Jumeaux somewhere and later learned he had been arrested. Eventually Lyon saw what he thought might be the Villa des Bois, but the man who opened the door, a Captain Ribollet, said it was the Villa Bernadette. Nevertheless, he knew who Turck was, for he said 'Mr Turck is in Paris.' Lyon went to a restaurant, where he was questioned by Vichy police, but not arrested. A few days later he went to the Villa des Bois. The door was opened to him by Vichy police, of which the house was full. He was seized, and dragged in. Then he was taken to a prison. In the prison he had found nearly all the agents of the French Section. He reeled off the names. All had been arrested at the Villa des Bois or Villa Bernadette, walking up to be caught one after another like mice in a trap. But Turck was not in the prison. It was Turck who had opened the door and said 'Come in' to each one as he entered the trap.

'Did you see Turck?' I asked.

'No'. Bégué had seen him, and perhaps one or two of the others. Most weighty was that Philippe de Vomécourt had had the prudence to telephone to the Villa des Bois, and had recognised Turck's voice. His answers had seemed suspicious, so de Vomécourt had not come to the Villa des Bois, and had not been arrested. After the war they had all wanted Turck charged. Turck had 'no network, no mission, nothing!' But the British had protected him/as they protected Déricourt'. Would I write a book on this affair? He would supply me with the material needed to expose Turck. He showed me identity cards bearing the photographs of Turck, his wife and mother. I wondered how he had come to possess these, and wondered if he had not reflected that to write such a book would lay me open to an action for libel.

I said I had met Turck, who said it was not him. I did not think of writing anything else on SOE at present. He was plainly surprised I had met Turck. After asking me to autograph his copy of *Double Webs*, he left.

After he had gone, though it was after midnight, I wrote to Déricourt recounting the interview. With regard to Bonoteaux, I was sure what Lyon had told me was true. I reminded myself that, as we sat side by side in Paris, he had told me the three men mentioned by Ernest as having been arrested after landing on his field at Angers might not be the only ones. There might be one or two more, that I did not know about yet, perhaps even that he did not know about. So, though they were shadowy figures, and this one had name and circumstance, there was really nothing new. I did not want to sound accusatory, yet it had shaken me up a lot, and there was a practical side to it. I wrote:

> If Bonoteaux was arrested in the metro after leaving his sister's house, that does not prove he was followed all the way from Pocé-sur-Cisse... more serious is the implication with regard to St Lazare. If you told me something that was untrue with regard to your movements on this date, it could make a bad impression. *Did* you invent the St Lazare story? And if so, why? You know I was suspicious of the St Lazare story (although I took your part tonight, as you were not present to speak for yourself); now I don't know what to think. You don't need to tell me what passed in reality, unless you want to. I don't insist, because I don't want to put you in an awkward position.

I put it that way, because I did not want to put him into the position of having either to lie to me or incriminate himself on paper. I did not want to seem to be rubbing in that I had discovered there was another death to his discredit, but I thought he should know I had been severely jolted and that there was a decision to be made. I added:

> Now, if you told me some 'story' it does not so much matter. I think you told me several... But this one has gone into print in the book, as a serious and deliberate statement by you, and if it is untrue that is very annoying, because it will make people think badly of you.

Obviously, the St Lazare passage could not be allowed to stand without comment in the paperback edition now in preparation. The most inconspicuous solution, I suggested, would be to delete from his list of points paragraph 5, and close up the numbering without drawing attention to it. In that case it would not be necessary to mention Lyon. Otherwise, I would have to say there was conflict of evidence.

The morning brought me an envelope containing a Chinese painting, inscribed by Déricourt on the back:

Hong Kong

Best wishes
for Easter
from Hens
eggs
and Henri
HD

It made me feel sorry he would receive such a stern letter from me.

Before I could receive a reply to it, I was re-turning the pages of the Abbé Guillaume's book when my eye fell upon the worst thing I could have found — the name Bonoteaux in an extract from the deposition of the French traitor Pierre Bony. Long ago the Abbé had sent me photostats of the depositions of Bony and Lafont. Since then Déricourt had sent me extracts from them, copied in his own hand, not realising I had photostats. I got them out. I had often pondered on them, but only now that I had Lyon's witness concerning Bonoteaux did they become deadly.

Bony wrote (I translate from the French):

> The services of Dr Kuhn, 74 Avenue Foch, in connection with Kieffer, utilised a double agent, 'Christian', a fair young man, twenty-eight to thirty, elegant, who went to the places where parachute drops were made, received the agents parachuted and returned with them to Paris, where they were trailed [from the station and either arrested in Paris or lost]. 'Chamberlain' was several times required for trailing

parachuted agents and under these conditions the following operations were carried out.

1. At Amboise, surveillance undertaken by Sartore, Jeunet, Chaves and a fourth; they distinctly heard an aircraft, the motor slowing down, then restarting. In the morning two men entered Amboise station, carrying suitcases. The informer made a sign; both boarded the train for Paris. One of them was trailed to a building with several doors, rue de Flandres or de la Vilette. The men were ordered not to arrest him. The second walked about in Paris, hesitated, took the metro to Auteuil, returned to the Gare d'Austentz where, thinking he was going to return by the train, the men arrested him. Conducted to the rue Launston, he was found to be carrying false papers emanating from Algiers, addresses of correspondents, and 4 millions. He gave his identity as Lieutenant-Colonel Bonoteaux, 'Chamberlain' had him taken to Avenue Foch with the documents and whole case.

2. At Angers: the Doctor asked 'Chamberlain' for ten men, with the mission to go to Angers to take on the trailing of eight agents parachuted. The informer had to take charge of them on the line from Le Mans to Angers. In order not to evoke suspicions, he sent two to the station of Tirce, two others to a neighbouring station. They got out at Angers Maître Ecole, and reassembled at the central station, from which at about fifteen hours they took the train with 'Chamberlain's' agent. Arrived at Montparnasse at about twenty hours, where 'Chamberlain' was waiting for them with a new team, an incident occurred; police asked the travellers for their papers. Confusion was produced, and 'Chamberlain' decided to arrest them all, including a German and a functionary. All were taken to Kieffer that evening.

3. At Angers: same operation, but the aeroplane did not come. We supposed the informer unmasked — which was

wrong, as was established from a message captured a few days later.

4. At Angers: same operation: several agents parachuted, one of them a woman. The tradings started from Paris with teams of two men. They went into a bar in the Gare Montparnasse where they separated; two entered a nearby hotel and a third went off. The informer said he would to Arles. Two others went to 45 (I think) Avenue Lamotte Piquet (block facing the entrance to the metro). Next day a taxi brought baggages [this seems to be argot; Déricourt renders 'two persons'] to this address, a young fair woman (im 65, head bare, blue coat, red belt, sporting type) followed by the informer, with whom, and with a man who had left them at the rue Tilsit, she had left the Café Colisée. The man went the next day to a new block on the Boulevard Murat. Two others went to the Café des Sports, Porte Maillot, and from there to the rue Bassano, into an hotel opposite no. 19. The affair dragged. Order was given to abandon it. I think the arrests were made directly from Avenue Foch.

5. At Angers: same proceeding, same informer, five men were trailed to Paris and arrested. They were two Englishmen who could hardly speak French; a workman who had worked in France and two Frenchmen of whom one was a Corsican. They were taken by Chamberlain to Kieffer.

None of these agents was interrogated by 'Chamberlain' or held at the rue Launston. 'Chamberlain' played only a role of execution.

The corresponding part of the deposition of Lafont, alias 'Chamberlain', read:

I know, having been told by Bony and my men charged with trailing, that Kuhn employed a tall young man as double agent. He had to receive the Allied agents on their landing, and conduct them to a station near Angers. There Kieffer's

255

men, and later mine, took over the trailing. Three times only Kieffer asked me for men for such work.

The first time Kieffer asked me for six men. I sent Sartore, Jeunet, Sazauba, Maillebaud and two others. They went to Angers — where; I do not know. The double agent pointed out to them six individuals. I know they were followed to Paris, and that there the trailing was taken over by German police. Of that affair I have no more to say.

The second time Kieffer asked me for six men, or rather Kieffer asked Boemelburg for them, and the latter gave me the order. I do not know who took part in that affair: I can only say that in these tradings, apart from those already mentioned, participated Salvatore, Discipoulo and two or three Corsicans, but I do not know if they took part in the first, the second or the third operation.

The six men designated at the request of Boemelburg had likewise to go to the neighbourhood of Angers, where they took on the trailing of some men. This second time I went to the Gare Montparnasse with some German NCOs in civilian clothes, and towards 8 p.m. the train came in. At that moment there was an incident: the police made a check and I saw that one of the men trailed by my team put down his case and made ready to fly. Immediately I made a sign to an officer in civilian clothes and he at once gave the order for arrest. Six persons were arrested; they were taken to the rue Launston. There they were searched, then taken to Kieffer's. I pointed out that one of the men arrested had absolutely nothing on him; I immediately released him and therefore only handed over five men to Kieffer.

The third affair was carried out in the same way: six men, for it was always six, were trailed from Angers. On their arrival in Paris their trailing was taken over by my men, each one coupled with a member of the German police. Three were lost. Kieffer was responsible for the others.

To the best of my knowledge my service participated only in these three affairs, unless during one of my absences Boemelburg used my men for a similar task.

I felt cold. Between heavy suspicion and proof is a gulf. When I had read these depositions before, the references in Bony's to 'agents parachuted' had prevented my feeling certain the reference was to Déricourt. Although Amboise and Angers were his fields, he never received agents parachuted, only agents alighting from aircraft that landed there. Lyon's evidence concerning Bonoteaux made it obvious that Bony's reference in the paragraph containing his name was to Déricourt. Déricourt was 'Christian'. When Déricourt had picked out the word 'the informer' and said that could not refer to a German, Placke or Holdorf, but must refer to 'a sneak', that meant himself. The words in Bony's first paragraph which I have enclosed in square brackets were missing from the transcript given to me by the Abbé, but present in the copy made by Déricourt from his own copy. Déricourt had a form of honesty which constantly surprised me. When he copied out for me these depositions, dreadfully adverse to himself, he was unaware I had copies from which I could check those in his hand, yet I found them faithful. He had taken only the small liberty of here and there substituting correct French for argot, either because I might not understand it or because, as he had said, he detested argot. Thus, for the argot word 'baggages' he had substituted the correct 'persons'.

I had to remember that Bony's and Lafont's depositions were, in respects already known, wild. Passages concerning Starr had been discounted by the DST, and the Abbé, though he had reproduced them in his book, had notified his *Commission d'Histoire* of the errors he now perceived in them (he had presented Starr, who came to see him, with an inscribed copy). There could, therefore, be equal inexactitude in the passages regarding Déricourt's operations. That they related them to parachute landings perhaps showed that they had never been on the field where an aircraft touched down. If they only waited at the railway station they would not know how the agents came, and Déricourt very likely referred to the agents as 'parachuted', in order to protect himself. After all, he did not want Bony and Lafont to know who he was. Bony's paragraph 2 and Lafont's first and fourth seemed to refer to the same operation, though the number of agents arrested was differently given as six and eight. I personally thought the operation was one that resulted in — according to Vogt — three arrests. These were the testimonies of corrupt men, who hoped that by giving as much information as possible to the DST they might stave off the execution which in fact befell them. All the same, I knew I was looking at garbled recollections of operations in which Déricourt figured.

If I could have seen him face to face at that moment, I would have said — confidentially, not aggressively — 'This is you, isn't it?' Having to write about it, I had to bear in mind that the written word, unsoftened by tone or look, could only appear as an accusation. In Déricourt's mind an accuser was an enemy; friendship should show in covering up for one. He would have no hesitation in lying for a friend. What I had to try to convey to him was that I was his friend, but must find a way to handle the matter that was right and proper. Could I get that over? I started and tore up a number of letters. Even to draw to his attention how bad the evidence was for him would be misunderstood; I would be reproached for trying to box him in.

To moralise would be repulsive, and he knew the moral anyway. In the end I thought best simply to own that re-

reading these depositions, in the light of Lyon's evidence, had given me a bad attack of the shivers — which of course was on his behalf:

> Last night I found something horrible in the deposition of Bony, Pierre, a paragraph mentioning the affair Bonoteaux... Imagine my horror on reading this account. You must already have the deposition of Bony because you quoted to me once from another part of it... Now we have one of the Bony-Lafont depositions *linked* with one of your operations... You see that 'l'Informateur' seems not to be a member of the Bony-Lafont team who had come from Paris. It seems to be somebody who took part in the reception on the landing-field; how else could he make a sign to the Bony-Lafont team? I think it is quite serious for you... You see the finger of accusation points very nearly to you ... I had in consequence of this a troubled night... my estimation of you depends not on what is proved or not proved about what happened in 1943 but on the 'you' as I know you today and since we met. I wear still your little silver bracelet with the Bangkok dancers; and I assure you of my best friendship.

I thought it useful to tabulate what I had been able to gather of 'Prosper's' movements and contacts from the time of his parachuting back until his arrest. I hoped that by setting out the dispersed details sequentially something might strike the eye. My table, of which I enclosed a copy for Déricourt, read:

> Night of June 19/20: 'Prosper'... received on landing-field by Culioli
> Afternoon of June 20: 'Prosper' meets Mme Balachowsky in Paris and sees her to Gare Montparnasse... they talk on steps and he tells her his suspicions about London
> Morning of June 21: 'Prosper' meets at Gare d'Austerlitz 'Gilbert' and hands over to him for repatriation the

Englishman Taylor... 'Prosper' looks at the same time and in the same situation for Culioli and two Canadians... does not find them.

Morning June 22 'Prosper' goes again to the Gare d'Austerlitz, still hopes to meet Culioli and the two Canadians, same rendezvous, same hour... finds nobody... Goes to apartment of Armel Guerne, arriving at 1 p.m.; and has lunch with Guerne and 'Denise' (deposition of Guerne).

BUT

Morning June 22: 'Prosper' lunched with Mme Guépin, 'Archambaud' and 'Denise' at Café Triadoux Hauseman to talk about a parachutage (deposition of Mme Guépin, 4–7–57).

Afternoon June 23: 'Prosper' goes to Gisors and spends the night chez Mm Guépin at Triechâteau.

Mornmg June 24: Marcel Charbonmer spoke with 'Prosper' at Triechâteau before he took the train. Mme Guépin saw him off by the 7 a.m. from Gisors, she understood he had a rendezvous with someone in Paris at 9.0...

This did not illuminate his arrest, but did show up that somebody's memory was at fault as to the lunch.

To show I had not crossed him off from my list of friends, I added first a comment on the world news about the flight of the Dalai Lama and asked him what he thought about it. Then I wrote:

> What I wanted you to understand most of all... was ... I would try to understand with sympathy any dilemma in which you had been caught, and that I would not turn against you. My relationship is not to you past but you present. You gave me your friendship and I gave you mine, and it *stays*.

Déricourt's replies came in a shoal. His letters of 3, 5, 10 and 27 April were all about what Lyon had said to me:

Villa des Bois — be careful.

... Don't shiver for me. I don't fear anybody. When we met at beginning I feared that the British services would let me down and throw away... but Buck covered me [BBC Television].

As regards his apparently having been in two places at once on the morning of 24 June, 'Lyon probably has his dates wrong'. I advised him against suggesting that. My impression was that Lyon had come very well documented, and although the SOE files were closed the Air Ministry permitted inspection of its record of flights, from which it could be seen when they put down 'two bodies' during that moon period. Was it possible, I asked, that an earlier train could have been caught from Amboise, enabling him to be at St Lazare at 9 a.m.? No earlier train, he said. Then, I suggested, the least conspicuous manner of dealing with the situation in the paperback would be silently to omit his St Lazare story. It would be a victory for Lyon but the ordinary reader would not notice. Otherwise, I should have to say there was a conflict of evidence. He said he would prefer that. He wanted to keep the St Lazare story. It had always been 'awkward', but he made it 'to help Culioli'.

Suddenly I understood. That woman Reimeringer had alleged Culioli led the Gestapo to the Hôtel Mazagran to arrest 'Prosper'. In court her testimony was broken down in cross-examination, but during the *instruction* a testimony that the arrest of 'Prosper' had taken place elsewhere would not have come amiss. It was Déricourt's way of making it up to Culioli for the doubt left in the Bony-Lafont depositions as to which of them was their subject of reference.

I quite saw that it would be mean for Déricourt now to withdraw the support he had given in this way. Because he was benefiting from something, he had given something. I did not want to take away from Déricourt one of the few gracious things he had ever done (to borrow a phrase from Michael Arlen's *The Green Hat*). Moreover, it was wiser just to say there was a 'conflict of evidence' between Déricourt and Lyon, without trying to account for it.

I warned Déricourt not to build too much on Buckmaster's television statement. I had sent it to him as something he could wave in front of anyone who was disagreeable (for instance, at his club), but I gave it no weight at all. It was just something Buckmaster had produced in answer to an unexpected question from the interviewer. There was nothing official about it.

Déricourt pretended not to understand me, and asked:

> How can you be sure Buck has no official approval to cover me? He could not speak on TV without permission. There is still a ban on that. And I am not so friendly with him to make him speak for me — against a ban. He does not fear me. He does not need me. So what?

I knew very well what. What was more, I knew Déricourt knew very well what. It was a silent joke.

Meanwhile, Irene had obtained from Profumo permission to correspond with Robin Hooper direct. She addressed him a number of questions, some of which had been set out by me, and asked him not to head his reply PRIVATE AND CONFIDENTIAL. He replied:

> Foreign Office, SW1
> April 1, 1959
>
> FZD/154/A
> Dear Dame Irene,
> ... About Nick Bodington — I haven't, I'm afraid, checked on what Buckmaster said on the television, but the point is that

he is a private individual. If he makes remarks ... he does so on his own responsibility, which is a different thing from HMG doing so — or being quoted as having done so...

[In the Phono or Garry circuit] there was no hint of trouble until October, 1943, when a report was received that Noor and her chief had been arrested. This remained unconfirmed... and shortly afterwards Noor (or so it was thought at the time) came up on the air again. Not many messages came through, but those that did showed no sign of abnormality ... At the end of February 1944 Major Antelme was parachuted into France with a wireless operator. Noor (or rather the pseudo-Noor) reported that Antelme had fractured his skull on landing... There is, I am afraid, no doubt whatever that Noor's wireless set was played back to us — with great skill — by the Germans for some months...

ROBIN HOOPER

So warnings were received, but disregarded.

I did not think I ought actually to quote to Déricourt from Hooper's letter, but tried to make him understand it was silly to waffle, because Irene had direct access to Hooper, and even to the Prime Minister, so that any bluff he attempted could immediately be called.

He replied (in English):

I try to take the way you think about Buck TV and Nick Court statement — anyway, they did not lied, they would not had dared that only on purpose to save me Buck tangled (correct?) with TV interview the way you explain clearly instead of Nick did it as a reward, a duty to me — because I saved his life nearly twice a day on his trip. Maybe but anyway I did that too. — if the real point is to know if I was authorised to do that — I answer yes, it was my mission and I told them (Nick and Buck) as less as possible — as I had been told before — They did not ask more than I told them

because they had been warned I was doing something else —
Elseway how do you explain that they did not explode when I
told Nick and Nick Buck, 'By the way, "Gilbert" is in German
hands'... and carry on with the pick up operations. So if Nick
covers me today it is by official permission may be not from
F.O....

Would he never learn? He added: *'Robin Hooper* — I should
be very pleased to meet him some time.' There is nothing like
nerve.

In his letter of 27 April he wrote (I translate from his
French):

Bonoteaux — I think it was. indeed me who received him at
Amboise. Of course I have read Bony's deposition about this
... I have even interrogated Sartore, cited by Bony, face to
face, alone. Needless to say the importance it had for me ... I
admit Bony etc spoke of the persons I received. Only I insist
one should not dissociate a single phrase from the depositions
of Bony and Lafont.

That, because in the deposition of Bony about Amboise,
Bony speaks of a double agent called Christian, young, fair,
twenty-eight to thirty, elegant; that does not sound like me ...
in another of his depositions Bony seems to know me, at least
by name.. As he did not like me, for reasons I do not have to
explain, he would have charged me, whereas he uses the word
informer, vague by design...

If you remember, I asked you a lot of questions about
'Christian'. I would like to know if Vogt knew him ... I would
like to eliminate the possibility it was 'Christian' who kept the
rendezvous in the empty flat.

Believe me, *all* the Germans spoke after the war. I was
present once when arrests were made at the Gare
Montparnasse. I was on the tram, having come from an
operation. The Germans arrested some people — who had

come from London — but they were not the ones we had
received, they were some others

I detached stones from their setting. Bony did not like him;
that was his way of saying he knew Bony. He knew Sartore. I
remembered his distinction between 'lying to be believed' and
'lying so as not to be believed', and his assurance that when he
lied to me he tried to make it obvious. I was sure that was what
he was trying to do here. To have been plain, in a letter, would
have been unthinkable, for letters may always chance to be
seen by someone not meant to see. But had he wanted to
deceive me he could simply have denied knowing any of these
people. Déricourt never gave himself away unintentionally.
This was a plea of guilty, presented in the form of a defence.

I offered him a get-out, asking if there was anyone but
himself and 'Marc' to assist on the field? I did not expect him
to charge 'Marc' (he was loyal), but they might have had some
casual assistants, whose names he had forgotten. He rejected
the get-out. Indeed, he behaved with so much care not to put
or leave anybody in the soup that it made it difficult to believe
he had done what he had done.

I remembered the passion with which he had pointed out
that his casualties had been fewer than Haig's. It was meant to
imply that he had had a strategy.

He had told me that the essence of his accord with
Boemelburg was that the agents arriving should not be
arrested. Could that be believed? The deposition of Bony made
plain that the arrest of Bonoteaux resulted from a mistake. The
instructions Bony had were to note where he entered and
report, not arrest. It was the fact that Bonoteaux did not enter
anywhere, but retraced his route to the station from which he
had arrived, that gave Bony, perhaps stupidly, the idea he was
going back to England; so he decided to make a catch.

Boemelburg might have been far from pleased to have this prisoner brought in. Was it possible the arrests of the three from Angers likewise resulted from a mistake? I did not understand what Bony meant concerning the incident involving police. Were the police acting in collaboration or, rivalry with Bony? Something unforeseen had apparently occurred, which left room for the possibility of another mistake. I felt that Déricourt would have put it to the Germans that so long as they only watched the operations, they had information, whereas if they arrested the agents they killed the goose that laid the golden egg. London would send no more agents through such a channel. But could it have been true that he made them believe he could give them the date and place of the invasion? Was it by this promise, that would never be fulfilled, that he had kept them content for so long with so little?

He had sent to safety more than had died through that compromised deal. 'What is a Bonoteaux? What is it in a war?' he wrote in another letter. I have to quote from memory because I burned it. What commanded my respect, even admiration, was the way he lived with his misdeeds afterwards; not humble because he had done wrong, nor yet cynical, nor even, now that I had come to know him, too embarrassed. I thought that most people who had done what he had done — if they had had the daring and the skill to do it — would afterwards have gone to either one extreme or another, taking either to drink or religion (in the weak sense), and becoming either repulsively repentant or else impenetrably brazen; in short, worsening, one way or another. He had improved. The tilt, when I met him, had been towards the brazen, but the mask was superficial; the skin had not thickened, or if it had, sensitivity was being regained, and a place that had been

266

desensitised began to hurt, to burn, although he would not bow his head.

It would not have been appropriate to send one so unprepared *The Secret Doctrine*. When I wrote that I thought, one day, to write a biography of Madame Blavatsky, he replied, 'In which network was she?' But I sent him *The Unity of Religious Ideals* by Inayat Khan, the father of 'Madeleine', and *At the Feet of the Master* by Krishnamurti. Later I sent him *The Idyll of the White Lotus* by Mabel Collins, commending to his particular attention the 'three truths' of the Master Hilarion:

> The soul of man is immortal, and its future is the future of a thing whose growth and splendour has no limit.
>
> The principle which gives life dwells in us and without us, is undying and eternally beneficient, is not heard or seen or smelt, but is perceived by the man who desires perception.
>
> Each man is his own absolute lawgiver, the dispenser of glory or gloom to himself, the decreer of his life, his reward, his punishment.

Because, I said, he knew them already.

12: SHADOWS FROM A FORGOTTEN WORLD

I had looked out my old notebook, in which I had scribbled at dictation my interview with Turck, and recapitulated it to Déricourt, for comparison with the opposing version of Lyon. He replied on 5 April (in English):

> *Turck* — I don't know anything about that story — even if it look like mine.
> *Humphreys...* never heard of them.
> *de Vomécourt* — *Sorry* not to help you — too dangerous.
> *Villa des Bois* — I have nothing to do with it.

I had asked him if the Villa des Bois was the mousetrap house in Marseilles, of which he had told me in Paris. He had said that it was so dangerous I must not even write the word Marseilles as an aide-memoire. I felt it must be this, could only be this. Probably he expected me to understand that. He went on:

> Be careful. They are trying to puzzle you — What for? To make me distrusted — or you. — because they fear something they don't like could happen or arise from the forgotten world of the de Vomécourt business in France!
> [When we met in Paris] I feared that somebody could be afraid of what I know or what I could say and take 'measures' to prevent it.

Referring to the Bonoteaux affair, he had said that all the Germans had talked now, there was nothing more to come out. He had nothing more to fear now concerning the 'Prosper' network and the Loire Valley.

This seemed to me a dangerous qualification. Did he mean me to understand he still had something to fear from the 'anterior' past?

On 30 April he wrote further:

> The de Vomécourt gang does not like me. Because they know I know. They need to make me distrusted before. Trust me. I know. But they can be quiet. I'll never tell what I know to anybody, even you. They too are dangerous. It could turn bad — it could arise to some killing — be careful — and be good for me.

I was careful, on his behalf as well as my own.

Irene received an abusive letter. Of all the mass of letters received by Irene, Elizabeth and myself about our books, this was the only one that was not on our side. It came from Benjamin Cowburn and the chief target seemed to be me. I no longer have the original (which was addressed to Irene), and it is only because Déricourt could not understand some of the slang, in the photostat I sent him, that I can reconstruct from my following letter the phrases I had to explain to him.

'When her stock of Germans ran out she turned to the next best... the arch-villain who flew rings round her.' Being descended upon both sides from British officers of the Regular Army, I recall being mildly vexed at the implication I was anti-patriotic. Anyway, why was Cowburn concerned? I had not mentioned him. The motive appeared to be to bludgeon Irene into dissociating herself from the authors of the two books and 'send them packing'.

I wrote to Déricourt: 'I was surprised not by the hostility (everyone has his right to be hostile...) but by the vulgarity. Irene and Elizabeth were also shocked from the same point of view.'

Irene did not even know who Cowburn was. In fact he was the third occupant of a boat — with 'La Chatte' and Pierre de Vomécourt — allowed by the Germans to 'escape' from the Breton coast on 27 February 1942. The idea was that when they arrived *in England* 'La Chatte' should there act as a spy for Germany. Cowburn's letter probably had something to do with the forthcoming de Vomécourt lawsuit. I would not have known when this came on, but somebody sent me from Germany copies of *Bild* and *Die Allgemeine Frankfurter Zeitung* for 21 April 1959. The former had a great spread of photographs, including pictures of Cowburn, the principal or only witness for Pierre de Vomécourt. The hearing was in Frankfurt. De Vomécourt's complaint was that Graf Michael Soltikov had, in a book *Die Katze*, libelled him in asserting he was this woman's lover. He had had to pay 7,000 D.M. to keep this out of English newspapers, and wanted 12,000 D.M. damages. Soltikov said he would be willing to omit some lines in another edition but not to pay damages, since he had treated de Vomécourt with chivalry in not putting into his book the far worse things that Bleicher had told him. Bleicher then went into the box, and said that when de Vomécourt was arrested in May 1942, after his return to France, he betrayed to Bleicher eight of his comrades, in return for an assurance neither he nor they should be killed or sent to a concentration camp, but kept in a prisoner-of-war camp until the war ended. This promise was kept on the German side. De Vomécourt admitted having given Bleicher some names, but said they were names that he knew to have been already given to Bleicher by 'La Chatte'.

Bleicher said they had not been given him by 'La Chatte'. He learned them first from de Vomécourt.

Déricourt wrote on 9 May (in English):

> *de V*: I don't mind of him — he was not so kind when he was supposed to be clean and pure. Now he is 'in'. C'est bien fait pour lui [He is done for]. He will never win — always doubt will remain — and it could be worse — his brother is phynancial [*sic*] inspector for the Government (a very strong ring), but if he see that his naughty brother could be dangerous he could let him down, so in that case anything can happen. You will test the temperature through the French papers — because they are allowed to print what suits the Government — There is a smell of carrion in the air — the vultures assembles and the rats leaves the boat.
>
> What is a sign is that Bleicher himself came in the court — and what he said and maintained — that means the DST (or 'Wybot') allowed him to go — because since the end of the war H.B. was in the DST hands. Now the staff of the DST has been changed ... is Bleicher really free or has he changed his boss? Anyway he can attack a friend of the French Government — that means a lot.
>
> Is he right? I don't know (!) I never have been in his business — the Cat and what is around her makes me fly away — too dangerous (now) for me — I won't take any side — but I think H.B. is right and tell the truth — Yes de V is mad.

Why did Déricourt say 'La Chatte' and what was around her could be dangerous for him *today*?

The case was adjourned until mid-May, in the hope that 'La Chatte' (now freed after serving twelve years) could he prevailed upon to testify. I think it was the judge who wished to hear her. But according to *Ici Paris* she declined to give evidence, though the *Frankfurter Zeitung* said she would make a statement to a French lawyer. I never saw anything in the papers about how the case ended. It was as though it were not resumed.

When the galley-proofs of the paperback edition of my book arrived, I was horrified to see written across them that the whole had to be submitted to Philippe de Vomécourt. This I forbade. The publishers said he had written, saying he was President of Libre Resistance and so had a right to vet all books on the Resistance for historical accuracy. I said he had not, and did they know his brother had been the plaintiff in a case in which he had been accused of giving away eight of his own agents? They did not know. Indeed, I think the *News Chronicle* was the only English newspaper to have reported the case, if only briefly. There was nothing in *The Times* or the *Daily Telegraph*. For that matter, there was nothing in the French newspapers either, that I was able to discover, save for the little paragraph in *Ici Paris*, and that did not mention the allegation Bleicher had made or explain why the judge had wished to hear 'La Chatte'. It can only have been that none of the French papers dared report it — for it would have been big news in France — and that seemed to answer Déricourt's question: de Vomécourt was protected by the DST or French Government and Bleicher was no longer in its service, but, since his return to Germany, free. Anyway, Pan Books struck off from my proofs the instruction they had to be shown to Philippe de Vomécourt.

The last I heard of the de Vomécourts was in a note by the Abbé Guillaume, enclosed with his Christmas card for 1960, the last he sent me before his death. I translate from his French:

'Lucas' [Pierre de Vomécourt] lies low ('ne se fait plus parler de lui'). He has been abandoned by all his defenders, who are suspicious of his true story.

His brother Phihppe has died, with the esteem of all the old *Résistants* and of numbers of friends.

Pierre Raynaud, who had been writing to me from West Africa, called to see me on 22 April 1959. He had been 'Alain', of Cammaerts's network. He had been parachuted to reception by Culioli and 'Jacqueline' only two nights after the two Canadians and before 'Prosper', and he said Culioli told him to keep his voice down as there were Germans in the woods round the field, apparently chasing boars. Raynaud thought they were there to watch the parachuting. To be sure I had not misunderstood, I had him write this out in his own hand. He was sure there had been a sacrifice of F Section from above, in the interest of some strategic plan, which I should make the subject of my next book. I should interview all the surviving agents and ask them what had been the terms and purpose of their missions.

'No!' I said. That would render me liable to prosecution under the Official Secrets Act. If I made so much use of the testimonies of Germans, it was precisely because they had not signed the British Official Secrets Act.

He suggested I should see Bleicher. Long ago I had expressed to Vogt the thought that I might see Bleicher. He had replied — 'He entrapped so many people, particularly women, so that they were hopelessly caught. Even though the war is over, I would fear he would find some way too involve you to your disadvantage.' If I went to see Bleicher, he said, 'I should feel that I ought to go with you, but I am none to keen on meeting him, myself.'

'I will go with you,' said Raynaud. 'He lives near Lake Constance. We could go together.'

But I really thought Bleicher was better left alone.

I wrote to Déricourt that same evening, detailing the interview and asking if the story was good or bad for him.

He replied from Laos (in English):

28.4.59

Dear Jean,

... You are so artless sometimes ... I got your 2nd letter tonight and I answer quickly to warn you once more.

Every time you discover a new information you start like a rocket, not even asking whether it is true or not — or better, what in it is true and what imagination...

He did me wrong. I always asked myself whether what I was told was true or not.

Even supposing the parachuting had been watched, as Raynaud said, he could not see anything wrong in the way Culioli handled the situation.

Culioli is not a coward. He played the game going on, that's all.

... Anyway, 'Alain' seems to me to be a little too expansif — You have better to be careful — and check first with care what he say — and that thing to offer you a travel — the first day that he meets you — What temper! that is not serious...

You change de V. wasp-nest for another.

... All that is not bad — not good for me. I don't mind... No, what I fear is people who think that I know too much and I can be dangerous for them and that I am informing you too much about them.

He meant the de Vomécourts.

13: 'YOUR GOOD FRIEND, HENRY'

Déricourt wrote to me on 1 June 1959. After touching on impending troubles in Laos, he went on:

> My book will be ready for Christmas. I'll see you in that time. I think mine is better than yours because I did not seek for history — although it is closer to the truth — people are not like what they ought to have been — they are what they were, with all their defaults, vices and so on — it is not history for class books, it is history without dates, but with fear, with courage, with hate and love, with money, with killing, with sex and so on, and it is like that — it was not your impersonal way of warfare — the history is not that — sorry not to understand you.
>
> I don't even try to whiten me — I am awfully black — but I prefer to be black and have saved hundreds of lifes instead of pure white and have done nothing. *Heureux sont ceux qui ont beaucoup péché, tl leur sera beaucoup pardonné.* [Happy are those who have much sinned, for much will be forgiven them.] I have a full life credit to haggle with him.
>
> Your good friend,
HENRY

He had re-read *Double Webs*, and enclosed seventeen pages of closely written notes. Petulantly, he rebutted Ernest's charges concerning the meeting in the empty flat, though he could not have forgotten that in Paris he had allowed me to understand they were true. But there were points. He wished, for instance, I had made more of George Starr's having warned London a neighbouring radio-circuit was German-controlled, and receiving the answer 'Mind your own business':

Why not stress this sentence, 'Mind your own business. We know what we are doing' — because London really knew what they were doing, sending planes, supplies, people to the Germans — it was part of a game — they were not abused — 'We know what we are doing' — they really knew — for me — I got once the same answer — and me ... I mind my own business — but that make me to think of my skin and that the reason why I took 'my own measures'.

I had not said it because it was what Colonel Buckmaster had said in the *Sunday Empire News* was 'monstrously and libellously untrue'. I knew of no radio-circuit being played back at Easter 1943, but Déricourt could have given unheeded warning about something else at that time.

Where had he been after his recall in February, 1944? At the Savoy, at The Swan in Stratford-on-Avon and at 'Burford in the Cotswolds'. The last was new to me. Why had they put him in that little country town?

He came back to the arrest of 'Madeleine':

The phone call from R.G. [Renée Garry] to give away 'Madeleine' was the fact that provoked the arrest. Elseway 'Madeleine' would have been arrested much later. As there was a double game on, from both sides, the Germans thought 'Madeleine' had been thrown away by the British, not by private interest. The Germans had lost the 'Madeleine' way... They were keen to find her but not to arrest her. When R.G. phoned, they thought the British did it on purpose — if they had not arrested her a German agent would have been unmasked as a consequence of it.

I was not sure what he meant, but it sounded uncommonly like what Mercier had suggested to me many years ago, that Kieffer was not really keen to arrest 'Madeleine', and only did it, when Renée rang, for fear that if he did not Renée would tell the British the German game. Déricourt bade me remember that message of which I had told him, 'May God keep you'.

He protested at my having seemed to defend the French police press release:

> The police invites the journalists... they take photo of you handcuffed with a non shaved face — elseway they make you look as villain as possible... Everybody who has been arrested once in his life will... laugh and hate you (not me).

Of his air-crash at Orly, and of my fear of finding myself attacking a dead man if he died of his injuries, he wrote:

> Why not attack a dead man ... it is a bourgeois error to think of the deads as you do. If I die tomorrow will you change your mind about me? The way you think of me? The way you speak of me? No.

But I had ceased to think unkindly of him already. He made a plea:

> Don't you see what a curious German agent I was? What could I have done to them, to be permitted to do so much against them?...
>
> Watt has never been German controlled. Once more, how to explain that I was a German agent? I should have given my radio operator. How can you imagine that I had enough credit with the SD to make the Germans leave me uncontrolled a radio operator?... What a bad German agent I was or what a powerful German agent! Add that with the people I did not denounce, that makes a lot — in balance with what? The mail?... Do you think I could have satisfied the Germans with 'Prosper's' mail and even Bonoteaux and one or two (unknown yet) more? No — See what happens with the others networks in German hands. 'Prosper' washed out.

Frager the same thing — North circuit (Pick, McAll)? — Nord Pole Nancy, 'Carte', Normandy Max and 'Leopold' — 'Phono' — Interallié — and so on — nothing left behind — not a chance of double crossing — May be after all they left the 'Gilbert' network and 'Gilbert' himself.

This I pondered long. It was one of those Sibylline or Delphic pronouncements of Déricourt, probably true yet capable of bearing diametrically opposed meanings. Did he mean he had been so artful with the Germans as to content them with very little, or that they were content with very little because they hoped for something much bigger from him, the date and place of this invasion? Surely he would not have been so wicked as to give them that, or if he had been so wicked even as to conceive the intent, so stupid as to say so, and on paper? What was I meant to understand? Of course, if the Germans believed he would be able to tell them the date and place of the invasion, that would give him the power to mislead them.

Our correspondence had always been interrupted by occasional periods during which he seemed to be incommunicado, but the longest was the one that followed this letter. I worried, because of the escalating unrest in South-East Asia, and especially in and around Vientiane and other parts of Laos. On 4 August I heard the BBC report a state of emergency in Laos, and I did not know whether letters addressed to him care of Air Laos would continue to be delivered.

Apart from concern for his life, there were matters of which I was sure he would wish to be informed. I received a series of letters from a Mr Lescender, in the United States, saying he was making 'an index to characters in books about SOE', and asking me for the real name of 'Gilbert'. I replied that I had promised 'Gilbert' not to give it, as he could see in my book. He said he had written to the two Croydon newspapers asking for the name of the pilot in the smuggling case, but they declined to give it — on instructions, he supposed from the British Government, but he would get it somehow. (Obviously he would, for he had only to get someone to look at the Paris papers.) Then I received letters from a Mr Bulhof in Holland asking for the real name of Déricourt. He said some not very nice things about Irene, and some phrases made me think he was in contact with Lescender. I supposed it was on the latter's behalf he wanted 'Gilbert's' name. I wrote to Bulhof pointing out I had promised 'Gilbert' not to give it, and received a reply saying it was obvious that it was on orders from the British Government that I refused to give 'Gilbert's' name. Then Elizabeth rang me and said she had just received a letter from Lescender asking for it and saying 'Miss Fuller, having obtained most of her information from the enemy, is unwilling to answer questions'. Next came a triumphant letter from Bulhof who had obtained the name Déricourt — from Lescender. I wrote about all this to Déricourt, sending copies to him at his QBG Club.

Apart from the fighting in Laos, there was another reason why Air Laos might no longer find him. He was coming up to his fiftieth birthday, and had always told me pilots were compulsorily retired at fifty. In one letter he had said he thought to retire to the Lebanon. In a later letter he had said he thought he would retire to Baghdad. I was on the point of writing to the *Daily Telegraph* Correspondent in Vientiane to ask if Déricourt was still there, when I received a letter from Déricourt, posted from Cambodia (in English):

Dear Jean,

Just receiving your 2nd Sept, letter. Thanks for the greetings. 50th but younger than ever. No I will not retire yet — I am in a job which pays, so, I will carry on a little while — Anyway I can retire when I like — It is up to me.

There is a lot of things I can't tell you by letter — even from a free country like Cambodia. I travelled these last three months everywhere in Far East. With all I saw, met and listen to, you could make ten books. Your dear friend Irene and her father Mac would certainly have been very interested. Will you tell them that? I wrote already a letter with some answers, but was not able to post it yet... Thanks for the book *Idyll of the White Lotus.*

No — no business in Beirut or Baghdad. I sold all my shares of the TL Lebanon. I think I will look more to Far East. Tokio interest me very much. Unfortunately I have not enough money to start what I like.

In Laos the situation is the biggest bluff I have ever seen. There are very few fights — of the two quoted near Vientiane, one was a looting from bandits come (probably) from Thailand — and the other a great fear caused by some shooting of rabbits by night (French people) — in North just guerilla and smooth infiltration — but no big fight — no modern weapons — Being on the spot *every day* I saw only one killed and one wounded by firearms in two months. What Laos needs is some activity, more business, so any UNO army coming (what for?) any American help (dollars) will be welcomed. The papers mean there (Laos) have nothing to speak of so they invent or at least emphasis (correct?) hundred times.

Sorry to have let you down so long time. I was busy on all fronts. I am working too much. I learn too much Chinese — and I sleep too few.

Your good friend,
HENRY

I showed Irene the letter when she came to dinner with me. Déricourt was not normally familiar, so his reference to Irene and her 'father Mac' referred obviously to her access to the Prime Minister, disguised in case of interception of the mail.

'Something he would think of!' she said, with a glint of humour, that had no malice.

We supposed 'smooth infiltration' to mean arrival from Russia or the Communist world of arms and equipment though not soldiers. We wondered if he flew over Communist territory.

'I don't want him back in Intelligence,' I said firmly. 'Not even in the service of our own government.'

Irene took my point.

A few days afterwards came a letter from Thailand, written just after receiving mine saying I was on the point of writing to the *Daily Telegraph* Correspondent in Laos. Déricourt wrote (in English):

17–9–59

Dear Jean,

No, I am not killed, wounded, prisoner or anything like that. I have been very busy and not often at home — does I have a home anyway? No, I'm not in Paris. I shall be in Paris for Christmas only, no QBG yet.

No I would not like to write for Papers and I know quite well Robinson — I'll check if he is not F. Robertson — May be I did not get his name properly — I brought him many times over there — I met too a cameraman — TV and pictures — Lennox. Don't worry about me. I am too busy that's all.

As I told you before I could give some help to Irene or her boss for their commercial business — I know prices of everything on all markets in the Far East — I could send you nearly every day the rates for the office dealing with his Foreign business — Let me know...

Sorry to leave you so quick

Very friendly,
HENRY

This worried me a bit. I felt it of paramount importance he should not get sucked back into espionage. On the other hand, if market prices were something innocent, I did not want to stand in the way of something that could be worth while. After some hesitation, I sent a copy to Irene, but I was really not sorry the matter went no further.

The end of September brought a bulging envelope from Déricourt, containing the long letter he had begun on 21 July and left at Luapg Prabang, which was the reply to a number of mine telling him things he would wish to know. He thought Lescender and Bulhof were not wasps but merely gnats. I had to tell him there was now another gnat, an E.H. Cookridge. He had sent a book of his, *Sisters of Delilah*, to Irene, asking her opinion of it. As she observed to me, this was plainly in the hope she would say something flattering about it, which he would use in publicity. She had not time to read it, and gave it to me to read on her behalf. I told her the stories were recapitulated from the published books of other authors, except where invented. What worried us was that he said in his letter to her he was writing the history of SOE. She checked with Robin Hooper, who assured her he had never even heard of E.H. Cookridge, and the historian they appointed would have academic qualifications. Irene told me she would not reply to Cookridge.

Then there were articles in *John Bull* by Charles Wighton entitled 'They Spied over England'. They alleged an Abwehr agent had been infiltrated into England by an aircraft leaving from Fleurines. Could this be vexatious for Déricourt?

In the *Daily Telegraph* there had been a piece about the smuggling of heroin from Laos. It was said to be almost impossible to stop, because almost all the pilots flying in and out of Laos carried it. I sent him this with a note scribbled across the top expressing the profound hope he was not one of them.

In his earlier letter from Luang Prabang, of 1 June, Déricourt had set out a number of questions which he wished I would ask Irene to ask Robin Hooper. They related to one we had discussed in Paris. Irene asked me to set them out in typescript. I seem not to have kept a copy, but the substance was: Did SOE really send a message to what it thought to be its Dutch Section, requiring that the agent 'Anton', whose return was desired, should contact in Paris 'Marcel' and 'Gilbert', as Huntermann had told me; and, if the answer was 'yes', by 'Marcel' did they mean Agazarian or Marcel Charbonnier, and by 'Gilbert' did they mean Déricourt or Gilbert Norman ('Archambaud'). If the latter, was a corresponding message sent to him, telling him to meet 'Anton' at Square Clignancourt? Déricourt was convinced the answer to all these questions was 'no' and I had hoped there might be something in the files which would refute the story if it were Christmann's invention. The reply, however, from Robin Hooper, which Irene gave me, was that he did not know and, short of interrogating all the persons concerned, did not know how to find out.

Then, a book had appeared, *Count Five and Die* by Barry Wynne (Corgi, 1959), a copy of which I sent him. Though presented as nonfiction, I believed it fiction. Addresses in London I checked did not exist. The theme was that agents had been sent into Holland with the intention they should fall into German hands and, under torture, break down and reveal the misinformation with which they had been briefed, that the invasion would be in through Holland. That it should have been written at all at least showed the idea that London was playing some kind of a game was beginning to catch people's minds. Russell, Jannsen and Baker are characters in it, mentioned in our correspondence.

Most important for me, the French publishers, Fayard, had made an offer for the French translation rights of *Double Webs*, conditional on 'Gilbert's' writing them a letter undertaking not to sue them for libel if they published it. Would he do that?

Also, there had arrived from Mauritius a young Daniel Antelme, nephew of Major France Antelme, 'Antoine'. His uncle, he told me, was not South African but Mauritian, though he had a business in Durban. During the period between his return to England in August 1943 and being parachuted back on his last — and fatal — mission, the letters which Uncle France had written to his brother (Daniel's father) were gloomy as though filled with foreboding. Daniel had learned from my books that his uncle had been parachuted straight into German hands and had come to ask if I could add anything to that. Really, it was all I knew. Irene, whom I told of his visit, had him to dinner at the House of Commons, but of course had not known his uncle. He came back to me and asked whether I would forward letters to Ernest and 'Gilbert'. This I did. Vogt replied direct to Daniel that he would be happy to receive him if he came to Germany. I thought this was a good offer, but when Daniel came to see me the last time he told me Miss Atkins, whom he had seen since, had advised him against going: the little Vogt would have to say would not be worth the expense and fatigue of the journey. By this he was discouraged, but still hoped for a reply from 'Gilbert' giving him at least some kind of idea of what sort of a man his uncle was.

Déricourt, in his long letter (in English), covered some of these recent questions, but first touched on an earlier point:

I agree about the dead but in a way it is very unpleasant to be accused in the place of a dead... unpleasant to bear the burden without any defense — everything is unpleasant — so, a rascal dead is a dead rascal. 'Prosper' was a hero — yes and a great one, but a mad hero — I don't want to carry on. Have you read *J'irai crachersur vos tombes* [*I will spit on your tombs*] by Boris Vian?

Pact — What a fool in all that is said of him is that 'Prosper' trusted more Kieffer — for rightness — than his own chiefs — no that is wrong. I knew him... 'Prosper' could have thrown away all his network in a moment of a kind of madness — to avoid any other Organiser to lead it after him. He had built it — he could not lead it to his end, he committed suicide, a collective suicide. There is a point which bothers me — it is that Darling was more than an agent for him — he was a felloe countryman — they were very alike — they liked each other — although Darling was an agent from Culioli and that there was some dissent between C and P. What doesn't fit is that Darling was the *first* the very first agent to be given by 'Prosper'. He gave him no chance to escape. So it looks as though somebody else had willingly — on purpose — tried to destroy the mind of 'Prosper' in giving the first blow to the best friend, the strongest opponent to the Germans — like in the chivalry times, when the King was killed the army flew. Really that doesn't fit... for me that *means something*, but I don't know what — yet.

What a fool is that de Vomécourt. That is a hero of the boasting kind of heroes. They boast that they are pure heroes — but nobody is pure — and de V less than the average hero.

He should have close his mouth like me … he is too French. I think I am a bit British (don't show your feelings) — an eel from the Channel waters, just in the middle.

OK for the editor. You can say that I have only minor things to add or change that does not import for the book — and about my name and about Gilbert on the jacket. I will cooperate and give my agreement as soon as I see the script in French. I have not changed my mind.

I am Knight of the Imperial Silent, double cross, 'sur fond de gueule' — with an eel circling round which bites his tail. That is heraldry.

Continued from Luang Prabang Thursday, 5.8.59

I let you down a little while because we had troubles hereabout. First we met with the worst weather I have seen for months — low clouds, continuous rain, no visibility and naturally no radio — secondly the opponent to the Lao Government get in open revolt — burned villages, killed soldiers and so on. Some people call them Pathet Lao (free Lao), someones Vietminh (Viet free) and others says others. I think the truth is a mixture of them — as usual — but anyway that makes everything difficult.

Barry Wynne speaks of the operation in the Pas de Calais area. I heard of it. There was one in Normandie too — they were deceiving actions with a certain action to deceive the deceiver. At the end of it nobody knows who was deceived. Did you read *Alice in Wonderland* from Lewis Carroll? about the false tortoise, she says, 'Ne croyez jamais ne pas être différent de ce qu'il pourrait paraitre aux autres que ce que vous etiez ou pournez avoir été n'était pas différent que ce que vous avez été qui leur avait semblé différent.' That seems a fantasy, but analysed is profoundly true. In my book I says something similar. 'Je sais que tu sais queje sais que tu sais, et tu es bête de penser queje suis assez bête de penser que tu es bête.' [I know that you know that I know that you know, and you are stupid to think I am stupid enough to think you are

286

stupid.] There is no stop, but if you stick very close to the meaning of it, you can control the situation.

So to come back to us — 'Prosper', me and others — we were not, far as I know, in the case of Russell, Jannsen or Bakker but all I can say is the position of SOE towards us has not always been fair. Probably 'Prosper' understood it on his trip to London in June '43 as I had understood it before. As I was the first I had time to take my 'own measures' instead of him, no time was left to him, the fruit was not ripe but already rotten. And anyway could he had the possibility to do anything?'...

I don't say my case was that of Russell — no — but SOE was not fair — that would explain some sentences — 'Mind your own business' [to George Starr] and 'Cut at once' and sending supplies and even people into German hands. I expect only that it was really for the victory and not for private revenge or private safety, but I am not sure — especially in operation 'Alceste'. I can imagine too what 'Prosper' understood in London in June '43.

I was surprised and delighted Déricourt should be a devotee of *Alice's Adventures in Wonderland* (obviously quoted by him from memory of some French translation). The passage from 'The Mock Turtle's Story' must have held a moral for Déricourt.

Lescender he seemed to confuse either with Cookridge or the yet unchosen official historian:

> ... the Lescender letter. So far as I can understand a new danger is arising at my horizon. An history of SOE! I can imagine how I could be represented in it! And by an American! So I think it is better I write to him the letter I enclose — could you forward it — that would avoid me to give my address and you could judge of the opportunity of doing it — (I am asking an advice).

The enclosed letter to Lescender began:

> Sir,
> I have been informed by Miss Fuller you have discovered my name and could print it...

It was the first time he had asked me to judge a situation for him. My advice was to do nothing, for the moment, as it was not yet clear Lescender intended to do anything. In fact we heard no more from him.

For Daniel Antelme he had enclosed a letter (in French):

> My dear friend,
> I am much moved by receiving a letter from a relative of 'Antoine'... I think I have told all I know of your uncle to Miss Fuller, and am sure she will have repeated it faithfully. No it was not indiscreet on your part to write to me. I can only repeat that 'Antoine' was magnificent, worked like a lion, people adored him. He knew how to take responsibility and how to command ... He was also a *bon vivant* and made the most of Paris... and as he was very good-looking, had much success with women...
> If you want precise details of the last times I spent with him, see persons with whom he was in contact, ask me specifically what you want to know...

Daniel Antelme was not too shocked by the hint of his uncle's affairs. His father had told him Uncle France was a *bon viveur* and did not get on with his wife, and I had told him rather more. Renée Garry had said at her trial she had been in love with 'Antoine', who had been her lover till 'Madeleine' came, and a very respectable English lady, not an agent, had told me she was expecting to marry him after the war, when his divorce came through. In a sense 'Antoine', by setting Renée against 'Madeleine', had provoked the drama which resulted in the radio-game to which he fell victim.

Daniel left it at that. Miss Atkins, he told me, had advised him not to pursue his inquiry; so he did not take up Déricourt's invitation to just specific questions.

October found us exercised over Charles Wighton's book, *Pin-Stripe Saboteur: The Story of 'Robin'*, which had just appeared from Odhams. Déricourt was not named, but was clearly identifiable as the character referred to on pages 213–15 as responsible for the betrayal of the whole 'Prosper-Robin' organisation. I had myself once thought that, but had long known the fall would have come without him. What made me indignant was that on the one hand he was incorrectly identified with a certain Abwehr agent (details about whom, in one of Wighton's other books, made quite plain he was not Déricourt), and on the other a British secret report on the French Section, prepared after the war was cited against him.

How had Wighton obtained the right to quote from 'a British secret report'? As it happened, passages from it had been read aloud to me by Elizabeth, who had obtained a copy from a source that was unlikely to have been Wighton's. Compiled neither for publication nor action, this 'dormant document' had poised question-marks over the loyalty of Déricourt, Gilbert Norman ('Archambaud') and Frager. Elizabeth and I had considered it impossible to quote from as it was not supposed to be in circulation, and it seemed to us iniquitous that a paper written under conditions of absolute privilege should be used in a commercial publication to condemn an individual who could not see the passage in context. We both talked to Irene about it. I said my feeling was that just because Déricourt's position was delicate, it was worse than if the attack had been made on someone who could collect enormous damages. Déricourt could not possibly sue; and yet the publication was unfair to him. Irene agreed; and asked a question about it in the House of Commons.[5]

Not wishing to increase the sales of *Pin-Stripe Saboteur*, she did not mention its title and unfortunately Selwyn Lloyd thought she was referring to *Odette* by Jerrard Tickell, which rendered his reply inconsequential. When she showed him *Pin-Stripe Saboteur* afterwards, outside the Chamber, opened at pages 214–15, he said he would look into it. Later he told her it seemed that former staff officers of SOE must have taken copies of the report into their homes and lent them to other people, and that as he did not know how many might by this time be in circulation it would not be practical to take action.

That being the position, I wrote to Déricourt telling him what else I could remember from it touching him: that the 'famous British officer... working for the de Gaulle Section', who first asked for him to be investigated was Yeo-Thomas, not now to be reckoned an enemy; and — since he was guessing wildly as to the authorship of the report — that it was by an academic called Mackenzie, of Manchester University.

Déricourt took the whole matter less heavily than I did. He thought anybody able to recognise the reference would see the exaggeration in the picture of himself as 'the Arch Villain who betrayed everything. Didn't you know he stole, then, the Waterloo Bridge and was never caught.' He wrote a mildly mocking letter for me to transmit to Wight-on, asking a few questions and saying he might call on Weil. For the real mystery of the book concerned the identity of its subject. Wighton had told me he was writing a book about Jacques

---

[5] *Hansard*, vols 6–7, no 58, pp 1258–9

Weil. Déricourt told me the adventures related were largely those of Jean Worms:

> 'Robin' was the code-name of Jean Worms not Jacques Weil. Jean was a British officer, he had sworn the Secrets Act Oath, tested and trained in the schools. He could be 'Organiser' and chief of a British network; Jacques, no.

He declared that Worms, the real 'Robin', had been made by Wighton into the second-in-command and called 'Jules'.

> The [account of the] arrival of 'Jules' is completely fantastic. We were parachuted blind together on 21.1.43 at Freville en Gatinais, Loiret. Jacques was not there.

I told Déricourt my strange story of Weil; of how I had written to him saying I first heard of him from Vogt, who was his interrogator whilst a prisoner at Avenue Foch Weil had come to see me and left it until half way through the evening to claim he had never been arrested. Déricourt replied, in English: 'Good for Ernest!'

It was a new note for him, and made me smile. But to be fair and eliminate any possibility of confusion with Worms, he asked me to ask Ernest the date of the episode. I did, and he replied that he thought it was about the end of January; but in fact I found in one of his earlier letters (12 September 1954), written before he knew the matter would become controversial, 'February or end of January' given as the date when they captured an Organiser who asked to be allowed to speak to 'Archambaud'. This quite put out of court the possibility of confusion with Worms, arrested on 1 July of the previous year; but even without the date, as Déricourt wrote, 'Ernest ... a [half] Swiss would have been able to tell another

Swiss!'. Vogt had first told me the story in 1950 as relating to a Swiss Organiser.

I looked at *Pin-Stripe Saboteur* to see what Weil was supposed to have been doing in January or February 1944, and oddly enough saw that, having left France at the time of the mass arrests in July 1943, he re-entered it and was held up by the local Feldgendarmerie 'in the early spring of 1944', though he said he bluffed them into letting him go.

What really surprised me in *Pin-Stripe Saboteur* was the statement (page 188) that in order to find out whether 'Prosper' had been arrested, 'Robin', meaning Weil, 'sent one of his men to the small hotel in the rue de Mazagran where he alone knew "Prosper" had been living'.

When I had made that table of 'Prosper's' known movements and contacts between his return to France and arrest, it had shown up that the only people he was known to have met were (apart from 'Archambaud' and 'Denise', both dead) Mme Balachowsky, Guerne, Déricourt, Mme Guépin and Marcel Charbonnier, all of whom had stated the Hôtel Mazagran address was unknown to them. I had not thought about Weil. By claiming to be the only person to have known it, he had placed himself in the front line of suspicion. (It could be, however, that Wight-on had invented this distinction for him, without realising what he was letting him in for.)

Further, Elizabeth had obtained a roll of the members of the Interallié, on which figured, to the astonishment of both of us, the name of Jacques Weil, with code-name 'Atin'.

It is only fair to add that Guerne, to whom I wrote about Weil, expressed himself revolted anyone should 'look for lice in his hair'. It was he who had undertaken the dangerous negotiation with a police officer for the freeing of the

Tambour sisters, and he had financed the 'Prosper' network 'from his private fortune'.

On 3 October a fuchsia flowered that I had grown in my flat. I made several studies of it in oil paints, and sent one of them to Déricourt. He replied (in English):

Vientiane
15 Oct, 1959

Dear Jean,

I received yesterday your painting. Thank you very much. It is really nice...

'Marc' was my second in command ... his real name (for you) is Clément, Rémy. He is still alive and still my friend.

... *Quiet American* — the book is very good [I had asked him if Graham Greene's novel gave a true picture of Saigon]... Weil was in the Interallié — he was not arrested — he did not fly — ... now if Weil is a friend of de Vomécourt it is full house... Operation Snails — no it was before Darling arrest...

We were developing our own shorthand. Re-reading this after so many years, I wondered to what it referred. Then I found on page 177 of the Wighton, in my own red pencil, 'snails'. It was against a story of Weil's having come to Gisors in May, found German troops there, taken to the woods and lived for twelve days on mushrooms and snails. Déricourt glossed, 'Snails, raw... a bit strong.'

We had a lot of fun from this book, as well as finding in it some serious matter. Déricourt arranged his pages of points under headings: *What Makes Me Laugh* and *What Does Not Make Me Laugh*. Under the latter he had written, 'The British Sacrificing the French (I know something about it. I was considered British!)' The reference was to railway sabotage entailing blowing up of locomotives without regard for their

French crews (Weil was stated to have refused to take part in this). Another of the things that did not make Déricourt laugh was a quotation from Sir Frederick Morgan's *Overture to Overlord* regarding a feint invasion, off France, in September 1943 — of which the Resistance was not warned. That was a plain sacrificing of whatever elements might rise, to support.

He emphasised the difference between people like Worms and himself, who were French but had signed the British Official Secrets Act, and those like Frager and Weil, who had not signed it. Of the latter's withdrawal to Switzerland he went on to say:

> The second difference between Weil and me is that I did not take cover willingly, letting down my agents. I was called back imperatively... My last BBC message was, 'Is my journey really necessary?', The answer came, 'For X (not "Gilbert") your last journey is really necessary.' So I understood at once. Anyway, I hoped to be back in France soon on another mission. I was wrong.

At the time I was shocked by Déricourt's not having wanted to escape from a situation in which he was obliged to inform to Boemelburg. There are things one understands only slowly. A double agent protects those working under him — but only so long as he continues working as a double. A double cannot withdraw without leaving his agents exposed. Only when I saw this did I realise how appalling the recall to London must have been to Déricourt. He would have needed to be able to see Boemelburg in the few days gained by prevarication with Morel; only then could he leave with any confidence that his departure would not be the signal for Boemelburg's giving the order to arrest 'Marc', 'Claire' and Watt.

I was surprised to hear from Déricourt, on 4 November, that he had received a letter from Weil, asking for an appointment. On his letter to Wighton he had put only 'c/o Miss Fuller', and my address, but of course Weil, being in Paris, had probably looked in the Paris telephone directory and found 58 rue Pergolèse. Mme Déricourt would have forwarded his letter. As it chanced, Déricourt was in fact once more expecting to return to Paris, and promised himself some interesting interviews in Europe:

> Well, Ernest.. I'll be in France in January — may be for Christmas — may be for Eve — I'll phone you on my arrival.

He sent me a pretty Christmas card, postmarked 'Hong Kong, 25 Dec., 1959'. Then he vanished.

I flew to Paris, and called at the Club QBG on 4 January 1960. The Secretary thought he must have re-entered France, though he had not yet called to pick up his mail. I dined *en famille* with Colonel Mercier, as he had now become, at his home in a leafy suburb. He begged me to consider it possible that Déricourt not only had been but still was an agent of the Foreign Office. I said I was sure it was not so. It would have been mean, I felt, to give away that he seemed to have been trying to make contact with it — with his offer of market prices — through me and Irene.

I called again at the QBG, and found the Secretary by now mystified. She had telephoned a number of times to the rue Pergolèse, but no one was answering. She was certain of his departure from Laos, yet he appeared not to have arrived in France. He must have left the aircraft on the way. Perhaps at Beirut.

On my return to London my mother, who had come in to make a meal for me, told me there had been a telephone call from a man who seemed to know all about my researches. He had said, 'I know all her friends'. She had not been able to get his name properly. Though he repeated it a number of times, all she could get was 'Kridge', or 'Cridge'. 'But we had quite a chat!'

I did not altogether like this. My mother did not follow my researches in detail, and could have been trapped into disclosing something I would not have imparted to a person unknown. I begged her to be guarded with anyone who claimed to know all my friends.

January passed into February. I continued writing — rather forlornly — to Air Laos. On 4 March I received a letter (in English) which had taken a long time in transit, posted from Siam but internally dated Vientiane. It began:

10.1.1960

Dear Jean,

I am a bit late to bless you Happy New Year … we had some parties which ended very late, mostly because the night is very cool (+10C)... there have been so many changes here that nobody knows what is going to happen now.

I delighted myself very much when in 'Pinstripe' I read the chapter against the Arch-villain … It is not my will to change a word of it. It helps me and shows the malicious permanent will … I am eager to know what is 'really' on the Lahousen Diary about Fleunnes — but the whole of it. If you meet W, please ask him in my name.

He had two questions about his novel:

1. Where — when — did W. Churchill (the P.M.) said 'Ma conscience est une bonne fille avec laquelle je m'arrange très bien' — in English evidently?

2. Secondly, during the war, how was he to be called when speaking straight to him: Sir, Your honour?

The quotation I did not know. For 'Your honour', I told him he must have heard it when up before the Croydon magistrates. I promised to catch mistakes of this sort when the manuscript reached me.

I had some qualms with regard to Déricourt's novel. I was sure it was a bluff, intended to give the impression he had been authorised in everything he had done from some inconceivably high quarter — doubtless Churchill himself, since he wanted to know how one would address him during an interview. Nothing of this did I believe. Nevertheless, my task would be to translate a work of fiction, not to say I believed it masked a truth. Perhaps he would agree to my putting in a 'translator's note', reserving my own position.

Elizabeth, about this time, conceived the notion he had been, secretly from SOE, a BCRA agent — the Gaullist organisation. 'An agent of his own government' she suggested to me on the telephone, and Irene later told me Elizabeth had suggested the same thing to her. I did not think it was so, yet it was an extra cover for him and I did not oppose it.

I did not think he was anybody's agent. I was sure he had no authorisation from anywhere. It was something he could not avow, because it would make him technically guilty. Yet I did not feel he was a devil without a conscience. As I thought it out to myself, he had found himself in some way trapped and had, by a bargain he could not own, done better for the French Section than it would have for itself, by sustaining the Lysander traffic. He would have put it to the Germans along the lines, 'You can look but not touch. If you arrest the agents, you kill the goose that lays the golden egg.' I hoped the arrests at the November moon had come about not through a planned sacrifice but through a mistake, but had no evidence to prove it.

On 16 February I learned the French rights in *Double Webs* had been sold to Fayard, and their M. Mousset came to see me. I told him 'Gilbert's' two conditions: that his real name must never appear anywhere, and 'Gilbert' not on the jacket — as it could catch his wife's eye from a shop-window. I also wrote to Déricourt.

He replied on 1 March 1960, enclosing a letter for Fayard (in French):

> c/o Miss Fuller
> 1.3.60
>
> Sir,
>
> I have a letter of Miss Fuller of February 16 that Editions Fayard have acquired the French translation rights of *Double Webs*, published in London by Putnam. I have the unfortunate honour to be the principal personage of this book and inform you Miss Fuller and I have made an agreement I am sure you will wish to take into consideration.
>
> I assure you I shall hinder you very little … I worked with Miss Fuller and the most large spirit of comprehension and even collaboration reigned over our discussions...

He set out his conditions — that his real name must never appear, 'Gilbert' permitted in the text but not on the jacket, and that the translation be submitted to his approval.

In his covering letter to me he wrote (in English):

> I answer to Fayard — through you as usual. I know a Mr Paul Mousset. Ask him in my name if he is Christian Scientist — if yes — he is the man I know — and you can tell him everything about me.

This gave me to think. I had read Baker Eddy's book *Science and Health* expressly in search of what it might be in her teaching that was meaningful to Déricourt; yet I could not catch a connection between his though and hers. Her teaching seemed to be that since God was good and the universe was in God, only good existed, and evil was an illusion. Translating that into theosophical terms, the terms of *The Secret Doctrine* of H.P. Blavatsky, I would suggest that by God she had in mind the One in its state of non-manifestation, or Pralaya, between universes, the poles of good and evil coming into being with manifestation, Manvantara, the birth of the physical universe. But I did not feel Déricourt regarded evil as an illusion. He had a terrific sense of the immanence of God, but the image that seemed to be before his eyes was of a pair of scales — like those in the *Papyrus of Ani* (the Egyptian *Book of the Dead*) — in which the good deeds of the deceased were going to be set on one side and the bad ones on the other. As he had, unfortunately, some big bad ones — the deaths of those who were trailed from his landing fields and arrested were heavy weights on the wrong side — he had to work hard to get the scales even. But now it came to me that his idea of Christian Science might have come not from the book but from an encounter. If he had met a man — Paul Mousset — who seemed to him of particularly pure and virtuous life, who said he was a Christian Scientist, who spoke of their being only God and therefore of the laws of God and Science being one, might that not have operated, or triggered, his 'conversion' — which Déricourt himself converted into terms of his own thinking? He knew he had to make reparation, yet had confidence his inner confession had rendered him already graced. That gave him his strength, his buoyancy, the ability —

however many times he re-descended into bitterness of recrimination over the past — to come up, serene again.

Meanwhile the paperback of the English edition was in preparation and I sent Déricourt a typescript draft of an additional chapter, which he returned to me interleaved with sheets of yellow paper on which he had written suggestions and comments (in English):

> The game was so intricate and so unfair that I had to take my own measures — first to save my life, secondly to save the lives of my friends I had recruited as agents, for whom I was responsible. I had pulled them into this fishy business; I had to pull them out.
>
> I add for yourself only — Do you think anybody has the right to judge me? Who betrayed first? And where does betrayal begin?

In the same envelope he returned to me an article I had sent him, by Nicholas Bodington, 'Dead or Alive', in *The People* of 21 February 1960. With it was a letter, 'not to be used or shown to anybody, any way'.

So long as Bodington was alive I never used or showed it to anyone. It consisted of thirty-one points upon which Déricourt was not quite in agreement with Bodington's account of how things happened during his visit to the field in July/August 1943. Most of them are without serious significance — for instance, that Bodington was not parachuted, as he said, but landed by Lysander or Hudson on a field near the village of Soucelles, near Angers, to reception by Déricourt and 'Marc'. Some of the other claims in the article were branded simply, but I felt probably truly, 'Fiction for newspapers'. The commentary becomes of serious import only where it touches the arrest of Agazarian, and now that Bodington has passed away, I feel I should make it available for history. Against Bodington's account, Déricourt wrote:

> No the arrest of Agazanan was not the fault of Frager — in spite of I disliked him — it is the fault of 'Archambaud' first and Bod second.

I knew what he meant here. 'Archambaud', since his capture, had given his code, his double security check and timetable to the Germans, enabling them to transmit in his name back to London. They offered Bodington an appointment in a certain flat — of a Madame Ferdi Filipowsky in the rue de Rome, said Déricourt — and Bodington had sent Agazarian to keep it in his place. Bodington himself had written that he and Agazarian both wished to go to the dangerous rendezvous, and had tossed a coin for it. Agazarian had the misfortune to win. Against this, Déricourt had written, 'No coin. I was there.'

That I believed. I was less sure I believed Déricourt had attempted to warn 'Agazarian'. Perhaps, but it would have jeopardised his chance of saving Bodington's life and his own. If nobody walked into the trap, Boemelburg would suspect Déricourt had warned them, and would have given orders for Déricourt as well to be arrested. If somebody walked into it, he would fume, but assume Bodington had sent a lesser man from natural prudence, not necessarily because of having been warned by Déricourt. In that case Déricourt could still hope to save Bodington. Agazarian had been sacrificed. It was not a happy thing. It could have been because of that that Bodington had given evidence for Déricourt at his trial. The only arrest which the prosecution had tried to pin on Déricourt was Agazarian's, whereas it was Bodington who, as much the senior officer, had sent him into the trap. Déricourt would have found himself obliged to explain that, had not Bodington gone

301

into the box and, by taking responsibility for having authorised Déricourt's contact with the Germans, in a global sense, rendered the Prosecution's accusations idle to pursue in detail.

Déricourt finished his letter:

> So, dear Jean, I ask you not to use that — please — I don't want any harm to Bodington. Thank you.

He enclosed a letter for me to send Bodington care of *The People*: (in French, using the familiar 'tu'):

> My dear Nic,
>
> I have just received extracts from *The People* about you. I am very glad to have indirect news of you. To my way of thinking you ought to have written something on this subject long ago and made a little money. 'Money had no odour,' said Vespasian to his son. You have too much proper pride and others not enough.
>
> As regards myself, I am back in harness in the Far East. I am almost happy. I work like a brute and have succeeded in re-establishing my situation which was not brilliant. I have used my hours of leisure to write a book about my war adventures. It is very daring. I should like to dedicate it to you, for I have always retained for you an admiration, but that might cause you a nuisance. In any case I shall let you read it, in about a month.
>
> Send me your address, quickly. I dare not ask after your wife.
>
> Je t'embrasse
HENRI

I had indeed supposed it was his own adventures he was writing under disguised form though till now he had spoken of a novel. I would have sent the letter care of *The People*, but realised it was published by Odhams, the publishers of

Wighton's book. In case of any crossing of the wires, I held it back and wrote to Déricourt explaining the reflections that gave me pause. He thanked me for not having sent the letter on.

In his comments on Bodington's article, Déricourt mentioned 'Claire', and I took the occasion to ask him if she had been his mistress. No, he replied; it was her husband, Aisner, who was a friend of his in the first place, though it was Jean Besnard, whom after her divorce she married, with whom 'Claire' shared the flat in which he installed Bodington, and who owned the house at Yerres where they lodged him during the latter part of his stay. Jean was not an agent but would hide a wireless. Before Jean, it was a M. Brulé, a cameraman, who was the friend of 'Claire'. She had been in the film business, her sister, Marie-Rose, being married to Emminente, a producer; their father lived in Hanoi. 'I sent her to G.B. to be trained.' She left before Easter and came back by the plane that brought 'Elie', 'Bastien' and 'Simone' to a field near St Martin-le-Beau, where 'Marc' and he received them.

In the new chapter I was preparing to be added to the paperback edition of *Double Webs* (retitled by Pan *Double Agent?*), I tried to make things better for Déricourt by saying something of the 'Denise' letters — and in other ways. I also referred to the novel *Count Five and Die*, and said that while I had found no trace of a deception plan designed to make the Germans think we intended to invade through Holland, a thought did occur to me. If the misinformation with which Starr was briefed in May 1943, that the invasion would be in two or three months, resulted from what Buckmaster disclosed in *They Fought Alone*, that he had been told from higher up that the invasion would be in the summer of 1943, this might mean that the high strategy was using the SOE agents — to suggest to the Germans the advisability of holding in France all that summer divisions which might with greater effect have been used in another field. This I wrote in 1960, simply out of my own head (though when I told Elizabeth on the telephone she said it had occurred to her too). It was, however, only a theory. It will be obvious that neither Elizabeth nor I had at that time seen General Sir Frederick Morgan's book *Overture to Overlord* (Hodder, 1950), save the brief citation from it in Wighton's *Pin-Stripe Saboteur*, in which the feint invasion of September 1943 was admitted but not really explained. That it was to protect our troops in Italy still seems to me as believable as another argument recently put forward, that it was to help Stalin and the Russians.

It was over a year that Elizabeth had had in her possession Mackenzie's 'secret' history of SOE — it had been given her in Paris when she went over in January 1959. I do not know why, therefore, it was only on 8 April 1960 that Irene, when she came to supper at my flat, told me she had been profoundly shaken by a passage in the Mackenzie typescript Elizabeth had shown her. It said that 'Antoine' (Major Joseph France Antelme), when he was parachuted on 29 February 1944, was on his return to have reported direct to Anthony Eden. She had always known de Guélis had appointed a successor; until now she had not known who it was. She recapitulated what had followed after she put the letter from de Guélis into Eden's hand. De Guélis had told her that Eden had given him an interview of twenty minutes and arranged for him to be received by Lord Strang, with whom his interview lasted two hours. Afterwards it was to Lord Strang he reported regularly, though to Strang on Eden's behalf. Then he told her he was being posted to Algiers, but had arranged to have a successor, who would make the reports in his place. Obviously, it was 'Antoine'.

Until now Irene had never known whether it was officially or unofficially that Eden had his 'man in SOE'. For the mention to be in the Mackenzie history, official sanction must have been gained for it, though when it was initiated by de Guélis, she felt that the liaison was unofficial. It was a curious twist that Eden probably learned what happened to his man — that he was parachuted into German hands — through chancing to overhear my telling Irene in the dining room of the House of Commons.

A few days after this, on 12 April, I received a telephone call from Cookridge. 'I know all your friends... Déricourt, the Abbé Guillaume...' He professed to admire my books, but said I had stopped short of a conclusion. I had not guessed which British service Déricourt was working for. He knew 'which Department'. He knew 'the whole secret'. He was writing a history of SOE and would like to see me.

I had not liked his books, his way of approaching Irene, or his conversation with my mother — for I guessed at once Cookridge was my mother's 'Mr Kridge' (and indeed when I told her the name she recognised at once that she had failed properly to catch), I did not want to discuss Déricourt with him. Yet if I refused him an interview, what he wrote about me in his book would probably be hostile, and that might affect Déricourt too. Under pressure, I gave him an appointment at the Bonnington Hotel for some days ahead, and wrote at once to Déricourt for counsel. Happily, he received my letter and replied quickly (in English):

Bangkok
19.4.60

Cookridge — let him down — he knows nothing — I never met him — Anyway he knows nothing on me. He is boasting... If he uses my name I will sue him on defamation — please tell him. And tell him too he will have 'other' troubles *too*.

I simply sent Cookridge a card, cancelling our appointment, on the ground the friend he had mentioned did not know him. This provoked a long letter:

April 19th, 1960

Dear Miss Fuller,

It was disappointing getting your note cancelling our appointment... My own reason for asking you to meet me as I told you honestly when I rang you: to 'pick your brains' on some matters that puzzle me and to ask you for advice ...

When I mentioned on the phone that 'we have some friends in common' (and I believe I mentioned the names of Déricourt, Culioli, Abbé Gauillaume and Hugh Bleicher), I really meant 'friends' very much in inverted commas! Apparently you decided to check on it, and I venture to guess that you wrote to Abbé Guillaume. With 'Gilbert' I have been in touch only by correspondence.

Had you asked me for some real references, I would have gladly supplied some. We ought to have some acquaintances in common — publishers, journalists...

Having read your three books I have a great admiration for you and I should hate to have created a very wrong impression.

... I am 52,... my family is of Greek origin, I was born in Bohemia, took my rerum politicorum degree in the University of Vienna... worked sporadically for the British Intelligence before the war, was arrested by the Gestapo in 1939, charged with espionage and sent first to Dachau and then to

Buchenwald... The British government got me out ... in May 1939 and I came to this country. During the war I was, let's say, specially employed (*not* with S.O.E)... Lt. Colonel Boxshall is now the custodian of such S.O.E. files as were salvaged. He gave me some assistance...

Perhaps being now in the position to check my identity, you may still decide it might be fun to have a chat ... I would regard it as an honour and a pleasure.

Yours sincerely,
E.H. SPIRO = E.H. COOKRIDGE

No, I was not now in a position to check his identity or career. Anyone can say they were in Dachau or Buchenwald or that they worked for the Foreign Office. Robin Hooper had told Irene he had never heard of him, and the files over which Boxshall presided were going to be opened only to the official historian.

I made a copy of his letter for Déricourt, which I enclosed with a letter of 23 April:

Should I see him or not? Elizabeth thinks I should see him, and that has unsettled me again, for I had decided not to do so. She thinks I should see him so that we should have him on our side. If he is writing a book that will certainly be published, and she offered to come with me... Perhaps I should see him in order to discover if he intends to use your real name and to try to persuade him not to do it, but I don't want to discuss you with him.

Déricourt replied from Thailand (in English):

... I have read the C/Spiro letter. In my opinion that man knows nothing. He expects to take from you enough material to make a book... His letter is amazing! If I had to write to somebody in that case, I would not tell him my whole life!

307

That is not references!... I never wrote to him. He never wrote to me. We never met... Both names mean nothing to me. He knows Boxshall but does Boxshall know him?

This crossed with one of mine telling him I had now received yet another letter from Cookridge, reproaching me for not having replied to his long one. I copied the new one for Déricourt, and said:

I had the same dilemma when Wighton approached me and wanted an interview. I gave him one but it did not prevent him from being disagreeable in his book.

Déricourt replied:

Luang Prabang
8.5.60

Cookridge — do as you like. You are the wisdom itself.

I replied to Cookridge:

11th May, 1960

Dear Mr. Spiro,

I have received your letters of 19th and 20th April and taken note of the contents.

Mr Déricourt has told me he does not know you under either name, Cookridge or Spiro, and has not been in correspondence with you.

Yours sincerely,
JEAN OVERTON FULLER

I was aware this made it likely any reference to me in his book would be hostile, but felt it better that way.

On 23 June I was surprised to hear from Fayard they had seen Déricourt, who had talked to them of his own book, which they would be interested to see. A few days later I heard from Déricourt (in English), from Vientiane, that he had been in Paris for two days and was sorry not to have telephoned me:

27.6.60

> In Paris I saw M. Page (Fayard). I told him I won't be a nuisance. We left very good friends and he promised to publish my book — after reading. But the trouble is that I wish to sign with my true name — and I speak of 'Gilbert' all the time — and your book will be printed just a few months before! What to do?

That he should even contemplate putting his own name to it seemed to me a miraculously good sign. I felt he was approaching a degree of unembarrassment such that, had he only himself to consider, he would not mind living openly with the story. But was it fair to his wife? (M. Mousset, when he came to see me, had expressed himself incredulous she did not know about *Double Webs* or that Déricourt trusted she could be kept from knowing when the French edition appeared.) I felt that, if Fayard took his book, they would insist on it being made clear the author was the subject of mine. Déricourt had spent three years in writing it — mainly in the air, he told me, while the aircraft was on automatic pilot. It was a feat of perseverance, and, for one who had never belonged to a literary milieu, an extraordinary achievement. He had an author's pride in his creation. It might even be good, for he had a gift for pungently pictorial phrases. But if he signed it 'Smith', or the French equivalent, its impact would not be that of a book by the subject of Dame Irene's motion in the House of Commons, the 'Gilbert' of my book, and I felt that it was *that* that Fayard wanted. Yet, if he signed it Déricourt, he would be doing what he had all along forbidden. I hoped that he would take the brave course.

I no longer felt it was *Double Webs* that was keeping him in exile. It was more than a year since he had first mentioned his Chinese mistress, Janine or Jeannine, who lived with him in the hotel at Vientiane. Now she made stronger appearances in his letters. Basically, he was loyal to his wife, Jeannot, but, as he mentioned a number of times, she suffered from nervous depressions. This was the cause of his overriding concern that nothing should occur to upset her. Nevertheless, the nervous depressions perhaps imposed a strain upon him. Though I later learned the relationship with the Chinese proved even more of a strain, in a different sense, and did not end well at all, I at that time thought it was probably more restful and therefore the cause of his not coming home.

Though he described his Chinese friend to me he never described his parents, or told me who or what they were. Although I told him something of my own and invited him to reciprocate, upon this point, he did not; and so, although in so many ways I felt I knew him very well, he remained always a being without an origin.

I was asked once, 'Do you trust him?' Oddly, I did. Not, of course, to tell me the truth about any particular incident, especially connected with his past in SOE, but to think for my good, for my best interest. 'If I were in danger of my life and only he could save me, I would trust him to do it; but not, afterwards, to tell me the truth about how he had been able to do it.'

I tried to widen our correspondence. Finding in some paper an article by an American scholar suggesting that at the Battle of Thermopylae Ephialtes had played the role not of a traitor but of a double agent in the Athenian service, I cut it out and sent it to Déricourt. He rejoined (in English):

29.6.60

Ephialtes! Amusing ... I don't think I was on the same plan. More I don't agree so much with the archaeological theory. Salamis was a trap by itself, from the sea — launched at the very last moment. The army by land, Persians or Grecs had very few to do with. Had the Grecs won at Thermopolae that it would have changed nothing. I don't see where the game is. Anyway Ephialtes was certainly killed...

Nevertheless, he developed the theme imaginatively. Doubtless he had found in the article itself the elements needed to refresh his memory of whatever he had learned at school (if anything) of ancient Greek history, but, without books in which to look it up, I thought he had risen to the unexpected challenge well.

I made references to my hobbies — painting, star-gazing. I had joined the British Astronomical Association, was doing a little observation for the Variable Star department — as well as researching astronomy's sister-study, astrology. I was using his natal horoscope for testing the comparative value of various systems of progression to the dates of happenings in his life — the undisputed ones, that is. It was nothing to do with SOE, but was giving me hours of arithmetic, and I would call it *Horoscope for a Double Agent*.

When the French translation of my book arrived from Fayard in July, I was delighted to find a footnote, inserted by the publishers, that 'Gilbert's' own memoirs were shortly to appear from their house. The English translation rights were, they wrote to me, reserved to me by his instruction. I made my own corrections, and posted it to Déricourt on 4 August —

the day he wrote that he had finished his own book and was sending it to be typed. The footnote about 'memoirs' had given him a start: 'Say book or novel... not memoirs — that word is enough to get me shot.'

He returned the typescript to me with twelve pages of notes on points of translation. He had not abused the opportunity of seeing the text to insist on any rewording that would be to his advantage.

I wrote to tell him I had received a letter from Christmann, who was now settled in Tunisia. Eva and he were now married, and if I came to Tunisia he would give me material for a book with a Tunisian theme. I did not want to write on a Tunisian theme, but thought I ought to hear again the story he had told me at Frankfurt, and take the occasion to press some of our questions. I heard from Déricourt:

Bangkok
24.8.60

... My script is on typing in Paris. I'll send you a copy as soon as possible So everything is all right — No war yet — yet, I hope — but not sure,

Your friend,
HENRY

He wrote again the following day (in French):

25.8.60

Dear Jean,

We have here some small troubles, but they have been settled, despite the activity of the American services, which have just failed to provoke a war Happily the Ambassadors of GB and France were here to bring about negotiation. Without that?

... My book is in Paris now, being typed. I will read through once more before sending it to Fayard. I hope you make a good job of the translation. Otherwise, look out.

Give my regards to Christmann, and tell him I should like to meet him some day to see if he is as good a liar as I am. I propose we should each interrogate the other for 30 minutes in alteration... and afterwards compare the notes taken down in shorthand. The loser — he who lied with least skill, to pay for the champagne.

Then there was silence for more than a month. Only from the newspapers was there news of Laos every day. There seemed to be a civil war taking place there. I cut and pinned together the reports, but could not understand who were the parties to the trouble and their names were almost alike.

I had, however, given Déricourt the dates of my Tunisian trip and the name of the hotel into which I was booked, in case there was still a postal service out of Laos or anywhere he was. It was my first trip to Africa, and I packed not only my typewriter but my oil-painting things, and my telescope, to see a few more southerly stars and observe in a dark sky without the impediment of London lights.

14: CARTHAGE

My plane took off as the sky darkened on the evening of 11 October 1960. A half moon and the three gold points of Auriga were constants through my window all the way, and when I stepped out at El Aouina and I looked up, I saw more stars than I had ever seen, huge, clear and bright.

Christmann was at the airport to meet me, thickened, he explained, 'from the Tunisian beer'. Then he drove me, through an avenue of date palms, into total blackness. His villa was in Carthage; the hotel he had recommended to me was the Byrsa, in Salambo. When we drew up, the place was in darkness with no one at reception. Christmann, however, shone his torch on the keyboard, and handed me the key to my room I had booked. Eva, he said, would call for me at eleven in the morning.

There seemed to be no switches in the passages but there was a light in my room which actually worked. I was too alive to sleep, and wrote letters to my mother and Déricourt describing my arrival. Then I kept getting up to peer through the window. At first I could discern nothing. As the darkness began to lift, a semi-circle of water became visible, with dun shores fringed by silhouettes of palms. At last the sun came up. The scimitar of water was now turquoise, and the smack of light reflected from the white verandah beneath almost hurt my eyes. Purple and magenta bougainvilleas cascaded, scarlet poinsettia thrust between palms heavy with bananas. The hill behind was crowned by the massive remains of Dido's castle.

Having stolen in, I was almost surprised when an elderly maidservant with one eye brought me coffee and rolls. Eva came. She said that the moat-like water was the remains of the old Punic port; outside brown doves flew. Richard was just setting off in his car for his office in Tunis. We went with him. His office was piled to the ceiling with packets of Complan and baby-foods. He showed me a letter from Glaxo, appointing him its sole representative in Tunisia. He wondered whether it might enable him to fulfil his dream of visiting England. Did I think he could even now be arrested, should he use the pretext to visit the firm's head office in Greenford?

Tunisia had not then been opened up for tourism. The Byrsa was a small commercial hotel, and in Carthage there was no one speaking English. The first time that I ventured out from it alone, I turned into what I thought was a garden, to find I was standing in the sanctuary of Tanit where the first male child of every family had its throat cut, as the acolyte told me, before being consigned to the oven and its ashes put in an urn. When I mentioned it on reaching the Christmanns' villa, Richard said euphemistically, 'We are here on the ancient cemetery. If one puts a spade in the garden one brings up urns. All these villas are built from stones stolen out of the ancient sanctuary and city.' I heard myself say, 'You must have been a Carthaginian!' — meaning, to stand it. He replied, 'I admire the Carthaginians.' I did not know if it was the water, or the vibrations from the Tophet, but during every day that I was there I was sick. Christmann said, 'It is le *mal du pays* — the sickness of the country.' Everyone had it for the first two or three years after arriving. 'It is what killed the Roman Legions. That is why they could not conquer Carthage for so long. As soon as they landed, they died of the sickness.' There was just one single remedy. I must drink a whole bottle of Vichy water every day. Certainly it reduced the sickness, but I was a little overpowered by the country and not at my best during our conversations.

I wrote to Déricourt:

Hotel Byrsa
25th October, 1960

Dear Henri,

I thought it would never be possible to talk to Christmann about your affair... I gave him verbally your message about the contest of lying... instead of laughing he looked very grave... Yesterday evening, to draw him out, I showed him your letter to me so that he could read for himself the passage about the contest in lying. This time he smiled, and said, 'He has kept his sense of humour. Me too.' And then it was possible to talk a little and I asked him some of your questions.

He assures me he went to no restaurant to get the address Sq. Clignancourt. 'It was London that gave me the address'... the first time Bodens went up the stairs alone ... as he could not speak French very well he asked Christmann to go the next time, for he had obtained a second RV for the afternoon... Then Arch, came down and presented himself. The correct passwords were exchanged... Arch, said it was he who had received the message from London telling him to keep this RV but the affair did not concern him...

As he was entering Kieffer's office, a man came out of it. He passed him in the doorway ... He (Christmann) had been arrested by the SD who thought he was a genuine Résistant of a party he was escorting, and this gave him a problem of how to 'escape' from the SD in a manner that would not seem suspect... London had invited him, as the Belgian guide Arnaud, to come to London... and he had to think whether he would travel to London really... Kieffer said, 'I have a man who arranges the departures for London, the one who just left my office.'

I asked him if he was sure the man he saw leaving K's office was the same with whom he was confronted by the French after the war ... 'It was the same,' he said... He thought he had been kind to you in not saying, 'This is a man I saw coming out of K's office ... I felt certain.'

Now he says he doesn't know what to think... He asked if you ever came to Tunis ... I said when you crashed in 1957 it was coming from Tunis. He cried, 'He could have come to see me!'

Tomorrow he will drive me (and Eva and their little girl) to Kairouan.

Your friend,
JEAN

I left the bad news without comment, because really I did not know what to believe, but hoped the signature was reassuring.

So I was driven across the desert to the second holiest place in Islaam. On the way back, he asked 'if Déricourt was still in correspondence with me'.

'Yes.'

'Does he know you are here?'

'Yes.'

'Have you written to him since you have been here?'

'Yes.'

This startled and seemed to worry him considerably. 'He was a Gestapo agent,' he said tightly. On the road into Tunis he insisted on overtaking every other car, alarming both me and Eva. 'I cannot endure to follow behind another car!'

He said he was not a Bleicher, to make depositions charging everybody — 'Bleicher ist ein Schwein!' His one regret was not to have killed Bleicher, during the war, when it would have been possible. At the DST Bleicher had a room to himself, in which he sat composing an extremely long deposition in which he gave away all the French who had rendered him service.

On the 25th I received a letter in English from Déricourt, addressed to me at the Byrsa. He had not yet received mine written since arriving, and replied to earlier ones, which expressed anxiety about the troubled situation in Laos.

18.10.60

Dear Jean,

... The local politics are so intricated that it is impossible — nearly — to understand anything. Anyway, we feel good and the city and the country is calm as usual — Only the papers — from everywhere report of troubles and fights. Any way I would like the end of it.

The most amazing thing happened the day before yesterday. As I was leaving for Saigon — as Captain of a plane — I was introduced to one of my passengers by the local French representative of the Ecole Français de l'Extrème Orient — an archaeological or historical organisation — so I was introduced to Mr Mousset and I answered that I heard already of somebody of this name in Fayard's and he answered, 'It is me.' Well — So I flew him to Saigon and had long talks and so on. Isn't it amazing — I told you already that Laos was the world's centre!!

My book is on typewriting in Paris now. I wait for a copy to make the last check. I will send one copy to you as soon as it is ready. I promised you to give you the script to be traduced and I did not change my idea but I will sell the rights in British language to an American editor. I have been told to do so because that way could lead to more profit. What do you think of it?

... To Christmann. Ask him to solve a problem: 'I am the biggest liar in the world and I can prove it in saying the truth.'

So — have a good time in Tunisia — my regards to Christmann.

Your good friend,
HENRY

318

I replied with the suggestion that — unless he had a contact with an American publisher — it might be best to let Fayard handle the placing of the English language rights, both in the USA and England. It was usual to let the original publisher handle translation rights. They would take a small percentage but would have a stake in getting him the best terms. They already understood that the English translation was reserved to me.

The annual Fair of Tunis was on. I was taken to the British, German and Jugoslav evenings, and after the last Christmann drove us all to a café at Gamat, where he ordered us champagne. On the way back he drove the car in diagonals, between the ditches on either side of the road. It was surely impossible he had drunk enough champagne to be *that* drunk, genuinely; he must be only pretending, to be funny... yet Eva was terrified too and I was weighing up whether the lesser danger would be to swing the door open and leap.

On the last morning he asked me not to tell Giskes I had seen him again, or that he was in Tunisia. I was not planning to tell Giskes, yet declined to promise in case I should ever want to.

He said he had been more nearly equal with Giskes than I realised — a member of his staff. That puzzled me, for it was not as such Giskes had spoken of him, and he had only been a *Sonderführer*.

On a sudden thought, I asked him if he know Jacques Weil.

'Jacques Weil of the all-Jewish network?'

Come to think of it, Worms, Cohen and Sonia were all Jewish.

Christmann obviously did know a lot about him, but was oblique and libellous. But that network interconnected importantly with 'Prosper's' and his knowledge of it was another suspicious link.

'Did you know Hélène, the mistress of Massuy?'

His eyes narrowed. 'She could have been Massuy's mistress before she became my agent'. I had thought he was going to say 'mine'. But Déricourt's big question was already answered. For good measure he added, 'Her husband was a diamond merchant... she must have betrayed about a dozen...'

Eva came in with cups of coffee. He seized the pretext to break the thread of the conversation and then it was time to drive me to the airport.

The instant I stepped down from the plane onto the tarmac of London airport, and took my first breath of the cold air, I felt well. I must get back to my flat, get out his old statements and compare with the new ones.

At my flat I found a slip from the Post Office saying attempts had been made to deliver a registered parcel. I called at the Post Office, but was told it had been returned to sender. No, they could not tell me from whom or from where it had come. It could not have been Déricourt's novel, for he knew I was in Tunisia and would never have it sent until he knew I was back; and he had written that he was having it returned from Paris to him for correction.

I compared Christmann's Frankfurt and Carthage statements. A number of discrepancies leaped out at me. At Frankfurt he had said Gilbert Norman had told him, when in the afternoon they had met for the second time, that he had made contact on his behalf with 'Gilbert', the Air Movements Officer. It was 'Gilbert's' evading an appointment that made him suspicious. In Carthage it was not Norman who had made contact with 'Gilbert' the AMO on his behalf, but Kieffer who had told him a man he had passed in the doorway was the AMO. I was shattered.

I wrote to Christmann saying I was horrified by the number of discrepancies I found between his Frankfurt and Carthage statements, and wrote to Déricourt, on 5 and 12 November 1960, setting them out. My letter crossed with one from him (in English):

7.11.60

Dear Jean,

I had written a letter to you and one to Christmann and I was at the Post Office to mail them when the postman called me and gave me your Oct. 27 letter. So I read it and come back to change everything ... It is amusing and it delights me to see that now you understand Christmann... He put himself in case similar with *Witness for Prosecution* of A. Christie.

He taxed me with having, at Frankfurt, trusted too much in the honesty of Christmann's feelings, and said it did not do, especially for 'people in our business'.

Over seven pages of close writing, he explained yet once more how impossible it was the appointment at Square Clignancourt should have been made by radio through London. He was certain it was Hélène, the mistress of Massuy, who had given Christmann the address of the restaurant, Chez Tutulle, in the rue Troyon, where he had gone and asked directions for finding 'Gilbert' from 'Tutulle, the tenant of the restaurant, who knew Gilbert for G. Norman and me as Henri but not as Gilbert!!'

Certainly the restaurateur, who was not a registered agent, should not have known anybody's code-name with London.

Déricourt suggested Giskes might cover up for Christmann, in order not to appear 'ridiculous' in having been abused and manipulated by a subordinate. No, I did not think Giskes would do that, yet I took his point about commanding officers not liking to appear ridiculous. Déricourt also pointed out that Christmann liked to play the fool with anybody for anything '— even pretend to be drunk when he is not for the pleasure to get people uneasy'.

On 21 November I mentioned to Déricourt I had received a reply from Eva, saying Richard was busy but would write me a letter later. It had not arrived.

Déricourt wrote that he was too bored with Christmann to write to him. Then he changed his mind, and sent me a letter to transmit to him (I translate from his French):

1.12.60

My dear Christmann,

I know through Miss Fuller that you have had the pleasure of a visit from her. I am desolated to have been so often in and out of Tunis without knowing you were so near. If I had known I would not have failed to call on you, for despite our different positions I have much esteem for you.

It would be interesting to discuss in private the points upon which we are not in accord...

It was not I who sent you that parcel, although it is a thing I could very well have done. I do rather reproach you for having leaned upon a psychological interpretation... However, I admit that each one does according to the circumstances in which he finds himself...

That is why today I permit myself to congratulate you on still being alive, and hope you are happy. I am, and glad to have escaped you, each morning as I see the sun rise. I said as much to you on a certain occasion when we met at Reuilly.

Believe in my sympathy,
H. DÉRICOURT

It was a generous letter. Unexpectedly there was a reply (in French), sent to me, which I sent on to Déricourt:

> My dear Déricourt,
>   ... Believe me, dear Déricourt, you have no reason to reproach me, for I have always had a great sympathy for you...

Referring to one of mine, in which I had assumed him to have been surprised at his arrest by the SD at the Capucines, he wrote:

> It was I myself who organised the party at the Café des Capucines with the accord of the SD. Present were Marcel, Alain and one of my German collaborators. The latter had to play the role of a Dutchman having to return to London. To get him out of his journey to London, we arranged this arrest, leaving the rest free, so that Marcel could signal to London the Dutchman had been arrested and therefore would not return to London...

Yes, but Giskes understood he was to go through Spain and that his mock arrest was to be by the Abwehr. The letter established 'Marcel' as Agazarian.

My correspondence with Déricourt was interrupted by civil war in Laos. I had always felt it was so that I should not worry about him too much that he had played down 'fights'. Now it was on the front page every day. I continued to write letters:

> 13 December, 1960
> If the troubles increase in Vientiane, there may again be a suspension of postal deliveries ... I think also of the manuscript of your book which is being typed in Paris. Perhaps you should warn the typist not to post it while the situation is so troubled.

I tried, from the papers, to understand the positions of three warring princes, Souphanovong, Boun Oum and Souvana Phouma, apparently Left, Right and would-be neutral. On 17 December *The Times* carried a headline: VIENTIANE IN FLAMES. It was being shelled. There was no water or electricity. It had been captured by paratroops of the Left.

On the 18th I wrote to Déricourt, worried by reports of... 'smoke over Vientiane, fires and fighting in the streets, the airport under fire'. I wondered if he was still there. The next day, the 19th, it had fallen to forces of the Right.

No letter came from Déricourt, even at Christmas or New Year. On 3 January 1961 I wrote: 'Do you think, after the crisis is over, from Vientiane we could do a book on Laos?' His eventual reply, in French, was written on 26 January:

Dear Jean,

I have just received several letters from you. They have followed me around to all the places where I have been during the period of troubles. Reassure yourself I am in excellent health and of indestructible morale. I have seen others!

Vientiane is trying to reorganise itself on a new plan. I hope it may succeed but fear it will have many difficulties.

He went straight back into the affair Square Clignancourt. 'Marcel' could not have been Agazarian. It was out of the question that London could have referred to Marcel Charbonnier as 'Marcel', since Charbonnier was not a registered agent and it was unlikely London even knew of his existence. He felt sure London had played no part in this thing at all. As he had said in Paris, his belief was either that Huntermann was in league with Bodens and Christmann against Giskes or Christmann managed to insert a false message composed by himself amongst messages from London decoded by Huntermann or his staff: 'I do not know how Christmann made Giskes swallow a concocted message through Huntermann, but he did it.'

Why? He wanted a pretext to go to Paris, obviously, apparently in the hope of obtaining a Lysander passage to England. As he had said in Paris, he felt it must have been Hélène who had obtained from some SOE agent the information that Lysander passages were arranged by 'Gilbert' and that this Hélène, who had very likely introduced Christmann to diamond smuggling, had told him he could contact the AMO at the restaurant, where the confusion of the Gilberts took place.

I believed he was right. Nothing had gone through London. Robin Hooper's answer to the whole set of questions we had asked him through Irene could have been 'No'. Unexpectedly, we had exonerated London. Giskes, who had so brilliantly deceived London, had been deceived by his own staff. Déricourt summed up:

> I affirm that he [Christmann] had the address of Alain from Tutulle, the proprietor of the café in the rue Troyon; that he had the address of it from Hélène, the mistress of Massuy, who got Marsac arrested; that this German infiltration came through the Jean-Mane [Frager] network, through the different contacts that they had with the Abwehr, as indeed 'Prosper' and his collaborators had through the Tambour sisters [negotiations for their freedom]. The Café Tutulle was recommended by Worms to 'Archambaud', and to Worms by me.

As to the imbroglio at Square Clignancourt coming from the arrest of Marsac, he was probably right. This was an idea that had kept on almost coming to the surface during the years of our correspondence. After all, when Bleicher arrested Marsac, he bamboozled him into believing he was a secretly pro-British German, who wanted to go to London, and it was as a means to that end he had persuaded Marsac to put him in touch with Roger Bardet — leading on to the arrest of the latter, of Peter Churchill and Odette and to the German control of their chief, Frager, left at liberty so that the Abwehr could run his network for him. But Marsac gave not only Bardet, he gave a crystal, money and a great deal of information. This may well have included the name of the Air Movements Officer, 'Gilbert', whom they should have to contact in order to obtain an aircraft to fetch them to London. Bleicher had no intention of going to London. But it was Hélène who had, on instruction from Massuy (Bleicher's chief in that operation), assisted Bleicher in the arrest of Marsac. She may have been party to some of the conversations between them, so learning that there was someone called 'Gilbert' who arranged aircraft passages to England, and passed this information to her other friend, Christmann. In that case, the downfall of the 'Prosper' network came, like that of the Frager one, from the arrest of Marsac — but passing from Bleicher to Christmann extra-service. Nordpol, then, had nothing to do with it, save inasmuch as Christmann used it to wangle out of Giskes an instruction that would take him back to Paris.

My satisfaction at having apparently solved this riddle was short-lived. It now struck me that if Christmann's story about the radio messages received from London and passwords exchanged with 'Archambaud' was false, then his claim to have learned from Kieffer that 'Gilbert' the AMO was his agent was valueless. Was it from some strange malevolence he had made it up? Had he made it up to please me? I could see it from his point of view, too. Here was this woman who came to him at

Frankfurt, wanting, as he thought, a statement to clear Norman and put the blame on Déricourt, which he had supplied. Now she had come to him at Carthage wanting Déricourt cleared. Could she not make up her mind which one she wished cleared? He had had a will to oblige, which was turning to exasperation. There was in him no idea of truthfulness as a value in itself.

And Mme Guépin. When first we had asked who she thought betrayed the 'Prosper' network she had said, 'Culioli.' Mr Norman and I had both shaken our heads. Then she had said, 'Gilbert.' Then, embarrassed because that was the name of Mr Norman's son, she had put it on to a Gilbert none of us knew. Suppose that I had gone alone, would she have said 'Gilbert-Déricourt'? I was appalled to realise how one could, unconsciously, lean on witnesses and influence their testimonies.

There remained Déricourt's submission of the mail, and the trailing from his fields. The admissions he had made were a comfort to me. I had 'convicted' him on testimonies, two of which were unsound; for this I apologised to him, not without emotion.

He replied with a very long letter from Vientiane (in French):

8.2.61

Dear Jean,

I have just received your letter of the 2nd, which is a record for-speed and seems to show the censorship has been stopped. I reply in haste because I have to go up North again tomorrow. I do not know if you have read in the stars that my fortune is better now than it ever was, even in the prime of my youth. I am on the point of achieving something extraordinary that will give me satisfaction. But it has to come off. But I am an absurd optimist — I should not otherwise know how to be happy.

... What makes me shudder is your way of presenting testimonies without too much warning they may not be veridical, leaving to the reader the burden of evaluating their authenticity...

I have lied to you sometimes but I have not dissembled from you. You have understood. I have meant you to know I was lying. I have never lied from boastfulness or pride — I have lied from prudence.

That brings me to other liars I have known. There are in espionage people who want to be valued... identifiable because they have always been chiefs, chief of a department, chief of a network ... I remember one who, when we spoke of the church at Auteuil, said, 'I know it, I was chief choirboy.'... Their activity has always led them to frequent high places and to have played an important political role... only their gifts have been badly used...

I come back to Christmann. You don't seem yet to see his psychology, simple though it is. He is a bitter liar, vexed at having been only the conductor on 'the way back'. He would have liked to be the key to North Pole instead of only the fourth executive (which is already not bad). He would have liked to go to London and play an important role, parading before the English officers, ridiculing them and disclosing North Pole to them.

His story of the medal is false. He could have staged a charade about that for Giskes as he must have done over the so-called radio message... His story of Kieffer is false ... He probably never met him and was never at the SD...

That he has it in for me is natural — it was I who prevented him from going to London, where he still imagines the role he could have played...

As to the position of Huntermann, Giskes and 'Anton' vis-à-vis Christmann, it is simple — they don't like your going to see a talker and a liar. Yet in case of need they confirm his lies in order not to appear ridiculous.

I enclose a rare document. I make you a present of it.

Everything is working itself out, even the political situation...

Thanks for all the sweet words but you have not to apologise. In this business it is often like that...

Your friend,
HENRI

What did he mean when he said it was he who had prevented Christmann from going to England? It came to me that it was perhaps he who had given away the meeting at the Capucines. It was only he who was so sure it *had* been given away. When he had pointed out to me long ago that he had the capacity to have done it, saying, 'Only I know it was not me', had that not been his way of drawing to my attention that it must be? Had he to spell it out before I saw it? Surely he could not have expected me to be so stupid.

I looked again at his letter of 22 September 1958 to Christmann, and the words 'I am very proud to have detected and countered you' leaped out at me. If I was understanding his message rightly now, he must specifically have persuaded Boemelburg to arrest the so-called Dutchman, taking him for an intrusive Abwehr man, and not to arrest Agazarian. The motive for arresting a German would have been simply to give him a fright and make him go away, lest his presence on some non-Abwehr business over-complicate an already complicated game.

If Christmann realised the Capucines rendezvous must have been given away, by one or other of the 'Gilberts', that would explain his attitude — and also his resentment. Now I understood why neither Déricourt nor Christmann could ever tell the truth about this episode openly; each of them was at the time on the wrong side of the fence.

The 'rare document' which Déricourt enclosed was a faded typescript yellowing with age, the copy of Bleicher's testimony for the DST of 15 October 1945, from his lawyer's file. I noticed that the woman who betrayed Marsac was designated as 'a Dutch woman, agent of Kaiser [Massuy] called Hélène'. In his published memoirs Bleicher had called her 'Claire', with no indication he did not mean Déricourt's 'Claire'. On the other hand, he referred to 'Claire', 'Gilbert's' radio operator'. 'Claire' was not a radio operator. Déricourt pointed to a possible confusion with 'Madeleine', who was sent out as supplementary radio operator to Gilbert Norman; he also wrote 'Archambaud' in the margin against a paragraph of Bleicher's asserting Kieffer told him he knew from 'Gilbert' of Bodington's presence in Paris and was determined to arrest him. Obviously it was through the messages exchanged with London over the radio circuit of 'Archambaud' (Gilbert Norman) that Kieffer knew Bodington was coming and offered him the fatal appointment which Agazarian kept in his place. While Déricourt pointed out in fairness that 'Madeleine' at one moment stayed in a flat of 'Claire's', the cumulative effect of these confusions did suggest an intent of Bleicher to frame Déricourt.

Déricourt did not believe in the alleged conversations between Bleicher and Kieffer — 'When did you hear a sergeant answer a major back?' And he scouted the claim in Bleicher's deposition that he had been of good faith when he persuaded Marsac and Frager he wanted to pass to the British side; Déricourt sent me a list, 'certainly not complete', of 103 in the British service arrested by Bleicher.

What I felt most was that Déricourt's parting with this monument of the prosecution's case — part of the furniture of his life for so many years — was like an offering to the winds, a freeing.

He also sent me, copied out in his own hand, two more of Christmann's depositions. One, of 25 February 1947 to the DST, read:

> ... I came to know at 84 Avenue Foch Stbf. Kieffer and one of his adjutants, Gutgesell (who had charge of Belgian and Dutch affairs). In our conversations there was several times mention of a certain Gilbert who worked for the SD.
>
> I do not know exactly how Gilbert entered into the German service, all I know is what Gutgesell told me. His activity being secret, all the same Gutgesell one day confided to me that Gilbert had been arrested by their service and at once spontaneously placed himself at their disposition ... I do not know at what date Gilbert entered into service of the SD Avenue Foch... what I am certain is that by the end of April or beginning of May '43 he worked already for the Germans and was registered as an agent.
>
> All I can tell you for sure is that Gilbert was arrested by the Avenue Foch service and according to what I was able to understand by Gutgesell it was following a parachute operation that this arrest took place ... he was chief of the reception of parachutings and had full liberty of action for his operations but on the other hand furnished the means to trail those arriving as well as the places of the arms dumps.

There were several details here that did not apply to Déricourt, most obviously — if this was an authentic copy — the reference to arms dumps, locations of which would have been known only to 'Prosper' and 'Archambaud', and those guarding them. The other deposition, made on 29 October 1947, before Captain de Résseguier, was vaguer, but said, 'As to Gilbert Déricourt, I never made contact with him at all, and all that has been said was related to me by Kieffer's department...' Déricourt had underlined this last phrase in red, and hazarded the guess that Christmann had never met Kieffer at all, only Gutgesell. Again, one had to remember the ranks.

I believed he had got it right. Gutgesell did exist; I had heard Ernest speak of him. Christmann had probably entered 'Kieffer's department', that is to say the building, 84 Avenue Foch, and there spoken with Gutgesell. Whatever Gutgesell had said or not said, in Christmann's conversations with me, both in Frankfurt and in Carthage, he had been changed into Kieffer. Raising the level of his contacts, he raised his own apparent rank, but also the importance of his statement, for Gutgesell could not speak with the authority of Kieffer, and if he did say anything about 'Gilbert', would probably only have been guessing.

I replied to Déricourt saying how relieved I was to read in his letter of 8 February that things were turning out so well for him. His reply (in English) was headed for the first time not from Air Laos but from his hotel:

> Hotel Constellation
> Vientiane
> Laos
> 2.3.61

Dear Jean,

... Yes I understand prayer ... I don't need to murmur or even to think of something. I *always tries* to do good. That is my prayer. The way I live is my permanent prayer. There is no special time, no special place, no special words, no special God. I do my best all the time — that is my prayer. I expect no answer. I never know when I do good, but I know when I do bad. That is my religion, and only that...

They were strange words, from one who had lived as he had lived.

Now I had to tell him something else. Irene had intimated the history of SOE she had proposed to Macmillan might be going to eventuate. Elizabeth and I were no longer so keen on it. Elizabeth had gone much further than myself in her suspicion of 'Archambaud', and we could not see how the downfall of the 'Prosper' network could be treated without either silences or unfairnesses. It would be unseemly to speak ill of the dead, impossible to speak ill of the living, because they could sue for libel (unless like Déricourt they had consented in advance) and we could both see Déricourt, because of what he had given me permission to publish, figuring as the scapegoat. There were, however, intimations we were to be favoured with some confidence; yet this posed problems:

> If we are to meet the person entrusted with the job ... we may be told things on the understanding we keep them in confidence. Now it would be terribly tantalising for me if I were told things concerning you that I could not tell you. What to do?

I wrote this chiefly to let him know that, if this went through, there would be things about which I would have to be silent in my letters to him. His file would be open to the historian. If I were told anything that really concerned him, I would ask permission to tell him and invite his comment. Even if this was denied, I still thought it better both Elizabeth and I should be 'in' on the matter.

I had to bother him for an authorisation for the new last chapter required by Pan. This he sent by a telegram from Bangkok, followed by a letter (in English) from the Hotel Constellation, Laos, dated 4 March 1960:

Dear Jean,

I forgot to make you notice my address has changed. There is no more Air Laos in Vientiane. I'll tell you later — but it does not affect my position here.

I never read any of the Abbé's books. Will you ask him — in my name — to send them (I will pay for books and transport of course). You can tell him it is for me — and if useful give him my address. I don't think I will be here long — may be one year — maximum — I need to change but there is no one to take my place... but I can be forced to go (by events).

He reverted to a quotation I had made from something the Abbé Guillaume had written, and ended:

Drive slowly...

I have no more fear of passing you the depositions... the risk I run is very small.

Amongst other enclosures was the list of British agents arrested by the self-styled pro-British German, Bleicher. This went up only to the time of Déricourt's recall to London in February 1944, and hence did not include the most odious of them all — the arrest of Frager, who trusted Bleicher.

This long letter, written plainly in leisurely style, was so level, normal and everyday that I was quite unprepared for the shock of his next and last (in English) which I received only on 18 March:

Hotel Constellation

Vientiane

Laos

8.3.61

Dear Jean,

I am very sorry — really sorry — but it happens I have to ask you not to write to me for some time. I can't tell you why and I ask you not to try to find out.

It is really a sign of great confidence to write you that, because I should not do it.

So after some time I shall write to you and explain everything, and you will understand.

Sorry to let you down,

your good friend,
HENRY

I enclose a procuration [power of attorney] you could use in any case for the best. H

Dismayed, I did not know whether to think he had gone off on a secret mission or had done something wrong and was obliged to disappear. I unfolded the paper attached. It read (in French):

I give by this present instrument power to Miss Jean Overton Fuller of 4 Guilford Place, London W.C.1, to act and sign in my stead and place in what concerns:
1. All facts concerning me, their relation and interpretation, from 15 August 1941 to 9June 1948.
2. All modifications, corrections, alterations, additions which she wishes to make to the original edition approved by me of her book 'Double Webs'.
3. id for 'Horoscope for a Double Agent'.
4. the utilisation of 2 and 3 in other domains such as cinema, radio, television etc.

On the other hand I formally forbid:
1. that my real family name shall be written or pronounced in any circumstances whatsoever.
2. that the name 'Gilbert' appear in the title or in display, the name 'Gilbert' being authorised in the text.

Signed at Vientiane, of effect to whom it may concern.

H. Déricourt

15: OFFICIAL CONFIDENCE

Loss of contact with Déricourt had indeed coincided with the granting of a measure of official confidence. Elizabeth and I had both received identical letters from Irene, inviting us to dinner with her at the House of Commons on 14 March 1961. Just back from a trip to Russia, with other MPs, she had to tell us the official history for which she had asked Mr Macmillan was probably going to be, and she had finally won permission from Mr Heath to make us party to her correspondence with him about it.

We said that if it was to please us, we were not pressing for it. The more we considered the confusions between Déricourt and Norman, the more it appeared to us impossible to treat the downfall of the 'Prosper' network. The dead had relatives living, to be hurt, so could not be treated with the detachment meted to historical characters, and as to the living, it was the least savoury amongst them who would be the likeliest to sue for libel and must therefore be spared real criticism. Elizabeth put it to Irene succinctly: 'One can't say anything about the dead because they are dead, or the living because they are living.' 'I will tell them what you say,' Irene replied. 'I think they will be relieved to hear it.'

Nevertheless, she would like to let us each have copies of a letter she had received from the Lord Privy Seal, which she had obtained his permission to disclose to us. In a letter dated 23 February 1961 Edward Heath agreed that she disclose to 'her two friends Miss Overton Fuller and Mrs Nicholas, on a personal and confidential basis, that a pilot project on the history of SOE in France was being prepared'. He said he would inform the author that Irene's two friends had information in their possession which was relevant to his work.

Irene had also obtained permission for one other party to be privy to this information. She had been under the impression Mr Heath was going to draw up a paper for the three of us to sign, but when I saw her again she told me he was going to accept our undertakings verbally, through her, not to reveal what we knew about there being a project for an official history until the eventual public announcement, if it was found satisfactory.

He wrote to her next that he had arranged for 'the author of our draft history of the French organisation' to be told of her interest in SOE's operations in France. He had suggested that he should get in touch in about two months' time, 'by when he should have read himself in and be in a position fully to appreciate the information which you and your friends wish to give him'.

Irene, much amused, wondered why the identity of the historian had to be a mystery.

Mr Heath replied as 9 May that 'in order to prevent his being distracted from getting on within the job, we decided not to reveal his name for the time being'. He could say, however, that it was not Bill Deakin.

On 28 July 1961 Irene came for dinner and told me she had an appointment with the Head of the Permanent Under Secretary's Department at the Foreign Office in a few days' time. Robin Hooper was going to present to her the historian who had been chosen. She still did not know his name. Then, on 31 July, she telephoned me to say she had just left the Foreign Office, where 'he' had been introduced to her. She had invited him to lunch with her at the House of Commons on 3

August. Would I come?

She presented him to me as 'the historian', and when I asked him his name, he pointed to his foot — which proved to be his name. I did not immediately understand. He said, 'My very existence is an official secret.' After we had lunched, we went out on to the terrace of the House. Irene told him the background to her concern with the affair. We stayed for tea with her. Then she had to leave us, called by Parliamentary duties, and he invited me to a second tea, with him, at a place in Bridge Street. He told me, which surprised me, that he had not permission yet to speak with SOE people, but had been recommended to see Elizabeth and me 'as you might be able to help me'. I gave him an appointment at my flat for 23 August.

At the same time, I asked myself what help I could give. Most of what I knew came from persons who were not of British nationality, and it was information given in the confidence I did not represent the Foreign Office and would not repeat in that quarter what was said to me. It would be a betrayal of that trust were I to pass such confidences on to Foot. I told him this, squarely. It was not a question of asking permission of my informants: we were pledged to secrecy. Also I gathered Foot had been chosen because he had served in SAS, not SOE. I suggested that the SAS commandos, being uniformed, were more like soldiers, whereas SOE agents lived lives more like those of spies. To judge them by military standards could be unfair.

One piece of information Foot gave me. Amongst the papers he had seen he found a momentary 'flap' had been caused by Déricourt's disappearance in September 1944. He had been flying a light transport aircraft for the Free French, carrying supplies to our army in France, and on 9 September, as he came down with his cargo, he hit a telegraph wire, crash-landed and was taken to hospital.

Déricourt had told me this had happened between Châteauroux and Isoudun, and that he sustained a broken radius and cubitus in his left arm, a broken or damaged right parietal (in skull) and occipital (base of skull), a broken right shoulder-blade, a broken rotule in his right knee, three broken right-hand ribs, a haemorrhage in his right lung, and a ruptured small vein in his liver (see my *Horoscope for a Double Agent*.) These injuries had kept him in hospital at Châteauroux for five months. He had also said he had been shot down while chasing a German fighter, which apparently was not the case, though Foot had now confirmed the fact of the crash and its date.

I mentioned Déricourt's assertion that he had come to London in July 1943, unknown to Buckmaster, for one night — which he spent in André Simon's flat. I suspected it of being a tease, but Foot might like to see if it could have been factual.

I showed him the handwritten originals of statements I had printed in my translation. I also lent him my card-index of dates — from which I had, the previous evening, removed the Bonoteaux card. Foot might find out about Bonoteaux, but I did not have to make sure he knew. I always hoped Déricourt would return some day, and did not want him to find I had sold the pass for him.

Ever since receiving Déricourt's last letter, I had wondered what had happened to him. Had he involved himself in the politics of South-East Asia? As a pilot, could he have been tempted into becoming a courier? Could he have accepted a dangerous mission that would take him behind the Iron Curtain, where he would be incommunicado? Or had he got himself into some kind of trouble, such that he needed to disappear? I tried to imagine ways in which he could fake an accident in which he had been killed. But would a crash out there be reported in the English papers?

On 18 January 1962 I woke from a powerful dream. A swordfish had been flying through the sky, over calm sea, ruddy purple like a catfish or some kinds of rock-fish. The sword shortening into the nose of a propeller, it became an aeroplane, of the same colour. Along the whole length of it was written in large white capital letters the name DÉRICOURT — as though it were the name of the airline. From flying level, gradually it lost height, began to point downwards, and at last went into the sea and disappeared. I fought away the words with which I woke: 'The poor flying-fish is going down.'

I have had in my life dreams that have told me, in symbolic fashion, what was going to happen, sometimes months before. The feel of them is different from that of ordinary dreams. I felt this was such a dream. But did it mean he was going to die, or to go under? There was nothing sudden, sharp, explosive or shattering, as to suggest an accident. The movement had been slow and controlled. There was no symbol suggestive of entry into an after-death state. Did it mean he had tired of the *persona* Déricourt, forgone his identity and submerged himself amongst the multitudinous peoples of China? It was his name I had seen go down. I knew only that I would not again receive a letter from him.

I did not at that time wish to interest myself further in SOE. I saw that a book had appeared, *Who Lived to See the Day*, by Philippe de Vomécourt. If Déricourt had still been accessible by letter, we would both have read it and gone over it together with a tooth-comb. Déricourt gone, I did not even bother to get it.

On 2 March 1965, almost exactly five years after Déricourt's last letter to me, I received one from Irene:

Dear Jean,

I have a very sad piece of news to tell you which came my way only last Thursday. 'Gilbert' is dead. Apparently it happened in South East Asia two or three years ago and was reported in *Figaro*.

I have no other information but this accounts for the fact that you had no news ... I am so sorry to send you this news but wonder if you had in any way anticipated it.

My love,

Yours affectionately,
IRENE

It was the death of a friend. I said a prayer for him.

Afterwards I went to the Newspaper Library of the British Museum at Colindale and found the obituary in the issue of 18 February 1963. It stated that he had been killed in an air accident on 20 November 1962 at Sayaboury, Laos.

Whatever he may have been in any other connection, to me his conduct was always honourable, generous, delicate. He never tried to exploit me in any way, and was sometimes wiser for me than I would have been for myself.

16: THE OFFICIAL HISTORY

On 13 April 1964 I had been installed in the private box of the Serjeant-at-Arms in the House of Commons. I heard Irene ask the Secretary of State if the Government would supplement the existing official histories with one of SOE French Section. I heard her receive the answer 'Yes'. Then I heard her ask the Minister to convey to the former Prime Minister, the Member for Bromley (Harold Macmillan), the thanks of Elizabeth and myself. There was a piece about it in *The Times* next day.

On 4 April 1966 I received a telephone call from Foot. I had not heard from him in a very long while, but he asked me to lunch with him in Soho on the 6th. His book would be coming out on the 28th, and he wanted to tell me his admiration for the integrity of my researches and prevent my receiving a shock when I read it. I had cited Déricourt as saying, to rebut Vogt's allegation three had been arrested on arriving at his field near Angers, three would not have formed a Lysander party: I would find he had referred to this as 'an interesting economy of truth'. It was a Hudson. This was not a shock. I had always known that for larger parties a Hudson was used, and that at a pinch three could be squeezed into a Lysander. Noor had gone as one of three in a Lysander. But Déricourt had behaved well over the whole and I did not grudge him the *ignoratio elenchi*. Then, said Foot, rather ominously I thought, Déricourt had told me Morel had come for him on 1 February, and he had gone on the 4th. In fact, Morel had come for him on the 4th and he had gone on the 8th. I would see the significance of this when I read his book.

On 28 April I bought *SOE in France* at Foyle's. At first opening I saw what Déricourt had always refused to permit — his real name used throughout, even displayed in capitals in the part titles. There was more about him than about any other officer, even 'Prosper'. It had been mainly to avoid pain to his wife Déricourt had insisted his name must not appear, and she still lived.

As I read, I wondered whatever he would have done. Foot had created a fight or flight situation. Yet I knew he would neither have fled nor sued. He would have sent me, to transmit to Foot, pages of contentious comments, with page and line references.

Foot said (page 290) that Déricourt was in Aleppo when the Allies arrived in July 1941 and was offered work for Imperial Airways. 'He said that he would like it, but had to revisit France on private business first.'

Foot had credited Déricourt with the mysterious trip to London for one night in July which he spent in André Simon's flat. He had even put a date to it. He made it the 19/20 July, by the aircraft which carried Antelme ('Antoine') and W.J. Savy ('Wizard'). Déricourt had told me he had parachuted back, but Foot had made him travel back on the 21/22 by an aircraft which set him down, in the Châteauroux area, with strangers to receive him. If correct, this would have been most inconvenient, seeing that he had to be back in one of his own fields to receive Bodington the next night.

I looked for the name of Bonoteaux, and was relieved not to find it. Foot said (page 293), 'Lyon was accompanied by an unidentified agent.' It had been worth withdrawing the Bonoteaux card.

Operations had code-names, and the fatal one on which three were arrested was 'Conjuror', on 15/16 November 1943.

The three were J.F.G. Menesson, P.B. Pardi and A.A. Maugenet. Maugenet had betrayed John Young and Diana Rowden. I had been told this first by Starr, who had it from Young, then by Elizabeth, after her enquiries amongst people with whom Diana had stayed.

It had been obvious to me from the depositions of Bony and Lafont that their instructions were not to arrest the arrivals, only to shadow them until they disappeared into a house in Paris or a station, then break off and report. The arrest of Bonoteaux had been an accident, brought about by his unexpected behaviour, which caused Bony, unfortunately, to act on his own initiative. Had something of the sort happened with regard to these three? I hoped their arrest was another accident.

Foot listed two other passengers who had arrived by this operation, V. Gerson and E. Levene. Both these had gone unmolested. Levene had at the end of the month walked into a Bleicher trap, when on his way to join the Bleicher-controlled Frager network, but that could have had nothing to do with Déricourt. This difference is blurred in Foot's wording, which almost suggests a complicity between Déricourt and Bleicher, which, as I wrote to Foot, 'is false to everything I know'. That Foot is 'Bleicher-minded' peeps out of his bibliography, in which he asserts that my *Double Webs* 'investigates Déricourt's career, mainly through the evidence of Bleicher...' I never sought evidence of Bleicher. Foot had substituted the name of Bleicher for that of Vogt. For me, Vogt was a man of honour, Bleicher not. The mistake was therefore vexatious to me, and I required and obtained its correction in the next edition.

Foot had found on the files no notification by Bodington that he knew of and had authorised Déricourt's contact with the Germans. Yet he did find a jotting in Bodington's hand —

'We know he is in contact with the Germans and how and why' — on the back of an office note concerning Déricourt dated 23 June 1943. It cannot have been at this date the jotting was made, for that was before Bodington's visit to the field; on the other hand, it must have been soon after his return, in the third week of August, for at the end of August he left the Section.

Most interesting is an extract (pages 298–9) from the citation of a DSO for Déricourt, for which Brigadier Mockler-Ferryman put him up in late October. This referred to his 'great ability and complete disregard of danger' in 'particularly difficult and dangerous circumstances' involving 'keeping up many very dangerous acquaintances, particularly with pilots of the Luftwaffe and Lufthansa'. This reads as though it had not been understood his German acquaintance included the SD and Gestapo.

It was bad weather during the December and January full moon periods which delayed until February his recall after the warning from Yeo-Thomas. It was on 3/4 February that Morel had come with orders to bring him back. A deposition from Goetz to Miss Atkins after the war said that on the evening of the 5th Déricourt dined with Boemelburg and himself, and told them he was going. I was glad to see that. To have gone back with Morel would have been to abandon Clément, Mme Besnard and Watt to certain arrest; morality obliged him to obtain the delay in which to see Boemelburg and Goetz before he went, tell them he was going, and so reconcile them to leaving the team to carry on in the hope of his return. Had he let Morel take him back to England, abandoning his team, he would have become, in his own eyes, a traitor in the lowest, meanest sense.

When he boarded a plane on 8/9 February, taking his wife with him, he knew it would not be the signal for Boemelburg to pick up the telephone and say, 'Arrest "Gilbert's" team.'

On 10 February SOE's chief security officer was writing: 'If in fact he has been working for the enemy... then he is a high grade and extremely skilful agent and no amount of interrogation will break him.' On the 11th he was questioned, with regard to the mail, and said even if he had shown it, it would have been worth it for the sake of continuing his operations unhindered. Gubbins was away. Sporborg could see no proof of his guilt, but on the 14th bowed to the opinion of Security he should not undertake a further mission. The decision he should not return to France was made on the 21st. Buckmaster protested the continuing immunity of 'Marc' proved Déricourt's innocence (Boemelburg was keeping his umbrella up). Even as late as 5 December 1945 Colonel Buckmaster was writing:

> ... when — if ever — the clouds are blown away, I am prepared to bet a large sum we shall find him entirely innocent of any voluntary dealing with the enemy. His efficiency in Lysander and Hudson work was staggering and it was his very success that raised the ugly idea that he was controlled. People who did not know him and judged him on the result of his work said, 'It's too good to be true. He must be a bad lot.' That kind of reasoning would of course be scoffed at by any country section officer...
>
> Suffice it to say he never once let any of our boys down and that he has by far the finest record of operations of any member of SOE.

That was before Kieffer and Goetz were brought as prisoners before Miss Atkins. Foot gave a too short extract from Kieffer's deposition to her, sworn on 19 January 1947, 'material which Boemelburg had photocopied by his agent Gilbert/Déricourt, and which was kept in my safe... was put to very good use during the interrogation of 'Prosper'.' On the other hand, Foot had quoted Placke for Déricourt's not having been directly concerned in the 'Prosper' disaster.

Foot used a new series of code-names for networks: 'Prosper's' was 'Physician', Garry's 'Phono', Déricourt's 'Farrier', de Baissac's 'Scientist', Robin's 'Juggler'. 'Robin' he identified as Worms, and he commented, 'Charles Wighton, *Pinstripe Saboteur*, attributes to Weil... the code name and the status of "Juggler's" commander.' Déricourt had told me truly.

Having always in my mind the mystery of Déricourt's 'anterior epoch' and of the mousetrap house in Marseilles of which he had knowledge, I eagerly thumbed through Foot's pages concerning the year 1941, to see if there had been more than one of these. I found, on page 173, an account of the Villa des Bois affair, from which I learned that the victims belonged to the earliest wave of agents sent over, of whom there were still very few. Foot wrote that J. B. Hayes, Jumeau, Le Harivel and Turberville had been parachuted together on 10/11 October. The last-named landed wide of the others and had been arrested separately, the others on arrival at the Villa des Bois:

> The same trap, manned by someone who resembled Turck closely enough in voice and figure to deceive several agents, also caught Robert Lyon, Roche, Pierre, Bloch, and — last and worst of all, on 24 October — Georges Bégué.

No other mousetrap house was mentioned. The one of which Turck had told me must be the one of which Déricourt had spoken as having been at the origin of the troubles of 1943. Which was the man he had known to have become, in

1943, a German agent? And how could Déricourt, not then a member of SOE, have known about it? And how could anything that had happened there have led to the *quid pro quo* between Déricourt and the de Vomécourts?

I also saw that Garel and Lyon had been recruits of de Guélis. That would have made de Guélis particularly vexed by their falling into the trap. Now, it dawned on me, that when Irene had said de Guélis had returned from France very much upset by the manner in which a lot of agents had been arrested in one house, it must have been this house and this disaster which he had in mind, and it was presumably about this he had written to Eden, in the sealed envelope he gave to Irene. The calamity must have been of signal magnitude and the manner of it perturbing.

Coming to the radio-game, Foot named four circuits which the Germans had played back to us: 'Valentin', 'Archambaud', 'Madeleine' and 'Leopold' (a French Canadian, M.J.L. Rousset). Further, on page 345, he tabulated nine networks, money intended for which had been parachuted month after month to German reception. He did not give the radio operators' names, but two of the networks, 'Bricklayer' (Antelme, 'Antoine') and 'Phono' (Garry), were controlled by 'Madeleine', whilst against those remaining I could (from Foot's text) set the names of D.H. Finlaison, A. Defendini, Marcel Defence ('Dédé'), R. Byerly and Adolphe Rabinovitch ('Arnaud'). That made nine radios. I believed one should add 'Hercule' (A. Dubois), who, Vogt had told me, had been operating his radio when he and Scherer came upon him. Anyway, Foot indicated, without estimating the total number, that it ran to more than he had picked out for mention. Rabinovitch and Finlaison had been dropped, with their radios, to circuits already German-controlled. Non-radio officers parachuted to radio appointments with waiting Germans included Antelme ('Antoine'), Madeleine Damerment, G.B. McBain, M. Lepage, E.Lesout and R.Sabourin. Defendini was arrested as a secondary consequence of the radio-game.

It was twelve years since Buckmaster had declared, on the front page of the *Sunday Empire News*:

> Miss Fuller states that … a number of our networks became German controlled. I know it was only one and I consider I am in a better position to know than she is.

It is not pleasant to live in the shadow of an *argumentum ad hominem* like this — repeated at intervals through other media — and, though Foot's references to myself were less friendly than I had expected, reading this sad catalogue, I felt justified.

Where I differed from Foot was mainly in character judgements. He was disagreeable about almost everyone who meant anything to me. I was surprised, too, to find no acknowledgement to Irene. When I went down to the House of Commons after we had both read the book, she asked me, 'Personal points apart, what do you think of it? I worked so hard to get it. Is it worth having got?'

I hesitated only for a moment, then said firmly, 'Yes.'

We were now in the period of a Labour Government, and on 11 May 1966 I received a letter from Irene, from which it appeared someone had said something about the *History* which gave the Foreign Office the credit for having initiated it. This cut out Macmillan, Heath and ourselves. She enclosed text of a parliamentary question she had addressed to the Secretary of State, and of Mrs White's reply that 'this Government' knew of nothing that had passed in the affair prior to the announcement of the (Conservative) Minister of State on 13

April 1964 — which I had been ensconced in the Serjeant-at-Arms's Box to hear.

I dined with Irene at the House of Commons on 4 May. She said the key phrase was, of course, 'this Government'. The Labour Government did not know, and it was not their fault, for nobody had told them. She was really rather dismayed by the rapidity with which history could vanish. She had spoken to Edward Heath about it and was quite relieved to find he remembered. Later that night I wrote to Timothy d'Arch Smith (today my partner in Fuller d'Arch Smith):

> I have just come back from having dinner with Irene at the House of Commons. Her chief news is that she has spoken with Ted Heath, and that he remembered the whole thing pretty clearly. In fact, he said, 'I was under the impression it was I who got you the book.' She said, 'It wasn't, it was Harold,' meaning Harold Macmillan, but that did not matter...
>
> I was quite relieved. There has been such an outbreak of amnesia, starting from Foot himself, that I had begun to feel we were living in that film *Stamboul Express* [in fact I meant *The Lady Vanishes*].

It was Heath, so I had understood, who had done the work of interviewing Chancellors of universities and obtaining their opinions of historians, though the impetus came from Macmillan, and it was, Irene told me, Macmillan who persuaded the Treasury to vote the funds for the cost of production and for Foot's fee. (He had a lump sum, but not a royalty on sales.)

On 16 May Irene telephoned to say she had had 'two letters from the Prime Minister'. Mr Wilson had asked her to come and have tea with him at Downing Street. She did not feel it would be quite right for a Conservative MP to have tea with a Labour Prime Minister at Downing Street, though she would naturally be pleased to have a chat with him in the Members' Tea Room of the House of Commons.

His problem was that he had found at Downing Street a file which he thought might be the right one, but he did not like to read it since it was marked on the outside, in Macmillan's hand, *Private* (or *Personal*, I forget which) and appeared to consist of a correspondence between his predecessor and Irene. Would she ask Mr Macmillan if he would write him a letter saying he would like him to read it? As for the other file, containing her correspondence with Heath, that was at the Foreign Office, and if he asked for it to be sent over, everyone there would think he was trying to 'get something on' Heath. To do it more nicely, would she ask Mr. Heath to write him a letter suggesting he should read that file?

Shortly afterwards, she told me both Macmillan and Heath had, with perfect good will, written the letters he asked for. Wilson now had the file in which my name and Elizabeth's were mentioned by Ted Heath as to be privy to the confidential correspondence. I really was quite thankful that the letters that for so long had been in my desk-drawer should be seen to exist by someone else — and that a Prime Minister.

At the end of the year appeared *Inside SOE* by E.H. Cookridge (Barker, 1966). As I had expected, the section concerning France was mainly cribbed from Elizabeth and me — though we were 'uninformed novelists'. Elizabeth rang up and said, 'To be libelled and plagiarised simultaneously is a bit much.' The book contained one point of interest. Cookridge said it was through Helen James, mistress of Kaiser, alias Massuy, of the Abwehr, that Christmann had obtained the name of the restaurant where he could meet members of the 'Prosper' network. Déricourt had guessed right. Cookridge must have had this from Bleicher, to whom Helen James had been lent by Massuy to help him in the arrest of Marsac. Only, Cookridge had the name of the restaurant wrong. It was not the Brasserie Lorraine, but the Tourets' Chez Tutulle.

I had feared to find Déricourt pilloried. On the contrary (page 221):

> Considering the fact he was found completely innocent, and acquitted, 'Gilbert' had suffered great hardship.. More tribulation followed. In 1958 Miss Jean Overton Fuller published a book...

Ah well! In a book of that sort, I would rather I was the villainess than Déricourt the villain.

17: CLÉMENT

I had moved out of the world of spies into one of poetry. I had written two straight biographies, *Shelley* (Cape) and *Swinburne* (Chatto) and had begun one of Sir Francis Bacon. I had written a good deal of poetry of my own. Then I received from George Mann three draft contracts, for reprint editions of *Madeleine*, *The Starr Affair* and *Double Webs*. I could only accept the middle one. *Madeleine* had just been brought out in a new hardback edition by East-West, and *Double Webs* I would never allow to go out again. It had ceased to represent my feelings about Déricourt even before it was published, but I would like to re-write it. Mann had hitherto done only reprints. He said it would be the first 'Mann Original'.

From the big trunk I got out the box-files of Déricourt's letters. Re-reading them was like going back into another incarnation. A sheet of ice had lain over it for so long. I wished I could ask him what he would like me to do with his story. The sense of his presence was very strong.

In his last letter he had asked me not to make enquiries. Even after reading his obituary I had made none, in case he had faked his decease. But after so many years it could hardly hurt. I wrote to the French Embassy in Laos. There I struck a vein of gold. The First Secretary, M. Denis Nardin, replied with so much kindness that I was emboldened to write second and third letters, explaining exactly the sort of information I was after. He made researches; he discovered that Déricourt, finding himself momentarily out of work following the closure of Air Laos, had hired his services to the small air transport companies at that time numerous in Laos. It was while flying a

Beechcroft bi-motor, belonging to a Mr Doncarli, that he crashed on landing at Sayaboury in North Laos, his four Laotian passengers being killed as well as himself. As far as was known to persons M.Nardin had questioned, there was no crisis in Déricourt's life in March 1961 (the moment when he had broken contact with me); although 'by nature solitary, he was not depressed'. He went at about that time to the plain of Jars, where the neutralist government of Prince Souvanna Phouma was encamped, and which was for a while completely cut off from Vientiane. At the time of his death he had had a project for the creation of a line of helicopters and was in contact with a sponsor.

M. Nardin had even been able to discover the name of Déricourt's Chinese companion — Janine. They had met at Hong Kong, where she was employed in or near the airport. She was about twenty, and already had a son at the time of her meeting with Déricourt, and had brought the boy with her when she followed Déricourt to Vientiane. After Déricourt's death she had gone to another country and re-made her life.

Déricourt's body, M. Nardin told me, had been flown to France for burial, at the request of his widow. He sent me a copy of the death certificate, which gave the exact place of his birth, Coulonges-en-Tardenois (which my atlas showed me to be a village near Château Thierry), and his parents as Alfred Déricourt and his wife Georgette, née Magny. (So the Baron de Malval had been mistaken in thinking Déricourt was not a real name, and that he might be a bastard of the house of d'Héricourt.)

M. Nardin told me Déricourt's executor was M. Rémy Clément, whom I could write to at the Secretariat General de l'Aviation Civile in Paris. I was overjoyed; for I knew that Rémy Clément was the real name of 'Marc', Déricourt's assistant in the field. I thanked M. Nardin for having done superlatively, and I wrote at once to Rémy Clément at the address given me — not without some anxiety, for a friend of Déricourt might have taken my book ill.

I wrote also to the Maire of Coulonges-en-Tardenois, asking for a copy of the birth certificate of Henri Alfred Eugene Déricourt, born 2 September 1909, and if possible for the names and addresses of any people in the locality who had known him as a child or could tell me in which house he had lived. I received a copy of the birth certificate, on which his parents were described as Alfred Déricourt, aged forty-one, postman, and Georgette Magny his wife, aged forty. So he came from the small people of France.

It was suggested to me that I could write to the widow Mme Marguerite Simard Henrie as the only person known who might remember the family.

Again, it was a very delicate enquiry, but I wrote at once to Mme Henrie, telling her I was writing a book about the war adventures of Henri Déricourt, who had given me his authorisation, and asking her if she could tell me anything about his early years or about his family.

Mme Henrie replied, 'Henri came from a very modest family...' He was the youngest of three brothers, of whom the eldest was born in 1899, the middle one two or three years afterwards. She could give me a letter from the eldest, M. René Déricourt, telling her of the death of their parents, who were buried at Jonquières (Oise), and she had a pile of postcards written by Henri's mother, one of which, posted from Neuilly in 1936, told her Henri had become a pilot for Air Bleu. 'I remember him as a child and little young man, charming, as were his brothers, too.' The house where he had been born still stood, though 'completely renovated after the two wars'.

I had always known I should have to go to Château Thierry — a compulsion. I wrote to Mme Henrie that I should like to come and see her, and perhaps she could show me the house where Henri had been born.

There was a little delay before I heard from Rémy Clément; he had been away when my letter arrived. But when a letter came from him — from 'Marc' — it was most warming: 'Henri occupied a great place in my life during the formative years... Henri often spoke to me of you.' I was surprised and affected.

There was some difficulty over arranging a date for a visit on which I could see both him and Mme Henrie. In the end we made a rendezvous by telephone for the evening of 24 April 1973. I overlooked the fact that to book a room in Paris just after the Easter weekend would be almost impossible. The only room which BEA could at last offer me was in the Lutetia. I supposed that for few people but me could that name have had such associations. I should wonder if I were sleeping in what had been an office of Bleicher, or one of his chiefs, or of Giskes, who had been at the Lutetia before he received his command in Holland.

I realised that I would be meeting for the first time a friend of Déricourt. To Tim, who saw me off, I said 'He might be deeply shocked by my book. Supposing he says to me, "Henri was completely innocent"...'

Clément called for me at the Lutetia, with his car. He was tall and thin, with still some dark in his hair, though born in 1900. 'Henri était un enfant,' he said as we drove off. 'One must never believe anything he said.'

'He told me not to believe him further than I thought I should.'

'He lived in a world of fable.'

357

'He loved the fables of La Fontaine.'

'I mean, he lived in fantasy. That overflowing imagination was beyond his control. He had mythomania.' He quoted from a definition he had found in a work of reference: 'Mythomania: form of psychic imbalance characterised by a tendency to fabulation, lying and deceit.' He quoted Malraux, 'His mythomania is a way of denying life…'

I did not think Déricourt denied life.

Clément said, 'He had paranoia.' He gave me a definition of paranoia, from the same work. 'The paranoic is characterised by a psychological over-estimation of self, falsity of judgement and social inadaptability.'

But I did not feel Déricourt was so characterised. It distressed me that his friend was so bitter. I tried to think of some fictional character prone to overflowing imagination but could only think of Anne of Green Gables. Anne was a waif.

'Do you know anything about his childhood or parents?'

'No. He told me his father was a *garagiste*. I ought to have asked where.'

I told him I was on my way to Henri's birthplace, to see friends of his parents, and he said he would be interested to hear what I learnt.

'Did he tell you he killed Germans?' he asked.

'No.'

'In his book he killed Germans.'

'That was a novel. But did you read it?'

He had read some of it in Laos, where Déricourt would show him bits of it as it was growing up. He had not found a copy among his effects. He had understood a copy had been sent to me. In fact he had found a receipt for a registration addressed to me.

'I never received it,' I said, perplexed.

358

I told him of Déricourt's last letter to me, telling me he would have to break contact, dated 8 March 1961. 'What happened at that time?'

'Nothing that I can think of.'

I said he spoke sometimes of going north, and I wondered if he had gone into Red China.

'Not so far north as that,' he said. He was sure Déricourt never entered Communist territory.

'Do you mean he went on living at the Hotel Constellation?'

'Yes.'

'And nothing changed?'

'Nothing... Wait a moment... March 1961 was just the moment when Air Laos closed down.'

'Yes. He told me, in one of his last letters.'

After Air Laos closed down, he went into something else. Clément hesitated, then asked in a significant tone, 'Have you heard of the Golden Triangle?'

'No.'

It was, he said, a district in the north-west of Laos, a district with hills. The poppy grew wild there, the poppy from which opium was extracted. The villagers cultivated it. The airmen arriving saw fields of it spread out beneath them. The villagers pressed the poppy upon them; it was common for the airmen to become carriers. Henri was not the man to refuse to take something aboard. 'I would not say he never carried it even while working in Air Laos. Most pilots did. But after Air Laos closed down, he went into it in a big way.'

I was shaken and distressed.

Clément said, 'There are people who smoke opium in moderation.'

I thought of De Quincey, but said, 'An opium den is not thought of as a health parlour.'

'Henri never smoked it himself,' Clément said.

'I am sure he would not. But that makes it worse, in a way, that he made it available to others.'

'It is the villagers' sole crop. If nobody bought it, how would they buy food?'

'But they can't live at the expense of others' lives! They should be helped to grow or do something else.'

Helped by whom? Laos was a poor country and could not afford social services. The country had only two exports, opium and antiquities — antique statues of Buddha — and it was not everyone who could deal in the latter. There was no industry or manufacture to speak of. On the low and swampy ground there was a little rice, but insufficient. Opium produced an income. Opium had a limited medical use, for which reason certain countries, including rich ones like the USA which had other resources, were licensed to produce it, whereas Laos, whose sole resource it was, was not so licensed.

It was not Clément but Tim, when I got home, who explained to me that one should distinguish between 'opium, which is smoked, and heroin, which is injected'. The untreated poppy-juice, which was presumably what Déricourt was carrying, was not in itself so deadly but it was from it that, by various operations, heroin was obtained.

Clément said, 'Henri must have known you would not approve.' Now that he thought of it, he felt sure that was why Déricourt had closed down our correspondence. Once he began fetching from the fields all the time, his activity must have been noticed, which could have led to his mail being opened by international police and the names of anyone in regular correspondence with him noted. 'If he had not told you to cease writing, your name could have been listed in a connection you would not have wished. It was from respect for you.'

To have continued would have meant lying to me, also. I was shaken, but I suppose a little consoled.

'You were his best friend,' I said.

'I was a friend of his. I do not know if I was his best friend.'

'He chose you as his executor.'

'He did not choose me. He made no will. Mme Déricourt asked me to settle his affairs out there, to pack up his things and send them to her.' There were no letters from me.

All this was in the car. We drew up in the Place Falguière, and he took me into a beautiful old-fashioned restaurant, where the lighting was only by candles.

I asked him whether Déricourt had any kind of mission from the French Government in Laos. Déricourt had said he was Commandant on the Reserve List and I told him I did not believe him, but then he gave me a (TOE) military network address at which I should write to him as Le Commandant Déricourt.

'Ah no,' he said. There were some French military stationed near Vientiane at one moment who became friends of theirs and offered them the use of their TOE number for their letters, to save them money and time. Writing to a TOE number, one had to put some invented rank or the people in the sorting office would have realised it was being used by civilians.

'Did he tell you how he got into spying?' he asked.

'In Spain, during the Civil War.'

'He was never in Spain. It was I who was in Spam during the Civil War'. Déricourt did only internal flying, except for a period in Turin.

He had said Spain. I told him the story he had told me, of his having carried a letter for someone from the zone occupied by the one side to an address in the zone occupied by the other, to find when he called at the house a reception different from that he had expected, meaning obviously that he had been arrested.

'The only place that could have happened was in France,' Clément said. After the Armistice there was the German Occupied Zone and the Unoccupied Zone. Déricourt had been at that time living in Marseilles, flying in later 1941 for SCLAM Marseilles-Paris, Marseilles-Vichy, Marseilles-Toulouse.

I had never been able to understand how something that had happened in Spain in 1936 could have connected him with Boemelburg and affected his whole life. Yet now I felt at sea.

'Was he a test pilot?'

'Yes.'

Clément must have met Déricourt first in the early 1930s, at Toussus-le-Noble, a flying club, at which they occasionally taught, umpired or took part in events. In 1939 they were both flying for Air Bleu. When the war broke out they were militarised. He was Déricourt's chief. They flew Air France aircraft requisitioned by the French Government. Then came the Armistice and they both returned to civilian employments. The sense of defeat made the atmosphere very depressing. One day Déricourt called on him and told him he was going abroad for his firm. Clément asked no questions. He thought 'abroad' meant England; that Déricourt had discovered some means of going there and meant to fly for the RAF. In the small world of pilots, everyone knew what everyone else was doing. If one was working for the Germans, it was plain. If one disappeared, one thought, 'He has gone to England.'

Sometimes he telephoned Mme Déricourt — Jeannot, as she was called by her friends — to ask how she was, for he was certain that, with Henri away, she must feel lonely. She was switchboard operator at the Hotel de Beauvais in Marseilles. Then one morning, 26 January 1943, she telephoned him and asked him to call. There was in her voice a triumphal note. When she opened the door to him her eyes were shining. Then he saw why. In the passage behind her stood Déricourt.

'I have come from England,' Déricourt said, straight out.

He said he had come with a mission to receive and despatch British aircraft. He had been parachuted and had gone to Paris, where he had recruited Julienne (later to be code-named '*Claire*'). He had come to Marseilles to fetch Jeannot, and, he hoped, to recruit Clément.

It was perhaps relevant that Clément had had some experience of clandestine work during the Spanish Civil War. A Lord Forbes had brought a Lockheed 14 from England to France, where he had sold it to the firm Gastelloix, which was buying aircraft for resale to Spain. Through this it came about that Clément flew aircraft from Paris to Barcelona, Figueras, Léon and Valencia. They had to be hidden. 'We were for the Republic, naturally.' France, like Britain, was formally non-interventionist, but a lot of Air France people must have closed their eyes to the clandestine supply of aircraft. He fancied that any stories Déricourt had told about the civil war in Spain had been borrowed from him, but anyway — Déricourt now gave him a few hours in which to think over the proposition. He would like an answer before he returned to Paris by the train leaving at 5 a.m. next morning.

Clément thought it sounded very dangerous. It would mean serving under a younger man, who had formerly served under him. On the other hand, it would be much better paid than the dull office job he had been doing in Marseilles since the Armistice. He came back and accepted on condition his services were limited to looking for fields suitable for the landing operations. He did not in the beginning intend to be present at the operations. He could not leave with Déricourt, as he had to serve out his notice with his naval office or his sudden departure could arouse suspicion. That was why Déricourt's first operation was from the Poitiers area, where the ground was found for him by Lise de Baissac. Clément moved to Paris in time to help Déricourt with the April operation.

How did I think Henri got all that money, he asked me suddenly — four million francs, according to the newspapers.

I said he had mentioned diamond smuggling.

At one moment he distributed six diamonds, said Clément; two he gave to Clément, two to 'Claire,' and two he kept for himself and his wife. Clément gave one of his to his wife, and the other he had a dentist insert in the cavity of a tooth that had to have a filling. Only later, when in need of funds, did he cash it in.

He was sure, however, the sum named could never have been made by smuggling diamonds. 'It was for *that*,' he said, without naming it.

'What do you believe about his wartime role?' I asked.

'What did he tell you? You go first.'

'He felt sure everybody was going to be arrested and went to Boemelburg and proposed a basis on which the operations could continue.'

He drew a slight breath.

I said I had been afraid it would shock him.

He said, 'Where Henri is concerned, I am past shock.'

'That makes it easier. Did you have no suspicion?'

In August 1943, he said, he was told to take something to the mother-in-law of 'Hercule' (Dubois). She ran a school near Tours. While he was there, German police entered and the whole school was placed under arrest. He never knew why. After a while they were all freed. There was a rule that if one was arrested one must report it, because of the possibility one might have been 'turned' and escaped with German complicity. He therefore asked Déricourt to meet him. They exercised extraordinary precautions over telephoning. They first let the apparatus give three pips; the caller then rang off and rang again, and asked, 'How are you?' The other must then moan about something. If he said, 'I'm very well,' it meant the worst, he was under arrest, and the flat was a German trap. Henri came out to meet him at the Etoile. They met at the Etoile because, being a large space, open all round, it would be easier to run for it if it looked as if one might be going to be arrested. At the Etoile Clément told Henri he had been arrested. He spoke of the fear he had felt.

'Henri was so marvellously compassionate, so understanding of what the fear felt like, it came into my mind he himself must have been arrested and said nothing about it. If somebody has appendicitis, somebody who has not had appendicitis may be very sympathetic but he does not know the nature of the pain, the suffering. Henri knew the nature of the fear that I had felt. It was a knowledge that could not be faked, or hidden. Even the colour of his skin changed.'

I did not know how to fit that into what Henri had told me.

He spoke to me of another occasion on which he himself had felt fear. When there was to be an operation, Henri and he always travelled down to the place in the morning. After taking a look at the field, they would lunch at a village hotel, in which they would take a room. After lunch they would go up to the room — to avoid being drawn into idle conversation down below — and read until the fall of darkness, not walking down to the field to join their passengers until about half an hour before the aircraft would come. They always brought a book each. But on one occasion, on 19/20 August, he thought Henri looked tired on the train down to Angers. At Soucelles, when they went up to their room, Henri did not read his book. He got into bed and stayed there all through the afternoon, until it was time to go out and meet their passengers — hiding in the bay in the bushes they had been shown earlier — and lead them the few steps down to the field. It was an unusually large party they saw off that night. Only one passenger descended from the plane, a man, carrying explosives. As though he knew where he was, he walked straight off, on his own, without asking them for directions. Therefore there were just the two of them to retrace their steps together. There was a small bank they had to remount, to regain the road. Henri was walking very slowly, and suddenly sank down on the ground. Then Clément felt fear. 'He was strong. What was the matter with him? Impossible to call a doctor.' He half dragged, half helped Henri to the base of a tree, against which he propped him. After a while Henri managed to get up. Clément put his arm round his waist and they walked back to the hotel, where Henri got straight back into bed. He had been all right in the morning, but it had been frightening.

There was another occasion on which Clément felt fear. It was the night Morel came and tried to take Déricourt back with him. Clément kept saying, 'If you take him, you leave me all alone here! Don't leave me here alone!' Morel returned without Déricourt, but a few nights later Déricourt boarded another aircraft and Clément was left alone. He still felt very sorely about it.

'Henri could not help it,' I said. 'It was an order. He had gained what time he could to make arrangements. You were safe, you and "Claire" and Watt. You were under Henri's protection.'

'I know that now. I didn't know it then.'

'He saved not only himself but the whole of his team. You were one of those whom he recruited. His own friends, whom he had recruited, came first with him.'

'It is for that I forgive him.'

'Henri told me it was you who sought out the witnesses for the defence.'

'Yes.' Clément had sought out all those who had passed to or from France through Déricourt's hands to safety. 'For two years I wondered what my own evidence would be if I were asked to testify.' He would give me a copy of his own deposition to the DST. He had refused to sign the summary of his statement written by the clerk, gone home, written his own and posted it to them. When reading Henri's deposition, which he would also give me, I should remember that it was not in his own words. The clerk always put what everyone said into officialese, always terminating with the stock phrase, '*Lu, persiste et signe*'.

After the trial, when he was freed, had he never asked Henri about any of the things that troubled him?

Only once did he try. It was in Indo-China. From 1957 on, Henri was flying for Air Laos, based on Vientiane, and he for Aigle Azur, based on Saigon. They would meet at Vientiane or at Saigon, or at other places to which their flights took them. Just once he asked something. Henri said, 'It is too soon.' He never tried again.

'Did he know you had come to believe him guilty?'

'Once, when we were having a row about something, I said, "I have passed my life in forgiving you." Henri didn't say anything. I knew he had understood.'

I asked him if he knew anything of the fatal accident.

He said it was he who had been asked to fly over the route Henri's aircraft would have taken, look down and try to spot the wreckage. He discerned on a hillside, just short of where it should have landed, what must be it. The Beechcroft, having insufficient range for two-way trips without refuelling, had four additional tanks fitted. When one was exhausted it was necessary to switch over to the next one and pump by hand to start the flow of petrol. On this flight Déricourt was not carrying a mechanic or other crew member to do this for him, in order to carry more payload. He had four passengers. The engines stopped on the approach to a landing and the aircraft crashed into trees, short of the strip, and burnt up.

Clément attributed the accident to meanness, in putting a paying passenger into the place that would have been occupied by someone he would have had to pay, to change the tanks over at the right moment, and pump; and to absence of fear. 'Henri was without fear. If one is too fearful, one isn't a good pilot, but if one becomes so confident as to assume nothing can go wrong, one ceases to be a good pilot.'

However that might be, to go up without arranging for a sufficient petrol supply did seem to me very strange. Was he sure it was Henri whose body was found in the pilot's seat?

'Impossible to identify bodies burned black.'

I produced from my bag the table I had made of Déricourt's air operations. Clément was most interested, as he had never had a record of their operations. Could he help me complete the passenger-list? Concerning one passenger in particular, I hoped for his help. Henri told me that Mme Felix Gouin left with 'Prosper' from Azay-sur-Cher in May 1943. She was just up from a miscarriage by Caesarian, and he had felt it a responsibility to take under his escort a woman who was really too weak to travel. 'Prosper' objected to the service being used to take a person who was not an agent. Her testimony had counted for him at his trial, for her husband had become Prime Minister of France. Foot, however, had made her leave from Angers, with a host of other passengers, on 4/5 February 1944. A newspaper reporting the trial had made her leave in February but, though probably Foot's source, could have confused her departure with Déricourt's.

Mme Gouin, said Clément, left from Azay-sur-Cher, on a warm, summery evening. The four of them dined together, then had to wait until it grew dark. Henri had had an order from London to go to Arles to fetch her from a clinic, in which she had undergone some grave operation. He escorted her personally all the way from Arles to Azay. Her sole fellow passenger was a man whose name he was not told, but who was some very big chief. He tried to give orders to Henri, who stood up to him, and said he was not under his orders. The big chief said that when he arrived in London he would protest at the use of the Lysander to carry a person who was not an agent. 'I was surprised he objected to Mme Gouin, as she was very sweet.' (Her husband had been in England for some time, and it was because he was an important French statesman the British had ferried his wife to him.)

I sought his witness on the quarrel between Déricourt and Frager as the latter was leaving for England. In Bleicher's book Déricourt had rushed up and tried to push Bardet aboard with him.

It was, said Clément, Bardet who travelled down with them in the train from Paris to Angers. He was one of the party to go. But as they left the station he saw Henri stop and look around, as though he felt he was being followed. Clément looked around too, and saw that Frager was following them. Déricourt bearded him and said he would not tolerate that he and his party should be stalked by Frager. Frager said he was of the party. Bardet had acted as a stand-in for him. Déricourt was furious, such things as stand-ins were never heard of. Bardet had given him the password, therefore Bardet was the one he had to put aboard the plane. Frager then repeated the password. Again, Henri was furious. Two persons in possession of the same password was a thing never heard of. He could not know which one of them had improperly passed it to the other. Now, since he could not know which one of them he had to board on the aircraft, he would have to board them both. The quarrel continued throughout their dinner. On the field Déricourt did try to force Bardet into the aircraft after Frager. Frager drew his pistol. Henri said it surprised him that Frager did not want Bardet with him in London, as they were friends. Bardet sidled off and disappeared. Frager lowered hrs pistol and held out his hand to Henri. Henri refused to take it.

'That is exactly what Henri told me,' I said. He added that people had asked him why he refused Frager's hand, and said it was because 'I would not take the hand of such a fool'. Frager would not sec he was being betrayed by Bardet to Bleicher. He would not see because he did not want to see. In the end it cost him his life. (In 1944 Frager was arrested by Bleicher and hanged in Buchenwald.)

I had set out my table of Déricourt's operations so as to show the fruits. Concerning the passengers to London, there was no question. They passed to safety. It was the fate of the incoming passengers in which his honour was reflected. I had marked with a star to the right those who were never arrested, or whose later arrest was not through Déricourt's fault. Those arrested through the trailings I had marked with stars to the left. When we came to the one with three stars to the left, Clément said he remembered it well. It was on the big field at Soucelles. There were, however, not five arrivals as I had it (following Foot), but six. The one missed out was Fille-Lambie, also known as Le Commandant Morlane. Fille-Lambie shook hands with Mitterand, one of the departures, as they crossed on the field. It was Fille-Lambie who told him the departing passenger, with whom he had shaken hands, was François Mitterrand (to become President of France). The other arrival, whom he recognised, was Pardi ('Filibert'). Pardi told them while they were resting on their way from the field that his mission was to carry out operations similar to Déricourt's in a different part of France. He asked if he could stay with them for a while, participating in their operations and learning their methods. 'Henri asked me what I thought. I refused categorically. Pardi was a boaster, and could endanger our security.'

Another of the arrivals was Gerson ('Vic'), who lived to testify for Déricourt at his trial, as did Fille-Lambie.

The six arrivals split into two parties. Three went with Henri to the nearby station at Tiercé, three cycled with himself to another small station, Etriché, where they split again. At Etriché station he noticed nothing abnormal, but in the compartment he entered with Dumesnil, their occasional assistant, he noticed that a passenger who pretended to be asleep covertly inspected the platforms of all the stations at which they stopped. It was a slow train, which they all left at Le Mans. Fille-Lambie, who was going to Rennes, parted from the rest of them. On the platform where they waited for the express to Paris, he noticed persons of an unmistakable

371

appearance, big men, without luggage, therefore with their hands free to seize one. He whispered to Henri, 'It's the rue Lauriston [headquarters of the Bony-Lafont gang].' They boarded the express without hindrance, but when he went forward to get tickets for the restaurant car, he noticed the big men distributed through the compartments. He came back and warned Henri, and they warned their passengers. The train was full, and on its arrival at the Gare Montparnasse Henri and he were amongst the last to leave. Ahead of them some people were arrested at the barrier, but then let go. 'I could have sworn they were not those we had met and escorted.' (So it was true, as Déricourt had told me, he had seen some people arrested there, but not the agents he had brought from the field.)

'They must have made a mistake,' I said. 'But three of the ones you had escorted were arrested all the same — Pardi, Menesson and Maugenet.'

That was the only occasion on which Clément was aware of their being trailed.

His reference to Tiercé enabled me to equate the fatal operation with paragraph 2 of Bony's deposition, while his reference to Pardi as Corsican linked it to paragraph 5. Bony had put this operation in twice. With this key, I could now identify all the operations on Bony's list: 1 related to Lyon and Bonoteaux, 4 to the reception of 'Madeleine' and others (all allowed to pass to their destinations unimpeded), 3 was void. This discovery reduced what had been for me a probability to a certainty that the arrests made through the tradings from Déricourt's field were exactly four, and no more: Bonoteaux, Pardi, Menesson and Maugenet.

Clément was agreeably surprised to find the ones arrested were so few. 'I thought it had been perhaps all.'

'The Germans could not arrest them without making Henri suspect in London. They had to be content with looking at the fruit, not taking it. The accord they made with Henri worked in the British interest.'

'Looking at this table, that cannot be denied.'

He said that just after the war he had been to England and spoken to Colonel Buckmaster, who said to him, 'What we reproach Déricourt for is not that he worked for the Germans but that he did not tell us about it. This is the only thing we reproach him for.' It was in a club, about six o'clock.

'He did not dare tell,' I said. 'He did not know if what he had done would be forgiven.'

'To shoot a lion, one must tie up a goat, and sometimes the goat is killed. Colonel Buckmaster would not have permitted the sacrifice of human beings.'

He thought, as I did, that it must have been Henri's pretence he could bring them the date and time of the invasion that kept the Germans content with so little.

'He beat them all!' said Clément. 'He beat the Gestapo, he beat the Intelligence Service, he beat our DST. I take off my hat. He beat Boemelburg, Buckmaster and 'Wybot'. Only he did not ask himself whether the wool remained firmly pulled over *my* eyes.'

We were special cases, I thought. So far as I was concerned, he had never really tried to deceive me.

Clément kept coming back to money, but although Déricourt had a lively commercial sense, I never felt that he was specially after money. He never concerned himself whether I had any. 'I offered him a percentage of the royalties on my book. He refused it.'

Perhaps it would not have been very much. Only a great fortune interested him.'

'What did he want it for?'

Clément had no answer for me.

'He wasn't a *bon viveur*,' I said.

'Not at all.'

'He didn't smoke.'

'No.'

'He seemed to drink very little.'

'Very little. I can truly say that in the thirty years I knew Henri, I never saw him the worse for drink. Neither did he use any of the drugs so easily obtainable in the Far East.'

He racked his brains, but could not think of anything in Henri's life-style that called for much money. He appreciated a good hotel or restaurant but did not grumble if there was only a poor one. He paused, sometimes, to admire a big, beautiful car but appeared happy with his small one. His wife had a fur coat but was not a woman who would be demanding. He had no mistress, known of. Just after the war, he appeared in a very good suit — 'Not loud. Not flashy. Henri was never flashy. But good. The stuff of the very best quality, the fit superb. It must have been made for him by a very good English tailor.' But a Savile Row suit hardly involved that sort of money. He really could not think of anything that Henri coveted that required a fortune. Then suddenly he exclaimed, 'A château! He wanted a château!'

'What? What for?'

'To live in. He wanted to be a grand seigneur.'

He did not live, or talk, like one who aspired to great gentility. Was there something about Déricourt I had never understood?

18: COULONGES

On the morning of 25 April 1973 I took the train to Château Thierry. When one leaves from the Gare de l'Est one feels one is heading towards Germany. The warnings not to lean out of the window are in French and German, instead of French and English, as on trains leaving from the Gare du Nord or St Lazare. The Marne is the Battle of the Marne. When I got out at Château Thierry the loudspeaker was talking about passports. The train was going on to Germany. Then the loudspeaker was saying, 'Will Miss Jean Overton Fuller go to the desk...'

An elderly M. Godbillon presented himself. Mme Henrie had asked him to meet me and drive me the twenty-eight kilometres to Coulonges. He could tell me his recollections on the way, for he had known Henri's father, and Henri as a child and young man. We crossed the Marne and I saw rise before us the great château from which the town takes its name. I saw the birthplace of La Fontaine, whose fables Déricourt had loved. Then we passed into an open, flattish, rather featureless country. I hoped he would not mind my coming here, penetrating to the origins he had kept from me.

The enquiries I had come to make of the people who knew his family were delicate. I could hardly represent the story which had brought me in the guise of 'Local boy made good'. I did not want to deceive these people, nor yet to cause pain. 'He had a bit of trouble after the war,' I said, feeling the ground. 'He was accused of being in intelligence with the Germans — which he was, though it is difficult to see what they gained from it.'

'Some people are imbecile enough not to understand one must be a little double,' said Godbillon.

Coulonges had been occupied by the Germans from 4 October to 13 October 1914, he said. In the village they thought they were going to be occupied again in 1918, so close the Germans came. I felt that he was still living in the aftermath of the First World War. I remembered the often unexpected detail in which Déricourt spoke of the way in which the battle line here had moved backwards and forwards, in days when he would only have been a child, and wondered if he was the transmitter of the memories of his people, people for whom the '14–'18 war was still the Great War, people for whom time had stood still.

'It would be from his mother Henri got his intelligence,' said Godbillon. She was an intelligent woman, though without advantages in life. She was brought up in an orphanage and the directors wanted her to enter religion but she had not the temperament to be a nun. Alfred Déricourt, whom she married, had little to offer her. At the time when Henri was born, he was employed by the post office. He had to collect the mail in sacks from Coulonges and another village and take them by horse-cart to the station; he set out at five in the morning, and as the round had to be repeated later in the day, did not finish until seven in the evening, and the pay was low. He and Godbillon's father, hoping to improve their lot, left Coulonges in 1911 for Chelles, near Paris, where they were taken on by an exporter of timber. They had to carry it all day; big logs, felled trees really; and the hours were worse than they had ever known. Sometimes they worked a twenty-hour day. As it was impossible to do with four hours' sleep, they were constantly falling asleep over their labour. Their employer would wake them roughly, saying, 'The night is for sleep', and make them go on carrying. It was far worse than what they had left at Coulonges. Later, Henri's father managed to obtain a better job, in an iron-foundry (*quincaillerie*), which made locks and bolts, belonging to a M. Fontaine. Later again, M. Fontaine moved Henri's father to Varenval, of which Mme Henrie would tell me more.

Henri was the youngest of three brothers, the elder being René and Marcel. M. Fontaine noticed Henri was intelligent and paid for his education beyond the age at which free schooling stopped. He saw Henri, since he was so good at school subjects, as cut out to be a schoolteacher, and paid for him to follow a qualifying course. But Henri did not want to become a schoolteacher. He said it was 'too sedentary' and too ill paid. He obtained for himself a position in the post office (PTT), at a much higher level than his father had had, as chief of the department which dealt with letters that had to be re-sorted and readdressed. It was better paid than school-teaching would have been, but still it was 'too sedentary'. What he really wanted to do, he now revealed, was to become an aircraft pilot. M. Fontaine paid for him to take the necessary pilot's training course, he qualified and became a pilot for Air Bleu, flying mail planes. It was curious how the mail haunted Déricourt.

'He was enterprising — ambitious even,' said Godbillon; but he was liked, despite his evident intention to rise in the world, for he had always a cheery smile and a wave for one. Later they heard he had married; he never brought his wife back here; none of them had seen her. When one had got away from poor beginnings, one did not come back. Godbillon said this without rancour, as one stating a fact of life.

We had arrived at Coulonges, a tiny village of virtually only a single short street. Mme Henrie pointed out to me one of the terraced cottages practically opposite but banked up slightly above her own. 'That is where Henri was born.' One could not say it was a picturesque cottage, but standing in her doorway I balanced a sketching pad on my handbag and made reverently the crude drawing from which I later made an oil painting.

At the top of the road was the church. Mme Henrie told me she had been to ask if they had the certification of Henri's baptism for me to see, but had been told the register had been destroyed in the bombing in the First World War. Nevertheless, she could assure me he had been baptised, and it was there.

She took me into her cottage, and said, 'Henri's family was very modest.' In the village, they were liked. 'Although they had little, they were generous with the little they had — which left them less.' Henri's mother was taught embroidery at the orphanage, but did not afterwards have the opportunity to be employed at such fine work. She loved her three sons, but her life had been hard. 'She was called Georgette.' Mme Henrie pronounced the name with tenderness, as though she were seeking for the way to express a delicacy, or refinement, which had not found encouragement to develop. Henri would have been about three when his parents entered the service of M. Fontaine. At first it was in Paris. Henri's father worked at the iron-foundry which M. Fontaine had there, and Henri's mother was employed as concièrge by M. Fontaine at his Paris house, in the rue St Honoré. 'It's shaming, isn't it?'

'No!' I exclaimed in protest.

Ah, but it is, she said. People think that it is. People say "*idées de concièrge*" as though a concièrge was the stupidest thing that could exist. Mme Henrie said this, turning away slightly, in the sickened voice of humiliation. They always dreamed of being able to scrape together enough to start a little business. But they never could manage it.

My distress deepened. In England, today, working-class intellectuals are often proud of their origins. In Paris, too. But Déricourt's parents had felt shame in their poverty. This was a strange corner of the country where time had preserved, museum-like, not only day-to-day moments of the First World War and the years that preceded it, but the class structure, the feeling about class, of the first decades of the century.

I understood now why Déricourt had said his feelings were for 'the small people' of France. It was not by chance he had instanced 'the postman, the concièrge' as examples of the 'small people' who — Germans come and Germans go — were, in peace as in war, 'always at the bottom'. That would have underlain his fury at the manner in which 'Prosper', the barrister, with his English public school background, had like a Pied Piper called out the Ismail people' of France into the most dangerous activities — and then delivered them all into the hands of the Germans. It was solidarity that produced that violent feeling with those 'small people' whom 'nobody considered'.

Henri must have been about ten, Mme Henrie said, when M. Fontaine moved the Déricourts out to his country property, near Compiègne — Varenval. Henri's father had a little house within the grounds, near the big house. On the lawn were some old rusted instruments, a ploughshare which had some history, and the wheels which had borne a cannon, captured from the Germans. Little Henri used to love to play on those wheels, and would bring his lively imagination to adventures in which the cannon had participated, ending in its seizure and transport to Varenval.

All three of the boys had done well. René, the eldest, had become a decorator; Marcel, who had emigrated to Dakar, had (as Godbillon had told me) become an *ébéniste*, a cabinet-maker.

When their parents retired, the three boys had clubbed together to buy them a flat at a house in a village called Jonquières, so their latter days had been happier than their beginnings. Mme Henrie said she would give me the letter from René that had told her of his parents' death.

With this, on the table, she had also a pile of postcards, written to her by Henri's mother. The first bore a photograph of Henri, taken at about fourteen, holding a book on algebra, of which he was very proud. He had just started it at school, and it must then have been his favourite subject. That, of course, was taken at Varenval.

Then she handed me the next postcard, on which was the photograph of a substantial château. On it was printed, *Le Château de Varenval*. 'His mother helped in the kitchen, and in the other rooms, wherever required,' said Mme Henrie, pointing to the lowest rooms. 'You can imagine little Henrie running in and out, playing on the steps and all about.'

It seemed too cruel. For a being of his impressionability, to be brought up in that magnificent place, and to have the run only of the lowest rooms. I knew that if I had been brought up there, the child of servants, I too would have wanted to own the château.

As soon as I got back to Paris, I telephoned Clément in a high state of emotion. He was at the Lutetia in half an hour.

I showed him the photograph of Varenval. 'That is where he grew up — he was the child of servants.'

'I had no idea,' Clément said. 'No idea at all. I never suspected. If I had known I should have been more understanding.'

Thoughtfully, he added, 'It was a château he bought after the war. But it was dilapidated.' The idea had been to rear poultry and game, but what came in from the sale of eggs and so on was very little. It needed capital, both to develop the farm and to put the château in order. That was why Henri went to Indo-China, where the pay was high, to try to make sufficient money to improve the place, while leaving his wife to manage it, in conjunction with Claude Jouffret, who had come to stay with them.

'Tell me about him. Where did Henri meet him? Was it in Fresnes, while they were both awaiting trial?'

He did not know where Henri met him, only that he became Mme Déricourt's lover. 'I tried to warn him. I said, "That Claude, he is a man, is he not, with needs like any other? If you leave him alone with your wife, for years, something may take place." He said if that should happen, he would be happy.'

I was puzzled. Everything had led me to suppose Déricourt loved his wife; probably it made him feel less guilty about living with a Chinese woman while he was away. All the same, I now wondered whether Mme Déricourt's liaison had been the reason he was vexed when I asked him about Jouffret. I had thought it was because Jouffret had been lover of 'La Chatte', and so formed a link with the drama of 1941. But it was Déricourt himself who had told me there had been a drama in 1941.

Clément talked to me also of the Chinese, Janine or Jeannine. She had a child by a previous lover, 'which was an attraction for Henri. He had never had a child of his own, so to be able to play with the little boy was a kind of consolation.'

'He told me she was better educated than he was. Is that true?'

'Yes.' Her father was a wealthy businessman and she had a degree in economics. The trouble was she was not content to remain Henri's mistress but wanted him to obtain a divorce from his wife and marry her. This Henri was unwilling to do.

He was very attached to Jeannot. He did not appear to feel supplanted by Jouffret, who he probably regarded merely as a consolation for her in his absence. Jeannot did not want a divorce. Henri did not want a divorce. So it was predictable a divorce would not take place. On the other hand, he was very taken with the Chinese. 'He was between Jeannine and Jeannot.' In the end he had not behaved well by the Chinese. After his death she tried to claim his whole estate, causing suffering to Jeannot, who had not previously known of her existence. As the marriage contract was on the basis of *partage des biens*, the estate went to the widow automatically.

A propos, could I tell him to whom in England Henri was sending, regularly, large sums of money?

No. I did not know that he was.

Clément felt responsible, as Mme Déricourt had asked him to help in settling up the estate. If that money was still Henri's, at his death — if for instance it was deposited in an English bank account in his name — then it formed part of the estate and he should get it in, because it should now belong to Mme Déricourt. But he had never found out where it was. Never discovered a trace of it. 'I wondered whether perhaps he was sending it to Bodington?'

'Not so long as I knew him. Bodington was in France, and Henri did not have his address.'

Would I like to meet Mme Déricourt? He could easily arrange it.

'Henri didn't want me to meet her.' It was because he did not want her to be upset. Now, that might have been partly because he did not want to be scolded by her for having consented to the book, or because an encounter might bring out that he had not given us the same versions of his wartime activities, but I still felt that concern she should not be upset was the dominant reason, and I had to respect it. 'He did not want her ever to read my book, or learn that it had been written. Does she know that *Double Webs* exists?'

'I don't know.'

If she knew that the book existed, then for me to call and see her could only do good. I could then assure her of my greatest regard for him, despite the things I had written. But if she did not know of my book about him, I could not go to see her without disclosing that I had written one; and that it was precisely what he wanted to avoid. Clément could only find out whether she knew by asking her; and if she did not know before, she would then. There was no way round this, so I had to refuse his offer of an introduction.

He produced something. It was the registration certificate of a parcel addressed to me at my London address. The contents of the parcel were described as 'Manuscrit' and the date stamped on it by the Paris post office was 1 October 1961.

That was just before I went to Carthage. It must have arrived after my departure on the evening of the 11th — I had found the slip about it on my return. What if he had thought from my failure to say anything about it that I had not liked it when I had read it? Yet he knew I was going to Carthage, had known it from August. It had probably been typed by that girl to whom he once had introduced me as his 'secretary'. But when it came back to her, surely she would have written to tell him? But then, as I verified when I got home, he had written to me at the Hotel Byrsa, on 18 October, that his book was in Paris being typed — he obviously had no idea it had already been posted to me. He was waiting to receive it, to check it through, and then would send it to me. The girl must have sent it direct to me by mistake, and when she let him know it had come back to her, he must have had her re-post it to him.

How he could have abandoned his book was the strangest thing to me. For almost four years he had laboured over it, and a lot of himself was vested in it. Something must have happened, of which Clément knew nothing.

Clément suggested the crash was a 'psychological accident' caused by his inability to choose between Jeannot and Janine. I did not believe that. Déricourt would have chosen between them, kept both on or dropped both. Suicide, no.

Clément opened his briefcase and gave me a mass of photostatted depositions to the DST — Déricourt's (in four fascicules), part of Placke's, his own and some contemporary notes he had made. I could keep them.

I began to read Déricourt's in the aircraft. He began by saying that in 1942 he was living at 50 rue Curiol, Marseilles. A person (whom he did not name) entered into contact with him ... he divined this person must be working for the British Intelligence Service, and therefore asked him if he could arrange for him to go to England or America. Following that (I translate from the French):

> ... I received the visit of a certain Pat... British agent in Marseilles, who announced that he had received the order to set me on my route. I was to meet him on 15 August at Marseilles Railway Station.
>
> I embarked secretly from near Narbonne, in the middle of the night on board a trawler, "Taranna", flying a Portuguese flag but really British, for Gibraltar. From there I was directed on to Glasgow...
>
> ... I enlisted in the RAF on 1 November... André Simon, Flight Lieut. RAF attached to the Air Ministry as liaison with SOE asked me if I would not like to join Buckmaster's organisation...

Pat O'Leary's book, *The Way Back*, which I had searched for Déricourt's name, contained nothing that could possibly refer to him, and it was for this reason I had decided not to put into *Double Webs* Déricourt's claim to have been embarked by 'Pat' in case it was false and 'O'Leary' would denounce it. But would he have dared to tell this story to the DST if it had been a fiction?

Déricourt had told me he had told a lot of lies to 'Wybot', so I was surprised to find he had admitted having given the Germans details of two of his operations — at Pocé-sur-Cisse and Soucelles. Why had he admitted so much? These were the two operations at which arrests were made, though it could not have been proved that the Bony and Lafont depositions referred to him. Déricourt had said: 'Culioli was on trial at the same time as me. My defence was clean. One should be given a good mark for the bad things one has not done...' He had not shuffled his faults on to another man, who was also fighting for his life. It would have been easy, as Bony had erroneously referred to '*parachutages*'. Déricourt could have said, 'It was not I but Culioli who received the *parachutages*.' He had accepted the odium, merely saying, 'I could not know what damage had been done in my wake.'

The postcards from Déricourt's mother were eight, dating from 27 August 1918, from M. Fontaine's house in Paris. The earliest from Varenval was dated 10 July 1924, when Henri would have been fourteen. I translate from her French:

> Henri's holidays begin on 25 July and I expect him Saturday ... so that he will be here for the Fête Nationale until Friday, because of the examination ... He asked me the other day if he could spend the whole of his holidays at Varenval, and he would like to visit Coulonges.

The last, dated 3 January 1936, said that 'Henri, pilot with Air Bleu, mail planes, is still with us, happy in his metier; unable to comprehend our torments whenever he is late.' René, she said, was still childless; Marcel had just left with his family for Dakar, where he had been appointed director of a school for cabinet-makers.

The letter from René Déricourt read:

Thursday, 13 January, 1945

On top of the death of my father, on 5 April, 1944, I have lost my mother.

My poor mother was taken ill on Christmas Day, with acute uraemia, with cardiac insufficiency aggravated by pulmonary expectoration ... in my presence she died on 11 January at 11 in the evening... She now reposes beside my father in the little cemetery of Jonquières...

R. DÉRICOURT

19: SOUCELLES

Irene had hoped that now it was 1973 the 1943 operational papers might be released to the Public Record Office under the thirty-year rule. She was informed they would not. In compensation, she obtained from the Joint Parliamentary Under-Secretary to the Foreign Office, Anthony Roy, permission for me to address questions to his Private Secretary, L. G. Davies, and the latter put me through to Colonel Boxshall. The first thing I asked him was Déricourt's rank, which had escaped mention in Foot's History. He replied:

[Déricourt was] appointed on 4 May (1943) to an honorary commission in the administrative and Special Duties branch of the RAF Volunteer Reserve in the rank of Flying Officer, which he relinquished on 19 August, 1944. After relinquishing his RAF commission he joined the Free French Air Force.

Next, I told him that whereas Foot listed only five passengers landed by 'Conjuror', Clément spoke of a sixth, Fille-Lambie. Could he confirm? At first he said there were only the five listed by Foot but, on my insisting, replied that he had looked in another file and indeed found a Captain Henri Jean Fille-Lambie, who had arrived on 25 October 1943 and was landed back in France on 15 November 1943.

Next, it had puzzled me that the lines selected by Foot for citation from Kieffer's statement for Miss Atkins included nothing about how 'Prosper' was arrested. She would have wanted to know. What did he say? Boxshall produced the lines:

> I remember that in the summer of 1943 I started the drive against 'Prosper'. He was arrested in his house after it had been watched for about a fortnight.

Probably Foot had omitted this because it was confused. 'Prosper' was arrested in a hotel and did not have a house. Triechâteau! Kieffer must have been thinking of Mme Guépin's house. Elizabeth had felt so sure it had been under surveillance, and Déricourt after reading her book suggested the police call there had been prompted by the Germans with the object just to probe and look around. Probably 'Archambaud' and 'Denise' had been followed there after their meeting with Christmann, though it was after 'Prosper's' meeting with them, on his return, that the hotel address had probably been shaken from them. Triechâteau was unknown to Déricourt, so that let him out.

Foot's citation of lines from Agazarian's statement concerning the arrest of 'Adrian' (*sic*) at the Capucines did not include any clue whether this was Bodens or Christmann. I asked Boxshall if the preceding lines contained a physical description. He copied out for me the lines:

> I met 'Adnan' for the first time about 17 May 1947 when he came with 'Arnaud' to the safe house, the address of which I had provided... 'Adnan' is about six feet, square cut and fairly stout, blue eyes, mousey to fair hair, fat rosy cheeks... fattish hands, a real Dutch type.

The rosy cheeks made it Bodens who had been arrested at the Capucines and, therefore, Christmann who had entered the flat at Square Clignancourt. Two more pieces of our jigsaw were in place.

Déricourt's deposition for the DST contained several — rather fanciful — references to a Major Warden, with whom he had been in contact after his recall to England in 1944. If this was a real person, could I be put in touch with him? Boxshall confirmed there was a security officer, Major R. A. Warden. He had tried to trace him for me but learned only that he had gone to Ireland.

The Times of 31 July 1973 carried an article, 'Tortured Officer Did Not Crack', by John Vader. It was from information from Mr Norman and Armel Guerne. Ostensibly a defence of Norman's son, as 'entirely innocent', it put the blame for 'hundreds of deaths' on Henri Déricourt, named in full, and wound up with the suggestion that Déricourt had been protected by 'Kim Philby, who was in SOE'.

My heart sank. There had been a time, long ago, when I had believed Déricourt responsible for the 'Prosper' disaster. It was like finding one's old clothes, picked up and donned by somebody else, as a hideous new fashion. To anybody who had seen 'Archambaud' handing round cups of tea at the Avenue Foch, or tuning the guards' radio to the station he wanted, reference to him as a 'Tortured Officer' would be ludicrous. Nor was Philby in SOE.

I said to Tim that since Norman had named Déricourt, I felt I should no longer protect the memory of his son. He agreed it was 'time for plain speaking'.

I wrote a letter to *The Times*:

31 July 1973

Sir,

I write to defend the memory of Henri Déricourt from blackening in your columns as the man who betrayed the 'Prosper' network. I probably know more about this man than anyone in the world, having researched into this subject over twenty years. I, too, at one time thought he might have been the big traitor, but have long known this was not the case. He was a double agent, whose case was of infinite complexity; he gave some things away but saved more and was acquitted by court-martial.

JEAN OVERTON FULLER

This was printed, after a delay, on 28 August; and it brought me a letter from William Kimber, asking me to write a book for his firm. So was commissioned *The German Penetration of SOE.*

From Boxshall, to whom I had written, I had a reply: 'Yes, I did see the article in *The Times* of 31 July and quite agree with you the theory expressed therein that Kim Philby protected Déricourt is complete nonsense.'

Clément, whom I had told of it, wrote that the prospect of a book by these people made him 'anxious for the memory of Henri, which I try to protect in the measure of the possible'. He proposed he should take me in his car on a tour of all the fields Henri and he had used, and suggested 12 September 1973: 'The moon will be full. Everything will be the same. Only, there will not come a Lysander.'

I took an early plane, which brought me into Orly at 11 a.m. Clément was there with his car, and drove me out through Chartres, Châteaudun and the beautiful old town of Vendome. 'Henri has become a historical character,' I said. 'I want to prevent him from passing into history as one of the great traitors.'

'What shall we do?' he asked. 'I should like to get him clear of this "Prosper"–"Archambaud" business. He was not a member of their network. He knew only the leaders, not the members. It is their affair. Don't let them put it on to Henri. He could become the scapegoat.'

It was my thought exactly. Only the leaders could have given away the hundreds in the network — 400 to 1,500 according to different estimates. They gave away members, whom they alone knew; demoralised, these gave away other members; and so it spread.

'When he came to recruit me, he was pure,' said Clément. 'When he recruited Lucienne, he was pure. If we could have worked on our own, he would have remained pure.' He had said to him, 'Get them to give you a wireless operator of your own.' It was so many months before they sent him Watt. During the early months, he had to use Agazarian, who transmitted also for 'Prosper' and for Frager, in both of whose networks there were German agents. 'If he had not had to share a wireless operator with contaminated networks, he would not have been obliged to become a double agent.'

We had taken a smaller road, through real country now, winding in the direction of Amboise. 'All these roads I cycled up and down,' said Clément. Cars were forbidden except to Germans and favoured collaborators. So he would cycle up every small road, peering over the hedges, looking for a field large and flat enough for an aircraft to land on. When he found one, he would memorise the position — never write down or make a mark on a map, in case of arrest — and fetch Henri to look at it. If Henri approved, he would have the particulars transmitted to London and the RAF would fly over, just to photograph it, in case there should show up from the air any disadvantages that had not been observable from the ground. If the RAF approved, then the field was homologated and an operation mounted.

'Did the farmers know their fields were being used?'

'No... yes...' They must have heard the aircraft coming down very low, then stop. Probably they decided to stay in bed, not to go out to see if it was on their land, and if it was a British one. All the people in these villages must have closed their eyes and ears.

Suddenly I read a sign 'Pocé-Sur-Cisse', and felt a slight shiver. We passed through the village and stopped by a wide open space. 'There! I did not know if I should be able to find the way.' We got out and walked about. It was larger than I had expected, a natural flat-land. There was no one else in sight. 'That's where we parked our bicycles.' He was pointing to a little bay in the hedge.

I was thinking of Bonoteaux, Clément of the two they had seen off, 'Xavier' and a little shot-down airman, Philip. He could not speak French, so, to prevent people from trying to talk to him in the train, and afterwards in the restaurant where they lunched, they said he had been in St Nazaire during the bombing and had been deafened. Two girls in the restaurant were somewhat over-sympathetic and looked as if they wanted to take Philip to bed. At last they got him away from them, and both men aboard the aircraft (which brought Lyon and Bonoteaux).

We got back into the car, and I told Clément a story I had found in *Watch for Me by Moonlight* by Evelyn Le Chêne (Eyre Methuen, 1973). It was the story of Robert Boiteaux, who had on 19/20 August 1943 formed part of a large party seen off by Déricourt and Clément. Boiteaux raised the security issue of sending so many agents at once, and criticised Déricourt and his assistant for their leisurely appearance only half an hour before the aircraft was due. He also complained that there were cows in the field.

Clément said it was London who decreed how many agents should go. That night there was Basin, extra, but he had just escaped from prison and begged Henri to board him on a plane for England. To have abandoned him to re-arrest by the Gestapo would have been inhuman. 'Henri and I met our passengers at the station in Paris. We travelled down with them in the train to Angers, escorted them from Angers. We cycled with them to Soucelles and showed them the assembly point, where we would expect to find them half an hour before the plane was due. They *knew* that, till then, we were in the inn.'

As for the cows, fields were used either for crops or for livestock. Since one could not invite an aircraft to land on a field of corn or cabbages, they chose a field used only for livestock. Henri and he would walk towards the cows spreading their hands out and making fanning movements and shooing noises to make them retreat. Besides, as soon as they heard the aircraft descending, they would rush to the far end of the field. 'Buckmaster did ask us if we would like him to buy us a farm, on which we could control the conditions, but it would have been too dangerous to have worked always from one place.'

We drove on, crossed the Loire with its silver sandbanks at Amboise, continued along the south bank, and suddenly I saw a sign, 'St Martin-le-Beau'. 'It's midway between St Martin-le-Beau and Azay-sur-Cher,' he said. 'We never knew which to call it.' We drew up again, beside another large field. 'It was here Julienne came back to us,' he said, meaning 'Claire'. 'With three others. It was from here Mme Gouin went with that big chief.'

He produced biscuits. To have lunched at a restaurant would have taken too much time, and he had by-passed the Pont-de-Braye. That and Le Vieux Briollay we would see tomorrow on the return journey. He wanted us to reach Soucelles in time to see the moon full, above the field, tonight.

We pressed on, past the Château de Chinon, and re-crossed the Loire. There were lines of poplars. The fields were full of maize, and the light was going.

We reached Angers, booked rooms at the Hotel d'Anjou, dined and returned to the car. It was dark when we passed through the village of Soucelles and, emerging from it, crossed a hump-backed bridge. I felt Clément's mounting excitement. 'There!' he cried. Beneath us was a wide expanse, absolutely flat. We stopped. First he showed me a hedge. 'That was the assembly point.' He was pointing to a very slight bay in its straight line. 'We fetched them from there and led them down the bank.' We picked our way down a faint track through thistles and nettles. 'This is the path we used... There! That is the tree against which I propped Henri the night he fainted.' It was separated now from the field by some bric-à-brac, which we made our way round or over. Then suddenly we were before the flat expanse. Above the trees on our left a clear full moon shone down.

'The fatal field,' I said.

He did not understand. 'No aircraft crashed here.'

I was thinking of Menesson, Pardi and Maugenet.

In the morning he drove me to Le Vieux Briollay, where he showed me a field on a surprising slope: 'That is where your friend, 'Madeleine', stepped down.'

He would show me the little railway stations at Etriché and Tiercé, but first we would go back to look again at the great field of Soucelles, by daylight. There was a heavy mist. I doubted if my photographs would come out and I did a two-minute sketch. There were brown and white cows all over it now, and a bull ...

'There is only one thing for which I reproach Henri,' he said, '— that he left me here. I am sorry to keep on about that but it sticks in my gullet. When Morel came for him, he should have said, "I do not go to London unless you take 'Marc' and his wife, too."'

But then, I said, 'Claire' and Besnard would have had to be taken as well — the whole team.

'As soon as he got to London, he should have told Buckmaster at once he was working with the Germans and asked him to send an aircraft to bring me back, or at any rate not to send more aircraft to me on the fields he had given them.'

'He was probably afraid he would be charged with treason.'

'He should have sacrificed himself,' he said with sudden hardness. 'He should not have left me exposed. He got me into it. He should have got me out of it.'

I realised suddenly there was something Clément did not know. 'He did fulfil his responsibility to you, in his own way,' I said. 'Between the time Morel tried to take him and the time he actually went, he went to see Boemelburg one last time. Why do you think that was?'

'To collect the money.'

'To collect the money perhaps, but also to ask him not to arrest you.' He looked incredulous.

'Why do you think you were not arrested?' I asked.

'I do not know. I have often wondered.'

It was obvious, I said. He went and told Boemelburg he had to go, but that he hoped to be back soon, and therefore that his team should be allowed to continue its functions without interference. 'If he had not done that, they would have been down on you at once, telling you your chief had always informed to them and asking you to do the same. You would have found yourself in an unenviable situation. By going back to talk to Boemelburg, he spared you that.'

He was silent for a while, and when he spoke again it was in a softened voice. 'The circumstances being as they were, it was the best thing he could have done. Il m'aimait un peu.'

20: ECHOES AND A LEAVE-TAKING

In the summer of 1974 I came on a book which had been published the previous year, *Histoire Secrète des Français, à Londres* by André Gillois (Hachette, 1973). I was shocked to find in it (pages 133–4) a statement attributed to Buckmaster that Déricourt had become cupidinous because enamoured of a woman who obliged him to extravagances and who permitted Bleicher of the Abwehr to penetrate two of his operations without his knowledge. This could not possibly be correct. The only woman for whom Déricourt had any known concern at that time was his wife. He had no relations with Bleicher or the Abwehr, only with Boemelburg and Goetz of the SD. Worse, the statement continued, 'Antelme, called "Antoine", warned us "Gilbert" had made excessive promises to Bleicher... unfortunately 'Antoine' was in his turn arrested and executed.' This read as though Antelme had been arrested through Déricourt's fault. Antelme was arrested through being parachuted back to a field appointed over the 'Madeleine' radio circuit, despite warnings from France she was under arrest, despite warnings even from Morel the set could be German controlled. For that fatal decision Buckmaster, alone, must accept the responsibility.

Gillois went on (I translate from his French):

> I was allowed to understand Bodington accepted money for his testimony. When I told Miss Vera Atkins, principal collaborator of Colonel Buckmaster, that he had committed suicide some years before, she replied simply, 'He did well to do so.'

The references for the interviews with Buckmaster and Miss Atkins were given as 8 November 1971 and 1 May 1972.

I was very distressed by the apparent news Bodington had committed suicide, and wrote to Boxshall asking him if it was true. He replied, on 8 July 1974, that he had made enquiries and established the story of Bodington's suicide was untrue. Indeed, at the time it was published he was still living: 'I have just been informed, on good authority, that he died in Plymouth last week, on 3 July.'

I received a letter from Group-Captain Hugh Verity — Déricourt's chief in the RAF Special Squadron. He asked if I would help him in some research, and lunch with him at the Lansdowne Club on 28 September (1974).

He told me the operational base of 161 Squadron was at Tangmere, in East Sussex near Chichester, where they repaired each month when the moon became full. The rest of the time they were at Tempsford, in Bedfordshire. He was posted to Tempsford on 15 November 1942, and Déricourt was sent to him for training soon afterwards. He spoke almost no English. Squadron-Leader Wagland remembered him as being at their 1942 Christmas Party, and Wing-Commander Pickard and his wife had him to dinner. Everyone liked him. Verity had found a letter he wrote to his wife on 10 January 1943, 'I have a very good friend called Henry. I have given him your telephone number.'

Verity was writing the story of his days with the Squadron, and sought my help in establishing the identities of the passengers carried to and from Déricourt. He was never told the names of the 'bodies' he carried, so his own log was of no use, neither was the log of 161 Squadron. Some names he had found in Foot's book. He showed me a table he was making, and I was able to fill in some of the gaps. I had not intended to give him Bonoteaux, but he said he had seen Lyon, and I knew what was coming. 'How could he have betrayed Bonoteaux?' Verity exclaimed.

He did not pick him as a sacrifice. The German orders to the trailing gang were not to arrest the arrivals. Bony's deposition showed that in the case of Bonoteaux he exceeded his orders.

Verity had summoned Déricourt back at Easter, after the episode with the tree. 'I had to make out a list of the parts of the aircraft that needed replacing. It was a long one.' He thought that Déricourt had perhaps felt strained doing a ground job, so during his days back with them at Tempsford, 'we put him into RAF uniform and I let him fly a Lysander around, to relax him'.

It was in early December that Buckmaster asked Verity to come and see him, and told him a member of the de Gaulle Section (Yeo-Thomas), had suggested Déricourt had contact with the Germans. Verity found that difficult to believe, but agreed they should bring him back for questioning. Déricourt was driven straight from Tangmere to Orchard Court, where the three of them had tea or coffee in Buckmaster's armchairs. Buckmaster, polite and embarrassed, told him it had been suggested he was in league with the Germans. This produced a silence, which lasted so long Verity felt nobody was ever going to speak again. Déricourt's face seemed to be carved in wood. At last he said, 'But, Major Buckmaster, how could I do my job for you without good relations with the Germans? I sell them black-market oranges.'

The enquiry was pursued at higher level. To cheer Déricourt, Verity and his wife invited Déricourt and his wife to dinner at the Savoy. Déricourt was in the uniform of a flight-lieutenant, wearing the ribbon of the DSO — prematurely, as although he had been recommended for it, the award was not destined to be gazetted. I wondered, suddenly, if this was Déricourt's only connection with the Savoy. From Verity's account, it did not appear that he was staying there.

'I shall spend the rest of my life trying to understand his motive,' Verity said.

He asked me for Clément's address, which I gave him, and he drove me to St Pancras. I was in the middle of selling my London flat to buy a house in the country, and had to take a train to Bedford that afternoon to see a house at Wymington, on the Bedfordshire-Northamptonshire border. I bought it. Back in London, I wrote to Verity:

29 September, 1974

About Déricourt there are many things I would like you to understand. You told me the discovery of his treachery was a shock to you because you thought of him as a friend. He had deep relations with the Gestapo of which he could not possibly tell you, but he was not going behind your back in order to do you down.

In the book for Kimber I had written a few lines about Turck, which I sent him, and he and his wife asked me to spend a weekend with them. I flew over on 7 January 1975. He met me at Orly, took me to their flat in the Auteuil district, and the next morning we drove out through the woods of the Oise and plains of the Somme to his magnificent Château de Frestoy Vaux near Montdidier, where he was mayor. He had won his long battle over the de Vomécourts. In 1963 the Conseil d'Etat had found for him, and in 1972 he had been invested a Commander of the Légion of d'Honneur. He had also become one of the leading architects of France. Would I write his story? I had been looking forward to returning to the *Bacon*;

nevertheless, I accepted his introduction to his former chief, Brigadier Leslie Humphreys, and on 8 February 1975 went to Bexhill-on-Sea to lunch with Humphreys and his wife. He had been head of D Section (Escapes).

He had told his people not to become involved with Buckmaster's. He asked me: 'Why ever did Turck get mixed up with the de Vomécourts?'

I left London on 18 April 1975 for my house in the country. I had been expecting proofs from Mann, but received instead a letter saying his firm was bankrupt. Might he keep my typescript in the hope he would be able to start up again?

I was soon occupied with the new experience of a garden, in which I was trying to become self-sufficient in fruit and vegetables, and I was in a creative stage of the *Bacon*. There was, however, a deeper reason why I let the Déricourt rest. I had ended it with my discovery of his childhood at the château. Yet that could give the reader the impression it was to buy the château he had committed treason. Clément seemed to have put it to Verity in that way. I did not believe it. Déricourt had probably taken M. Fontaine for his model of the speech and dress of a gentleman, and would doubtless have liked to be Varenval's owner. But he was not Heathcliff.

I needed something further.

Publication of my book *The German Penetration of SOE* (Kimber, 1975) brought me a letter from Michel Pichard. I had often heard of him from Yeo-Thomas, who had died, sadly, on 26 February 1964 with Barbara beside him in their flat in Paris. Pichard had, for a while, done for RF a job analogous to that of Déricourt for F. He wrote to me that in February 1944 (just after Déricourt's recall to London) he was asked if he would board on one of his planes an F Section agent, 'Hercule'. The man he detailed to meet 'Hercule' thought him genuine, but Pichard did not care for some of his reported remarks and did not go to the offered rendezvous, at a café in Lille, on 27 February 1944. 'You will no doubt agree the man was unlikely to be A. Dubois.'

Indeed, yes! The real 'Hercule' had been arrested on 19 November 1943, after killing Scherer and wounding Vogt. So 'Hercule's' radio, too, had been played back to London and could have led the radio game from Buckmaster's section into de Gaulle's.

There now appeared *Bodyguard of Lies* by Anthony Cave Brown (W. H. Allen, 1976). Before reacting to this, one should first remind oneself of what had already been disclosed by General Sir Frederick Morgan, COSSAC (Chief of Staff Supreme Allied Commander) in his book *Overture to Overlord*. He wrote that in 1943 a deception plan had been mounted — Cockade/Starkey, the pretence that the main British invasion would be in the Pas de Calais on 9 September 1943, and Cockade/Wadham, the pretence that this was to be followed by American landings in Brittany. There was some anxiety lest fake preparations, intended to deceive the Germans, also deceive the Resistance. Now, it appeared, a quantity of COSSAC files had been released in Washington, and an American journalist, Anthony Cave Brown, had perused them. He had come to the sensational conclusion that to deceive the Resistance was the intent — and that Déricourt had been the instrument of the intent. He had, theorised Cave Brown, been ordered to betray to the Germans mail in which the misinformation was planted. He had been an agent of MI6 planted in SOE to do this, and the hundreds lost in the 'Prosper' and de Baissac disasters were the sacrifices to Cockade.

I was sure this was not true. A very long time before, 29 November 1949, Lise de Baissac had come to tea with me. She had told me her brother Claude controlled a large network in the Bordeaux area and she had one in Poitiers. After she and her brother returned to England in August 1943, there were disasters in both the networks they had left behind. This they did not learn until after the war. It was a member of Claude's network, Grandclément, who after being arrested had gone over to the German side and taken the Gestapo to the houses of the Resistance supporters in all the villages. For this he had been killed by the *Résistants*.

Nor had Vogt seen any reference to the invasion in the photostatted mail. Neither had Starr. Moreover, the theory was right out of line with Déricourt's private confession to me (which of course I had not put in my book, which was Cave Brown's main source for Déricourt's case), and his reaction to the quotation from Morgan's book in Wighton's — which prompted him to criticise the risk to the Resistance under the heading, 'What does not make me laugh'. He was out of sympathy with it. Further, I noticed mistakes in the book. Some were trifling — Cave Brown got Germans' Christian names wrong, spelt Déricourt's name without its accent throughout and followed Cookridge into giving Mme Déricourt's name as Janine — her husband's postwar Chinese mistress. What struck me as far from trifling was when, puzzled by quotations from my own book, I checked with it and found that in two places the words 'the French Section,' had been substituted for 'Prosper' in my veritable text. Excusably, perhaps, my inclination was not to take the book seriously at all; but it was destined to have consequences.

I seldom came to London except to see Tim or read at the

British Museum, but I wanted to see the Woolsack, on which Bacon sat. Irene invited me to lunch with her at the House of Lords on 11 November 1976 — since her retirement she had been elevated to the peerage as Baroness Ward of North Tyneside. She was, that day, quite her bonny self, but after that her age began to tell. Christmas 1979 brought no card from her. I rang the Helena Club, where she stayed while in London, and was told she had left. I rang her house in Tynemouth but nobody was answering the telephone. I wrote to the Clerk of the House of Lords. This brought a telephone call from David Greenslade, her nephew. He said she had fallen over a fender in the Helena Club and broken a thighbone. She was in Knaresbrook Nursing Home.

When I went to see her, on 13 January 1980, she was so emaciated it shocked me. Her once bouncy hair, now white, scraped back and made into a bun on the top of her head, left her face unexpectedly narrowed and sunken. She assured me she was 'very well', but when I kissed her goodbye, I knew it was for the last time.

I learned of her passing from the 5.45 News on ITV, on 26 April 1980. Then her nephew rang, to ask me her age for the obituary. I was able to tell him she had been born in London, close to midnight, on 24 February 1895.

21: COLLINS AND RUSBRIDGER

As I dug my garden and fed my hens, my thinking was going into my current books. *Bacon* was out, *Saint-Germain* was finished and delivered to East-West. I had started on the *Blavatsky*.

Then I received a letter from a Larry Collins. He said he was writing a novel inspired by the Déricourt story and would like to meet me. I read this with a mixture of feelings. I hoped this was not another Wighton or Cookridge. A novelist would, anyway, not be a rival, and if the portrayal was to be recognisable, I could perhaps protect Déricourt from vilification. I offered Collins an interview. On 24 March 1982 he arrived by car and set up a microphone.

He was a big, confident American, mainly resident in France. Arthur Watt had lent him my *Double Webs* and suggested he might find in it a theme for one of his historical novels. He told me he had seen Mme Déricourt.

I told him I had given Déricourt my promise never to approach his wife, from which I did not feel his death absolved me, and he said he would let me have a tape transcript of his interview with her.

He said he had seen Parks, the door-keeper at Orchard Court, who told him Déricourt was paid in diamonds. I do not like microphones but suddenly I was glad this was on tape. Long ago Déricourt had told me, 'The key is diamonds.' I thought he meant he was smuggling them to France for Bodington or Simon. It had not occurred to me he might have been paid in them openly. I supposed they must have been for industrial use.

No, said Collins, beautiful gem-stones. 'A form of highly portable liquid currency.' It was thought he could sell them in France.

Because I had worked in the Censorship, I was extremely conscious of the Trading with the Enemy Act. This was contravention of it. Was SOE above the law? I was sure Déricourt thought the traffic in diamonds illicit.

Collins's idea — which he put forward with an air of great authority — was that Déricourt was an agent of MI6, briefed to contact the Germans, to mislead them as to the invasion plans.

This placed me in a quandary. I knew it was untrue, because Déricourt had admitted to me his approach to the Germans had not been authorised. I had been poised to protect him from vilification, but if somebody believed in the legend he had worked so sedulously to weave, was it for me to destroy the fabric?

Later, Collins telephoned to say he had obtained an interview with Boemelburg's son, Rolf Gunter. He would send me the transcript, though brief and disappointing. He did not limp (as Déricourt had described), though he had lost an arm on the Russian Front. He had not attended aerobatics or car races, and he had not met Déricourt. He had spent 1943 at Neuilly with his father and knew his top agent was 'Gilbert'. Their chauffeur, Braun, had picked him up from the street in a car to bring him to the secluded rear entrance of the villa and on the last occasion had given him money. Braun had said to Rolf, 'Just think, I could have killed him and kept it for my self!'

That was all I heard of Collins's evidence for some time.

In October 1983 I received a letter from the BBC, telling me a series on SOE was projected. Might Christopher Riley, who was producing the programme on the Dutch Section, come and see me? He came with an assistant named Jane Callender. The series was screened in September 1984. The programme on France did not mention Déricourt.

The series provoked a number of letters to *The Times*. One was from Christopher Woods, who appeared to have taken over from Boxshall, whose obituary I had read. One, on 4 October, was from me, and one was from James Rusbridger, from St Austell, Cornwall, who mentioned Déricourt in a manner that showed he had read my *Double Webs*. I therefore wrote to him at his Cornish address.

He replied, enclosing a photocopy of a letter Buckmaster had sent him direct, in response to his in *The Times*, and also a copy of a very long letter he had written Buckmaster in reply to his, asking him whether, when in mid–1943 he briefed 'Prosper' that the invasion 'might be closer than we thought', he knew this was only a ruse (Cockade). He quoted from my *Double Webs* and asked if Déricourt had been allowed to sacrifice 'Prosper' and de Baissac to the Germans 'to enhance the credibility of the deception plan'.

I did not know who Rusbridger was. He told me he had not been in SOE but had had some experience with the postwar 'Intelligence fraternity', and had become involved with SIS as Greville Wynne had, though less dramatically. Field-Marshal Earl Wavell had been a cousin of his father. Cautious of saying too much to anyone who might have in mind to write, I asked him if that was his aim. He replied, 'No — I am not planning to write about any of this. I am not clever enough with words to do so.' This reassured me, as did his family connections. I thought that a retired Intelligence man might be able to throw a professional's light upon some of the dark holes in the story.

He showered me with photostats of letters he had received from his other correspondents. I asked him to keep sensitive points from my letters to himself. He sent me a photostat copy of a long letter he next received from Buckmaster. It was dated 12 October 1984 and stated categorically that I had no access to F Section information. My books, Buckmaster said, were 'based mainly on biased stories from German sources'. Then followed an amazing claim: 'When she and others commissioned M.R.D. Foot to write his so-called "History", one of the conditions imposed upon him by her and her colleagues was that he should never on any account consult me'.

In the same letter Buckmaster said that 'Prosper' had no contact whatsoever with Claude de Baissac ('Scientist'), so it was incorrect 'to link the two *réseaux*'. 'Scientist's' trouble had arisen through the treachery of Grandclément, who was subsequently 'put to death by the French Resistance'.

There was also in this letter a reference to 'Prosper' which I will keep over for another chapter. About the de Baissac network I believed he was correct, but I was stunned by the references to myself. As Déricourt once said to me, in another context, 'You are crediting me with more power than I have ever had.' I wrote to Rusbridger: 'Buckmaster is going off his head if he thinks I commissioned the official history or gave instructions to Foot.'

Rusbridger then sent me a copy of a further letter from Buckmaster, dated *26* October 1984. It was a fact, wrote Buckmaster, 'to my certain knowledge', that I and Elizabeth had prevailed upon Irene 'to intercede with Macmillan for an "official" enquiry into the "misdeeds of the French Section"'... Irene had approached the Prime Minister on the day the Profumo scandal broke, and Macmillan had told her that he 'was too busy to deal with the question and she could "do as she wished"'. Buckmaster was 'not aware' that Edward Heath was in any way involved. 'Foot's brief was laid down by Overton Fuller.'

This grossly misrepresented both Irene and Macmillan. The scandal that caused Profumo's resignation did not break out until June 1963, four years and eight months after Irene tabled her Motion and suggested to Macmillan there should be an official History. Lest Rusbridger think I had invented the role of Heath, which I had mentioned to him, I sent him photocopies of some of the letters that passed between Irene and Heath.

Rusbridger must have sent a copy of Buckmaster's letter to Foot, for he sent me a copy of a reply from Foot, flatly denying as 'simply untrue' Buckmaster's statement that 'Foot's brief was laid down by Overton Fuller'. Such brief as he had had — 'a directive to draw up the clearest account I could of what SOE had done in France' — had been verbally delivered by the head of the Permanent Under-Secretary's department in the Foreign Office, 'not a person who held any brief for Miss Overton Fuller at all'. Rusbridger would see from the bibliography of the official History that Foot was 'no great admirer of Miss J.O.F. or of her supposed patroness, Dame Irene Ward'.

Thank you.

Rusbridger pressed on Buckmaster letters in which he continually harried him with questions concerning Déricourt. These Buckmaster first parried by referring him to Verity's book, but in his letter of 26 October he wrote:

> Déricourt. The handling of double agents is always tricky. I was greatly helped in my decisions by a very senior officer of MI5, who worked closely with me on this.

I was sceptical. Rusbridger, however, kept on at Buckmaster, who on further pressure gave the name of this officer as Sir Dick White. White was living. Rusbridger wrote to him, and sent me a copy of his reply. He had never even heard of Déricourt. Incidentally, he did not seem to know who Bodington was either.

Rusbridger had become 'hooked' on Déricourt, the way Desmond Young used to be. For Rusbridger, Déricourt was either an agent of MI5, or else a straight German agent — or 'a brave crook... playing both sides against the middle'. He was impressed by a passage on Foot's page 305:

> Boemelburg said to Goetz in Placke's hearing of the news of Déricourt's flight to England, 'Ah well, that's four million down the drain.'

Rusbridger had worked out that was now the equivalent of £3,000,000. I had to admit it sounded too much to be Déricourt's commission on selling in France diamonds obtained by Bodington in London, even if it was to Boemelburg he sold them. It sounded more like the price of the invasion.

Rusbridger was not flattering about Bodington — 'In effect... you had two opportunist crooks propping each other up like drunken sailors' — and my efforts to explain Déricourt more sympathetically seemed to have only the effect of hardening Rusbridger against him. He spoke of Déricourt's 'reporting back' to Boemelburg as soon as he was parachuted. Why, he asked rhetorically, had he not brought his wife with him when he came to England? Because he knew he would be coming back.

I thought it might not have been possible to bring her — but the point worried me.

22: MOUSETRAP HOUSE

Déricourt's 'anterior epoch' haunted me. What had been the drama sealed in that phrase? What was it he had done wrong? What was it Philippe de Vomécourt had done wrong? What was the 'bad thing' each knew about the other — the basis of the *quid pro quo*? Had they been doing different 'bad things' when, by chance, each glimpsed the other? Or had they been doing the same 'bad thing' when each saw the other doing it? It was on a November morning of 1984, soon after I had woken, but while I still lay in bed, asking myself, as so often, these questions, that I saw a waking vision. On a hillside, densely wooded with tall trees, in the top right-hand corner of the view, was a low log-cabin, in very dark, old wood. It looked dank. From under it leaked unwholesome, slimy water, which trickled away downwards towards the left, over not boulders but sodden, rotting, wooden steps, almost obscured.

For a moment I did not understand. Then it came to me. Villa des Bois. The French means, literally, House of the Woods. Mousetrap House! The imagery was of course symbolic, for the real villa would have been one of those luxury ones, painted white or in light colours, which one finds along the Riviera coast. But that was *it* — a pictorial pun on the name, with its sinister overtones — I felt certain.

Yet what did it mean? The Villa des Bois had a connection with Philippe de Vomécourt, in as much as he had stated he had telephoned to it, distrusted the voice that answered his call, and not gone in. Suppose that he had done otherwise than as he said? Suppose he had gone in, and something had happened? But how could Déricourt have had knowledge of

411

that? He had not been an agent of SOE at that time, had no business to be at meetings of its agents, no business at the Villa des Bois.

Christmas and New Year passed. I was still in correspondence with Rusbridger. Then, one Sunday evening, 17 February, I suddenly asked myself if Déricourt could have been the man within the house who opened the door and said 'Come in' to those arriving to be arrested. It had been said the man looked like Turck. They were of about the same height. Both were slim and wiry figures. Both had blue eyes, and both had a crest of rather strongly upstanding, wavy hair. Déricourt's was fairer and more curly, but was it possible that in a half light those who only knew Turck could have thought they saw him? As though in a click within my head, I saw Déricourt in a dim doorway. I was shocked to have had the vision, assured myself he could have had no motive to do a thing so wicked. He did not belong to that group, did not belong to the Resistance at all at that date. Why should the Gestapo pick on an airman, a pilot on the Paris-Marseilles run, and take him to this villa, to perform this role, for which they could have found one of the agents of the Milice? There seemed no reason to capture and involve an airman.

It was a week later, just after midnight on the night of 23/24 February, that it came to me quietly; came to me he had told me himself, long ago. He had been at the airport, walking towards his aircraft, when a man had come up to him and offered him banknotes, together with a letter in a sealed envelope, which bore on it an address in the town to which he was flying, which was in the other zone. If he delivered it, he was told, it was likely the recipient would give him something further, for his pains. He had found his way to the house, and rung or knocked on the door. It was opened, but his reception

412

was not that which he had been led to expect. He was seized and found himself a prisoner within. Then he had been made to do things, a whole series of things. 'I was the prisoner of a situation.'

It had been in Spain, he had said, during the Civil War, but then he had added, 'Sometimes I change the place and the date, but the story is true.' I had thought he had meant that when he told the Tribunal Militaire he had been arrested in Paris in June 1943, it had been in Spain, in 1936, that this had happened. I had wondered how this had affected his whole life, creating a situation that lasted into the war and, as he said, could never cease, since, as he had also said, there was a sense, because pressures could be put on him, in which he was still prisoner to it — in respect of its being impossible ever to say what had happened. To be sure, the Civil War in Spain had attracted volunteers from other nations to one side or the other. There could have been Germans in Spam. Would they have taken prisoner the occupants of a house and seized any who came to call at it — and how could that make him prisoner for life? If he had not wished to be used by one side against the other in the Spanish Civil War, he could just have avoided returning to Spain. But then there was Clément's reaction to the story when I told him. Déricourt had never been in Spain, that he knew of. Certainly he had never been flying in and out of Spain, or between zones in Spain. It was France that was divided into zones, the Occupied and the Unoccupied Zone. Airmen, like train drivers, could cross the line. 'That could only have happened in France. It could only have happened while he was on the Paris-Marseilles run.'

He had been in the Paris-Marseilles run during the 'anterior epoch'.

Now, almost eleven years after Clément's having given me that clue, and twenty-three and a half years since Déricourt had tried to tell me what I now knew was the truth, it came to me. It had been at the Villa des Bois he had presented that letter and been seized.

The two stories he had told me — the story of the letter he had carried to a house at which, instead of being paid, he was arrested and made to do things, and the story of the mousetrap house in Marseilles of 1941 and the *quid pro quo* with de Vomécourt were one story. How had it taken me so long to understand?

Suddenly I felt very relieved. I could see what must have been the awkwardness of his situation. The Vichy police, when they opened the door and seized him, would have supposed that, since he was bearing the letter, he was a member of the group. He would have explained that he had received it from a stranger, to carry to a stranger, only for a wad of banknotes, not knowing what it concerned. He would have had difficulty in convincing them he could have been such a fool. When he was made to open the door to others, as they came up, in procession to be arrested, he would not at first have known who or what they were. Marseilles is a great port, receiving ships that have come from the East, and now and again one reads that French police have raided a house there used by drug smugglers. His first thought might have been that this house was being used for something like that. How was he to know those arriving were British agents, parachuted from London? They were the very first lot sent. Only bit by bit would he have come to understand the nature of the affair in which he had become a participant.

It was a pity he had not told me this story without veils. I would have kept it to myself, not reacting with scorn and contempt. But he could not have felt confident of that. Also, to have known — then — would have placed me before some awkward moral problems. Perhaps he had been right only to give me intimations.

I asked London Library for *Who Lived to See the Day* by Philippe de Vomécourt (Hutchinson, 1961). I read it very closely, and certain things struck me. There was only his own word for it that he had telephoned the Villa des Bois, recognised Turck's voice, distrusted his answers and gone away without calling. His account of his activities during the ensuing year was remarkably sketchy. The space allocated to the period was occupied by general descriptions of conditions in France and particular anecdotes illustrating the heroism of individuals, called only by their Christian names. On the other hand, he had been arrested or taken into protective custody by Vichy police on the eve of the German occupation of the hitherto Unoccupied Zone, to keep him from arrest by the Gestapo. He had been in prison until, at a date not given (and which I could not find from Foot's History), he escaped and came to London, whence he was parachuted back into France at Easter 1944. Thereafter his service was apparently regular and honourable. Even if his encounter with the Villa des Bois had been otherwise, he could not have been the person arrested in the mousetrap house whose membership of SOE French Section gravely menaced it, as Déricourt had told me, in 1943. That was himself! When he used his visit to London at Easter 1943 to seek out that high up person to divulge what was within his knowledge — was he proposing a confession and deterred by the reaction?

I did not impart to Rusbridger my knowledge of Déricourt's 'anterior epoch'. Rusbridger was too hostile to him and might have seized upon it as proof that when Déricourt first came to this country, in 1942, it was as a German agent. That did not follow of necessity, though certainly I wondered.

23: CORRESPONDENCE WITH RUSBRIDGER

Rusbridger had been in Washington, seen the Cockade/Starkey papers in the archives, and talked with Cave Brown. I saw he rated the latter's book higher than I had. I told him I had found so many mistakes in the parts I had the means to check that I did not feel I could rely on it for a description of documents to which I had no access. I could not build upon the notion of Cockade/Starkey unless I saw primary documents. For answer, he sent me fourteen sheets of photostatted typescript he had obtained from the Public Record Office at Kew. All bore the reference CAB/80/71 5360. They were marked MOST SECRET, and by six parallel lines ruled across, intimating the restriction of circulation. The fourteen pages formed two separate documents, of the same reference number. The earlier was dated 17 June 1943 and headed OPERATION 'COCKADE', and the significant paragraphs were:

> 11 The object of the plan... is to convince the enemy that a large scale landing in the Pas de Calais area is imminent and to bring the German airforce to battle. 23... General Morgan estimates that there will be a wastage of 450 fighters during the 14 days' preliminary preparation. The British share of this will be 340 fighters.

If they were preparing to waste all those fighter aircraft and their crews on the arousal of a false anticipation of the invasion in 1943, Rusbridger argued, it could hardly be supposed they would have regarded with less equanimity the wastage of a large part of the Resistance. At the date on this document 'Prosper' was on his visit to London, from which he returned to the field convinced that all his people were doomed.

In the second part, dated 18 July 1943, one read:

> 16 The object would be: To assist the deception by promoting the symptoms of underground activity, prior to [Starkey] D Day, which the enemy would naturally look for as one of the preliminaries to a real invasion.

I had always said the July date made it impossible it could have caused the 'Prosper' disaster in June, but Rusbridger supposed the plan had been discussed between Churchill and Roosevelt when they met at Casablanca in January, and had been acted upon before the date on the documents. That would, indeed, explain Starr's having been told, in May, to drop some of the security as the big day was coming soon. Could Noor have been sent to join a group that was being deliberately 'wasted'? Buckmaster's letter of 12 October carried the lines:

> 'Prosper' was a brilliant and forceful officer, who was summoned by Churchill to activate the Resistance in the Paris region, regardless of security breaches in order that Stalin might be appeased.

If this was true, I felt deeply for 'Prosper'. To have been summoned to an interview with Churchill — who had in those days almost a nimbus of deity about his head — and to have sensed he was being lied to, would have been enough to unbalance his mind. It would explain those words he had spoken to Mme Guépin. But was it true? I had seen in what Buckmaster had written about the Official History having been commissioned by myself how wildly his imagination could run. Again, I had a loyalty that shrank from attacking Churchill.

Rusbridger wrote (5 November 1984):

> I wouldn't worry about attacking Churchill. He did the dirty on lots of people (including my father's cousin Archie Wavell) and let their reputations and careers suffer.

I have never thought of Churchill as saintly. Probably he had a streak of the roguery and opportunism evident in his forbear, the Duke of Marlborough. There have always been those who felt he treated Admiral North unfairly. He may have been unfair to his military commanders, including Wavell. But to have summoned 'Prosper' and told him a he that would send him and all his people to their deaths would come into a different category. I wrote to Rusbridger, suggesting that if Churchill really had received 'Prosper', the name Suttill ought to appear in the diary of his engagements, which his Secretary would have kept for him. Rusbridger wrote to Martin Gilbert, as Churchill's biographer, but the latter was unable to confirm.

I should have liked to be able to talk about all this to Elizabeth, but she had long been too ill, and when I received a letter bearing the Dover postmark, addressed to me in her husband's hand, I knew before I opened it the sad news it contained.

With Starr's New Year greeting was enclosed a note saying he had spoken on French television on the fortieth anniversary of D Day. I sent him photostats of the Cockade documents. He replied that if it was Churchill's bluff, 'I bear him no grudge — we needed him.'

It was not stated on the document the plan was Churchill's. It would probably require the Prime Minister's approval, but I thought there was a Colonel Bevan who was Controller of Deception. Buckmaster replied to Rusbridger about this:

Cockade... In my minor capacity as merely head of F Section, I was not made party to high level decisions, nor to such things as plans to deceive... Please don't bother to send copies [of the Cockade documents].

Rusbridger nevertheless pressed them on him. He also sent a set to Foot, with an expression of surprise Foot should in both his books have said SOE was not involved with deception plans. Foot replied that he thought it probable F was involved in Cockade 'unconsciously' — so far as it was involved at all: 'I know Bevan did not intend to use SOE as an active deception agent.' And where was the Chief of Staff's approval of the plan? 'Without that, plans were only plans... One after report is as a rule worth a dozen plans.'

Rusbridger replied, 'Of course there was an after report.' He did not, however, produce it, and I thought it possible there could have been a modification in respect of the paragraphs in question. On pages 109–10 of his book General Morgan said they were worried lest the Resistance be deceived by their 'antics' into emerging from cover. It was impossible to warn them, beyond telling them not to move until they received the signal from London, which of course did not come. That showed a very different spirit. Though Cockade was a failure, for the Germans were not deceived by it (Charles Cruikshank, *Deception in World War II*, Oxford, 1979, p.73), the 'Prosper' disaster having convinced Hitler we could not invade that year (Kopkow interrogation, Foot, p. 505), I could not see that a single arrest had been caused by it. None the less, Morgan admitted it caused confusion on the home front, and agents who sensed we were playing games not disclosed to them could have become suspicious and sought to protect themselves.

Rusbridger wrote to me on 24 January 1985:

> One report has Déricourt working for MI5's XX Committee
> ... in February, 1944, Operation Fortitude, the deception
> scheme for D Day was getting into full swing... was
> Déricourt's claim to Boemelburg and Kieffer he could bring
> them the date of the invasion, for which they paid him 4.0
> million francs, his own idea or was it inspired by MI5?
> ... Déricourt's treatment after the Tribunal [of 11 February
> 1944] certainly suggests he had done someone a favour and
> was being rewarded.

Indeed, if they thought he was a German agent, why did they
release him so that he could join the Free French Air Force?
He could have flown straight to join the Germans.

Irene had been informed by Lansdowne and Hooper that
Déricourt had never been on a Foreign Office pay-list, and he
himself had told me it was without authorisation he made
contact with the Germans. Yet was it possible his hint of
retrospective authorisation related not merely to Bodington's
approval, but to cooperation after his recall, with MI5? MI6
was under the Foreign Office, MI5 under the Home Office. As
related in *The Double Cross System in the War of 1939–45*, John
Masterman (Yale, 1972), MI5 had an offspring, Double Cross
Committee, XX or Twenty. It was claimed that every German
agent in this country was either executed or used by XX to
feed misinformation back to Germany. Rusbridger thought it
was run from Northumberland Avenue, and Déricourt had
certainly hinted that by the time he reported there, in February
1944, something more than usually secret and exciting seemed
to be going on. Could his role have become, as he himself
suggested, consultative?

Nigel West, who had come to see me in connection with a book he was writing, and who had written histories of both MI6 and MI5, did not think there was anything in this.

Rusbridger was greatly intrigued when I mentioned that Placke said in his deposition for the DST that Déricourt had wasted their time, claiming that his big field at Soucelles was to be used for the landing of troops on D Day — because Rusbridger recalled, the pretence we intended to invade through the south of Brittany was Fortitude/Ironside. Rusbridger could not credit that Déricourt thought of it for himself — coincidentally. He must have been put up to it by MI5. I was sure he thought of it for himself.

Of Bodington's visit to the field Rusbridger wrote:

> It is very odd that F Section's second-in-command should have been allowed to go because it is a cardinal rule with most clandestine organisations that those in charge who have access to innermost secrets ... do not place themselves in jeopardy. If Bodington had been caught, then it would have made the Dutch Englandspiel look like petty cash, and F Section could have packed up for the rest of the war.

I replied that in that case, in saving Bodington Déricourt saved the Section. This must have riled Rusbridger, for he replied: 'By any definition, Déricourt was a traitor. The argument that his liaison with the Germans saved Bodington's life is fortuitous...'

It was not fortuitous. He risked his own to do it. What was getting lost in these theorisings was the Déricourt I knew.

Rusbridger next wrote suggesting Bodington had perhaps had a homosexual relationship with Boemelburg before the war, which, if Déricourt knew it, 'would have given him a very powerful lever against Bodington', sufficient to compel his appearing as witness at his trial. I was sure this was false. Cave Brown referred to Boemelburg as homosexual, but how could Cave Brown know? I had never heard it from anyone who had known Boemelburg. No one ever referred to Bodington's sex life so I supposed it ordinary. Déricourt was not a blackmailer. I felt I must kill this. On 25 January 1985 I therefore wrote to Rusbridger of Bodington's visit to the field. Déricourt told him the Germans knew of his arrival:

> But then there is this rv [rendezvous] in the rue de Rome to think about. Bodington must of course not go to it. I used to wonder why anybody should have gone to it. It was a trap. Why not just keep away. But then it came to me... Boemelburg would be waiting for Bodington to be caught ... If his men waited and waited at the trap flat in vain, and nobody walked into it, Boemelburg would be livid with fury. He would know Déricourt must have warned Bodington to keep away, and [would have] ordered the arrest of *both* of them. They were, then, both dead men. So Bodington sent Agazanan to keep the rv. He was seized... Déricourt would not have to answer to Boemelburg, for why Bodington had sent Agazanan in his place. Bodington's having done that would not necessarily imply Déricourt had warned him ... It was probably better for the Section poor Agazanan was sacrificed, but Déricourt felt it rather badly because he had known Agazanan personally. The affair of Agazanan was brought up against Déricourt at his trial. The prosecutor tried to charge him with having let him go to his death unwarned. Déricourt got out of it without charging Bodington ... He did not say, 'It was not me but Bodington who sent him,' which was the truth, but if Bodington had not come forward to give the evidence that obtained his acquittal, he could not have been expected to keep quiet about it ... By giving evidence that obtained Déricourt's acquittal, Bodington assured his

own responsibility for Agazanan's death would not be heard of.

In my mind I was still reserving to myself whether I should or should not make this exposition of what Déricourt had called 'the knot of the problem' in my new book. It was therefore a shock to me to receive from Rusbridger, in May, a copy of a letter he had written to a person he admitted he had never heard of, but whose name had been given him by a friend of his — it was in fact a briefly serving agent, D. Turberville, who had been parachuted with but wide of the agents arrested in the Villa des Bois and arrested before them. In this letter Rusbridger had set out all the things that were going round in his mind about Déricourt, needlessly bringing in what I had told him of this most delicate matter of Bodington's having sent Agazarian to his death, complete with the suggestion I had made that this had necessitated his witness at Déricourt's trial. I wrote to Rusbridger on 9 May 1985 saying I no longer dared pass him sensitive material. He replied, on 13 May, saying he was sorry he would not be hearing from me again as he had enjoyed our exchanges. He had, as he reminded me, sent me a good deal of primary source material and he added, generously, 'You may use any of this as you wish.'

24: FRESH OPENINGS

I re-started by writing to Christopher Woods at the Foreign Office, telling him of the permission the late Lady Ward had obtained for me to correspond with the late Colonel Boxshall, to whose functions he appeared to have succeeded, and asking if he could let me have information from the files on the same basis. From Déricourt's PF, could he tell me his height (a subject of differing estimates) and his *curriculum vitae*. He replied in detail:

> Déricourt gave his height as 1.72m (that is 5ft. 8in. less 1 cm) and his weight, in February 1944, as 74 kilos
> According to his cv, as given by himself:
> — after completing his education he was first employed from 1927 with the Postal and Telegraph services,
> — he first took up flying in March, 1930 when under an Air Ministry scheme for men wishing to become pilots in the Air Force he entered the Ecole de Boursier de Pilotage at Toussous-le-Noble, where he obtained his 'brevet militaire' on 9 August, 1930,
> — on 15 November he was called up for military service and sent to a pilots' school at Istres for training and four months later was posted to a squadron with the rank of sergeant After his year's service he was released on 15 November 1931 with the rank 'sergeant-pilote de reserve';
> — he then decided to continue flying on a free-lance basis which he did for the next two years, instead of returning to his previous job with the PTT;
> — from about November 1933 for another two years he was chief pilot with the Aero-Club de Paris,

— in about November 1935 he joined Air Bleu with whom he was employed until the outbreak of war, working on their postal service from Le Bourget;

— on 2 September 1939 he was mobilised with the rank Sergeant-pilot;

— on 20 April 1940 he was seconded from the Air Force to the SNC ASE as a test pilot and continued to work for them until after the armistice;

— in or about July 1941 he joined Air France and was sent by them to Aleppo with spare parts for two of their planes which were grounded there; he arrived on 12 July and was still there when British troops entered the city about 17 July; — about 27 July he and most of the other Air France personnel went by tram to Beirut where they stayed for nearly a month awaiting repatriation to France;

— he finally sailed about 20 August and reached Marseilles about a week later;

— he was then employed by Air France as a pilot, mostly on their passenger services Marseilles-Vichy and Marseilles-Toulouse, and as an instructor at Marignane;

— on 1 June, 1942 he was sent with two other Air Force pilots to inspect pilot training schools in North Africa;

— after his return about 19 July 1942 he was attached as a pilot to the Commission Française d'Armistice at Turin and flew members of the Commission between Marseilles and Turin;

— he left Marseilles on his journey to the UK on 15 August 1942.

There was no mention of his having flown Paris-Marseilles in the autumn of 1941. It was, I thought, not impossible that the fatal letter to be delivered to the Villa des Bois was handed to him in Toulouse or Vichy, but Paris seemed to make better sense — and Clément had believed Déricourt did fly to Paris.

He might have thought it prudent not to mention Paris in the *curriculum vitae* he made out for the authorities in England.

I did not see the Spanish Civil War in it. Otherwise, everything was in line with what I had been told by himself, Mme Henrie, Godbillon and Clément — except for the piece about Aleppo. That I had seen only in Foot, plainly working from this source.

In further letter, Woods wrote:

> He is recorded as having joined SOE on 1 December 1942 and on this date he signed the Official Secrets Act ... he was then recruited to be 'an agent in the field after training'. He was described at the time as a 'commercial pilot with BOAC'... I conclude from the negative evidence that he did not go through any of the normal courses at SOE training schools... The only other document relating to his training is a Security Declaration which he signed for the Training Department on 15 December 1942 ... he was destined from the start for early despatch: 'to be engaged in the field on a special mission this moon' (which I take to be the December moon period). Indeed he was allocated the code-name 'Farrier' on 3 December together with the field-name Marius Fabre. And from the F Section War Diary for 1942 it emerges that telegrams were sent to 'Actor' (Roger Landes) for 'Artist' (Lise de Baisssac) early in December asking her to provide assistance for him ... as from 14 December. She replied in a telegram dated 19 December she would be ready to receive them from 22 December onwards. The operation was in fact attempted on 23 December but failed because of fog. It was again unsuccessful due to bad weather on 29 December. Unfortunately there is no F Section War Diary for 1943.

Larry Collins wrote to me again, saying his novel was already out in France and would soon be out here. He was convinced Déricourt was employed by the Intelligence Service 'for purposes of deception' outside of his service with SOE:

> As you will see from my book, I have put my imaginary
> character, inspired by Déricourt, into the role which I believe
> he was intended to play in 1944, but which Déricourt was
> prevented from playing because he had to be repatriated to
> England in 1944.

Here was the inverse of my conception, that the only time he could possibly have been taken into consultation on deception was after his recall to England in 1944. He had told me himself his approach to the Germans in 1943 had not been authorised.

Collins added:

> I must tell you that Buckmaster, whom I interviewed
> extensively, is now singing a rather substantially different tune
> on Déricourt than he was a few years ago, when he was... less
> aware of his activities than he is today.

Was this resultant on the extensive interviewing by Collins? Collins's joy at having made a convert was naive, but in my experience it was dangerous to let one's own ideas and feelings transpire to one's witnesses, as it could colour their testimony. People are only too ready to reframe their ideas to accommodate the questioner.

Collins offered me the tape transcripts of his interviews and offered me an appointment in London on 24 May 1985. His flat in Exhibition Road was palatial, though his home was his villa at Juan-les-Pins. 'MI6!' he exclaimed triumphantly, as we met.

The first transcript he showed was Sporborg's. On 18 April 1983 Sporborg had said Déricourt had declared his German contacts before he was sent on his mission:

I think it emerged during the initial questioning before he was engaged, before he was taken on by SOE. I think he'd put it forward as an advantage... something he could contribute ... he put that forward as a plus point. That he'd be able to get information for us whereas others couldn't. That was knocked on the head and he was told he would not be expected to do anything of that sort.

This was confirmation of what Irene had told me Lord Lansdowne had told her. Lansdowne must have questioned Sporborg.

Miss Atkins had spoken of Déricourt as 'rotten', but had answered a question as to what the mail from the field consisted in:

It wasn't bulky. An envelope. Not a life history. A few happenings and requirements.

In that case, as Thackthwaite had surmised, Déricourt's having shown it to the Germans would hardly have done much harm.

Buckmaster had spoken of Déricourt as a venal man, pushed by his wife's demand for fur coats. But the interview was dated 28 March 1983, and Buckmaster had moved since then.

Passing from British to French witnesses, Clément had dug out for Collins a Robert Marotin, who had known Déricourt during the prewar period I was anxious to fill in. I afterwards wrote to Marotin, and combine with the tape details he gave me in his letter of 6 June 1985.

In November 1935 the air line Air Bleu had lost a pilot and a radio operator in an accident and therefore recruited replacements. On 11 November Marotin was engaged as radio, and about ten days later Déricourt was engaged as pilot. They were put together as pilot and radio at the beginning of January 1936.

Déricourt told Marotin that this ended for him a few years of freelancing, giving flying lessons at aero clubs and organising *fêtes aériennes*. He would take a field, for Saturdays and Sundays; sometimes it was the small airfield of Toussous-le-Noble, but more often just some farmer's field. A few francs would be charged for admission, and stunt flying exhibited. Déricourt did not himself perform aerobatics, but he had with him two pilots who did loops, low fly-over and wing-edge. He had also someone who made parachute jumps, and he himself helped with the parachuting. Then the villagers would be offered *baptême de l'air*. Anybody who had not flown before could, for a few francs, be taken up for a few minutes' joy-riding. The viability of the business depended on the weather; nobody wanted to stand on a field in rain, and that was why Déricourt had taken the employent offered by Air Bleu — he still kept up the *fêtes aériennes* at weekends.

For Air Bleu he piloted a silver single-engined Simmons, with enclosed cabin. As the pilot he received 8,000 francs (six times the SMIG rate), and Marotin as the radio received 4,000. Air Bleu was a postal transport company, taking neither passengers nor freight, and was new, having been created only in 1935, by the former directors of the Compagnie Aeropostale France-Amérique de Sud, which later became incorporated in Air France. Air Bleu, however, performed only internal flights. Déricourt flew Paris-Rouen-Le Havre. They flew out in the morning, spent the night at Le Havre, and flew back the next day.

When they first joined, the company had no uniform. Then, by informal consent, everyone wore blue trousers, white shirt and blue tie — everyone, that is, except Déricourt. He wore white trousers, blue shirt and white tie. 'It's more amusing,' he said.

430

He was one of the company's best pilots. He was brave. Once, when it looked as though they were going to crash-land, he said to Marotin, 'Get back! There is no point in our both being killed!'

Answering the question whether Déricourt was interested in money, Marotin said he was interested in money without being obsessed by it. If he made any one day, he usually spent it the next, taking a girl out. About the airfields, there were usually girls, hoping to be picked up by airmen.

Had he any political ideas? None. Marotin had, at that time, some right-wing ideas on which he endeavoured to engage Déricourt's attention, but was laughed off. Déricourt was not attracted by Hitler or the Nazis. He thought them absurd. If there was a foreign nation that attracted him at all, it was the British.

Did Marotin know if Déricourt was ever in Spain? He never heard of it. Nevertheless, Air Bleu lost its subsidy from Renault at the end of July 1936 and suspended its operations, while retaining its precious assets, particularly human. The personnel were sent on leave, on pay that was reduced but still very acceptable, for eleven months, during which they had no duties. Some used the time to prepare themselves to sit for examinations. He himself took a temporary employment with a line plying Nice-Bastia. He could not remember if, when they reassembled, Déricourt had told him what he had done with the time.

When they resumed, it was a night postal service, Paris-Pau-Bordeaux. They would fly out from Paris at 8 pm, reaching Bordeaux about midnight. This route they flew until September 1939 when the war broke out and they were militarised to liaise with the General Staff HQ. Soon after that Déricourt left to become *'pilote réceptionnaire chez un constructeur'*, which involved flying for a plane manufacturer. At any rate this corresponds to the period during which, according to Clément, he had such a flying job with SNCASSE. The head office of the company was at 6 Avenue Marceau, Paris, but Déricourt's days in its employ were spent — according to his deposition for the DST — at a great centre for engineers and mechanics at Carry-le-Pont or Carry-le-Rouet, near Marignanne, Bouches du Rhône (therefore near Marseilles), testing a new autogyro.

To return to Collins: naturally, I was keenest to hear of his interview with Mme Déricourt. First, he had heard she had since died. Then, there was something about which he would like to consult me. She had shown him Déricourt's flight log, from which he had copied down details. There was a break in the entries between 15 November 1940 and 30 July 1941, when the flying hours recorded picked up from the previous number. Could I shed any light?

No. Was there any reason to suppose he had left SNCASSE? After doing his stint as a test pilot, he might have done some ground job the firm had to offer. According to his deposition for the DST he was still at Carry in 1941.

Collins suggested I should ask the heir to the estate for the flight log, flying licence and passport of Déricourt, together with any other memorabilia. (This I did immediately upon my return home, I addressed a letter to The Heir to the Estate of Mme Déricourt, 58 rue Pergolèse... and in case that was not forwarded, wrote also to the Gréffier of Paris 16, asking to be put in touch with the heir or with the notary who settled up the estate.)

To return to Mme Déricourt. She had shown Collins a receipt for that fur coat. It predated her first meeting with Déricourt. She met Déricourt on 19 May 1940, just before the French capitulation. She was then switchboard operator at the

Hotel de Beauvais in Marseilles. He was then flying between Marseilles and various places within France. He was always certain the English would win in the end. They became lovers within three weeks; she became pregnant in the autumn of 1940, but was unable to keep the child as it was extra-uterine. On 13 December 1941 they married.

She thought he must have been in Spain during the civil war because he talked of the horrors. She had not heard of his going to Aleppo. 'He was always coming and going.' Nevertheless, he was living with her all through 1941. He was flying Marseilles-Morocco daily. (According to himself and Clément he was flying between Marseilles and other places in France, but his route may have varied.)

Here must be brought in the story of Léon Doulet, another airman Clément had dug out for Collins. In 1941 Doulet had been flying Aleppo-Athens, and he was there in July when the British arrived. A Lord Forbes (later 9th Earl of Granard) interviewed him, and told him the Intelligence Service needed a new line, to be based on Stockholm and organised in conjunction with Imperial Airways (BOAC). Only three or four would be in the know. Forbes would like Doulet to fly for this. He told him to return to France for the time being but said, 'I will contact you, perhaps through the American Consulate.' (America was still neutral). Doulet returned to France, where he called at the American Consulate in Marseilles and saw Donaldson (Admiral Leahy's adjutant), MacPherson and George. Doulet was now flying Marseilles-Vichy. Also flying Marseilles-Vichy was Déricourt. No, he had not met him in Aleppo, nor did Déricourt say anything about having been there. As aircraft captains, they talked. Doulet told Déricourt he was hoping to go to England. Déricourt exclaimed, 'That interests me terrifically!' He asked Doulet if he could arrange for him to be taken to England with him. Doulet, therefore, gave his name to the American Consulate, saying this was a fellow airman wanting to come too.

A year passed, during which there was constant consultation. Then George called on Doulet and said, 'It's all arranged.' On 1 August Déricourt and he were to rendezvous at the Saint Charles Railway Station, Marseilles, where someone would take them in charge. (I take into this narrative details from a long letter Doulet later wrote to me.) Déricourt's wife came to the station to see him off. He was very much upset by the parting and kept on kissing her goodbye. As he and Doulet continued their journey, however, he regained heart. From Narbonne they were escorted to St Pierre Plage, where they were boarded on a British trawler flying a Portuguese flag. This took them to Gibraltar, where they had a longish wait for another boat to take them to Glasgow. They arrived there on 8 September and travelled down to London together. They saw each other at the Patriotic School, where their particulars were taken; afterwards, their ways diverged.

Doulet's story thus confirmed Déricourt's in every particular, except that it was obvious that Déricourt had falsely attributed to himself the bit of Doulet's story about having been in Aleppo when the British arrived and recruited by British Intelligence for secret work. Probably this was just for glamour, like his borrowing of Clément's experience in the Spanish Civil War, but it is surprising that the interrogators of the Patriotic School (made famous by Pinto's books), whose business was to check on the stories of foreign arrivals, failed to check on this. They had only to have asked Lord Forbes. (I did, now. From his reply it was obvious he had never heard of him.)

I now wrote to 'Pat', in real life a Belgian, Dr Albert Guérisse, GC. He replied from Waterloo on 28 August 1985. I translate from his French:

> It is true that, *on orders from London*, I embarked Déricourt and Doulet at St Pierre Plage les Narbonne, on 15 August 1942, on a vessel bound for Gibraltar. I boarded them personally, on account of the great interest London took in them, as Air France pilots. Their names and coordinates had been transmitted to me by radio.

Mme Déricourt passed a lonely five months in Marseilles until Déricourt returned, in January 1943, to collect her and take her to Paris. They stayed, she said, for the first three nights with Julienne — who was later 'Claire'. Then, while looking for a flat, they went for three weeks to the Hôtel Bristol, near the Gare du Nord. At that time, though it remained a 'free hotel' — that is, had not been commandeered, as were the Majestic and Lutetia — it was full of German military and French collaborators. They found a flat to let, 58 rue Pergolèse, but a lot of work had first to be done before they could move into it. Not being able to stay at the Bristol any longer, they took a furnished flat at 4 rue Colonel Moll until their future home was ready.

Collins had met Besnard, who was already the friend of Julienne though not yet sharing a flat with her. Julienne told Besnard she was going to the country for a few days, then telephoned to say she was back. As soon as he saw her again she told him she had in fact been in England and that she was now an agent, with the code-name 'Claire'. Her chief in France, she said, was Déricourt. She arranged for them to meet and Besnard agreed to help in their work.

When Bodington arrived, Déricourt installed him in a large flat, with eight rooms, which Besnard and 'Claire' were now sharing. Besnard had the impression that at the moment of Bodington's arrival the relations between Déricourt and Bodington were very tense, as though each were trying to sense where the other really stood; then suddenly there was a relaxation and intimacy. Bodington told Besnard that Déricourt had told him he was working with the Germans, though without specifying in what manner. They decided not to tell 'Claire'.

Besnard made a comment on Mme Déricourt: 'She was not the *femme fatale*, or specially seductive — almost the woman who would put one's slippers out. She was the woman with whom Déricourt found the calm he needed in his adventurous life.'

Mme Déricourt told Collins that during the eighteen months of her husband's imprisonment Bodington had called several times, to ask if she was all right and if she needed money. She was able to tell him she did not, for she had taken a job again and could manage to pay the rent. She showed Collins a rent-book going back to February 1943. 'It was only a two-roomed, rented flat,' Collins said to me. 'If there had ever been any money in that household, I saw no sign of it.'

When she went to Fresnes to visit her husband, he assured her 'They have nothing with which to reproach me.' He paid the expenses of his defence himself. It was she who obtained Moro-Giaffen. After the trial they gave a huge party. 'He was not bitter at all, but very sweet.' He had never for one instant doubted that he would be acquitted (*not* what he said to me), but as to the events that had led to the accusation, what had happened was just what he had told the court and he did not want to talk about it any more. Neither during the war nor after it did he tell her any details of his operations or adventures.

I had not expected to find much on the Clément tape new to me, but one thing that did surprise me was his claim that it was when he was going to London in August 1943 that Déricourt told him to ask André Simon for six diamonds. He had also expanded another point: *all* the money Déricourt made from his eventual commercial flights he received in American dollars but regularly took to Hong Kong, converted into sterling and sent to England (presumably less whatever it cost him to live at the Hotel Constellation). I wrote to Clément asking him when Mme Déricourt died, as I had just heard, and how he knew Déricourt had done this with his money.

He wrote back that Mme Déricourt had died in November 1984 and had been buried beside Henri and one of his brothers at Vitry-aux-Loges. He had attended her funeral. As to the money (I translate from his French):

> In Laos, where Henri was working as an independent pilot for local clients [patrons], he made a great deal of money. At that time I was flying for the Commission Internationale de Controle and slept three nights a week at Vientiane, so I saw Henri often. It was during that period he told me several times that he converted everything he made into English pounds and transferred it to England.
>
> Henri never let out of his sight a brief-case containing his personal papers, cheque book, money etc... It was burned in the air-crash in which he lost his life.
>
> Despite all my enquiries, I have never been able to discover where that money went.

If it had been to Beirut, Baghdad, Tokyo or anywhere but England, I would have thought it was to constitute the capital of a business he intended to found on his retirement from flying. But it is of no use to one to have money in a country one cannot enter. If he had hoped to have the ban lifted, I would have thought he would have got in touch with me, if only to ask me to ask Irene to have a word with the Home Secretary.

Collins attached the greatest importance to Déricourt's one-night trip to London in July 1943. It was, for him, the proof Déricourt was in MI6. I was sure he was not, but said, 'How so?'

Foot's History (page 295) put him aboard a Lysander which left France on 19/20 July 1943, taking also Antelme and a W.J. Savy, and said Déricourt spent one night in André Simon's flat in London and returned to France on the night of 21/22 July, by a Lysander that landed its passengers near Châteauroux. The last detail always seemed to me strange, for why would Déricourt have been set down so far from his area, to reception by a team that was not his? If there was not an aircraft that would set him down nearer to where he wanted to go, would he not have jumped, as before, to reception by his own team, or blind as twice before?

'Buckmaster assured me he *did not know* Déricourt was in England that night,' Collins said, in significant tones.

'That does not prove he was in MI6,' I said.

For answer, Collins showed me the transcript of an interview he had had with Tony Brooks ('Alphonse'). There I read:

> You've only got to read Verity's book. You've only got to look at the list of his operations to see that there are sometimes 'and three bods'. Even to this day he doesn't identify them... When it was an MI6 chap it was always 'a bod'...

No. Brooks had got it wrong. Verity's book does not tell its readers that he built his table up piecemeal. He makes an acknowledgement to me for some things I said about Déricourt, but nowhere mentions that it was primarily with the request that I should place at his disposal my knowledge of these operations to help him fill in gaps in his passenger-list that he asked me to lunch with him. He showed me the list of his operations, as he had it from his own log. It showed the number of passengers — or as they called them in the RAF 'bodies' or 'bods' — to or from France on the dates he had down. To some of these he had been able to put names, from perusal of Foot's book. Amongst these were the journeys of Déricourt on 19/20 and 21/22 July. He had copied them from Foot's page 295. He had already met one or two people who had been able to tell him the nights on which they travelled, but there were still long white gaps in his list where he had been unable to match sufficient names to his note of the number carried. Could I fill in some of those gaps? I filled in some for him, but not all. He had down three for the 'bods' to Châteauroux on the 21/22. Déricourt he had filled in from Foot. Could I tell him who were the other two? No, I could not.

Brooks, knowing none of this, had assumed Verity to have known the identity of his passengers. From this he had deduced that wherever their names were not given in Verity's printed table, it was because MI6 had required their suppression. This must be because they were agents of MI6. From this it followed that as there were two unnamed bodies on the flight to Châteauroux on 21/22 July, with Déricourt, that was an MI6 flight. Therefore Déricourt was an agent of MI6. This was the fallacious reasoning Brooks had imparted to Collins, with heavy consequences. I told Collins I was sure that gaps in Verity's table represented only gaps in Verity's knowledge, not MI6 suppressions.

Collins informed me there was 'a real live Frenchman very much alive and able to witness', who had been aboard the plane that left for England on 19/20 July, with Antelme and Déricourt: W.J. Savy. That was one of the earliest Resistance names that I had gathered, for Robert Gieules had told me, when I saw him in 1949, that a W.J. Savy had left with 'Antoine' (Antelme) aboard an aircraft bound for London in midsummer 1943. I had never known Savy's address. Collins gave it to me; it was in Cannes.

I wrote to Savy. He replied on 4 June 1985 (I translate from his French):

> It is correct I left on 19/20 July 1943 by a Lysander operation organised by Déricourt, but Déricourt, having seen the aircraft off, remained on the ground and must have gone back to Amboise.

Here was a surprise. In Foot's book Déricourt was a passenger on that flight; in Verity's also, though he had taken the names of the three passengers from Foot. Clément must have been at Déricourt's side, so I wrote to him asking whether Déricourt boarded the aircraft. He replied (I translate from his French):

> Déricourt did not leave for London with Antelme. I do not believe he went to London for one night. At any rate, not by Lysander in my presence.

I wrote to Verity about this. He replied, on 25 June 1985:

> I do not *remember* Déricourt coming back for one night in July... However, I do remember him going back through the

hole of the Halifax on 5th May 1943 and I have that flight in my log book.

Since his book was published, Verity had learned (and included in the French edition) the identities of 'the two other passengers to France on 21/22 July '43 as Commandants Peretti and Cazenove'. Peretti and Jacques Robert, whom he picked up from Châteauroux, were BCRA men, so he supposed it a BCRA flight.

I wrote to Woods, who could find nothing that shed any light.

I wrote to the Public Record Office. Their David Ellis replied:

> I have searched the Operations Record Book of 161 Squadron for July 1943 (AIR 27/1068)...
> The mission of July 19/20 to Azay-sur-Cher resulted in three passengers and six packages being picked up. The names of the passengers are not given.
> Squadron Leader Verity flew to Châteauroux on the 21/22 July carrying one passenger and four packages.

So, here was a discrepancy between Verity's private log and the official log of 161 Squadron. Verity thought he had now established from his own enquiries the identities of two out of his three passengers of that night as Peretti and Cazenove. According to the Squadron's log, he had only one passenger altogether. As he did not *remember* Déricourt as having been that one, I supposed that one was one of the other two — unless he had made two out of one double-barrelled name.

In any case, Déricourt had told me he had parachuted back. My feeling was that he had only been teasing and had not come at all; so Foot had incorporated a mythical episode in his book on the strength of a story for which I was his source.

However that might be, there were too many contradictions in the evidence for Déricourt's having made this trip unknown to Buckmaster to constitute, as Collins contended, proof that Déricourt was an MI6 agent, who had come that night to confer with his 'real' chief.

25: THE TRIAL PAPERS

It was over thirty years since I had tried to obtain the DST papers relating to Déricourt's trial, and subsequent attempts had been fruitless. Déricourt had given me a bundle, others I had had from Clément and the Abbé. Now Collins handed me, with an air of triumph, an enormous wad. I quickly saw that it was not, as it appeared, complete, for the depositions of Bleicher and Christmann, as well as some other bits, were missing; but these I had, and here was much that was new.

The Acte d'Accusation presented an extract from the Penal Code, Article 75, para 5:

> Shall be guilty of treason and put to death any Frenchman who, in time of war, shall entertain relations with a foreign power or its agents with a view to favouring the enterprises of that power against France.

The last clause was all-important in this case. To be in conversation with the enemy was not in itself an offence, only to be so with the intent of helping the enemy's designs.

I remembered Mercier's telling me the paper drawn up by the *juge d'instruction* for the President of the Court was not necessarily condemnatory; it just said there was an issue for the court to try, and set out what that was. One saw that here. Déricourt's own story, about having been lured into the car by the two German pilots, was presented, not challenged. What the *juge* considered to be worst feature of the case was that Déricourt, by his own admission, had not informed his British chiefs in London. Notwithstanding that he was thereby in breach of Article 104 of the Penal Code, he did tell Bodington,

443

when he arrived in France, and Bodington confirmed this and said he had authorised continuance of the German contacts.

The *juge d'instruction* drew to the attention of the President of the Court a peculiarity of this case, that much of the evidence was invalidated by the uncertainty of witnesses whether by 'Gilbert' they meant Déricourt or Gilbert Norman. (Some examples of apparently confused statements were given.)

With regard to the statement of Roger Bardet, there was something the *juge* thought he should tell the President. Bardet said that he had given a letter and papers to 'Simone', telling her to give them to 'Gilbert', and later saw copies of them in the hand of Bleicher. At the DST, however, they had taken a statement from a person who would not be heard in court, since neither Déricourt nor the Prosecution were calling her. That was Suzanne Laurant. She deposed that it was she to whom Bardet had given the letter and papers in question, and she who had given them to Bleicher. Plainly this would have been for the Defence, it came back to me that Déricourt told me he preferred not to call Bleicher's mistress. (Suzanne Laurant was later tried, along with Bardet, Kiffer and Jouffret, but received the lightest sentence — three years and a fine.)

The *juge d'instruction* summed up — apparently on the cover or title sheet — 'The evidence favours Déricourt.'

The witnesses called by Déricourt were listed as: General Zeller, General Ely, Pierre Bloch, Gerard Morel, Bodington, Georges Bégué, Ben Cowburn and Rémy Clément. The witnesses for the prosecution were listed as: Germaine Aigrain, Louise Brioux, Bleicher, Goetz, Knochen, Roger Bardet.

Of Brioux nothing more seems to have been heard.

I had not realised Mme Aigrain had been a witness. Apparently she had not only told of the Andrès report but, in the office of the *juge d'instruction*, claimed to recognise a photograph of Déricourt as that of a man who had taken part in her interrogation, but then said she did not. This explained to me something in his attitude towards Mme Aigrain that had always puzzled me — his allegation that she had borne false witness, told the *juge d'instruction* she recognised him, then in his presence broken down and avowed she did not. My feeling about this was that she had been trying to support Mme Touret, who had assured her Gilbert (Norman) had been present at her interrogation, though 'Gilbert' had after the war told her he knew what she had said at it.

Julienne Besnard ('Claire') said that as courier she was the link between Déricourt and Watt. If Déricourt wanted to see his radio operator, he told her. 'He never asked me where Captain Watt lived.'

The depositions of Bleicher and Placke I knew already. What I wanted to see was the deposition of Goetz. I should first mention that there was one from Knochen, but as it was only hearsay from Kieffer, it did not amount to much. He had understood from Kieffer that he was always informed about the landings of aircraft by the officer responsible, but it was to Kopkov, in Berlin, Kieffer reported and received his instructions concerning this.

Now to the meat of the matter: Goetz.

Goetz said he had gone on leave on 19 June 1943 and was on 29 June recalled. While he was away, arrests had been made and there were prisoners. (Here I would point out that Goetz's having been allowed to go on leave just before the arrest of the 'Prosper' group supports the view Giskes had put to me — that it had not been planned to arrest them at that moment, but that some accident had rendered the arrests suddenly necessary.) Two of the prisoners taken were radio operators, 'Valentin' (Macalister) and 'Archambaud' (Gilbert Norman), and Kieffer wished Goetz to compose radio messages in the names of these two, to be sent to London over their respective circuits, as though they themselves were operating. In this way, over 'Archambaud's' circuit, Goetz made an appointment with London for an officer to come and meet him in (an apartment in) the rue de Rome. It was thus his service knew Bodington was coming, though actually it was Agazarian who presented himself at the rue de Rome to be arrested.

Most of his meetings with Déricourt took place in an apartment somewhere in the neighbourhood of the Avenue des Ternes — the exact address had escaped his memory.

Déricourt would furnish the particulars of forthcoming aircraft landings, but there was an accord between Déricourt and Boemelburg that the agents arriving should not be arrested. Normally this accord was respected, but there was an occasion in November or December 1943 when, as all got out of the train at the Gare Montparnasse, Henri Chamberlain, alias Lafont, who was leading the party shadowing the agents, noticed that there were French police making a snap check of the passengers, requiring them to show their papers and open their luggage. Not wishing the agents who had come from London to fall into the hands of the ordinary police, Lafont signalled to his own men to arrest them. Boemelburg, when he heard about it, was furious, because it risked making Déricourt suspect with London and they were saving his real utility to the end, for he was to tell them the date and place of the invasion. The damage, however, had been done, and would not be undone by setting the agents free.

At last here was proof of what I had always hoped, that the arrest of Menesson, Pardi and Maugenet, like that of Bonoteaux, was an accident. Pardi must have been arrested when his briefcase was opened, for he was carrying a million

— in banknotes. I do not know what the other two may have been carrying. Why had not Déricourt sent me Goetz's deposition? It would have done him so much more good than some he did send me.

Answering a question, Goetz said the designation BOE 48 was unknown to him. He had not been shown any photostatted mail of the 'Prosper' network. Déricourt had passed him only three reports. One concerned the political activity of Edouard Herriot, perhaps mentioning that he would go to England. One was a general review of the political situation in France, and one concerned the effects of the bombing of Boulogne-Billancourt (— so Madame Aigrain told truly).

None of these reports contained addresses. Déricourt never gave him the addresses of any persons in France. He said that he had three assistants, 'Marc', 'Claire' and, later 'Geoffroi', his radio operator, but he did not provide their addresses. He promised to give the key to the code of 'Geoffroi', but did not do so. At one moment they thought they should arrest 'Claire' but Déricourt protested so strongly they gave up the idea.

Most of the arrests were made through the radio-game. Déricourt played no role in the radio-game. He knew nothing about radio. Concerning 'Antoine', he was dropped to German reception by appointment made by himself, Goetz, with London, over the 'Madeleine' circuit.

On the question of money, he heard Boemelburg say he had in mind to give Déricourt a million, or perhaps buy a property for him, but he did not know if Boemelburg in fact paid him any money. On the contrary, he heard Boemelburg offer Déricourt some money and Déricourt refuse it.

At the last meeting, which was at Boemelburg's villa, Déricourt gave them the BBC message which would be broadcast as an assurance to his team that he had arrived in England safely. It was 'La lampe verte est toujours allumée'. This they later heard broadcast.

The main deposition is followed by *Additional Questions to Goetz*. In this he comments upon a deposition of Placke. Placke had said:

> After the departure of Déricourt for London, Boemelburg and Goetz would have meetings to discuss him. During one of these I heard Boemelburg emit this reflection, 'That makes 4 million francs lost!' to which Goetz replied, 'That is just the price of a property he wanted to buy in the Midi.'

Goetz commented:

> The deposition of Placke is inexact, in particular with regard to a supposed conversation with Boemelburg in which were mentioned sums of money paid to Déricourt. As I have already said, Déricourt received nothing from Boemelburg — at any rate, not in my presence.

Following these testimonies to the DST was a brief abstract of the evidence given at the trial itself — not a transcript, but an attempt made by some clerk to summarise the burden of what the witnesses had said, with obvious mistakes, and less detailed than the reports in the newspapers. Collins had written below this:

> The differences between what was said at Déricourt's trial... and the detailed accusations focused on him at the DST's pre-trial investigation are so great one has to ask oneself whether there was a concerted effort by some authority to see that he was acquitted.

He had seen what I had seen when I got the newspapers out, all those long years ago, that the German accusations, so heavy at the time of Déricourt's arrest, had in the court-room become as snowflakes in the sun. Desmond Young had been convinced the German witnesses had been interfered with — he had thought by Bodington, whom he suspected of some treasonable league with the Germans which obliged him to cover up for Déricourt. Collins, on the other hand, thought it was MI6 which had persuaded them the British wanted them to drop their charges. What Collins could no more explain than Desmond Young was how anyone could have got at them for improper purposes, since, even if the French allowed them prison visitors, any interviews granted would have been in the presence of a guard — precisely to prevent interference.

What did, however, strike me was that Foot, on his page 305, quoted Placke's allegation of the money paid to Déricourt but not Goetzs refutation of it. I wrote to the Foreign Office, that is, to Woods, asking whether that page of Goetz's deposition was missing from the copies of the DST papers laid before Foot. Woods replied:

> ... as to the depositions of the DST, a complete set of these is not on the Déricourt file (nor anywhere in the SOE archives) and was therefore not available to Foot. Déricourt's file contains a copy of the depositions by Placke, from which Foot quoted, but there is no copy of any deposition to the DST by Goetz.

In 1955 Yeo-Thomas had mentioned to me that the DST had received back the files bearing upon the investigation of agents in the British services which it had lent to the British Government for copying. I had understood from him that the whole of the relevant files had been lent. At any rate, he specifically mentioned the index, or indices. How had Goetz's statement got missed out?

26: GOETZ

At this moment I was given the address of Dr Goetz. For more than thirty years he had been, for me, the brain of the Avenue Foch — unfortunately impossible to trace. As the person who gave me the address asked me not to divulge my source of information, I had to begin my letter by apologising for being 'a little mysterious'. I had never been an agent — of SOE, the Foreign Office or any secret service — but I had been a friend of a young girl he would have known as 'Madeleine'. I was now writing a book, a further book, on Henri Déricourt, whom he would have known as 'Gilbert'. Could he answer some questions?

I was thrilled to receive a reply from him, in French:

20 June 1985

Madame,

... I can no longer remember the date from which I knew Gilbert Déricourt. One day, my chief (Kieffer) told me to contact Gilbert, agent of Boemelburg, and I did so ... I never asked Gilbert how he had entered into contact with Boemelburg. I am convinced that he had, of his own initiative, sought that contact, in order to protect his clandestine activities, to the profit of the English, and he succeeded admirably, one must admit.

I do not believe that the English, learning of the German penetration of their service, conceived the idea of sacrificing the network in France in a strategic interest. I know that after the war they tried to make that believed by those who criticised them for having been tricked by the Germans. In reality, the British service has never been willing to admit that it was tricked by the Germans for long months, and was a little imprudent in its work...

No, he misunderstood me a little. Buckmaster was always adamant they never dropped people into German hands on purpose, and repudiated that suggestion. But now I wanted very much to see and talk with Dr Goetz. I invited him to spend a weekend as my guest and, to my delight, he accepted. We spoke on the telephone. His voice was a deep bass. He would arrive at Heathrow on Saturday, 20 July at 1.10 p.m.

If I drove to meet him, I would have to divide my attention between him and the road; therefore I engaged a taxi, from the local firm. In case the conversation going on behind him should sound strange, I told the driver on the way down a bit about who it was we were going to meet. I had posted Goetz a small photograph of myself to assist in identification, so while Eddie, the driver, was standing holding up a card on which he had written 'Goetz', it was towards me that I saw a tall man approaching hesitantly. He had a high domed cranium and brown eyes behind glasses. He was clean-shaven, his hair was white. He looked younger than I had thought he might.

'Have you been in England before?' I asked, as we sat back in the taxi.

'In 1952, for one night, in transit to America. Before that, in 1945, as a prisoner.' He spoke in English, slowly.

'How were you captured?'

'Placke gave to the English my address in Hamburg ... I was arrested and brought to Colchester.'

'How was it?'

'The food was abundant, but I was interrogated by Miss Vera Atkins. Beautiful, but haughty. She sat on a chair, and left me standing in front of her. *Never* I had a prisoner stand in front of me. Always I offered a chair. At the side of the room, I saw some chairs. I went and I took one, and I sat in front of her. She was annoyed. She took out a cigarette, put it in her mouth and lit it. I took from my pocket a cigarette, and asked her to give me a fire for it. She was still more annoyed. But she gave me a fire — and then she began to laugh. It went on better. She began to ask questions. She wanted to know from me *which* English agents had worked for the Germans. I had not to answer.'

'Did you see Colonel Buckmaster?'

'No... Do not tell Colonel Buckmaster I am here.'

'I won't. He doesn't like me. I am not in contact with him.'

'Do not tell Miss Vera Atkins I am here.'

'I won't. She doesn't like me either. I am not in contact with her.'

Did the British, after they had finished with him, hand him over to the French?

'I had from the English my clearance. I was being released. Bleicher told the French where they could come to take hold of me.'

In the Prison du Cherche-Midi he had suffered extremely. Bad as it was, he was nevertheless glad, afterwards, to have been through it, because it ended with his having a French clearance too. 'Without that, I could always have felt something hanging over me.'

How did he get into Kieffer's service?

He taught German, French and Spanish in a school in Germany. When the war came, he was called up. In 1940–1 he was in the army. He was taken out of the army to do something in Spain which required his Spanish. He expected afterwards to be returned to the army, but was told they wanted him in Paris, where his French was needed. He did not wish to serve with the SD but was told that if he refused the

Paris posting and insisted upon return to the army, it would not be to his former unit but to one for criminals and other disadvantaged persons, with a high risk of getting killed. 'I was threatened.' So he accepted the service pressed on him. In fact Kieffer proved a nice chief to work for, and he settled in.

I asked how he became the radio expert. That had made me expect a science background, whereas his qualifications were plainly on the arts side; he was a languages man. He was not a radio expert, he said. It was only on the job he learned about radio and coding. He had, to work for him, a team of radio technicians who did the transmitting on the sets of the captured radio operators. 'Never I asked a prisoner to transmit. I would not put a man in that position. It would not be fair. Also, it would be foolish. I should always have to fear he would work into his messages some warning to England that he was under German control. I had my good set of German technicians, who imitated the captured operators' manner of sending.'

He talked about captured agents. 'Some of them should not have been sent. Marcus Bloom should not have been sent. Marcus Bloom got the wrong gender of every word. Never he could have been taken for a Frenchman.'

For a moment I could not place Marcus Bloom. He is mentioned in Foot's History as the radio 'Urbain', Cockney Anglo-Jewish cinema proprietor, who was arrested, together with his chief, M. Pertschuk, in Toulouse in April 1943. Goetz told me he was sent to Toulous to interrogate Bloom. After two or three days Bloom confided to him, 'Dr Goetz, for the first time since I was landed in France, I feel safe.' Perhaps he was aware how bad his French was and had all the time felt terrified it would give him away. Now the blow had fallen, possibly he felt relatively secure; but in the end he was hanged at Buchenwald. That, however, was not Goetz's doing.

The first radio circuit Goetz played back was Bloom's, but not for long, as London detected the trick. The first successful one was that of 'Valentin' — 'Macalister'; he pronounced the name as though remembering across a great distance of time, but correctly. There followed 'Leopold'... 'Madeleine'. He gave names to the operations over each of the radio circuits he controlled, that over the 'Madeleine' circuit was his Operation Diana. After 'Valentin', it was the most successful. They multiplied. He no longer remembered the names. In all there were fifteen. His work was to compose the messages sent as from all these radio operators, with texts responding to the texts from London. This demanded a certain psychological sense of the sort of message each of the captured agents would send, also the coding. This was exacting and tedious. He arrived in his office at eight each morning and did not leave until ten in the evening. He worked a fourteen-hour day, even Sundays. Meals were served to him on a tray in his office. He lived in an hotel, but hardly used it except to sleep. Berlin took close interest in the radio game. Every day he had to send to Kopkow, Kieffer's chief, copies of all the telegrams (teleprints of radio messages) received from London. This increased his work, and indeed in the beginning he had to send for approval drafts of all the messages he proposed to send in reply. It was impractical, however, to send to Berlin for approval because the replies had to be transmitted at once, so he composed the replies, had them transmitted, and sent the copies to Kopkow. He therefore had complete records of the messages exchanged over every circuit. Under the strain, 'I lit one cigarette as I put the other out. I smoked forty a day.'

'Was it while interrogating you that Miss Atkins learned of the radio-game?'

'No.' He confirmed what I already knew. 'After the Normandy landings, we gave ourselves away. We sent messages: "Thanks deliveries arms and ammunition... signed Gestapo". I was against it. I said to Kieffer, "Is this not a mistake? Should we not keep this to ourselves, still, and continue?"' But the order to send the mocking messages, over all the radio-circuits they controlled, came from Hitler. Hitler thought it would cause dismay in London to offset 'the landings'. In the end, 'We sent the messages signed "Gestapo" over twelve of the fifteen circuits we controlled, and kept three for ourselves. These three we continued to play, fruitfully, during our retreat, from Nancy and from Lake Constance, up to the last days of the war.'

'I know. Vogt told me the last delivery, at Lake Constance, was of three unfortunate Americans.'

'And a hundred Camel cigarettes, for which I had asked. That was the last.'

'Did you ever assist at a parachute reception?'

'A few times. To participate in the danger. If the English had come to understand that it was we who formed the reception committee, they might have dropped a bomb instead of containers. It did not seem right always only to send other men to stand under an English aeroplane and wait for what it would drop.'

'There was never a bomb?'

'No.'

We had turned from the M25 and into the M1, which was exciting his interest. 'What is this magnificent autobahn?'

Eddie could tell him it was built in 1959.

He was the perfect visitor, appreciating everything. When we left the M1 for the small roads, he exclaimed with pleasure every time we passed a whitewashed cottage with black beams and thatched roof.

We were beginning to talk of Déricourt as we descended the hill into Wymington, but were keeping our serious conversation until we were settled. My house, thank goodness, had just had its windows newly painted, and the roses round the door were in bloom. I arranged with Eddie to collect us on Monday and took Goetz inside. This was the first English home he had entered. Amongst the array of paintings on the walls were portraits of my father and grandfather, uniformed and be-medalled.

I took him upstairs to show him his room, and there came the moment I had been waiting for. On a wall of the landing was a small, framed photograph of Déricourt. He stopped before it, and exclaimed with keenest delight, 'It is *him*!'

'Our friend!'

He also recognised the portrait of 'Madeleine', but this time his reaction was shaded with sorrow. 'She should not have been sent,' he said. 'She was too straight, too emotional, too naive, too transparent. Every thought and feeling showed on her face and in her movements.' She had a school exercise book in which she had transcribed all the messages she had exchanged with London, in code on one side and decoded on the other, showing the security check and everything.

I knew. Vogt had told me. He picked it up in the flat in which he arrested her. A Resistance colleague had warned her, but she had misunderstood an instruction she had been given in London and thought she had to keep them filed.

'Did she want to be sent?' he asked.

'Yes.'

He asked it again, as though he found it impossible to believe, and said, 'She could have served the Allies in some less dangerous way.'

How could I explain her romantic wish to do something heroic, self-sacrificing, testing?

I took him out into the garden behind the house, invited him to smell the old Bourbon roses, especially the Madame Perière, led him to make the acquaintance of my bold and clamorous hens, and, in the measure of the possible, my three cats, Bambina, Tiutté and Cleo, who, devotedly affectionate to me, fly the intrusion of any stranger, and two shy goldfish, Rhodophis and Flo. Then I brought him in and made and set the tea.

'Your questions!' he said 'Have you your list prepared?'

I suggested he begin with his first meeting with Déricourt — or first knowledge of the 'Prosper' network.

He had been on leave in Hamburg since 19 June, when a telegram from Kieffer recalled him. 'My wife wept.' She had just given him a son. When he got back, Kieffer told him they had arrested the chiefs of an important group. He agreed with me Kieffer could not have expected to make those arrests just then, or he would not have allowed him to go on leave. Kieffer had not told him how he learned of 'Prosper' and his team, but he had heard it was through a restaurant. Some members of the 'Prosper' network had been overheard speaking English as they sat back after a meal. This puzzled me, because during the time 'Prosper' was in London 'Archambaud' had nobody English to eat with. Would Agazarian or 'Antoine' have talked in English for greater ease, or had 'Prosper' been heard talking in English with 'Archambaud' before he left for London?

I asked him if he had heard of Christmann. At first he did not think so, yet the name was not quite unknown to him, for he queried 'Abwehr?' I told him the story of Christmann's intervention. It was new to him.

As to the two Canadians, he had heard their arrest was purely accidental (which was what I had understood from the Abbé Guillaume). Police or Feldgendarmerie were stopping all cars to make a snap check, and in the car of the Canadians was found 'Valentin's' radio transmitter, together with crystal, code, everything. It could have been their arrest that decided Kieffer to take in those he had been watching, in case news of the arrests caused them to flee from their usual places.

Kieffer told him that in Holland Colonel Giskes controlled the whole of the English network, and said, 'We must achieve that here.' But Goetz said, Giskes had the advantage of having caught the very first radio operator parachuted; he doubted whether it would be possible to break into something already established. But, the radios of Macalister and 'Archambaud' were set before him, and he started.

The first he heard of our friend was when Kieffer asked him if he would meet an agent of Boemelburg, called 'Gilbert'. He had often wondered why he was chosen and thought it must have been for his French. 'Vogt's French had an accent that would be recognised as German or Swiss.'

The first meeting with Déricourt was in a car, which gave him the idea for the story he later told at his trial. 'He gave me the particulars of a forthcoming air operation.' After that, their meetings were in an empty apartment, somewhere near the Avenue des Ternes. Kieffer kept the key and would give it to him when he needed to use it. He would arrive first, let himself in and wait for Déricourt. 'I do not know if Déricourt also had a key. He would leave first, I would lock up and return the key to Kieffer.' Then came Bodington...

'Your meetings with him had begun before Bodington's arrival?'

'Yes. Between 19 June and whenever Bodington arrived.' They had agreed with Déricourt none of the agents landed by his aircraft should be arrested, but they had expected Bodington to keep the appointment at the rue de Rome, made over the radio. When he failed to do so, they asked Déricourt where he could be found. Then Déricourt led them a dance. 'He is here … he is there... always telling us some place where he was *not*. And so he kept him from us. It was very skilfully done.' He said 'us', and I remembered that Placke, in his deposition to the DST, said that he had been asked by Goetz to meet 'Gilbert' in his stead on some occasions, and that on one he had waited in vain with him at the Bar Lorraine for Bodington, who should have come (to be arrested) but did not.

I understood now what Déricourt had meant when he said he was grateful to Anthony Brown for giving me a small taste of what it felt like to be under pressure to give something away. I understood now, also, Clément's story of Déricourt's exhausted, half-somnolent condition on 19/20 August 1943. It had been on the 16/17 August he had put Bodington aboard the plane that took him back to England. He had spent nearly a month keeping him in hiding while pretending to the Gestapo to be trying to help them catch him. Now he had finally to say, 'Sorry, he is gone' — and wonder if he would be killed for it. No wonder he showed signs of strain.

Goetz thought it probable that Déricourt continued to have direct meetings with Boemelburg. Indeed Placke said that on one occasion it was Boemelburg and he who went to the empty apartment.

'Tell me more about your meetings with Déricourt.'

They lasted for perhaps half an hour. Déricourt would give him the date of the next operation, co-ordinates of the field, type and number of aircraft, code-names of agents departing and number of agents arriving. 'It was already interesting for us to know the number, because we had the idea that before the Landing the number would increase.' (I supposed that would be why the shadowing team had orders to follow the arrivals after leaving the Gare Montparnasse until they either entered a house in Paris or another railway station, and report; it would be to have an idea whether they were going into the provinces or remaining as near as possible to the forbidden Channel area.)

Déricourt's proposition was in effect: 'You can send your people to watch, from a distance. You may look, but not touch. You must not arrest the agents, or the game is over.' In return for their forbearance he offered to give them eventually the date and place of the invasion. This was a promise so big it could not be neglected. What were a few agents against that? In 1943 it looked already as though Germany would lose the war, but it was Boemelburg's hope that the invasion details would make all the difference. Déricourt's information was to save the war for them. 'I was always suspicious.' What guarantee had they that Déricourt would perform what he promised? They had to agree everything, in advance, without surety as to what they would receive at the end. Perhaps nothing. Or worse, misinformation. Kieffer, too, was suspicious. But 'Kieffer was very, very dutiful. Never would he disobey.' Boemelburg was his chief. Déricourt was to make Boemelburg's glory.

Déricourt would arrive and say something like, 'I have a Lysander coming on such date,... such co-ordinates... Now, you will make sure there is not a catastrophe!'

'Then', said Goetz, 'I would telephone the Luftwaffe, tell them to expect it, and tell them not to attack it. Next, I would telephone to the anti-aircraft batteries on the ground and give them the same instruction. So, the aircraft had a protected flight.'.

He suggested that this was something positive, which should be set against the small number of agents arrested 'through mistakes of the shadowing people', of which it was improbable Déricourt had been told. The aircraft, its crew and passengers came and went in safety. They would otherwise have been likely to have been attacked, for on nights when the moon was full, the Luftwaffe were very active, especially over the area facing England. (Indeed, I had noticed from Verity's table that against flights made to reception by agents other than Déricourt enemy action was sometimes noted. On three occasions the aircraft was shot down, with loss of crew and passengers.) Goetz said that the only thing that used to worry him was lest the contrast cause the English to suspect Déricourt must have German permission for his operations. He was sure now Déricourt duped the Germans.

'He achieved what no other agent has ever done,' he said, 'he obtained German cover for British operations.' Putting his fist to his forehead, as if to indicate cerebration, he said, 'I am convinced it was his own idea. He must have said to himself, "I have to do such and such things. What is the best way to do them? The best way is to obtain German cover." He must have weighed up the risks and advantages of an accord with us. It was his firm belief that Déricourt himself had sought them out. He must have made enquiries who was the best person to approach. He supposed that Déricourt had obtained an interview with Boemelburg, and said something like, I can be of use to you. Do you want me?'

'Would Boemelburg give blind credence to someone of whom he knew nothing?'

'He knew how to present himself!' — 'Il savait se presenter!'

Déricourt allowed them to understand he was 'not of the Left. The opposite — Conservative.'

Well, I was sure he believed in private enterprise. I said, 'He told me he had known Boemelburg before the war, when he was at the Embassy.'

'I did not know Boemelburg was at the Embassy.'

'What was Déricourt's manner to you?'

'He always looked me straight in the eyes. His regard was direct and penetrating. He possessed an exceptional degree of intelligence, a mind that could see all sides of a question at one instant. He saw the consequences of a move, and the consequences of the consequences.'

I remembered Déricourt enjoyed chess.

'The relationship between us was one of respect. Little was said between us, but it was dense. Very dense.' He meant condensed. 'There was in him a terrific energy. His build and walk were sportive. He was very self-possessed, controlled, careful. Every word was weighed. On my side, also. In meeting each other, we had each to get the most possible, and to give the least possible.' Goetz was on his feet, his whole attitude expressing what he meant — hands outstretched and grasping, as if to seize, yet hips back and on his toes, as though to evade, in case Déricourt, instead of giving anything, should whip out a pistol to shoot him. Every sinew was tense.

Once, in the empty apartment, the telephone rang. It was in a corridor and he went out of the room in order to answer it, leaving his jacket over the chair that was the sole piece of furniture. When he came back, it was not exactly as before. 'I said to myself, "Now, you have done a foolish thing. Now he has been through your pockets. He knows who you are. He has read your Identity Card, looked at everything that you carry.'"

It was a relationship in which each regarded the other as dangerous. He always felt Déricourt was setting his wits against his own, ready to exploit any carelessness; never for one moment relaxed, even when his manner appeared so.

'He was a born agent,' he said, putting up his finger and thumb to make a circle. 'The model of an agent!' The pattern of what an agent should be.

He felt sure Boemelburg would have paid him, yet felt that money was the last thing to consider in his motivation. 'It was his sense of adventure!' In the affair at Croydon, also.

I said, 'What he said to me was, to have accomplished his mission in the way his chiefs wanted, without the Germans' knowing, would have been impossible.'

'Impossible!' he. agreed. 'He did it in the only way, the way he thought of himself. But,' he added 'if Kieffer had been the chief, he would not have succeeded. He would have been arrested!'

One thing he had never known how to interpret. On one occasion Déricourt said to him, 'Would you like to come to England with me, for ten days, to have a look round?' 'Was he serious? Was it a joke? I didn't say no! I said, "I will think about it", and I told Kieffer. Kieffer said, "On no account whatsoever."'

'What did Déricourt tell you about me?' he asked 'How did he describe me?'

He had said very little of Goetz, perhaps from prudence.

'Did you ever visit any of his fields?' I asked.

'No.'

'Did Déricourt ever go to the Avenue Foch?'

'Never! *Exclus!* The possibility is to be excluded.' (So Christmann did lie.)

He was asking himself now how Déricourt made the appointments. He did not know Kieffer, and Kieffer did not know French. 'He must have telephoned each time to Boemelburg, to ask if he might have another appointment, then Boemelburg must have told Kieffer the date and time that had been arranged. Then Kieffer told me and gave me the key.' He was not given Déricourt's number.

Then came the last evening. Kieffer told him he was invited to dine with Boemelburg at his private villa in Neuilly. Although their offices were next door, he did not think he had met Kieffer's chief, face to face, before that occasion. Of the dinner, in February 1944, he could remember only a round table and the three of them sitting round it, Boemelburg, Déricourt and himself. Déricourt explained to them that he had been recalled to London. He hoped it was to outline to him what would be his duties as the time for the landing approached. He had already gathered that his big field was to be used in a big way, and as the particulars of what he had to do were given him, so it would become apparent what was intended.

'What impression did you have of the personality of Boemelburg?'

'He liked good food and good wine.'

'Nothing else? Nothing beyond that?'

'After the dinner he sat back and left Déricourt and me to do most of the talking about details.'

'Is that all you can remember of him?'

'He was not impressive.'

'Can you describe to me the interior of the villa? Were there paintings on the walls? Were there books?'

'I do not remember. If it was good taste, if it was bad taste, I have no recollection. I see only that round table, the three of us sitting round it.'

The atmosphere was cordial, Déricourt very poised, very self-possessed. Yet, though his manner might appear easy, Goetz thought he was not really relaxed, not as with genuine friends. Behind the apparent ease was always that weighing of every word, that care, as though he were mentally editing his every phrase for its possible content of danger. The ease was very well acted, but yet there was inner tension behind that self-possession. Eventually he rose to go. He hoped he would not be kept in England for too long. When he came back, he was sure to have his invasion mission. So they parted.

I referred to Placke's tale, that when the BBC message was heard by which they knew of Déricourt's safe arrival, Boemelburg had said to him, 'There is four million down the drain...'

'That is fiction,' said Goetz. 'Placke has a very active imagination. At the Avenue Foch once he told me a long story in which I could never find one thing that was true.'

After that he heard no more of Déricourt until after the war. He was a prisoner in French hands when at the DST one day Inspecteur Coupaye put before him a French newspaper carrying a report of Déricourt's arrest, in which it was stated 'Le Capitaine Gilbert' had explained how he was lured into a car, in which was a Dr Goetz, who claimed to know all about him and threatened him with consequences unless he cooperated.

'I was furious! For some moments, furious!' It was an accusation of blackmail. 'Never I blackmailed anybody!'

But during Déricourt's trial there was a moment when the court was cleared, probably because the *juges* wanted to discuss some legal point, and the witnesses were all put into one room, near the court. Bleicher had already testified, he himself not yet. He sat next to Déricourt. He reproached him: 'Why did you make up that story involving me? You know that I never put pressure on you! Why did you put that on my back?'

Déricourt said, 'I had been told you were in Spain. I thought it could not hurt you. If I had known you were in French hands, I would not have put that on to you. Excuse me. Forgive me.' The way in which he said it was so nice. For the first time he felt that Déricourt was natural with him, without that air of being innerly on guard against him, relaxed before him, just simply friendly. They were both in the same boat now. Both prisoners of the French. Déricourt said, 'I have already taken it back. It is now someone I heard addressed as Doctor, not Dr. Goetz.'

Then, confidentially, Déricourt said, 'I have already started a new network. In the prison.' 'I did not know what he meant,' Goetz said, 'but I believed him.'

Then they were all summoned back into the court, Goetz feeling much relieved that he was not going to be charged with having impressed Déricourt. In fact Déricourt referred only to 'a civilian'. He, Goetz, had next to give his evidence. He did it in a way to help Déricourt. He said that always he had distrusted him, mistrusted his intent to do anything good for the Germans. Déricourt gave them only promises. He made them promise not to arrest his agents, as he was going to give them the date and place of the invasion. This promise he did not fulfil.

'His counsel, Moro-Giafferi, was quick to make the most of this.' Pointing first to Bleicher, who had been trying to get Déricourt convicted, and then to Goetz, he said, 'Here you have two Germans. There you have one who ever since the war ended has been working for the French. Here you have one who during the war did his duty. I leave to you, officers of the jury, to decide which is the more honest man.'

So the mystery of the discrepancy between the newspaper reports of the German evidence at the moment of Déricourt's arrest and at his trial was dispelled. It was not the British Intelligence Service which had interfered with the German witnesses to pervert the course of French justice — a notion that had played no small part in the building of the myth that to have been so protected by the Intelligence Service Déricourt must have been its agent. In the press release at the moment of his arrest, it was Placke's tale of the millions paid to him that had captured the headlines. During the subsequent interrogations, to which the press were not privy, Goetz had contradicted Placke's assertion. That is probably why Placke had not repeated his story when he went into the box at the trial. At the trial it was Goetz's evidence that had made the strongest impression, and Goetz, though called by the Prosecution, had been moved by compassion for his old 'contact' and was trying to help save his life.

At the mention of Bleicher, Goetz's face hardened. 'Bleicher!' He made a horizontal, cutting movement with his hand, an erasing motion. 'Mean!'

'He was a liar,' I said.

'He was a liar, and so mean. He is dead now.' He made again the same gesture, as though he would erase his name from the tablets of human memory. 'He was during the war a traitor to Germany. After the war, he gave away all his agents and all his friends.'

As Bleicher never met Déricourt — admitted in his deposition to the DST — how, I asked, did he come to hate him?

'Because of the rivalry between the SD and the Abwehr.' From the window of his mistress, Suzanne Laurant, Bleicher could see Déricourt going in and out of the next-door house. He could not bear that Déricourt worked for the SD and not for him. It was envy and greed. He wanted to be the only one with agents working for him. Since the SD had one, he had to be destroyed. 'Bleicher worked always to destroy Déricourt.' To have told Frager, who though controlled by him was a British agent, that 'Gilbert' was an SD agent was a treason against Germany. Déricourt was the agent upon whom the SD pinned all its hopes. Probably Bleicher was preparing to defect to the British, if he had not done so already.

'Bleicher arrested at least 104 agents by the end of 1943,' I said. 'That is too many for him to have been a British agent! And Frager he arrested in July 1944.'

'Perhaps he had to do that.' He was sure Bleicher was preparing his *après-guerre*, preparing to ensconce himself comfortably with an Allied service after the war'. He would plead that he had informed the British about Déricourt and so rendered them a great service.'

'He fabricated circumstantial evidence against him — at the DST and even in his book.'

Suddenly Goetz asked me, 'Did Déricourt know about my radio-game?'

'I don't know if he knew during the war... He knew 'Archambaud' had been arrested, and yet that an appointment had been made with Bodington over his radio, so he must have divined the Germans worked it. I do not know if he knew it was controlled by you. In 1957, anyway, he knew it from me.'

'Who told you?'

'Starr. Afterwards, Vogt.'

This interested him. He had been given *Madeleine*, but had not seen my subsequent books. I showed them to him, and after supper brought down some of the albums of press cuttings. He plunged into the one devoted to reviews of *The Starr Affair* and saw the furore created by my disclosure of the radio-game, which was causing us to drop people into German hands. He said, 'Reading this, I feel that I am in danger, in being here.'

'You are not in danger.'

'But really, I feel that I am.'

'English people are not vengeful.'

'Truly, nobody knows that I am here?'

'Truly.' (Except for Tim, of course.)

I showed him the *Double Webs* reviews album. He said with surprise, 'Your book is very hard on him [Déricourt]!'

'It was,' I said. 'But I am wearing something I would like you to see.' I showed him the bracelet with the Cambodian dancers. 'He sent me that, from Laos, when the book was published, in token of "non-aggression feeling". It is because it was too hard on him I am writing another.'

He looked at his watch, 'My wife is in bed now.' It was the signal to let him retire.

In the morning, after breakfast, I brought down the photographs of Déricourt, in Laos and as a boy. 'The book he is holding is on algebra. He was proud to be starting algebra.'

'Algebra!' he exclaimed, as though that were an illumination. 'There are in algebra some things which have correspondence with his way of thinking.'

'And chess. As you said last night, the consequences of the move, and the consequences of the consequences.'

'Yes, that is chess.'

'He thought of himself as playing chess with the Germans. But his chiefs in London did not play chess.' I put something to him. 'After his return to England, you left his team to continue its operations under the direction of Clément.'

'Because we expected his return. We wished him to find his team still functioning when he returned to resume the direction.'

I told him Morel had been ordered to bring him back *with* him, on the night of the 4/5 February, 'without giving him time to tell you he was going. If he had done that — gone back with Morel — without coming to tell you he must go — if he had just vanished, what would you have done with regard to his team?'

'We would have arrested them. No point to let Clément continue if Déricourt would seem to have abandoned us, without coming to tell us he must go but would come again.'

'Quite so.' Not one of them had seen it. Not Buckmaster, not Foot, who wrote that Morel's judgement failed him in granting Déricourt the delay he asked for; not Sporburg, not Verity, not Miss Atkins. I excuse Verity. He was an airman. His training had been to know about aircraft, not agents. But the others should have seen it.

The mention of Laos brought him to ask me if it was true Déricourt had been killed in an accident in Laos.

I told him the story Clément had told me.

'How could he know there was no petrol in the tank?'

'I don't know.' I got up, fetched the two box-files of Déricourt's letters and showed him the last one. 'That is the last one. If you had been me, and you had received that, what would you have thought?'

'That he intended to start a new life.'

'That is what I thought.'

I told him what Clément had told me about his sending all the money he made to England. 'Why would he do that?'

'Perhaps to repay a debt?'

'Even if he had a debt, he would not send all he earned.'

'I think he is here!'

'That is what I have been thinking. If he wanted to start a new business in a new name, it would be in England people would least think to look for him.'

'Perhaps, one day, you will hear a sound at the door. You will open, and he will be standing there.' He made a gesture down from his chin, as though to indicate a long white beard.

'It would be nice.'

'Perhaps when your new book about him is published.'

'I have been thinking of that.'

'And tell you the *truth*.' This was uttered with mock schoolmasterly severity. 'Does he know your address here?'

'I came here only ten years ago.' He could find me through my publisher, through my London bank, or through my own publishing company, Fuller d'Arch Smith Ltd. The address would be at the Registrar of Companies.

If Déricourt did consider faking his own decease, I reflected, it would explain something that had puzzled Clément — that he had not taken out life insurance in favour of his Chinese friend, as she had asked him to do. He was not normally mean but the last thing he would have wanted would have been to have insurance people making enquiries and perhaps trailing him.

It was a bright sunny morning, and I asked Goetz if I might take some photographs of him. He agreed, but when I said, 'For the book?' declined.

'My mother did not like me to be in that service.'

There was no arguing with a reason like that. He allowed me to take some for myself only, and we went out on to the patio.

'I did my duty,' he said, as though something needed to be explained. The arms and explosives parachuted by SOE were for use against the Germans. When they blew up a factory or derailed a train, people would get killed. Sometimes the agents assassinated a German soldier. For every German soldier assassinated, a number of members of the French civilian population were taken and shot, in reprisal, though they had done nothing wrong. Therefore, to make it possible by his radio-game to arrest the agents, as they arrived by parachute, before they had the opportunity to do any of their work, though it cost (in most cases) the lives of the agents, saved not only the lives of the persons they would have killed, but the lives of French civilians who might have been shot in reprisal for their acts. 'It seemed to me that by my radio-game I was preventing the number of lives lost from being so high!'

He was therefore very sympathetic to the intention of 'the arrangement which "Prosper" and "Archambaud" made with Kieffer and Vogt.'

So he knew of the pact. I was thankful, because Vogt had been very conscious of being the only surviving witness.

'I will say something that will shock you,' he said. 'All that SOE achieved did not equal the suffering of the French people.'

I had thought that for the last twenty years.

'It was like a civil war,' he said. 'In France and in all the countries we occupied, between the ones who worked with us and the ones who worked for you.'

I had long ago thought of it as a 'civil war'. 'I know. The bitterness remains to this day — between the ones who worked for you and the ones who worked with us. The hurts are never forgiven. The suspicions and the accusations remain. There are those who can never hear kindly the name of another.'

Yet I had to remember that in England, at the time, it had cheered us. We were depressed when we heard that in Norway someone called Quisling was governing on behalf of the Germans, depressed when Darlan handed over the French fleet. When we heard there were some people resisting the Germans, it lifted our spirits, assured us we would still be welcome when we returned.

We reverted to the radio-game. He had asked 'Archambaud' for his security check and composed a message to London using the one he gave. A reply had come from London: 'You forgot your double security check be more careful.' I had heard this story three times, from Starr and from Yeo-Thomas, both of whom had been told by 'Archambaud', and from Vogt, who had been told by Goetz. It was still worth while to hear Goetz tell me himself — unprompted.

Then, he said, there was the Canadian Rousset ('Leopold', arrested in September 1943). 'I asked him: "In which language do you transmit to your chiefs, French or English?" I composed a message in whichever he said. The reply from London began: "Why have you changed your language?" He spread his hands. 'It is something you cannot conceive, how all the attempts of their agents to warn them failed. There was another one — one of the ones we met as he parachuted. I asked him, "What is your mission?" He said, "I do not know". "What? They parachuted you without telling you your mission! I do not believe that." He said it was to be transmitted to him. I did not believe that. But he would not tell me, so I asked "What is my mission?" The reply came from England, "How can you have forgotten your mission?" Then it was detailed.'

He did not believe SOE dropped people into their hands deliberately. There was one, a specially important agent, whom they met as he parachuted, who was in a terrible rage. He said, I did not think they would have dropped me straight into your hands! He did not think this was an accusation that they had done it on purpose, only that they had not been clever. Then he said, "I will tell you nothing!" I said, "Let it be so." To avoid having to invent supposed activities for him, he composed a message as from Madeleine saying this important man hit his head on a container as he landed, and was unconscious. A message came from England saying this was serious, because he had a cold and so could come to suffer meningitis. I consulted a physician. He told me a blow to the head of somebody with a cold could cause the germs to rise in a certain way and produce meningitis. I asked him what were the symptoms of meningitis, and what he told me, I told London that he showed. London must have also have consulted a physician, for instruction came as to how to treat him. So he sent messages: "All that you tell us we do but still he sinks"; finally, "He is dead."'

I showed him, in Foot's book, the profile photograph of 'Antoine'.

'I remember his face from the front. I cannot be sure.' But Robin Hooper's letter to Irene, mentioning the story that he had hit his head on a container, confirmed the identification.

'They warned us about the D/F vans, and about the D/F belts,' he said. 'They warned us against ourselves; and they instructed us every time they changed the system of coding.' If on one or two circuits they had kept up communications only in order to pretend they were being deceived, they would not for this purpose have told him every time they changed not just a particular agent's code but the whole system of coding used throughout all the circuits. 'First, it was letters. Then it was numbers. Then it was one-time pad.' The one-time pad is called the unbreakable code, because by looking at the transcripts for however long you cannot decipher it. It is just necessary to have possession of the small physical object, the pad. But if you give the pad not to your agent but to your enemy... 'They parachuted the pads to me.' He received pads for every circuit he controlled. With instructions.

What proportion of the F Section circuits did he think he controlled?

'One evening, out of thirty BBC messages, twenty-seven were for me.'

Quietly, he added, 'I did get the date of the invasion.'

I looked at him quickly.

'Through the BBC messages,' he said.

'Les sanglots longs des violons d'automne...?' I suggested. According to Foot (page 388), the meaning of the two BBC messages, consisting of the opening lines of Verlaine's poem (misquoted), had become known to the Germans. This, Foot supposed, was because, although intended for Philippe de Vomécourt, they had earlier been given to Garel, so that the Germans might have learned them from his radio, Rousset, when they captured him.

'That was only one of them!' exclaimed Goetz. 'There was a different pair for every circuit. An A message, meaning invasion will be within fifteen days, and a B message, meaning invasion will be within forty-eight hours, or twenty-four hours, I do not remember which now. Whenever a prisoner was brought to me, I asked him, "What is your A message?" and "What is your B message?" I collected together all the A messages and B messages.'

Because it was important to have this exactly as he explained it, I later asked him to write it out, which he did (in English):

> When an agent and his radio were sent to France to build up a sabotage organisation, they were given an A and B message (the same for the two people). They were told to listen, every first and fifteenth day of the month, to the personal messages sent by BBC after the evening news. If the A message came out on the first or the fifteenth of a month, it meant that, during the following fifteen days, the invasion would take place. If the B message came out, it meant that the invasion would take place that same night [actually, within forty-eight hours, I think]. As we had about fifteen radio plays (with fifteen A and B messages given us by the arrested agents and radios) and as there were other agents and radios who had been captured by the service or the army, we had, as far as I can remember, about 25 A and B messages. In fact, on the first of June 1944, all these 25 A messages were sent out and we knew that the invasion was imminent. And when, on the fifth of June, the 25 B messages were sent, we knew that the invasion took place the same night.

He told Kieffer, and the information was sent by despatch-rider on a motor-bicycle to the HQ of the High Command of the Army. 'I was told, later, it lay all night on the table of an officer. He was shot.'

A thought rose in my mind that would have been inappropriate to express, that perhaps some beneficent and holy power had wafted from the officer's mind that his duty required him to do something about it.

Rommel was on leave.

In a very small voice, Goetz asked, 'If my information had been acted upon, would it have changed something?'

I tried to picture what it would have meant if the whole might of the German army had been waiting for us. I remembered, also, 6 June 1944. I woke that morning, dreaming the words, 'They're over', meaning our troops were over the Channel. There was a noise of aeroplanes going overhead, southwards, which could have caused the dream, but they had been doing that for weeks now. I turned on the eight o'clock news. There was no mention of our troops having gone over. So my dream, it seemed, had not been a psychic intelligence. Yet, as I went to the office, where all was as usual, I was still on tenterhooks, unwilling to believe the dream was wrong. At about eleven in the morning, on the internal loudspeaker, Edwin Herbert, Director of the Postal Censorship, told us there had been a newsflash. Our troops had landed in Normandy. I prayed, we all prayed, that the Germans would not be there, waiting for them, that the slaughter would not be too great. I tried hard to visualise the answer to Goetz's question. Could they have pushed us back into the sea? If we had been pushed back into the sea, however long would it have been before we could try again? I thought that on 6 June, when we came, we came to stay, through however much blood we had to wade.

I said, 'The result would have been the same, but at the cost of very much greater loss of life.'

These words he repeated, low. I hoped that any lingering trace of regret that might be there had died.

'Shall we make a little promenade?' he suggested.

'Yes.' He would like, first, to see the church, with toothed, castle-like tower, he had looked out on from his window. So I took him round St Lawrence's and told him it was as old as it looked — begun in the fourteenth century. Then I led him up the lane past the riding school, and showed him the little oak

478

tree, which was the subject of my poem, *The Great Adventure of the Much Travelled Little Oak Tree*. Shirley Warner, with whom I had ridden for a while, was taking her class, in the ring where I had ridden round. We stood for some minutes watching the riders. Then I waved to her, and we began to walk back.

As we turned to the wheat-field, we came to be talking about Kieffer. I said it was a pity we hanged him. This provoked Goetz to utter the only violent words I heard from him. Naturally, he had been very much shocked and upset by the hanging of his chief. 'His poor family...' He was sure that whatever Kieffer had done he must have been ordered to do. Suddenly to have ordered the execution of six commandos, who when captured were in uniform, was outside the character of the Kieffer he knew.

I told him Starr had gone to Wuppertal and given evidence for Kieffer. He had been told by the Judge Advocate General in London that Kieffer was asking for him. He found himself the sole witness for the Defence. Vogt would like to have given evidence for him, but probably Kieffer did not think to ask for members of his own staff, supposing their evidence would be discounted. When Starr reached the court, in March 1947, the evidence for the Prosecution had been already given, so he did not know in what it consisted, except that two comrades of the fallen men had testified. Here we stood, Goetz and I, in an English country lane, trying to debate something without access to the data from which to see the points to be debated. It was unfortunate there was no transcript of the trial available.

In consequence of this conversation with Goetz I wrote to the Ministry of Defence asking if I could see the record of Kieffer's trial, and was given the file reference at the Public Record Office. I obtained photostatted copies of the 333 pages. Kieffer, born 4 December 1900 at Offenburg, swore that in July 1940 he was directed to change his service and report to Dr Knochen in Paris. In July 1944 he learned through the radio-game of a parachute drop to be made and sent men to receive it. Instead of the expected containers there descended uniformed SAS men, of whom some were brought back as prisoners. He asked Berlin what to do with them. After an interval occasioned by the attempt on Hitler's life, he was on 8 August summoned by telephone to Knochen's office. Dr Schmidt was also there. Knochen showed them a teleprint order signed 'Muller', which had come from the RHSA, that the men should be shot in civilian clothes within twenty-four hours. Knochen ordered him to have them changed into civilian clothes and boarded on a truck and Schmidt to organise the firing party. There was no difference between the Prosecution and the Defence as to the facts. Knochen's statement tallied with Kieffer's, as did those of the other accused (Schmidt not among those arraigned). Serge Vaculik and Thomas Jones, survivors of the SAS party, said they were taken to a wood, where a paper was read and translated to them saying they were judged guilty of collaboration with terrorists. Then the automatics were raised. They made a run for it — and so appeared for the Prosecution. The Defence pleaded obedience to orders. The trial at Wuppertal opened on 7 March 1947 and ended with the passing of sentences on 12 March. All were found guilty, and Knochen, Kieffer and two of the firing party, Karl Haug and Richard Schnur, were sentenced to death. All appealed. All their appeals, together with attached appeals on their behalf from the two Archbishops of Cologne, Evangelical and Catholic, were dismissed by Lord Russell of Liverpool. On 26 June Kieffer was hanged at Werle, with Haug and Schnur. Knochen had been lent to the British for this trial by the French, on condition of his being afterwards returned to them for trial on other charges, and was so returned. Eventually he was graced and released.

'Was Kieffer a Nazi?' I asked Goetz.

'I do not know. Not fanatical, anyway.' He thought it must have been his sense of duty which carried him from his position as Chief of Police in Karlsruhe, his home town, into the SD. He behaved with consideration to his staff. 'I was lieutenant. He was major. He called me Doctor.'

He asked me where Vogt was now.

I thought he must have died. I used to receive, every year, a Christmas card from 'Ernst and Lily'. Then they ceased. 'I sent him my change of address when I came up here, but there was no answer. He never looked to me very strong...'

'He was very heavily wounded, by that man who killed Scherer... Vogt was a good man. I mean, he would not have hurt anybody.'

I knew what he was thinking. I never thought 'Madeleine' had been hurt at Avenue Foch. It was afterwards, in Germany.

We returned to the house. I got out my red Fiat, Robin, and took him for a drive through Rushden, then out into the country.

'In your estimation, Kieffer was a better man than Boemelburg?' I hazarded.

'Certainly. If you wish for my opinion, most certainly. But Boemelburg was his chief. What could he do?'

'Can you tell me any more about Boemelburg?'

'He ate much red meat, drank much red wine. And he had a red face. Like all people who eat much red meat, drink much red wine.'

He had never heard anything about his personal life or career. 'We did not speak about him.'

At Knotting we got out and I took him into the church of St Margaret of Antioch. He appreciated the Saxon arch. Then we got back into the car and I drove him down between the two oaks that lean to kiss each other across the road, then round by the moated castle remains at Yielden, and so back home for tea.

'Hitler was a maniac,' he said, out of the blue. 'I knew it the first time I heard his voice, on the radio, not having seen him. I said to my sister-in-law, "If that man ever comes to power, we are lost." That was from the voice only. In 1932. How millions of so intelligent people could follow a maniac is a mystery.' From a silence, he said, 'For me, the war was a long *cauchetnar*, a nightmare. To have the certainty of that defeat, to be able to do nothing about it, and yet to have to do my duty...'

'When did you know the war was lost?'

'After Stalingrad.' (February 1943.)

He apologised for not being able to remember all the details of things that happened over forty years ago. After he received his clearance from the French, he said to himself he must put the war from his life, to resume his interrupted career: 'It is a big bite out of one's life.' As an inspector of schools he visited the USA, Mexico, Paraguay, Tokyo and Nepal. He had a Tibetan prayer-wheel like mine. Like myself, he had done some study in the history of sound changes in Indo-European languages.

'With what do you occupy your leisure?' I asked.

'I play the mandolin. I used to play the organ. My wife and I are both very fond of swimming.' It was their equivalent of my yoga. She was a water-colourist who painted flowers and landscapes. I had feared my meatless table might be too light for him, but he was well read in health and diet, preferred a tea of mint or sage from my garden to any other beverage. He was a non-smoker.

'How did you stop smoking?' I asked.

'In one instant. I lit a cigarette. I said, "That is the last." I put it out.'

He had said he used to play the organ. The church connection prompted me to ask if he was a believer.

'I try to be a believer. Catholic Church. I think religion is one of the bases of our life.'

I asked him — wondering whether we had more in common than would have been suspected — whether his having a Tibetan prayer-wheel meant he had a feeling for the Buddhist philosophy.

'Buddhistic teaching interests me, as every attempt to explain the sense and aim of this life interests me. I think atheism cannot be such an explanation.'

So we did have a deeper common ground. I told him a little of my studies in *The Secret Doctrine*.

To revert from sacred mysteries to profane, could he throw light on one concerning 'Madeleine's' phantom recall? She told a number of people, both agents and personal friends, she was being fetched back to London by the October moon. The Garrys were expecting to go too, by the same plane or another leaving by the same moon. She was expecting to be contacted on 14 October by the man who would escort her to the secret field and board her. She told Vogt, when he arrested her, that she would have been on her way to England the next day. Miss Atkins said there was no plane to fetch her. Déricourt assured me he received no order to contact and board her — or a couple either — and nobody reproached him with having put aboard too few. Verity told me there had never been an operation for which the number to be picked up did not come. I could see from the table we went through together that the aircraft that left by the October moon had no unoccupied places. So what was the explanation?

Goetz had read all the messages exchanged between 'Madeleine' and London from the day she arrived to the day she was arrested, in that copy-book. What was said about it there, in the messages from London?

Nothing, he said.

But then, how could she have got the idea?

Goetz suggested that perhaps she misunderstood something someone had said to her — as she misunderstood the instruction about 'filing' messages.

'Impossible,' I said. There was no one to give her messages from London. It was she who was the radio link with London. Other people sought their instructions from London through her.

Someone told 'Madeleine' something untrue?

Same reasoning applied. Then, I passed in review through my mind all the persons in France with whom she was in contact. Only Déricourt had, in Watt, a wireless link other than herself, and he had no motive to invent a pick-up he would be unable to perform. And she would have suspected a message that did not come to her. Then it struck me there were two people I had been leaving out of count. Placke and Holdorf. They were in contact with her all the time and she still thought them the two Canadians whom they were impersonating. Supposing Placke told her they were all to go in one big party, himself and 'Valentin', she and Garry — for Mme Garry asked for inclusion only when told by 'Madeleine' that it was for a long time their chiefs wanted her husband in London. Placke could have told her the message had been sent to 'Valentin', for oral transmission to her, instead of sending an identical message to her as well. The object, then, would have been to meet Garry. Placke would next tell her they should all be together when 'Gilbert' came to fetch them — only it would not have been Déricourt who came to fetch them. The meeting-place would have been a trap, in which the Garrys as well as herself would have been arrested.

Goetz thought this might, indeed, be the explanation. He remembered that Placke had been hoping to meet Garry, and his only way was through 'Madeleine'.

I remembered Mercier's saying, all that time ago, that he did not believe Kieffer really wanted to arrest 'Madeleine' at that moment; he would have let her run, perhaps until he had got some more. But when Renée rang up, it forced his hand. He could not let a stranger know they sometimes preferred to leave an agent at liberty.

So, if 'Madeleine' had not been arrested on 13 October, and the Garrys on the 18th, they would all three have been arrested together on the 14th. It had come to the same in the end.

Could he resolve a chronological problem? He and Déricourt had dined with Boemelburg on 5 February 1944. But according to Jacques Delarue's *The History of the Gestapo* (Macdonald, 1962), page 244, late in 1943 Boemelburg was transferred to Vichy. 'Had he been to Vichy and returned?' I handed Goetz the book.

'He did not return from Vichy to Paris. In February he had not yet gone. There is a mistake in the date. I notice one or two mistakes.' But he read aloud the description of Boemelburg's deteriorated condition in 1943 and said, 'That is how I remember him.'

Delarue made no mention of Boemelburg's having been at the Embassy before the war. He said he had been in a central-heating firm in Paris, then in the IKPK, forerunner of Interpol, studying with the French measures to combat terrorism, then 'settled in as head of the Gestapo at the rue des Saussaies'. It now struck me that Déricourt had told me at our first meeting that he had known Boemelburg before the war in order to pre-empt an accusation that he had met him prior to 1943, while giving to the meeting a date and setting that made it innocent. 'Do you know where Boemelburg was in 1941?' I asked.

'No. In 1941 I was in the army.'

'Déricourt told me that in 1941 he committed a folly. I am wondering if he met him in that connection.'

Vogt told me that when, in 1940, he was drafted into Kieffer's service, it was at the rue des Saussaies, from which it moved to the Avenue Foch early in 1942.

I asked Goetz if he remembered Agazarian. There was a passage in Foot, page 323: '... he refused to talk, in spite of brutal torture promptly and long applied.'

'I vaguely remember Agazarian. I never heard that he was tortured. At any rate that was not the way I talked to the radios or others with whom I had to do. I am sure you know it.'

I had never been satisfied with Foot's source reference, in a footnote to the same page, 'Note by an SOE officer, 4 April 1945, of interview with Bodington on previous day.' How could Bodington know? I wrote to ask Woods this. He replied, 'I have checked the record of this interview, from which I find the interviewer himself asked the same question.' Bodington's explanation had been that he got it through Jean Maurice Besnard, 'a lawyer with good police contacts'. He got Besnard to make enquiries through these police contacts. In this way he got confirmation of Agazarian's arrest and 'subsequently ascertained through the same source that Agazarian had been brutally questioned for 48 hours, but that after that he had apparently been left alone'. So Foot's account was stepped up from a source which was at best fifth hand and ultimately unidentifiable.

I turned to the plan to mislead the Germans over the date of the invasion. I asked Goetz, 'Did you ever think the invasion would be in 1943?'

'No.'

'You did not think 'Prosper', Starr and the others had been stirred into activity, dropping security, because the invasion was imminent?'

'No.'

'An attempt was made to make you believe the invasion would be in September 1943.' He looked disbelieving. I said 'Yes, really. There are papers which show it. Nothing in the messages you received from London made you think that?'

'No. You should see the telegrams — from England to me and from me to England.'

'They have disappeared.' I was sure the Foreign Office staff were telling the truth when they said they had not got them, had never had them. There was a fire in the headquarters of SOE French Section, after the war, before they had to hand their papers to the Foreign Office on closing down. It was generally supposed the telegrams had been amongst papers destroyed.

'But there is another set!' he said. 'Every day I sent to Kopkow copies of all telegrams I received from England and all telegrams I sent to England. I addressed them to "Kopkow, Reichssicherheitshauptamt, Prinz Albrechtstrasse, Berlin". Where are they now?'

'Is Kopkow still alive?'

'Yes.' He advised against seeking him out, for the same reason Vogt had advised against it.

It was growing dark again and I put on the light. 'The window!' he exclaimed. Even if he thought villagers might look at us, that seemed hardly to account for the urgency in his voice. As I moved to pull the curtains, it struck me that with his training, his instincts told him we were a lit-up target for a marksman. Could he be serious? Now Goetz asked: 'That lady to whom you waved? She will not tell anybody I am here?' Had he been thinking about that all. the afternoon? It was a woman's wave that was the signal for Marsac's arrest.

'She did not know who you were.'

'When I said goodbye to my wife, I said, "If I do not return, you will know it was a revenge-killing." That was joke.' Play-acting now, he said, 'They have not many hours left. Do you think Miss Atkins will poison me or Colonel Buckmaster will stab me in the back?'

It cannot have preyed on his mind, for in the morning, when I asked if he had slept, he said, 'Ten hours.'

He gave me his final impressions of Déricourt. 'His game was always to the profit of the English. He chose an unusual way, a complicated way... He was not ruthless ... He had a morality, even very much sense of responsibility.'

Eddie came back with the taxi. As we drove off, I said, 'It was brave of you to come.' I felt sure he was the only member of the staff of *that* place to have spent a weekend in an English home.

'Now, I suppose Déricourt would have been pleased to make a fortune,' he said, 'mais pas au prix des bêtises.'

Suddenly I remembered a minor puzzle. In 1944, shortly after Déricourt and his wife left for England, some Germans went to his address at the rue Pergolèse, asking the people in the other flats and in the nearest shops where he was, and telling them he worked for the Germans. 'Who could they have been?'

'Bleicher's people. Probably led by Bleicher. Only Bleicher would do a thing like that. To ruin Déricourt.'

It had been my guess also. Clément had told me. He was told by Mme Déricourt, who was told by the neighbours when they returned after the war.

'How did Bleicher learn Déricourt was working for the Germans?' I asked. From Suzanne Laurant's window he could see him enter and leave the house next door, but could not know from that he worked for the Germans. Somebody must have told him.

'Perhaps Placke. Placke and Bleicher were friends. They had the same tastes, habits. Both kept mistresses in Paris. They went to restaurants together, Placke, Bleicher, Hélène Leduc and Suzanne Laurant.'

This was a new piece of information. Placke could have boasted about 'Gilbert', making Bleicher envious.

'But Placke was not mean,' he said. 'Bleicher was mean.'

He asked, 'How old was Déricourt?'

'He was born on 2 September 1909.'

'Then he was older than me! I was born on 7 March 1910. I thought he was younger than me. It was because he did more... was more athletic. So, we were of an age! I would have loved to have met him after the war, when we were both free.'

Relaxed, we had fallen into a silence, as between friends. Out of it, I said, 'Déricourt would be surprised if he could see us now, side by side.'

'He would be surprised ... You can say he was a friend we had in common. Je l'estimais.'

We were at the airport. After we had set him down, Eddie Cunnew said, 'I don't usually get on with Germans, but what a charming man he is.'

My quest was ended. I had only a pilgrimage to make. From Wymington to Varenval is a winding way. My train from Paris got me into Compiègne at 10.32 on the morning of 21 September 1985. I checked in at the Hotel du Nord, breakfasted and came out again, armed with a large-scale map, found the station's taxi rank and asked to be taken to Varenval. At first we followed the north bank of the Oise, then as we left the smooth and shining river the road ran through fields of maize — small fields, a patchwork of tiny pieces. We climbed. Oak-leaves swished the windscreen and on either side of us was every kind of broad-leaved tree. We must be in the Forêt de Compiègne. Suddenly we were in the village. Cottagers of whom we stopped to ask directions identified me at once. Months before, I had written to the owner of Varenval asking if he could tell me anything about the Déricourts. A M. Miroche had replied saying he had not been the owner very long and was trying to sell it, hoping for about £250,000. Did I know anyone who would like to buy it? (Déricourt should have been with me, his pockets bulging with the ill-gotten £300,000 Rusbridger thought he had!) He had shown the cottagers my letter but they had not been there long enough to know the Déricourts either, but he knew M. Déricourt had been *régisseur*. We would see the *régisseur*'s house within the grounds, beside the Château.

M. Miroche was in Paris, but the cottagers directed us. The great gate was open, so we were able to drive in. Dark against the sun, the Château rose out of the morning mist and the enshrouding trees, its tall towers uneven in height and shape.

We circled round to the sunlit front, with a prospect of long waving grass and giant hogweed. The rose-garden mentioned by Déricourt's mother must long have been overwhelmed by nature. But there in the front, encrusted with rust, side by side, were a ploughshare and an enormous pair of wheels, on an axle — the wheels on which Mme Henrie had told me Henri had played as a child. He believed they belonged to a German cannon captured in the Great War. My taxi-driver thought they pulled the ploughshare; indeed, one saw the driver's seat. But to me its long rake-like teeth suggested a harrow.

Beside the Château stood a substantial house. The wife of the occupant of that did not work as a maid. How had Mme Henrie imagined it? She and M. Godbillon had known Henri's parents in their poor beginnings. In M. Fontaine's service they had probably started at the bottom, but they had risen to the top.

The *régisseur* would have managed the estate for its lord, represented him in his absence. Henri's father was the bailiff of Varenval. The bailiff's wife was probably the housekeeper. Henri did not grow up in the basement; he lived in that house, in an upstairs room, for the shape of the doors suggested the ground floor consisted largely of a garage.

The description of Henri's parents' position which I had given Clément on my return from Coulonges, which Clément had passed on to Verity when the letter came to interview him, and which Verity had included in his book (p. 167) with acknowledgements to Clément, was therefore false. Henri may have felt it would be nice to be 'le grand Seigneur', but his parents would have been respected in the village.

I told my taxi-driver to take me on to Jonquières. When Henri's parents relinquished the tied house, he had joined with his brothers in settling them into one of the houses of this pleasant village of seemingly only two streets; but M. Fontaine probably gave them a golden handshake. We stopped at the churchyard and looked for their grave. It was my taxi-driver, Pierre Guibert, who found it. The inscription was simple:

ALFRED DÉRICOURT
1868–1944
GEORGETTE MAGNY
1869–1945

Excepting in social parlance, a wife keeps her maiden name in France. I should have brought flowers to lay beside the china flowers. I had only my meditation to offer to two unpresuming people, who had tried to bring up three sons to lead proper lives, and never dreamed someone from England would look for their tombstone.

27: 'TIMEWATCH: ALL THE KING'S MEN'

In Paris, I looked at the Hôtel Bristol (near the Gare du Nord, which explained its English name), refreshed my memory of the Café-Restaurant Royal-Capucines (opposite Lloyds Bank) and the Avenue Foch. Then I walked up the rue Pergolèse. I had never done this while Mme Déricourt was alive, as Henri did not wish me to go near her. Since her death, however, I had been trying to find out who had inherited her estate. I had written to Clément, but he did not know. I had written to the Gréffier du 16e Arrondissement (Town Clerk to that part of Paris) asking to be put in touch with the notary who had settled the estate. I had also addressed a letter to the Heir or Executor of the estate of Madame Déricourt, at 58 rue Pergolèse, saying I would like to buy Henri Déricourt's flying licence, flight log, passport, papers and memorabilia. As I received no reply, I had telephoned the Gréffier's office from Wymington, fruitlessly. Tim had also telephoned the Gréffier's office from London on my behalf, got a better line and was told I should write a further letter, setting out the whole matter again, from the beginning. I had done so. This time I received a reply from the Gréffier's office advising me to write to La Direction Generale des Impots, 11 rue Tronchet. This sounded like the Income Tax office, but I wrote to it, and at last received an informed reply (I translate from the French):

> ... regarding the inheritance of Mme. PATURAL, Jeanne, widow of m. Déricourt, Henri, domiciled in Paris 16 at 58 rue Pergolèse, deceased 29 November 1984, I have the honour to

inform you that, no heir to the estate having manifested, I was named administrator...

In this capacity, I held an auction of her goods on 2 July, 1985, at the flat of which Mme. Déricourt had been the tenant.

Kindly accept the assurance of my distinguished sentiments.

for the principal inspector

(signed) R. SAVIGNON

If only the Gréffier had directed me to R. Savignon when first I wrote, I could have attended the auction and bid. I wrote again asking who had bought these things, as I would like to make that person an offer. I had no reply. Perhaps they had not been sold but thrown away.

Now, standing in the rue Pergolèse, I rang all the bells at No. 58. The concièrge was away and no one could tell me anything. Then, continuing up the rue Pergolèse, I noticed a small restaurant, over which the proprietor's name was given: IGNACE. That was the name Déricourt had used in the story he had told at Croydon.

I walked on, to the Place des Ternes. There I sat down to rest my feet at one of the pavement tables of the Brasserie Lorraine. Before me stretched the flower-market, its stalls filled with flamingo gladioli. Déricourt's words came back to me. Across that expanse of low flowerstalls, nobody could creep towards him unobserved — unless by dropping on all fours, which would attract attention — so that, providing his back was against something, he could sip his aperitif relatively at ease.

Yet at one of these tables Déricourt had sat with Kieffer's men, the decoy in an ambush set, again, for Bodington, in succession to the failed ambush at the rue de Rome. There Agazarian had been the sacrifice. This time there was no sacrifice, and Déricourt must have wondered if they would murder him for having tipped Bodington not to come.

My book, I felt, should end with Goetz and myself seated side by side, as friends, in the taxi, or perhaps with my finding Déricourt's parents' grave. Anyway, on a note of harmony and healing.

Destiny had a different turn in store. It began with the arrival, soon after my return to Wymington, of Larry Collins's novel, *A Fall from Grace* (Granada, 1954). It was nice of him to have sent me an inscribed complimentary copy, yet I found it troubling. It was in a genre strange to me, fiction, yet with the names and roles of real people, only recently dead or even still living, mixed into it. Scenes set in brothels and torture chambers were probably to procure it a ready sale, but the theme was that a 'Sir Henry Ridley' of MI6 briefed SOE agents with false information as to the place of the invasion and ordered the Air Movements Officer to betray them to the Gestapo, so that under torture they should break down and unconsciously plant that false information on the enemy. I was sure this was untrue. It was meant to be kind to the fictional AMO founded upon Déricourt, in that, by making him do everything in uncomprehending obedience to orders, it lifted all moral responsibility from him — but by making him a tool, it made him a fool.

It was presented as fiction, yet an 'Author's Note' at the end implied that though the characters were 'creatures of my imagining' the underlying story was true — that the Foreign Office Secret Intelligence Service, MI6, had wickedly violated SOE.

The book was not only anti-German but anti-British. The only innocents were the Americans and the French. Collins was an American living in France. In my book I had striven, despite all the bitterness of things past, to heal and offer a spiritual dimension. This could only make hate more bitter.

One passage, however, startled me. On page 293, where real names were suddenly used, was a reference to Starkey and to 'Francis Suttill's summons to Churchill's office in May 1943... Churchill's message to the young SOE officer that day had been simple — and untrue. An invasion in the autumn...' Now where had Collins got that? It appeared like support for that line in Buckmaster's letter to Rusbridger of 12 October 1985, yet did not figure in the script of Collins's interviews with Buckmaster on 28 March 1983, though it showed Collins as insisting to Buckmaster that in July 1943 Déricourt had made a flight to London unknown to him to confer with chiefs in MI6. I re-read Collins's letter to myself of 1 March 1985, telling me Buckmaster was now singing a different tune. Buckmaster had condescended to learn from Collins, and at a date prior to the commencement of his correspondence with Rusbridger.

Then I received a letter from the BBC, dated 26 September 1985, and signed 'Robert Marshall, Producer, "Timewatch"'. It said, 'We on "Timewatch" feel the truth about Déricourt should be properly told', and asked for an interview. This was tantalising. A television tie-in with my new book would be ideal, but I could not provide information to be used in a programme that would be screened long before my book came out. I gave myself a few days' delay, in which to consult first Tim and then another friend, both of whom were of the opinion I must refuse.

Before I had replied, Robert Marshall telephoned. I explained that I was only just finishing writing a book on Déricourt. My old one lacked a mass of information that would be found in my new one but I could not give away secrets from the new one so early.

He said, 'It's an important chapter in British history and must not be suppressed.' He began talking about non-availability of files. I said the person to write to at the Foreign Office was Woods. He scoffed. Woods presided only over SOE files. What he wanted was MI6 files on Déricourt.

So that was it. It was Collins with whom they had the tie-in. He had convinced Marshall that Déricourt was an MI6 agent.

In a further letter Marshall invited me to appear on the screen, but I felt I could not do that without giving away material the reader should learn only from my book; so again I had to refuse. In yet another letter he said they would not begin filming until February 1986, by which time he hoped I would feel differently. In February I received so many telephone calls from 'Timewatch' I began to replace the receiver every time it was 'Timewatch' on the line. I had just hung up on Roy Davies, the series producer, when I received a telemessage from him, saying they had Déricourt's flight log. If I was interested I should ring.

Since May I had been trying to obtain that, being referred from one French official department to another. I felt that I could not accept it from 'Timewatch' but I wondered how they had obtained it.

Christmas had brought a card from Rusbridger, inscribed, 'I miss your letters'. I had felt sure he would be against the 'Timewatch' programme, so I sent him a card in return, asking if he knew about it and assuring him I was having nothing to do with it.

His reply surprised me:

Yes — I do know about the Timewatch film on Déricourt, and have made a significant contribution ... I am quite satisfied Déricourt did work for MI6 while he was in SOE.

I did not write to him again.

I wrote to Woods, warning him to look out for the 'Timewatch' programme, assuring him I was having nothing to do with it. Woods replied that he feared Robert Marshall had 'been beguiled by the farfetched theories of Mr James Rusbridger'.

The *Radio Times* for the week beginning 28 April carried on the page bearing the programmes for 1 May the trailer for the 'Timewatch Special — All the King's Men'. Below, in the middle of the page, was a photograph of 'Prosper' with the word BETRAYED stamped across his forehead, between photographs of Déricourt and Lieutenant-Colonel Sir Claude Dansey. The text implied they were going to say Déricourt betrayed 'Prosper' on orders of Dansey, deputy head of MI6 under Menzies. There was an accompanying article by Larry Collins, leading up towards the advertised idea. For this he offered only two props. The first was 'the deafening silence London offered to French pleas for help' in the prosecution of Déricourt.

No! It was to Buckmaster, not to MI6, the French would have written, notifying him they were prosecuting one of his people and asking if there was anything he would like to tell them. It was Buckmaster from whom they had no reply — and not solely in the case of Déricourt; in every case, including that of Renée Garry. By this reasoning Renée Garry should have been an MI6 agent.

Collins's second reason was that 'Pat', through whose escape route Déricourt left France for England in 1942, would recall on 'Timewatch' that it 'was the only time during the war he was specially instructed by the War Office in London to bring out an ordinary French civilian. Who in London wanted Déricourt out of France and why?'

498

But Déricourt was a pilot. A pilot is not an ordinary person. In war, a pilot is an asset to the side possessing him. When the programme was shown, on 1 May, 'Pat' appeared on screen but said nothing about Déricourt's being an 'ordinary French civilian'. What he said was that the order from London to embark Doulet and Déricourt stuck in his memory as the first occasion on which London had ordered him to embark two 'foreigners'. Till then all the orders he had received were for the embarkation of 'Britishers'. Indeed, the 'Pat' line was used by London for the clandestine repatriation of members of the RAF shot down over any part of France or Belgium. They were filtered out through Paris, Marseilles and 'Pat'. From his point of view he was picking up two locals, whose addresses in Marseilles were supplied to him, yet certainly (as he had said in his letter to me) because they were airmen, wanting to fly for Britain. Thus a particular link between Déricourt and Dansey was not demonstrated by 'Pat's' statement. All escape routes were handled in London by MI9 and Dansey was responsible not only in MI6 but in MI9. Even that would not make a stronger link between him and Déricourt than between him and all the other airmen who came out through 'Pat'. Nevertheless, from this point on in the programme, it was just assumed by the narrator to have been proven Déricourt was Dansey's man.

On his arrival in England, it was asserted, Dansey had confronted Déricourt with having lied about having been in Syria and put him into SOE. Now, I think it probable that 'Syria' was a bit of Doulet's story which Déricourt had borrowed, for glamour, but if he was Dansey's man already why need he have invented it? Was Marshall insinuating that Dansey had blackmailed Déricourt into penetrating SOE?

More significant, said the narrator, was what Déricourt had really been doing. He had been flying for Air Bleu. This was said in such sinister tones as to imply there was something wrong with Air Bleu, that it was a dark secret, brought to light by the penetrating researches of 'Timewatch'. Everybody had always known he flew for Air Bleu. I saw it for the first time in the account of his arrest in the issue of *Le Parisien Libéré* for 29 November 1946 which I had brought home thirty years before. Déricourt did not emphasise having flown for Air Bleu simply because, in snobbish flying circles, to have been flying mail-bags had no cachet. That was why to be flying Vichy Ministers (and other humans), as he was from the beginning of August 1941, was, as Clément had explained, a move up from mail-bags. Nevertheless Air Bleu was perfectly respectable.

Robert Cecil, a retired MI6 officer, whom it surprised me to see appear in a programme such as this, said Dansey disliked Churchill's direction to Dalton to 'set Europe ablaze', disapproved of sabotage in principle and apprehended that an amateur organisation such as SOE, in making noisy bangs all over the place, would get in the way of his own people, who needed to work at their collection of information silently.

Quite. I had always understood from Irene that that was exactly the way Anthony Eden felt about SOE, but nobody had therefore concluded Eden arranged to have its agents sent to their deaths.

We were moved on to the 'Prosper' disaster. This was attributed solely to Déricourt's submission of the mail. *Suppressio veri suggestio falsi* ('Suppression of the true implies the false') is a legal adage that might be applied here. The arrest of 'Prosper', 'Archambaud' and 'Denise' was laid to Déricourt's door. That Christmann and Bodens had met 'Archambaud' and 'Denise' and that the SD had been involved in the affair by

Christmann was suppressed; that Pickersgill and Macalister when arrested had been carrying new crystals and instructions addressed to 'Archambaud' was suppressed. The arrest of the two Canadians, Pickersgill and Macalister, was laid to Déricourt's door; that they had been caught with their equipment in a random road check was suppressed. The arrest of Noor Inayat Khan, monstrously, was laid to Déricourt's door. That her betrayer was known to be a woman and that Renée Garry had been tried for the offence was suppressed. The disaster in de Baissac's network was laid to Déricourt's door. That this resulted from the betrayal by Grandclément, as Buckmaster would have told them, was suppressed. Even the arrest of Robert Benoist was blamed on Déricourt. It was suppressed both that Benoist left France as one of the large party seen off to safety by Déricourt on 19/20 August and that he had returned to France on 2/3 March 1944 — after Déricourt's recall from the field. Benoist had not been arrested until 18 June 1944 — after the Normandy landings and a whole year after the 'Prosper' disaster of June 1943, of which it was made to seem a part. Dowlen's arrest was made Déricourt's fault. That Dowlen, a radio operator, had been caught by D/F while operating his set was suppressed, as was the whole radio-game. Why?

Déricourt having been made into the one great traitor and author of every disaster that befell SOE, the blame was suddenly lifted off him and placed on Dansey, the architect of the holocaust — now revealed as obviously the 'Sir Henry Ridley' of Collins's novel. Apart from Dansey's having had nothing to do with it, Déricourt would have said, 'Thank you for nothing!'

The phantom flight featured importantly. It was asserted that Déricourt had returned to England, in July, for one night only, unknown to Buckmaster, to report on his handiwork to Dansey, 'his real master'. A few words spoken by Verity on the screen were preceded by the voice of the narrator, which Verity might not have heard (in fact he did not hear them) saying that Déricourt's return to France by an even more highly secret MI6 flight, on 21/22 July, was remembered by the pilot who flew him.

After the programme I telephoned Verity, pointing out that this was at variance with what he had written to me on 25 June 1985. He replied that what he had written to me was correct. He did not remember Déricourt as having come over in July, he had taken that from Foot's book; he could hardly expect to remember who was on every flight. The flight of 21/22 July was a BCRA flight. That was what he had meant by 'another service'. Further to this, he wrote to me on 9 June:

> Robert Marshall shocked me by introducing a response to one of his questions, 'There is a pilot who remembers...' When challenged on this, his justification was my reply to a later question, 'Do you remember anything else about that operation?' I replied that Déricourt had gone off on his own after landing. (I remembered reading that.)

So it was as I had surmised when I heard it on screen. Verity had been answering Marshall from out of Foot's book, instead of from his own eyewitness. Here was an example of the difficulty, well known to legal people and historians, of obtaining uncontaminated witness on any matter that has been written about. The power of the printed word can even affect those who were participants in the events. People approached as witnesses think to increase their helpfulness by adding recollections of what they have, read to what they saw and heard at the time. They insufficiently appreciate their status as primary sources. Interviewing them, one really has to make sure; 'This you saw with your *own eyes*?'

The corner of what I recognised as the Cockade document from the Public Record Office was shown on the screen. This will have been Rusbridger's 'significant contribution'.

Buckmaster appeared on the screen. He said he had been commanded to 'summon' 'Prosper' back from France for an interview with Churchill. He said that at that interview Churchill had told 'Prosper' to overlook — forget — all the security he had been taught in SOE and produce a lot of explosions. Buckmaster did not claim to have had an interview with Churchill himself, but he was, after all, 'Prosper's' commanding officer; it would have been rude of Churchill to talk to his man but not to him. Was the Cockade D Day, 9 September, supposed to have been confidential from Churchill to 'Prosper' or was Buckmaster saying 'Prosper' had told him the substance of the interview? Buckmaster sounded hurt that Churchill should have abused 'Prosper' and sent him to his certain doom on a false promise the invasion was imminent. Yet what he was saying now was in direct contradiction to what he had written in his first book, *Specially Employed* (Batchworth, 1952, pp. 186–7) — that he had called 'Prosper' back to tell him that, as he and his people would have to endure for a long time yet without support, they should not over-expose themselves by rash actions; it was a difficult message to give, that 'Prosper' had to restrain the expressions of the *Résistants'* enthusiasm without killing their spirit. Which was correct? One might think the first book, written so much sooner after the event, when his memory would have been fresher and as yet unimpinged upon — though he had begun to go into reverse with the second book, *They Fought Alone* (Odhams, 1959). Yet where could he have got this idea

503

Churchill had instructed 'Prosper' to jettison security? It really was a very grave allegation against Churchill.

Furthermore, in a trailer for the programme signed 'Lawrence Marks' (though obviously composed from what the writer had been told by Robert Marshall), printed in the *Observer* of 27 April, Buckmaster said that 'Prosper'

> was I believe — I cannot prove this and have no knowledge of it other than what I have deduced from other people subsequently — encouraged by Churchill to run enormous risks, to overlook the security training which he'd had over several months, and produce violent explosions ...

The 'other people' to whom he owed this idea were, presumably, Collins, Rusbridger and Marshall. If he explained this in the interview recorded, it had disappeared in the editing, and the viewer was given the impression he came out with this assertion, unprompted, as if from his own knowledge. One must remember that Buckmaster was by this time eighty-three.

Buckmaster was followed on to the screen by Jacques Bureau, a survivor of 'Carte' whose technical knowledge of wireless had been useful to 'Prosper'. He said that when 'Prosper' returned from London, in June, he told him the date of the invasion had been settled. Speaking very rapidly in French, he said, 'I don't know if he said the 9th September, but at any rate the beginning of September.' So the interviewer, whose lead-up one did not hear, must have mentioned 9 September, the fictitious Cockade Starkey date. Bureau's testimony, therefore, seemed to confirm the Cockade thesis, only it was at variance with what Guerne and the Balachowskys had understood from 'Prosper' on his return. Bureau himself said his immediate chiefs were 'Gilbert-Archambaud and Armel Guerne' and it hardly seemed to me credible 'Prosper' would have told Bureau what he kept back from his higher-placed lieutenant — the invasion date, as he had been given it by Churchill. The Abbé Guillaume had cited Bureau only for what 'Archambaud' had said to him when they met as prisoners at Avenue Foch.

In an article in the *Listener* to accompany the programme 'Wartime Secrets', Robert Marshall said that the Cockade date was 'confirmed by two survivors of the "Prosper" network, Jacques Bureau and Pierre Culioli. Both have the clearest recollection of Suttill returning from London with the news that the long-awaited invasion was now just a few months away.' The Abbé had told me Culioli had helped 'Prosper' out of his parachute harness and handed him his bicycle, on which he made for the railway station from which he would take the train to Paris, but that there had not been time for anything that could be called conversation.

Conversation was to have taken place when Culioli joined him in Paris, bringing the two Canadians that were in his house; only he and they were arrested on the way. Culioli had given all his papers to the Abbé, but though Culioli had been twice tried on a charge of having betrayed 'Prosper' and it was therefore incumbent on him to be very exact and complete in the statements he made, neither at the preliminary examination nor in court had he ever mentioned 'Prosper's' now having given him the invasion date. Something funny seemed to have been happening with people's memories, or else they had all been brainwashed.

It remained that Starr was told in May he could this time drop some of the security as the big day was coming soon. For the support of a fake invasion in September, May or even June seemed a bit early for throwing security to the winds.

I will not deny that I enjoyed seeing old friends popping up on the screen — Starr, Rémy Clément... but did all of them understand the theme of the programme? Clément had felt so deeply that Déricourt's posthumous reputation must be protected and he must not be used as scapegoat for the downfall of the 'Prosper' network.

Miss Atkins appeared on the screen and said she had always distrusted Déricourt. In January 1947 she had questioned Kieffer about various people and he had told her Déricourt was not his agent but Boemelburg's, and that photostatted copies of 'Prosper mail had been passed to him bearing a Boemelburg reference number. She had sent Kieffer's statement to London through the usual channels. The inference of the programme was that its not having been acted upon, either to bring a prosecution against Déricourt in England or assist the French in their prosecution of him, proved his protection by Dansey and MI6. It seemed to me none of those responsible for this programme appreciated a point of law. Neither in England nor in France can prosecutions be brought upon a basis of dead men's depositions or hearsay. Kieffer had been hanged at Wuppertal on 26 June 1947. Even had he been preserved until Déricourt was brought to trial, so that he could give his evidence from the box, never having set eyes on Gilbert or BOE 48, he would have been unable to identify Déricourt as either. Had he started to tell the court that Boemelburg told him they were one and the same, he would have been stopped by the President of the Court. As a witness he would have been under the disability Mercier had indicated to me in the case of Vogt. '"Kieffer told me" is not evidence,' Mercier had said, defining hearsay, and he would have added, '"Boemelburg told me" is not evidence either.' The reason why the British had not used

Kieffer's statement was probably nothing more sinister than that it was unusable.

It was not reassuring that Cave Brown had been followed in getting both Boemelburg's and Kieffer's Christian names wrong. One heard from the screen of 'Hans Boemelburg' and 'Joseph Kieffer', instead of, as it should have been, Karl Boemelburg and Hans Kieffer. On the trial papers I had obtained from the Public Record Office Kieffer's own deposition was signed at the foot of every page 'Hans Kieffer'.

Déricourt had been used as a bullet in a gun aimed at Dansey, who was convicted of iniquity on the basis of Déricourt's having arrived in the United Kingdom by the 'Pat' escape line, his supposed flight to England and back in July, which never took place, and the failure of the British to use Kieffer's deposition to prosecute him — which was unusable for the purpose. In this effort Larry Collins was cited as the 'adviser', though Rusbridger figured among the additional credits. I really was staggered by the irresponsibility, and sent off a sheaf of protests to newspapers that very night.

The one to the *Daily Telegraph* appeared on 7 May and began:

> A monstrous allegation was made on BBC 'Timewatch' that Henri Déricourt... betrayed 'the 400' agents of the British 'Prosper' network to the Gestapo, on order from Sir Claude Dansey, deputy head of MI6, in furtherance of a deception plan, Cockade Starkey.

I went on to say that 'Prosper's' network had been penetrated by Christmann, the two Canadians, Pickersgill and Macalister were arrested when a random road check revealed the radio in their car, and Noor Inayat Khan had been arrested on denunciation by a woman.

Robert Marshall's reply on 9 May ignored the Canadians and 'Madeleine', and said merely that Christmann was Abwehr (which I knew) and the arrests were made by the SD. Then came a most extraordinary paragraph:

> It is coincidental that the 'Prosper' network, the one so badly damaged by Déricourt's relations with the Germans, was also involved in a deception plan. To date there is no evidence that Dansey was connected with the plan.

I had certainly thought the whole argument of the programme was that Déricourt did these dreadful things, on Dansey's orders, in furtherance of Churchill's deception plan. If that was not the innuendo, it was misleading to have treated both themes in a single programme, weaving them in and out of one another. If the allegation was that Dansey had ordered Déricourt to betray the 'Prosper' network *not* because the order descended from Churchill, through the High Command, but simply because he, Dansey, disliked it as getting in the way of his own people, that was an allegation of treason, for which he could have been hanged. If that was what Marshall had meant, I would rather he had come out with it roundly.

My reply, though posted that night, did not appear until 19 May, and was then cut down to its first paragraph, explaining that Christmann involved the SD.

The *Observer* of 11 May carried a letter from Foot:

> The 'Timewatch' programme... can only be characterised as imaginative fiction; an ingenious story, but not a true one ... I asked Commander Cohen, the head (under Dansey's distant supervision) of SIS's French Section, whether Déricourt had been an SIS agent; he was sure he had not...

Lieutenant-Commander Kenneth Cohen had had, under

Dansey, the particular charge of Marie-Madeleine Fourcade's organisation, L'Alliance.

From Nigel West I received a welcome letter, saying he had appreciated my protest in the *Telegraph* against 'the BBC's calumny...' He said a lot more, too, which perhaps it would run me into legal difficulties to print.

The *Listener* of 15 May carried a letter from Lord Gladwyn, saying neither Sir Charles Hambro nor Sir Stewart Menzies (Dansey's chief) 'both of whom were honourable men', who had been in the same house as himself at Eton, would have allowed so dreadful and scandalous a thing as the sending of hundreds of Frenchmen to their deaths. Also published was a letter from Anthony Read, on behalf of David Fisher and himself, as authors of the biography of Dansey, *Colonel Z* (Hodder & Stoughton, 1984), saying that while it was true Dansey regarded the weak security of SOE as posing a threat to his own operators,

> ... to suggest... that he would deliberately sacrifice the lives of 400 or more SOE agents is quite monstrous... What we were offered was hardly good enough to indict a man who, however many people disliked him, served his country faithfully and well for over 50 years.

I wrote to Read, assuring him Déricourt had never claimed to have worked for Dansey and I doubted if either man was aware of the other's existence. Read replied, on 27 May:

> I am glad you agree with my assessment of the 'Timewatch' programme as a monstrous piece of mischief... Robert Marshall had been pursuing David Fisher and me, too, but gave up when it became apparent that anything we had to say would cut the ground from under his feet. In all the several years during which we were researching for *Colonel Z* and for

Operation Lucy, which preceded it, we never came across a single mention that Déricourt may have worked for him.

I studied *Colonel Z*. The few lines in an article by Robert Marshall in the *Listener* which had given the appearance of having possibly been founded on inside information had been taken from Read and Fisher's book (without acknowledgement). Marshall had taken *Double Webs* and *Colonel Z*, and married them.

Another point struck me. What people of his own did Dansey have in France in the summer of 1943? From *Colonel Z*, as from Nigel West's *MI6, British Secret Intelligence Service Operations, 1909–1945* (Weidenfeld, 1983), he appeared to have had only L'Alliance, under Marie-Madeleine Fourcade (with whom I had had a memorable tea on 4 June 1954) and those who were on the intelligence collecting side of BCRA, under Dewavrin, 'Passy', Yeo-Thomas's chief. I felt quite sure that from neither of these quarters would there have come a petition to Dansey to have the Buckmaster people betrayed. Between all these organisations was occasional friction, but Yeo-Thomas had been appalled, absolutely appalled, by Guerne's suggestion that 'Prosper' and 'Archambaud', however they had behaved, could have been sent to their deaths deliberately by anybody in London; and Mme Fourcade had seemed to me to have only goodwill towards the Buckmaster networks, though, as she said, without knowing very much about them as they did not have occasion for contact.

On the cover of the May 1986 issue of *Encounter* was a descending parachutist, against the legend, 'Bluff, Deceit & Treachery: An Imperfect Spy Story, by James Rusbridger'. Inside, the subtitle was: 'The Story of Henri Déricourt and an SOE Disaster in France'. This was a piece in which the author described the Cockade deception plan and declared: 'Central to the whole appalling affair was the shadowy figure of Henri Déricourt...'

Much was made of the flight log. (From a letter of Rusbridger's in the *Listener* of 29 May I learned that this and other documents, including Déricourt's flying licence and passport, had been 'unearthed' by Robert Marshall and another in the flat which had been the Déricourts', where they had lain 'undisturbed' since his death in 1962. Does this mean they were picked up in the flat before or after the auction, and did Marshall notify the auctioneer or other authority that they were being removed? When I called, there was nobody with authority to open the flat for me.) I knew most of what was in the flight log already, but it gave the date on which Déricourt commenced flying for SCLAM as 1 August 1941 and confirmed that he began training flights with the RAF in September 1942, within a few days of his arrival in the United Kingdom.

Rusbridger's article contained one point of interest, which he had obtained from Washington — that between October 1941 and June 1942 Déricourt visited H.M. Donaldson at the American Consulate in Marseilles weekly. October 1941 was the date of the affair at the Villa des Bois. I was thankful not to have told Rusbridger about that. He went on:

> It is clear that Déricourt's escape was not something arranged on his own — which has always been his story until now — but was carefully planned by MI9 and SIS.

Whatever gave Rusbridger the idea Déricourt pretended to have escaped 'on his own'? He was proud of having been fetched by 'Pat', following arrangements made between the American Consulate and the British Intelligence Service. He detailed the story in his deposition to the DST and told it to me when first we met — though as I did not see it in 'Pat's' own book I did not then know if it was true. Why did he go to the American Consulate so often? Perhaps just to ask whether there was any news yet from London.

Rusbridger went on:

> Before Déricourt left France, he had somehow acquired enough money to settle his parents outside Paris and to give his wife a substantial sum of money. How Déricourt obtained this sudden and convenient wealth has never been explained... the money might have come from MI6 in London or have been an advance payment from Hans [sic] Boemelburg.

This is nonsense. Déricourt's parents (notwithstanding Foot, p.290)[6] were settled not 'outside Paris' but outside Compiègne. Jonquières, to which I had so recently made a pilgrimage, was a modest village, where the cost of anything could not have been high. According to Mme Henrie, it was the three brothers, René, Marcel and Henri, who clubbed together to settle them. Moreover, since it was when they reached retirement age they had to vacate the house within the grounds of Varenval, and Alfred Déricourt was born in 1868, it would have been well before the war that their sons settled them in Jonquières. Besides, M. Fontaine would have given his faithful *serviteurs* a golden handshake. To imagine the resources of MI6 or Boemelburg or both needed to provide a couple of rooms in Jonquières was ludicrous.

As for the substantial 'sum of money' said to have been given his wife before leaving France, I am sceptical. Doubtless he gave her what he could afford, but she kept on her job as

---

[6] It is always possible that Foot had as his ultimate source some tale told by Déricourt on his arrival in England to make himself a little grander to new friends

hotel telephonist and Rémy Clément's impression was that she was having a lean time.

Then, continued Rusbridger, in January 1943 'he was dropped by parachute near his parents' house outside Paris, where he stayed for a few days...' No, he was not parachuted near his parents' (nonexistent) house outside Paris, but at Prithiviers, in the Loiret, near Orleans, and there was no one for him to stay with there.

Then, Rusbridger went on, after collecting his wife from Marseilles:

> the two of them travelled to Paris with his close friend Rémy Clément. There the Déricourts spent three nights with a SOE agent, Georges Besnard, who sent a message to London telling F Section of Déricourt's safe arrival.

No, Clément did not travel with them, having to work out his notice. Jean (not Georges) Besnard was not and never became a radio operator. He was not and never became a registered agent of SOE F Section. He was already the lover of Julienne, and perhaps already paid the rent of the flat in which she had the Déricourts to stay for three days, but did not call during those three days and so did not meet the Déricourts or learn that such persons existed — until four months later, when Julienne slipped off to London and returned as 'Claire'. Rusbridger must have got his idea of the three nights' stay at the Besnard flat from Collins's tape transcript, but garbled it; or perhaps, as he made no acknowledgement to Collins, it was passed to him by Robert Marshall already garbled.

Then, Rusbridger went on, Déricourt and his wife moved 'to a flat he purchased at 58 rue Pergolèse'. No, not purchased. Here, again, was the implication of wealth. Mme Déricourt was still paying the rent on that two-roomed flat when she died.

One could only smile at Rusbridger's assertion that Boemelburg had been reluctant to testify against Déricourt at his trial. Rather more than reluctant — he had died during the war. But there was an error far worse than any of these. Rusbridger referred to Déricourt as giving the Germans 'details of messages passing between London and the "Prosper"... networks'. The papers Déricourt passed the Germans have always been referred to as 'the mail' (in French, '*le courier*'), the term 'messages' being reserved to radio messages. By treating the terms as interchangeable, Rusbridger had blurred the distinction. Indeed, what could he mean by 'between'? The mail was only one-way, from the field to London. That Rusbridger had fallen into the trap set by his own loose verbiage appeared lower down, where he wrote, 'As a result, captured agents were frequently shown copies of their own signals.' No, they were not. They were supposed to destroy the written texts of the signals as soon as they had transmitted them — not save them up and send them by hand to London at the end of the month (the signals went continually). What went by the planes that touched down at full moons were handwritten reports of background conditions, personal requests and letters to relatives. What 'Madeleine' was shown, for instance, was a photostat of a letter she had written to her mother. As her mother did not even know she was a secret agent or in France, this would have been passed to her by Miss Atkins without indication of where it came from, and the content would have been only an assurance she was well and some expression of daughterly affection. Worse, Rusbridger went on to speculate that Déricourt might have given Goetz 'Archambaud's' security checks. Déricourt was not a radio operator, and therefore knew no code and no security checks. He would never even have seen a radio message. Rusbridger was trying to implicate Déricourt in the radio-game. That Goetz, who ran the radio-game, was also Déricourt's contact was purely coincidental.

Also incorporated was the information I had given him in my letter of 25 January 1984, concerning Bodington's having sent Agazarian to take his place in the trap in the rue de Rome, and the role which that had probably played in bringing Bodington to appear as a witness for Déricourt's defence. I did not feel Bodington's behaviour 'a disgrace'. It could not have been easy to have to stand up in court and say one had used a brother officer to spring a trap, yet I remembered Spooner's comment that if one of those two had to be arrested it was better it should have been Agazarian than Bodington. Bodington knew the composition of every network in France, and had he been broken under interrogation *everyone* would have been arrested. Rusbridger's *Encounter* piece was not merely riddled through with mistakes but without compassion.

The *Listener* for 8 May carried a letter from Rusbridger, in which he referred to the ancient 'Panorama' programme when Buckmaster 'told John Freeman that he had authorised Déricourt's liaison with the Germans', and added:

> ... in October 1984 Colonel Buckmaster told me he had been running Déricourt as a double agent with the help of Sir Dick S. White... but Sir Dick White has told me this was not so.

Déricourt's manner of speaking of Buckmaster precluded, for me, his having regarded him as his chief-in any sense other than that he was the head of the Section.

The *Listener* of 22 May printed a longish letter from myself, in which I stated that both Savy and Clément had assured me that Déricourt was not a passenger aboard the aircraft that left France for England on the 19/20 July. I sent a copy to Verity.

The *Listener* of 29 May carried a letter from Rusbridger, entering the lists on Marshall's side. He used it against me that I had never met or corresponded with Mme Déricourt. This was something Déricourt had bound me not to do, and I had not felt his death absolved me from my word. Rusbridger went on:

> ... it was Robert Marshall and Miss Daniella Dangoor, of 'Timewatch', who unearthed Déricourt's personal papers... These had lain undisturbed in his Paris flat for over 25 years, unseen by Miss Fuller.

Presumably he was inferring I had been slack and had not searched for them. The irony was that I had applied to the proper official authorities; the phrase 'unearthed' did not evoke the atmosphere of the auction room and the making of the successful bid. I had the impression that the 'Timewatch' team had had the good luck to call just when there was someone to let them into the flat. At what date, I wondered, had they made this coup?

Rusbridger's letter continued:

> One still unexplained facet of this intriguing story is the alleged contact between Colonel Buckmaster in F Section and Sir Dick White and Guy Liddell of MI5, who are said to have authorised Déricourt's contact with the Germans. The combination of Guy Liddell, with Anthony Blunt at his elbow, promoting a double agent within SOE to appease the Russians, raises some fascinating possibilities, and might explain how the Communist networks in France were tipped off that the Cockade invasion was a fake and kept their heads down and escaped arrest.

Guy Liddell was not named by Buckmaster in the letter naming

Dick White of which Rusbridger had sent me a photostat.

Rusbridger's concluding sally appeared to take its rise from his imperfect memory of a letter of mine in which — as he seemed interested in Communism — I told him Burdet's story. But that related not to 1943 but to 1944, not to the Channel coast but to the Riviera, not to Cockade but to Dragoon. Rusbridger, quoting from memory, had changed the year, the theatre of war and the code-name of the operation, presumably to feed his obsession with Déricourt and Cockade.

The *Listener* of 5 June contained, in addition to a further letter from myself, one from Marshall criticising Rusbridger's of 15 May for having resurrected an 'old chestnut' that 'Buckmaster... might have been the man who ran Déricourt as a double agent'. Marshall wrote: 'With all due respect to Mr Rusbridger, he has never met Colonel Buckmaster, nor anyone else concerned with the Déricourt story.' It was, Marshall continued, always 'rather curious why Colonel Buckmaster should have made such assertion to Mr Rusbridger', but now, having come to know Buckmaster, he felt he had the answer. When doubts were first raised concerning Déricourt, in 1943 and 1944,

> Colonel Buckmaster encouraged by his delinquent second-in-command Nicholas Bodington, became a tireless defender of Déricourt's record. After the war, as the truth of Déricourt's involvement with the Germans was winkled out, this regard for Déricourt turned to bitter embarrassment. Burdened with a sense of having been doubly betrayed, it was perhaps only human of him to try to protect his credibility by claiming he knew all about Déricourt all along.

Precisely. That was what I had supposed when the 'Panorama' interview took place. Moreover, it was what

Déricourt himself supposed — and found so hilariously funny. Buckmaster, as he now seemed to have authorised Marshall to admit on his behalf, to save face for everyone had given Déricourt an extra layer of cover.

Marshall was now satisfied that Buckmaster 'was *not* the man who had run a double agent in his own outfit'. But why did these people — Marshall, Collins and Rusbridger — assume somebody had to be 'running' Déricourt? I was sure nobody had been 'running' him. It was as if the 'Timewatch' associates were attempting to impale their followers upon the horns of a dilemma: either Déricourt was merely a mean and mercenary traitor, who had somehow got away with his treason, or some Macchiavellian person in London was 'running' him. Now, the dilemma is but a special form of what logicians call the Categorical Disjunctive — fallacious if the opposed propositions presented as the only possible alternatives are not such as to preclude another solution to the problem.

Following my letter in the *Listener* on 22 May I received a personal letter from Verity, pointing out, as though I might not have noticed it, that according to Foot (p. 293) Déricourt spent the night of 20/21 July in André Simon's flat. I wrote in reply, that Déricourt had told me he made a flying visit to London, 'unknown to Buckmaster', which he spent at André Simon's flat, but I remembered the roguish, sidelong glance with which he said it, and thought it to be — not a lie exactly, but one of his whimsical sallies, intended to amuse and confuse, a tease. I told it to Foot, for what it was worth, when he came to see me in 1961, and it turned up in his book.

This brought me a letter from Foot, the first in a very long time. He said Verity had sent him my letter. It was twenty-five years since he had done the research and he could not remember his sources in detail. Yet, so far as he could recall,

André Simon was his source, which he had confirmed from consultation of the log of 161 Squadron. At any rate, he would not have put the story into his History just from me. I could understand that might have nettled him, but it did not dispose of the problem. The log of 161 Squadron did not give the names of the passengers, and it was for that reason Verity had taken them from his (Foot's) book, and from me. The Squadron log would have shown there was a flight from one of Déricourt's fields on 19/20 July, but both Savy and Clément said Déricourt did not travel on it. If he was in Simon's flat on 20/21 July, how did he get there? The preceding flight, of 18/19 July, carried only three persons, all of whose identities were established — Marie-Madeleine Fourcade, with two of her people, Lucien Poulard and Marcel Gaveu. It did not go from Déricourt's area but from near Paris. It was not an F Section flight but an MI6 flight — since it was laid on for L'Alliance — and Déricourt would not have known it was going. Similarly, with the still earlier operations in July one had a number of names equal to the number of passengers, and none of them were Déricourt operations. What the Squadron log would have shown was that there was no flight by which Déricourt *could* have come, save that of the 19/20. He did not come on it; *ergo*, he did not come.

I could only surmise that Simon had misled Foot. He would have gathered from Foot's putting the question that the story was one Déricourt must have told, and perhaps felt he should back it up. His memory may have been genuinely confused, but he had also some motivation. It was he who had recruited Déricourt into SOE, for which reason, as well as from some lingering sense of camaraderie, he may have been disposed to cover for him.

On one issue at least Foot and I were in total accord. He sent me the complete text of his letter to the *Observer*, from which 'the crucial sentence was left out'. It was: 'I discussed with Colonel Bevan, the head of the deception services, what use he had made of SOE; he convinced me he had made none.' Foot concluded his letter to me: 'At least we can agree on one thing, "All the King's Men" was a deplorable programme.'

28: FURTHER DIVERSIONS

May 1986 brought me an offer from a producer, Léon Vitali, for the film rights of *Déricourt*. I remembered Déricourt's having written, 'Films, I don't like them, they distort too much.' So I said the script would have to be submitted for my approval. This did not seem to me an unreasonable condition. It had been happily accepted by Duncan Ross for the BBC in respect of their television play, *Madeleine*, screened in May 1955. Moreover, another producer, Ahmed Jamal, with whom I signed a contract in June 1986 for the film rights of *Noor*, invited me to write the screenplay myself, or, if he did it, to look his script over and tell him if he had made any mistakes or done anything I did not like. So as not to appear merely negative and obstructive in my correspondence with Vitali, I put forward a positive suggestion as to how the sinuous and elusive theme of Déricourt might be handled — along the lines of the classic Japanese film, *Rashotnon*, in which a mysterious event is reconstructed on the screen according to the testimonies of each one of the participants — each time with a difference, so that the viewer is all the time asking himself, 'What *did* happen?'

Vitali said he could not make his offer conditional on my approval. I therefore asked him, through my film agent, if he would, before a penny was spent or the contract signed at all, agree to the following conditions:

> That Déricourt shall not be represented as an agent of Sir Claude Dansey or of the British Foreign Office, or of the Soviet Union, or as a German agent pure and simple, or as an out-and-out villain...

That his wife shall not be replaced by a glossy fictitious heroine.

That the Germans, Vogt and Goetz, shall not be made into 'baddies'. They have received clearances from the Allied authorities, and gave me a great deal of confidence... and I do not want them... libelled, made into brutes or represented in any way they would not like.

That there shall be no torture scene introduced. There is no call for it, as none of the characters in the story was tortured, but I know how some film people love torture scenes.

On 4 December I received a reply from Vitali, saying images of Déricourt, Vogt and Goetz could not be controlled, and my conditions were 'impossible'. He hoped I would accept his last offer — which was by now more than double the original, and seven times more than I accepted for *Noor*. It was the biggest sum of money to which I have ever said 'No', but I instructed my agent to refuse it for me.

On 17 July 1986 I received a surprise telephone call from Pierre Raynaud, surfacing after more than thirty years. He was in England for a few days and would like to see me; he was making an inquiry of his own. He came with a lot of questions and after his return to France sent many more. He also disclosed that he was in contact with Louis Dujardin, who had recruited Bardet into the Frager network, and Dujardin, who proved to be the 'Petit Louis' of Bleicher's deposition, wrote to me that he was collecting material which he hoped to make into a book rehabilitating Bardet. To start with, he did not attribute his own arrest (on 23 June 1943) to Bardet. Bardet had come to see him immediately after his fictitious 'escape' from Fresnes, and told him frankly that he had feigned to Bleicher that he would work for him in order to procure his release. Dujardin told Frager at once, before Frager met Bardet again. Frager was, therefore, not duped for an instant. He hoped, through Bardet's association with Bleicher, to learn something of the Abwehr. Frager warned only one other, Sager, a coal merchant. When he went to London, in the autumn of 1943, and had the opportunity to tell Buckmaster, he kept it from him. Dujardin sent me a copy of Bardet's appeal against execution of the death sentence, in which Frager's failure to tell Buckmaster was explained (as Frager had explained it to Dujardin when they met in Buchenwald):

> London insisted on a very strict separation of the services. Colonel [sic] Frager, as chief of an action group, had not the right to go in for intelligence.

In this case Frager was culpable. His failure to disclose the true situation was clearly a sensitive point, for Raynaud wrote to me that Dujardin had not wished to let him see

> the letters written by Frager to Buckmaster, during his stay in London, as in all those letters, urging on him his conviction of the treachery of Déricourt, he lied to him, on the subject of Bardet, in as much as he did not disclose to him that Bardet was, on his orders, in relation with Bleicher.

In this light I re-read a copy of a letter sent to Buckmaster by Bardet and Kiffer ('Kiki'), jointly, on 10 November 1944 — that is, while they were still awaiting trial — telling him they were charged with intelligence with the enemy and asking him to give evidence for his 'German liaison agents'. They supposed Frager to have registered them as such on his visit to London. Mme Balachowsky, who sent me the copy, had been disappointed at Buckmaster's not coming forward. It was now evident he knew nothing about their position. Frager must also have been less than frank with Balachowsky when they met in Buchenwald: Balachowsky was left with the same impression Frager must have given Bardet on his return to France — that while in London he had told Buckmaster the true position.

Frager's motivation remains obscure. Perhaps he just wanted to keep the game in his own hand. I asked Dujardin if it was true the relationship between Frager and Bardet was homosexual. It was not only Déricourt who had told me this; Collins had also heard it from Culioli. Dujardin repudiated what he considered to be an unworthy smear. All I was thinking was that if there were a special relationship, it could, as Déricourt suggested, explain Frager's closing his eyes to Bardet's faults and covering up for him — though, on the new evidence, he had really landed him in the ditch. Dujardin did confirm that in the First World War Frager had received a wound that prevented his having children; so Déricourt had not made that up.

Nevertheless, when Elizabeth interviewed Bardet, he admitted to her that he knew Vera Leigh was going to a rendezvous at a café where she would be arrested by Bleicher. He offered alternative excuses: that he had warned her, and that it was best she be arrested by Bleicher, which would make her a prisoner of the Abwehr; otherwise, if she were arrested through Déricourt, she would be a prisoner of the SD. This explanation had not made the best impression on Elizabeth.

I grudge no man his rehabilitation, in the measure it can be achieved without injustice to others. In this case, I felt, it was not. It was incidental that Dujardin reproduced the old canard about 'Buckmaster's own secretary hanged for high treason'. This he had been told by Frager at Buchenwald. So Déricourt was not the only one to have misinterpreted poor P's disappearance from the office. The real gravamen of

Dujardin's attack was against Déricourt. Here again he brought out old canards.

Bleicher's deposition contained an assertion it was Bardet who had passed him 'Bastien's' code and wavelength, so enabling him to monitor his transmissions. This Dujardin sought to rebut on the same grounds that Bardet had sought to rebut it at his trial, by a story. The story, urged upon Buckmaster by Frager, was that when 'Bastien' arrived (on 13/14 May) to reception by Déricourt, he left his baggage for some time, on instruction from Déricourt, in the care of 'Marc' (Clément), who must have filched from it his crystals, codes, schedules and workplan and given them to Déricourt, by whom they were given to the Germans. At one of our first meetings Clément had shown me a copy of the allegation, together with a copy of his reply to the DST, which was simply that he had done no such thing. Indeed he had not. What was not known until Foot's book appeared was that after 'Bastien's' departure for France, his crystals, codes, schedules and workplan, which should have been put in the baggage he took with him, were found to be still in England. Thus 'Bastien' was unable to work for four months, until these things were sent on 10 September — and not to reception by Déricourt; they were parachuted. How they then came into Bleicher's hand is a question for Bardet's defenders to answer without reference to Déricourt.

In the whole of this correspondence I had the feeling that while I was trying to be fair to both sides, for Bardet's champions, Déricourt had to be all black. The trouble was that justification of Bardet's double-agency could only be attempted along the lines that it produced some fruit and the one fruit it produced was Bleicher's tip that Déricourt was in relation with the Germans. Therefore, to make the most of this, Déricourt had to be placed in the worst light.

After the 'Timewatch' interlude I never expected to hear from Robert Marshall again, but in September 1986 I was much surprised to receive a letter from him. He, too, was writing a book, on the theme of the programme and proposed a cooperative exchange of information. This seemed to me impossible in as much as our themes were totally opposed. He referred, however, to the Déricourt papers he had. From Rusbridger's letter to the *Listener* of 29 May 1986 I had learned that it was in Mme Déricourt's flat, after her death, that Marshall found the log book, flying licence and other papers, lying 'undisturbed'. My own letter to the *Listener* asking on what date this had been was not printed. Now Marshall mentioned that the papers included Déricourt's novel. I was overjoyed to learn that it had survived. His typist must have put as the sender's address neither her own nor Déricourt's in Laos, but 58 rue Pergolèse, so causing it to come into the hands of his wife, who he had hoped would never learn of its existence. I replied to Marshall telling him that Déricourt had wished me to make the English translation and that I had a letter from his French publisher telling me the English translation rights were reserved to me, by the author's wish. I told him the story of the registered parcel which had arrived while I was in Tunisia and been 'returned to sender' and so lost, and I asked him to be so kind as to send it to me. Without either promising to send it or refusing to do so, he wrote to say it was being translated (perhaps this meant only for his personal perusal as I understand he did not know French), which would take several months. He then asked me questions about Déricourt, including whether I knew what it was that

Déricourt had told Cookridge. Déricourt never told anything to Cookridge. Cookridge (now dead) pretended to know people he did not, including Déricourt. I held Déricourt's letter assuring me that Cookridge's claim to his acquaintance was false; but Cookridge must have lyingly boasted to Marshall he knew him, and Marshall had fallen for his bluff. Marshall's letter ended with a quotation from one of those Cookridge had written to me, saying keeping information to oneself was 'a deadly sin'.

I read Marshall's whole letter over the phone to Tim, who thought it simplest not to reply; so I left it unanswered.

My apprehension that somebody would conceive the idea of representing Déricourt as a Soviet agent was justified in time to include mention of it within the present covers. The spring of 1987 saw the publication of *The Secrets of the Service* by Anthony Glees (Cape). The chapter on SOE could have interested me for the idea it floated that the Communists might not have been averse to the weakening of SOE networks that left their own in control after the war. It was something that had entered my mind as a possibility as, on 3 September 1954, I listened to Burdet telling me his story (which, had he heard it, would have caused Glees to be cock-a-hoop). Glees, however, threw away all credibility when, on the strength of Rusbridger's letter to *The Times* of 4 October 1984, and a trailer for the 'Timewatch' programme, he launched (p.108) the hypothesis:

> It is possible, then, that Déricourt was not directly involved with the Nazis (indeed a French court found him innocent of this in 1948) but only indirectly via Moscow, taking orders from Soviet Intelligence about which particular French resistance leaders ought to be betrayed to the Germans.

Happily, Foot, in his review of the book in the *Sunday Times* of 17 May 1987, dealt with this nonsense:

> Mr Glees, overtrumping Déricourt's own cover story, that he was an agent planted inside SOE by MI6, fantasises that he was really a Russian agent instead. There is not a scintilla of proof.

29: THE DATING OF THE PACT

In July 1987 I received a letter from Jacques Bureau. I had wished I could ask him some questions from the moment of hearing him speak from the screen on 'Timewatch', but had not known how to make contact with him. Now, having talked to Pierre Raynaud, he had written spontaneously. His letter was dated 1 July. He told me he had transmitted for 'Prosper' from March 1943 and also knew 'Archambaud' and Guerne. After his arrest on 14 July, he met 'Archambaud' again at the Avenue Foch, where, together with Vogt (for whom he put in a good word as having behaved kindly) and Starr, they listened to London on the ordinary radio, kept in the guardroom for entertainment. They were cheered by the news of the Allied landings in Sicily.

'Archambaud' had already told him about the pact. I translate from his French:

> His attitude in front of Goetz was remarkable. One day they exchanged a few words in front of me. Goetz asked him:
> 'How goes it with you today, Gilbert?'
> 'As with Sicily!'...
> He said to me, loudly enough to be heard by Goetz (or anyone):
> 'You can give them your material [Bureau had hidden two quartzes]. That has hardly any importance any more. We shall not be here much longer and everything will have ended, for the best!'
> That signified he had given the autumn for D Day. He added, winking, so that Goetz could not see: 'Shed *some* light.'
> I followed his indications, plus those given me by 'Prosper' from a long time back [*depuis longtemps*]:

'Lie but little... Confuse everything. The invasion is close (beginning of autumn).'

Now, it is only fair to say that Bureau thought the story he was telling me was in line with Robert Marshall's Starkey thesis, but in fact it took away the legs from under it.

The 'Timewatch' programme, by introducing Bureau to follow Buckmaster, with his story of 'Prosper's' having been summoned to an interview with Churchill, had certainly given the impression that it was on his return from this momentous interview that 'Prosper' passed on to Bureau the intelligence that the invasion would be in September. Marshall, in his 'Wartime Secrets' article in the *Listener*, had said that Jacques Bureau had 'the clearest recollection of Suttill's return from London with the news the long awaited invasion was now just a few months away'; and Lawrence Marks, in his trailer for the programme, had written:

> Suttill's wireless expert, M. Jacques Bureau, one of the few members of the network to survive the war, says, 'When he [Suttill] returned to France he said, "It's for the beginning of September."'

I had felt an instinctive doubt whether Suttill ('Prosper') would have given intelligence of the highest secrecy, just received by him from Churchill, to Jacques Bureau, who was not an officer of SOE, had not come to London for registration and training and had not signed the Official Secrets Act. Bureau was a local man who had been drawn in, to the 'Carte' network in the first instance, as someone who had the technical knowledge to repair radio sets that were not merely receivers but transmitters. He also had the patriotism to keep quiet about it.

He was, he explained, an engineer. During the first six months of 1940 he was in Lebanon, where he used to listen in to Italian naval stations. He obtained the radio materials he needed from a British contact in Jerusalem, to whom in return he passed on the information he gained. When France capitulated, he asked the contact what he could do to remain active in the war. The contact took his Paris address and advised him to return there and wait. This he did, but London did not get in touch. In the beginning of 1942 someone introduced him to the Tambour sisters, of the 'Carte' network. They lived at 38 Avenue de Suffren, he at 44. In the autumn of 1942 Germaine Tambour told him two English officers had arrived, whom she would like to bring to him. They proved to be 'Prosper' and 'Archambaud'. He never operated a radio set, but they brought him an S phone which had been dropped in a pond and was therefore not working, and, over the months, sixteen radio sets, in order that he might improve their performance. He adapted them, removing some of the parts and replacing them with others, in particular with 'beam aerials', which should be less detectable to the Germans whilst giving almost three times better reception.

From the way he expressed it to me, 'Prosper' could have been telling him for months the invasion could not be far away, just as his own idea, not as a secret briefing from Churchill. I therefore wrote back to Bureau, asking him whether this was something 'Prosper' had been telling him all along, or whether it was something he had told him for the first time between his return from London in the small hours of 20 June and his capture on 24 June. The reply I received from Bureau, dated 30 July 1987, was even more of a surprise. I translate from his French:

531

Between the end of May and the end of June I received a confirmation the invasion would be in the autumn, and that by one of the two Englishmen whom I saw regularly. Was it by 'Prosper', between the 20th and 24th? You have caused me to doubt, now, but I am sure that someone (perhaps 'Archambaud') told me, in the middle of June, something like *London confirms the imminence of the invasion*. Perhaps, after all, it was 'Archambaud', whom I am sure I did see during those last days.

Now this is the letter of an honest man, admitting that after forty-four years he cannot wholly rely on his memory of a detail which had not, until now, seemed to him of such crucial importance. It is certainly not 'the clearest recollection', as Marshall claimed, that it was 'Prosper' between the specified dates. It is not a statement to pit against Churchill's reputation, not the proof that Churchill told Suttill a momentous lie, deliberately betraying him and his into actions likely to cause their deaths. If it was 'Archambaud', he had certainly not been favoured with an interview by Churchill. Moreover, one has to weigh this impression of Bureau against the quite contrary one of Armel Guerne, that 'Prosper' had come back from London raging with despair because the invasion was not, after all, going to be at once. Even if one doubts Guerne's assertion that 'Prosper' intended to call the Resistance out so as to force the hand of the High Command and make them mount the invasion at once — which may have been something 'Prosper' exclaimed that he 'felt like' doing — one may incline towards the recollection of Mme Balachowsky, that whereas 'Prosper' had been very eager for the invasion to be that summer, when she saw him on the afternoon of 20 June, the day of his return from London, she found him aged and depressed because the invasion was not going to be yet — and he did not think he could keep his network intact for another year. The summer of 1944 would be too late for him, and all the people of whom he was chief. They would all have been arrested before then — as indeed it turned out. Hence his gloom at the last meeting with Mme Guépin, the night of 23/24 June.

As for Déricourt's alleged role, as the kingpin in the Cockade/Starkey deception plan, Goetz, who has kept in touch with me by letter and telephone, feels he has the complete answer. If it had been as Collins, Marshall and the rest of the 'Timewatch' people believe, that Déricourt had been briefed by the British Intelligence Service to plant misinformation on the Germans concerning the invasion plans, 'He should have been telling us, Calais! He did not.'

On 6 January 1988 I received unexpectedly a letter from Pierre Raynaud saying that after years of trying to discover the date of the 'Prosper' pact, he had at last thought of writing to the Hôpital de Gisors, to ask the date on which George Darling was admitted with the gunshot wound of which he died there. He was told it was 25 June 1943. Now, when I called at the Hôtel Mazagran on 26 November 1956, the proprietress, Mme Esther Fèvre, told me it was about 1 a.m. on 24 June 1943 that a party of Germans entered, asked which room was occupied by M. Despret (the name under which 'Prosper' had registered), seized the register and saw that it was No. 15. Then some of them sat with her, while others went upstairs, presumably to 15. They had to wait until between ten and eleven in the morning, before he came in, went up to his room and was brought down a captive. It was, therefore, after not forty-eight but only about twenty-four hours that 'Prosper' concluded the pact with Kieffer. Given that Vogt remembers an interrogation through the night, it was probably around the breakfast hours of the 25th that the pact was concluded and

'Prosper' wrote the letter to Darling which Placke and the escorting party took to him at Triechâteau, resulting in his being shot as he tried to escape. 'Prosper' had concluded the pact and written the letter to Darling pretty quickly: Déricourt had been right.

30: NAMES TAKEN IN VAIN

Robert Marshall's book, *All The King's Men*, appeared in January 1988. I cannot say worse of it than that it resembled his television programme. He appeared to have worked mainly from the papers Larry Collins had handed over to him, with Rusbridger's Cockade papers as an insert — not really integrated in his theme, which seemed to be that, not on orders from Churchill but moved by some personal dislike of SOE, Sir Claude Dansey had taken it upon his own initiative to instruct Déricourt to betray to the Germans nearly a thousand men and women. The papers supplied to Marshall by Collins and Rusbridger did not prove this, and he presented his own suppositions as facts. Some of his source references did not bear examination.

On page 102 Marshall wrote:

> Déricourt and Bodington always referred to Boemelburg not by his real name but by the soubriquet 'notre ami'.[28]

Curious, I looked up the reference and was astounded to read:

> 28 Déricourt correspondence with Jean Overton Fuller, undated.

My correspondence with Déricourt had not been seen by Marshall, or by anybody (except for the last letter, which I showed to Goetz). Neither had Déricourt written to me anything of the nature 'sourced' to our correspondence. On the other hand, as we sat and talked he had told me that, when trying to intimate to Bodington, during their stay at the country place Besnard had taken for 'Claire', that he was in contact with the Gestapo, he had said to him, in the kitchen, something about having seen 'old friends' again. I had written this into the first draft of this book, then taken it out, in case his apparent counting on Bodington to know what old friends he meant might appear to incriminate Bodington, in a way that Déricourt would not have intended. How had something I had never published become known to Marshall? I looked through the file of my correspondence with Rusbridger and found that on 28 December 1984 I had written to him concerning the days Déricourt and Bodington had spent together under Besnard's roof:

'He [Déricourt] said, "I have been meeting old friends again."'

Continuing my perusal of Marshall's notes, I was further astonished to read, oh his page 283;

> Déricourt writes a great deal about the 'little people' in a series
> of letters to Miss Overton Fuller during 1959–62.

There was nothing about 'little people' in any of the letters Déricourt had written to me, but again there was an aural reminiscence — something he had said to me in the street. I looked through all my files and found in the tape-transcript of the interview I had given Larry Collins on 24 March 1984 that I had said concerning Déricourt's attitude:

> He did feel that it was the British old school tie brigade who
> were making use of the little people in France.

I was extremely vexed that Marshall should have claimed to have found these bits in Déricourt's letters to me, because such 'sourcing' must convey the impression I had granted him access to my house and papers, whereas he was the very last person I would have allowed to see them.

Had he really seen them, he would have known that Déricourt's letters to me ran not from 1959 to 1962 but 1957–61. He would also have seen that for three years I wrote to Déricourt c/o Air Laos, and not made the mistake of writing that Déricourt only pretended to be working for Air Laos.

Fortunately, an opportunity was soon afforded me to make public that I had not granted Marshall access. *All The King's Men* was the subject of a review in the *Sunday Times* of 24 January, by Professor Foot, beginning, 'Bad books on SOE abound. Alas, here is another.' Marshall, he observed, omitted to say how he supposed Déricourt and Dansey to have been able to communicate. The point was well made, for Déricourt was not a radio operator, nor had he a radio. But the review made some mention of my name, and this gave me the occasion to write to the *Sunday Times*, 'I should like it known that whereas Robert Marshall cites as source for some of his statements,' Déricourt correspondence with Jean Overton Fuller', my correspondence with Déricourt has never been seen by Robert Marshall or by anybody.' This was published on 31 January, under the heading 'Unpublished Correspondence'.

I found a piece of obvious fiction on Marshall's page 106, where he represented Déricourt as having, on the afternoon of the day he was first parachuted (23 January 1943), gone to Coulonges-en-Tardenois to visit his parents: 'He waited in the small bar until his mother returned from work ... on departing left his mother a large wad of notes.' It suited Marshall's theme to have Déricourt rich at that time, but Déricourt's parents left Coulonges-en-Tardenois when he was a child. Marshall was plainly ignorant that during most of his childhood and youth they had been at Varenval (where his mother's post was a live-in one) and that by this time they were retired to Jonquières. Had Marshall realised Déricourt's mother was born in 1869, he might have reflected before representing her as going out to work in 1943.

Continuing my inspection of Marshall's book, I saw that on page 250 he wrote of the B messages (from which Goetz knew the invasion would be on the morrow) that 'many of them came from Déricourt, who had handed them over to Boemelburg in the back of the car'. Even I knew this must be wrong. It was certainly not what I had understood from Goetz. Moreover, Goetz had ceded to Marshall's petitions for an interview on condition of not being questioned concerning Déricourt, since he had given me his word not to talk about Déricourt to anybody else until after my book was out. I posted him a photocopy of the page, and he replied at once, repudiating Marshall on ten points:

16.1.88

Dear Jean,
  Have my answer — as fast as I can.
  1. I never gave Marshall the informations he pretends having from me...
  2. Déricourt may have known that every agent had an A and B message. But I think it absolutely impossible that he knew the text of the messages of the different agents, except those he had for his own use (if any).
  3. Every agent was given an A and B message (for himself only) before leaving England. Déricourt could not have known them.
  4. Déricourt *never* gave me *any* A or B message.
  5. The story about handing over messages to Boemelburg must be ridiculously wrong, because he could not have known other agents' messages.

6. The 15 A and B Messages Marshall refers to were the messages of the agents who has been captured and in whose place I made the Funk-spiel with London. The agents, when captured, had given them, during their interrogation, to Vogt, who informed me of them.

Best wishes and regards,

JO

Funk-spiel is German for radio-game.

Marshall's pages 261–2 carried what was given as Goetz's deposition to the DST. I got out my photocopies of the original and found the translation not exact. For instance, Marshall cited him as saying:

He [Déricourt] handed over agents' mail en route for London. Technical reports, political reports.

What Goetz had actually written, on page 6 of the original was:

[lines 9–16] I remember only one occasion on which he handed me a political report... concerning Edouard Herriot... Another concerned the bombing of Boulogne-Billancourt. It was a purely technical report on the effect of the bombing. I do not know where it came from. A third was a general review of the political scene.
[lines 19–20] I think I can affirm that Gilbert [Déricourt] never gave, in my presence, reports with the addresses of agents in France.

It should be noticed that these lines, which will have been noted by the *juges* as favourable to Déricourt, are omitted from Marshall's transcription, without omission marks to show that anything has been left out.

Against the code-names 'Marc', 'Geoffroi' and 'Claire,' Marshall has written in between round brackets — as though they figured in Goetz's deposition, which would suppose them to have been supplied to him by Déricourt — (Rémy Clément), (André [sic] Watt) and (Juju). Both Goetz and Vogt had told me they never knew the civic identities of these people or where they lived. Julienne Besnard was by her husband, Déricourt, Clément and Watt given the dignity of her name in its proper form. Marshall's insertion into Goetz's statement of this nickname implies a misleading familiarity.

There is worse. On page 4, lines 27–9, Goetz wrote:

> D'une façon générale, lorsqu'une opération était dévoilée par GILBERT [DÉRICOURT] et mis à pied par BOEMELBURG, il était établi qu'aucun des arnvants ne devait être arrêté.

This means:

> As a general rule, when an operation was disclosed by GILBERT [DÉRICOURT] and set afoot by BOEMELBURG, it was agreed the arrivals should not be arrested.

Marshall, however, renders it:

> By his information on his air operations GILBERT enabled us to carry out our arrests.

Goetz does indeed go on to suppose this had been agreed between 'Gilbert' and Boemelburg because the 'brutal and immediate arrest of the agents as they arrived upon the soil of France would grill Gilbert'. On the following page he also cites the instance when, in despite of the general rule, some time in November or December some of the agents arriving were arrested at the Gare Montparnasse, but he makes it clear that this was on the initiative of Henri Chamberlin ('Lafont') because he saw that there were French police checking the papers of all passengers and looking through their things, and he thought Boemelburg would not wish anything carried by the agents to fall into the hands of the French police. Goetz adds that 'Boemelburg was absolutely furious over that, because it risked grilling Gilbert.'

Significantly, this is not a passage reproduced by Marshall. It is very important, because it gives the lie to the allegation often made that it was for the arrest of the three agents taken that night that Boemelburg paid Déricourt a tremendous sum of money. So far from being willing to reward anybody for it, Boemelburg was furious that it had occurred. (As Goetz put it to me, the trailing-people had, in an emergency, misjudged what Boemelburg would want them to do, being ignorant of the order of priorities in Boemelburg's mind, as nobody had explained the game to them.)

It is also true that on page 8, lines 15–18, Goetz permits himself the surmise that Gilbert 'sacrificed some men and some information, in order to work more surely with others'; but that is imputing to him a strategy not in the German interest. What he told the DST is not really out of line with what he said to me so many years later. His deposition was thoughtful and nuanced. It was not at all the simple, damning piece tailored to suit the prosecution which is presented by Marshall. Nor does Goetz make any reference to B messages in the parts of his statement that concern Déricourt.

I was considering the passage in Marshall's book that purported to be an extract from Goetz's deposition when it occurred to me that Goetz might never have been given a copy of that deposition — which of course would not have been in his own words but those of the interrogating officer. I had a set of photostats made, which I posted to him with photostats of Marshall's pages 261–2, bearing his very free translation. Goetz replied, on 7 February 1988, to thank me and make some comments. The first few concerned the deposition itself. He could not remember going with Déricourt into Boemelburg's villa at the end of the ride in the car during which he first met him. 'I only remember that the first meeting of the three of us was the last one in February 44.' He thought something had gone amiss in the DST formulation. As to Marshall's rendering of it, he wrote:

> Marshall's book, p.261: I never told anybody that 'I had deduced that the massive arrests which had occurred in the Buckmaster networks were due in part to information previously supplied to Boemelburg by Gilbert or Déricourt', this is a pure invention of Marshall...
>
> Marshall's book, p. 262: It is wrong to say that 'By his information on his air operations Gilbert enabled us to carry out arrests'. On the contrary our service was urged not to make arrests.

31: THE CHEQUERED SPY

I had seen the evolution of so many theories concerning Déricourt — from the deplorable traitor to the MI6 agent. Yet none of the theorists had really known him. He was, for them, a two-dimensional piece to be fitted into their jigsaw. I, on the other hand, had known the living person.

What I remembered always was the man who, relaxed at the luncheon table, confided to me that had he told the truth to his court-martial it must have meant the firing-squad. He never would have said that had he been innocent, authorised and ordered to do all that he did by a senior officer of the British Intelligence Service. Finding himself charged, Déricourt would surely have said to his *juge d'instruction*, 'Ask Sir Claude Dansey for a reference' The very name would have created a stir. The Secret Service may be secret, yet not so secret that at the DST that name would have not been known. Mme Fourcade told it to me openly. Had she, her OBE notwithstanding, found herself charged by the French with the murder of Blanchet, I am sure she would have had no hesitation whatever in telling them, as she told me, 'Dansey told me to kill him.' When Déricourt was charged, Dansey was still alive, though retired to the country. He could have been reached through the Foreign Office. Yet Déricourt did not ask his wife to go to England and find Dansey. He asked her to go to England and find Bodington.

There was that chapter in his life unknown to anyone but me. The mousetrap house in which he had done 'something bad' in 1941 was the Villa des Bois. The 'person of weight and consequence' who had told Hérissé that Déricourt had been

543

arrested at a very early stage of the war must have been Philippe de Vomécourt — careful not to expose himself to questioning as to the role he himself was playing when he came by such information. But was he correct in adding his conclusion that when Déricourt had left France in August 1942 it was with German permission, therefore to act in Britain as a German agent?

Had Déricourt been obliged to reveal to the Vichy police or Boemelburg his contacts with Doulet, the American Consulate and 'Pat'? Had he betrayed the 'Pat' line? I re-read the book about 'Pat' by Vincent Brome, *The Way Back* (Cassell, 1957). The 'Pat' line had suffered at the end of 1941 from the treachery of Harold Cole, but though a number of his people were arrested and the Germans were, thereafter, on his trail, 'Pat' managed to continue right up until March 1943. Had the Germans *let* Déricourt 'escape', they might have abstained from arresting 'Pat' at once, so as not to cause Déricourt to be suspected. But for how long? Not from August until March, surely. 'Pat' had no doubt his betrayer was a person calling himself 'Roger le Neveu', later killed. Was it not possible, therefore, that after the affair of the Villa des Bois had died down, Déricourt had been able to make a genuine escape with Doulet by the 'Pat' line, without informing the Vichy police or the Germans?

His having started making training flights with the RAF in September supported what he had said to me, that his first intention had been to become a pilot for Britain. Had he done so, his record would have remained clean. It was the transfer to SOE that was unfortunate.

I tried to check with Woods whether it was Simon who had introduced him. There was no record of who had introduced Déricourt, but Woods (who had missed the 'Timewatch' programme) looked out André Simon's record for me and found that he had been commissioned in the RAF before being introduced to SOE by de Guélis, whose job as Briefing Officer he later took over. He would have been in that job when Déricourt actually joined SOE on 1 December, though they could have met earlier. There was also a regular liaison officer between the Air Ministry and SOE.

To me, it seemed all important that Sporborg vouched for Déricourt's having told him he had contacts with German Intelligence. Sporborg will not have realised how deep, but it was Sporborg's fault for not having asked Déricourt how deep. There was no record of Déricourt's having been to Ringway and he told Clément he had declined the offer of a course because he could as easily break a leg on a training jump as on the real thing. Had he been a German spy, he should have welcomed the chance to attend the parachute school, in order to be able to report on it. Even his having been at the Bristol seemed to me to tell in his favour. Had he returned to France as a German agent, he would have taken an obscure lodging, such as *Résistants* chose. To go straight to an hotel full of Germans and collaborators was a defence, for it would enable him to say to any awkward acquaintance from the past, 'I have not been hiding from you!' Then he could tell some story about having been to the mysterious place whence he obtained the black market oranges he sold them. It was a good bluff.

But then something went wrong. It could even have been when those two German airmen called on him at the first flat, on the rue Colonel Moll. He could have felt they were suspicious, and that he could come to be under pressure. By chance Verity recalled him to England. He told me that while he was in England at Easter he managed to speak with someone higher than Buckmaster, and — without being too plain, because he needed to feel the ground before unburdening himself of what was in his mind — spoke some words which ought to have caused this officer to understand there was in the organisation a person who had been in German hands through the affair at the Villa des Bois... words which ought to have caused the officer to show a very considerable reaction. The way in which what he said was received, without alarm or perturbation, as if its import had not been grasped, caused him to suppose that the officer already knew. It was this that gave Déricourt the idea that some game was being played. His attempt to warn London of a situation 'very grave for the French Section' had failed, and he took his 'own measures'.

Who was that person? Could it have been Sporborg? Sporborg was higher than Buckmaster, and how indeed did Déricourt come to have met Sporborg? No other agent in the field that I know of did. Starr met no one higher than Buckmaster and his rank was higher than Déricourt's. Yet it is from Sporborg we learn Déricourt told him he had contact with German Intelligence. For him to have dismissed this disclosure in so cavalier a manner he cannot have taken it seriously. Perhaps he thought it was only a claim to be selling them black market oranges, and did not realise much more would come out, given a little encouragement. Did this strange snatch of conversation take place before Déricourt was first parachuted into the field, or during this Easter period? This, according to what Déricourt told me, was crucial. Cockade seems to me a side-track. If Déricourt got any sniff of it, it would have confirmed his suspicion the English were playing games; and one should remember what he said, 'We were open to tales.' Whatever it was that happened, he assured me that it was during those days in England, before he parachuted back, that he decided what he would do when he returned — go to Boemelburg, with a proposition that would prevent his being brought to him willy-nilly. If he left it for the Germans to arrest him, he would have no scope for manoeuvre. By offering them, against immunity for his operations as Air Movements Officer, the eventual invasion date and place (a promise he had no intention of keeping and would not even have had the information to keep), he preserved his team in safety, for the very small sacrifice of the handwritten mail — mainly background reports concerning conditions in France, effects of RAF bombing raids, requirements, personal letters to relatives and so on, plus some details of the training schools he recalled from André Simon's careless talk. The massive arrests of June were not foreseen by him and not caused by him. The casualties of his confidence trick on the Reich were four, not four hundred, and he regretted them. They resulted, Goetz assured me, not from deliberate violation by the Germans of their accord with him, but from mistakes by their French underlings, the trailing people. The deal which Déricourt did with the Gestapo was not authorised by British Intelligence, yet it would have paid them to authorise it. In his dealings with the Germans he was careful to give away only what would do the least possible damage. He was a better chess player than his chiefs.

It was a loyal treason.

APPENDIX A: DRAMATIS PERSONAE

Germans

At the Avenue Foch (SD)
Boemelburg
Kieffer
Goetz
Vogt (Ernest)
Placke

Abwehr in Paris
Bleicher

Abwehr in Holland
Giskes
Huntermann
Christmann
Bodens

British and French

'Prosper'
'Archambaud'
'Denise'
'Madeleine'
'Phono' (Garry)
Culioli
The two Canadians, Pickersgill and Macalister
Starr
Yeo-Thomas (RF)
'Carte' (independent)

Frager (independent)
Basin
de Vomécourt brothers
Turck (Escapes Section)

Double Agents

Déricourt

'La Chatte' (former head of Interallié, later controlled by Bleicher)

Kiffer (former agent of 'La Chatte', controlled by Bleicher)

Bardet (agent of Frager, controlled by Bleicher and rival and enemy of Déricourt)

APPENDIX B: DATES FOR REFERENCE

1909
2 Sep: Déricourt born.

1930
9 Aug: Sergeant-pilot on Reserve List.

1935
Nov or Dec: Joined Air Bleu: Paris-Rouen-Le Havre.

1936
end Jul: Furloughed from Air Bleu.

1937
c. Jun: Resumed flying for Air Bleu: Paris-Pau-Bordeaux.

1939
2 Sep: Mobilised.
3 Sep: Britain at war with Germany.

1940
20 Apr till Armistice: Test pilot.
After Armistice: Returned to civilian flying, based on Marseilles, living with his future wife.

1941
Still living with his future wife in Marseilles, flying between there and other places in France.

4/5 May: Bégué parachuted, 'blind'.

6 Aug: Jurck and de Guélis parachuted, 'blind'.

17–24 Oct: Arrests at Villa des Bois and Villa Bernadette.

18 Nov: 'La Chatte' arrested.

11 Dec: Cole arrested.

13 Dec: Déricourt married.

1942

26 Feb: 'La Chatte', Pjerre de Vomécourt and Cowburn take boat for England.

6 Mar: Operation North Pole begins in Holland.

1 Apr: Pierre de Vomécourt parachuted back.

25 Apr: Pierre de Vomécourt arrested.

Jul: Doulet in Aleppo.

15 Aug: Déricourt and Doulet leave France from Narbonne by 'Pat'.

8 Sep: Déricourt and Doulet land at Greenock, Glasgow. Déricourt, after clearance at Patriotic School, posted to RAF station at St Mawgan, Newquay, Cornwall. At Tempsford some time in the autumn.

1942

24/25 Sep: 'Denise' and Lise de Baissac parachuted, to reception by Culioli.

1/2 Oct: 'Prosper' parachuted, to reception by Culioli.

2 Nov: 'Archambaud' parachuted, to reception by Culioli.

10 Nov: de Guélis reports his arrival in Algiers.

1 Dec: Déricourt signs the Official Secrets Act and joins SOE. Attempts to parachute him by the December moon fail because of bad weather; he is at Tempsford at Christmas.

1943

22/23 Jan: Déricourt and Worms ('Robin') parachuted, 'blind'.

26 Jan: Déricourt at Marseilles to recruit Clément and fetch wife.

Feb: First three weeks at Hôtel Bristol, then at r. Col. Moll.

17/18 Mar: Déricourt's first operation, from Poitiers.

23/24 Mar: Marsac assists Peter Churchill in receiving a Lysander, by which Churchill and Frager depart.

27 Mar: Marsac arrested by Bleicher. Marsac puts Bleicher into contact with Roger Bardet. Bleicher obtains address of Odette, at St Jorioz, where he visits her.

14/15 Apr: Accident with tree on Déricourt's field.

15/16 Apr: Peter Churchill parachuted back, to reception by Odette. They are arrested by Bleicher on return to their hotel at St Jorioz.

22 Apr: Tambour sisters arrested.

22/23 Apr: Déricourt returns to Tempsford for refresher course.

5 May: Déricourt parachuted back, 'blind'. Move to rue Pergolèse about this time.

13/14 May: 'Prosper' leaves for England.

19/20 May: John Starr parachuted, 'blind', into Jura for work in Dijon area.

20 May: Intervention of Christmann and Bodens. Sq. Clignancourt imbroglio.

20/21 May: 'Antoine' (Antelme) parachuted on second mission.

9 Jun: Royal Capucines imbroglio.

15/16 Jun: The two Canadians, Pickersgill ('Bertrand') and Macalister ('Valentin'), parachuted, to reception by Culioli.

16/17 Jun: N. Inayat Khan ('Madeleine'), Diana Rowden, Cecily Lefort and C. Skepper received by Déricourt.

'Madeleine' begins to work with Garry and 'Archambaud'; Rowden goes to work with Starr; Lefort goes to Savoy to work with Cammaerts, Skepper goes to Marseilles to organise new network.

20 Jun: 'Prosper' parachuted back, to reception by Culioli.

21 Jun: The two Canadians, Culioli and 'Jacqueline' arrested.

24 Jun: 0.00–0.15 'Archambaud' and 'Denise' arrested; 10–11 'Prosper' arrested. Lyon and Bonoteaux landed to Déricourt, Bonoteaux arrested later in the morning.

25 Jun: Darling shot, arrested and hospitalised.

29 Jun: Goetz returns from leave and begins radio-game.

1 Jul: Worms and Guerne arrested.

2 Jul: Balachowsky arrested.

18 Jul: Starr arrested (through local betrayal).

18/19 Jul: Antelme ('Antoine') seen off by Déricourt.

22/23 Jul: Bodington and Agazarian landed to reception by Déricourt. Agazarian goes to appointment made over 'Archambaud's radio, and is arrested.

16/17 Aug: Bodington seen off by Déricourt.

7 Sep: Arrest of Fox and Rousset ('Leopold').

13 Oct: 'Madeleine' arrested.

18 Oct: Garry and wife arrested.

30 Oct: Vera Leigh arrested.

15/16 Nov: Operation Conjuror. Maugenet betrays Rowden and John Young, probably next day or day after.

end Nov or early Dec: Yeo-Thomas reports suspicions of Déricourt.

1944

13 Jan: Y. Beekman arrested through D/F (wireless direction finding instrument) or local betrayal.

3/4 Feb: Morel tries to bring Déricourt back.

8/9 Feb: Déricourt and wife return to London.

29 Feb: Antelme ('Antoine'), Lionel Lee (another wireless operator) and Madeleine Damerment parachuted to German reception by appointment over 'Madeleine's' radio (supposed to be received by Garry).

29 Feb: J.T.J. Detal (a Belgian) and P.F. Duclos parachuted to German reception appointed over 'Leopold's' radio (supposed to work with Fox).

2/3 Mar: MacBain, Finlayson (another wireless operator), Lepage, Lesout, Sabounn and Rabinovitch (another wireless operator) dropped to German reception, by appointment over the 'Valentin's' radio (supposedly to work with Pickersgill); Defendini arrested at contact house for Sabounn.

17 Mar: Octave Simon and Defence (Dédé) (another wireless operator) parachuted to German reception by appointment over 'Leopold's' radio.

27 Mar: Skepper, Eliane Plewman and Arthur Steel (another wireless operator) arrested in Marseilles, through local betrayal.

6 Jun: D Day: Invasion.

8 Jun: Robert Benoist arrested.

2 Jul?: Frager arrested by Bleicher.

17 Aug: Avenue Foch staff withdraw from Paris.

20 Aug: Allies enter Paris.

1 Sep: Déricourt enlists in Free French Air Force.

9 Sep: Déricourt hospitalised after crash-landing.

1945

8 May: Germany surrenders.

1946

26 Nov: Déricourt arrested.

1948
8 May: Déricourt acquitted.

APPENDIX C: DÉRICOURT'S CROIX DE GUERRE AND LÉGION D'HONNEUR

To obtain the text of the citation for a French decoration is not easy. As it was explained to me by the Assistant Army Attaché at the French Embassy in London, in a letter dated 14 March 1985, information about decorations is given only to the recipient or, in case of his being deceased, his next-of-kin.

I explained that the deceased, M. Henri Déricourt, had no children. His widow was deceased. His mother and father were deceased. He was the youngest of three brothers, of whom the two elder, M. René and M. Marcel Déricourt, were deceased. The difficulty of this situation was appreciated, and I was referred to French official departments in Vincennes, in Paris and finally in Pau. From Pau I received a letter of 15 September 1986 from a Lieutenant-Colonel Gulka-Tarroux, saying that if I would send them a photocopy of the procuration of 8.3.1960 given me by Déricourt, which I had mentioned, satisfaction would be given to my request. I sent the photocopy, and on *22* November 1986 had the joy of receiving not merely a typed text of the citation for the Légion d'Honneur, which was all I had expected, but a certificate for his Croix de Guerre with Palm, with red, white and blue border and golden replica of the medal encircled with laurels, and a similar certificate for his Légion d'Honneur. He had told me (even in writing) he had no medals, but the Palm is the highest embellishment that can be added to a Croix de Guerre. He thus had France's highest gallantry medal.

RÉPUBLIQUE FRANÇAISE
Guerre 1939–1945
CITATION
Extrait de la décision no. 160
Publiée au Journal Officiel de 22 Juin 1946

Le Président du Gouvernement provisoire de la République française cite à l'ordre de l'armé
Déricourt, Henri
capitaine des Forces françaises de l'intérieur
'Officier pilote d'une grande valeur professionelle, ay ant fait preuve d'une magmfique courage et d'un bel esprit de décision pendant deux ans en travaillant dans la résistance en liaison avec la R. A.F.

'Abattu par la D.C.A. allemande le 9 Septembre 1944 en mission de guerre pres d'**Issoudun**, il réussit malgré ses blessures graves à rejoindre son unité dans le minimum de temps et à sauver le matériel qu'il transportait.'

CES CITATIONS COMPORTENT L'ATTRIBUTION
DE LA CROIX DE GUERRE AVEC PALME
à Paris, le 21 Novembre, 1944
Signé: DE GAULLE
EXTRAIT CERTIFIÉ CONFORMÉ
Pau, le 27 août, 1986,
Le Commandant, GARNIER
Commandant par l'intérim le Bureau central d'archives administratives militaires

EXTRAIT
du décret en date du 27 juillet, 1946
publié dans le J.O. du 18 août, 1946

portant nominations dans la Légion d'honneur
ARTICLE 1er: sont nommes dans l'ordre nationale de la
Légion d'honneur
AU GRADE DE CHEVALIER
Déricourt, Henri
capitaine engagé dans la R. A.E

'Officier pilote de valeur, patriotique, ardent et clairvoyant, évadé de France en juillet 1943, s'engage dans la R.A.F. pour missions en territoires ennemis. Parachuté à deux reprises, chef de réseau, monte une organisation modèle de résistance qui a fonctionné sans interruption de janvier 1943 à la Libération. A participé personellement à trente-sept opérations d'atterrissages de nuit. Par sa maîtrise et son courage, a mené à bien toutes ses missions se devouant sans réserve à la cause de la Patrie. Chargé d'une mission aérienne d'infanterie, lors du débarquement, a été abattu par la défense allemande et grièvement blessé.'

CES NOMINATIONS COMPORTENT
L'ATTRIBUTION
DE LA CROIX DE GUERRE 1939–1945 AVEC PALME
à Paris, le 27 juillet, 1946
signé: BIDAULT
EXTRAIT CERTIFIÉ CONFORMÉ
Pau, le 27 août 1986
Le Commandant GARNIER
commandant par l'intérim de Bureau
central d'archives administrations militaires
[signed]

A BIBLIOGRAPHY OF DÉRICOURT

BOOKS IN WHICH HE FIGURES IN ORDER OF THEIR PUBLICATION

Guillaume, Paul, *La Sologne au Temps de l'Héroisme et de la Trahison* (Orléans, 1950). In French.

Borchers, Erich, *Monsieur Jean* (Sponholtz, Hanover, 1951). In German. Déricourt figures as Gilbert.

Colvin, Ian, *Colonel Henri's Story* (Kimber, 1954). A translation of the Borchers, with annotations, in which Gilbert is identified as Colonel Buckmaster's Air Movements Officer, though not named.

Fuller, Jean Overton, *Double Webs* (Putnam, 1958). Déricourt is called Gilbert, by his own request.

Wighton, Charles, *Pin-Stripe Saboteur* (Odhams, 1959).

Fuller, Jean Overton, *Double Agent?* (Pan, 1961). Paperback of *Double Webs*, revised with an additional chapter.

Fuller, Jean Overton, *Horoscope for a Double Agent* (Fowler, 1961). He is called Gilbert.

Coulette, Henri, *The War of the Secret Agents* (Scribner, New York, 1966). A long narrative poem, which won the Lamont Poetry Award of 1965. Though fictionalised, carries an acknowledgement that it is based on my *Double Webs*. Déricourt is called Hilaire, and I am called Jane Alabaster.

Foot, M. R. D., *SOE in France* (HMSO, 1966).

Cookridge, E. H., *Inside SOE* (Barker, 1966).

Noguere, Henri, *Histoire de la Résistance en France, 1940–45* (Laffont, Paris, 1968). In French.

Heslop, Richard, *Xavier* (Hart-Davis, 1970). Déricourt is called Claude. Clément is called Auger.

Fuller, Jean Overton, *Noor-un-Nisa Inayat Khan GC* (*Madeleine*) (East-West, Rotterdam, in conjunction with Barrie & Jenkins, London, 1971).

Goldsmith, John, *Accidental Agent* (Leo Cooper, 1971). Brief mention.

Gillois, André, *Histoire Secrète des Français à Londres* (Hachette, 1973). In French.

Fuller, Jean Overton, *The German Penetration of SOE* (Kimber, 1975).

Le Chêne, Evelyn, *Watch for Me by Moonlight* [the story of Robert Boiteux] (Eyre Methuen, 1975). Brief mention.

Verity, Hugh, *We Landed by Moonlight* (Ian Allen, 1978).

Gib McCall, *Flight Most Secret* (Macmillan, 1981).

Collins, Larry, *A Fall from Grace* (Granada, 1985). This is a novel. The character inspired by Déricourt is called Henri Le Mair, alias Paul, alias Gilbert. He is designated the Air Movements Officer. His mission is, however, transferred to 1944, and the plot is totally fictitious.

Marshall, Robert, *All the King's Men* (Collins, 1988).

A NOTE TO THE READER

If you have enjoyed this book enough to leave a review on **Amazon** and **Goodreads**, then we would be truly grateful.
Sapere Books

Sapere Books is an exciting new publisher of brilliant fiction and popular history.

To find out more about our latest releases and our monthly bargain books visit our website: **saperebooks.com**

Printed in Great Britain
by Amazon

35164538R00311